GOVERNORS STATE UNIVERSITY LIBRARY

W9-BFU-781

3 1611 00224 4108

CHILDREN WITH CANCER
The Quality of Life

GOVERNORS STATE UNIVERSITY
UNIVERSITY PARK
IL 60466

CHILDREN WITH CANCER
The Quality of Life

Christine Eiser

Cancer Research UK Child and Family Research Group
Department of Psychology
University of Sheffield
Sheffield, UK

LEA LAWRENCE ERLBAUM ASSOCIATES, PUBLISHERS
2004   Mahwah, New Jersey   London

RC
281
.C4
E335
2004

Copyright © 2004 by Lawrence Erlbaum Associates, Inc.
All rights reserved. No part of this book may be reproduced in
any form, by photostat, microform, retrieval system, or any other
means, without the prior written permission of the publisher.

Lawrence Erlbaum Associates, Inc., Publishers
10 Industrial Avenue
Mahwah, New Jersey 07430

Library of Congress Cataloging-in-Publication Data

Eiser, Christine.
    Children with cancer : the quality of life / Christine Eiser.
        p.   cm.
    Includes bibliographical references and index.
    ISBN 0-8058-3544-X (alk. paper)
    1. Cancer in children.   2. Cancer in children—Patients—Family relationships.
3. Cancer in children—Social aspects.   4. Cancer in children—Psychological aspects.
5. Quality of life.   I. Title.

RC281.C4E335   2003
618.92'994—dc22   2003061279
                                                             CIP

Books published by Lawrence Erlbaum Associates are printed on acid-free paper,
and their bindings are chosen for strength and durability.

Printed in the United States of America
10 9 8 7 6 5 4 3 2 1

Contents

List of Figures and Tables

Acknowledgments

I would like to thank the many people who have worked with me over the years. In particular, I am grateful to Cancer Research UK (formerly Cancer Research Campaign), who have funded me for the last 10 years or so, and I would like especially to acknowledge Jean King and her team at Cancer Research UK. A number of research staff have worked with me—Trudy Havermans, Imogen Cotter, Sheryl Kopel, Annie Ellis, Yvonne Vance, Anne-Sophie Darling, Rachel Morse, Linda Sheppard, Marcelle Crinean, Sally Clark, Kate Absolom, Sarah Adams, and Jo Lawford—and I am grateful to them all for their hard work and inspiration.

I have learned a lot from opportunities to work with colleagues in pediatric oncology. In particular, I have enjoyed working with Mike Stevens, Meriel Jenney, and Helena Davies. I would like especially to thank Mike Stevens for his advice, and bringing to my attention the example of decision-making in rhabdomyosarcoma. I would like to acknowledge especially Diana Greenfield, Vallo Tillman, and Dick Eiser for commenting on earlier drafts of the book, and Laura Monument and Aimèe Bryant for help with preparation of the manuscript.

The most heartfelt thanks go to all the children and families who have welcomed me into their homes and shared their experiences. It is not always clear what individual families gain from taking part in research, but many I know are hopeful that their experiences and comments can be used to help children in the future. I hope that they are not disappointed with this book, and that it does make a contribution toward improving quality of life for children with cancer.

—*Christine Eiser*

Glossary

Allogeneic: A graft or tissue from someone other than the patient; usually a matched sibling (a brother or a sister) but may be a matched unrelated volunteer donor.

Bone Marrow Aspiration (BMA): The removal of the marrow from the cavities of the bones by suction.

Autologous: A graft or tissue from the same source; that is, taken from the patient and then returned to the patient.

Bone Marrow: A soft sponge-like material in the center or cavities of the bones that produces blood cells.

Chemotherapy: Drugs stop cancer cells from growing. Chemotherapy can be given in different ways, either by mouth or by an injection into the blood stream through *the Hickman line or Portacath.*

Clinical Trials: Research studies to find ways to improve health and cancer care. Studies are conducted to find out whether promising approaches to cancer prevention, diagnosis, and treatment are safe and effective.

EMLA Cream: A topical anesthetic, or cream that numbs the skin and decreases the sensation of pain.

Hickman Line or a Portacath: A narrow plastic tube through which blood samples can easily be taken. This avoids the need for repeated blood tests using a vein in the arm. Drugs and transfusions can also be given through the line. It is inserted into a major blood vessel in the chest.

Immunosuppression: Reduction of the functions of the immune system to prevent a reaction against donor marrow and to prevent graft-versus-host disease.

Lumbar Puncture (LP): A procedure in which a small amount of the fluid that surrounds the brain and spinal cord (cerebrospinal fluid or CSF) is removed and examined. They are used to place chemotherapy medications into the spinal fluid.

Lymphocyte: One of the major groups of white blood cells. B lymphocytes directly attack virus-infected cells and other foreign cells, such as cancer cells.

Magnetic Resonance Imaging (MRI): This type of scan uses magnetism to build up a picture of the inside of the body instead of X-rays. The MRI scanner can be used for cross section views of the body, like the CT scanner.

Methylphenidate (Ritalin) is used to treat attention-deficit-disorder in children.

Neutropenia: A severe drop in infection fighting white blood cells (neutrophils). It is a common side-effect of chemotherapy and has serious consequences for treatment, since chemotherapy has to be stopped or postponed.

Neutrophil: The most common type of white blood cell in the bloodstream. It helps to defend against bacterial infections.

Prednisone: A hormone-like drug used to treat and prevent graft-versus-host disease.

Radiotherapy: X-rays used to kill cancer cells.

Why Write a Book About Children With Cancer?

QUANTITY AND QUALITY IN SURVIVAL

The Good News

Cancer in children is a very rare disease. Because it is so rare, many people know almost nothing about it, and assume that a diagnosis is effectively a death sentence. One reason for writing this book is to increase public awareness of the progress that has been made in treating childhood cancer. A diagnosis of cancer in children is very frightening, but does not carry the death sentence it once did. There is good news, as well as bad, about the disease.

How can news of childhood cancer be good? Before the 1950s, there was virtually no effective treatment, and children were likely to die within weeks of diagnosis. New treatments introduced in the 1950s and 1960s brought renewed optimism. Over a relatively brief period of time, survival improved from virtually none to approximately 50% (C. M. Robertson, Hawkins, & Kingston, 1994). These trends have continued, and current statistics suggest that up to 80% of children with cancer can be cured. The good news, then, is that with modern treatments, many children can be treated, and go on to live happy and fulfilled lives.

The Bad News

Improving survival statistics is excellent news. However, survival often comes at a price. During the course of treatment, many children experience difficulties and restrictions in almost all areas of their lives. They can be limited in their physical functioning, and have reduced energy or poor motor skills and balance; in social functioning especially in relating to their friends; and in their ability to learn. The good news is that survival rates have improved, but there is still bad news in terms of the potentially adverse implications of the disease and treatment for the child's quality of life (QOL).

This raises the question about what exactly is meant by QOL. For the moment, readers are asked simply to think what is important to their own QOL. Somewhere comfortable to live, access to running water and food are basic requirements, though most of us take these for granted. Good health, too, is a universal requirement. Beyond this, individuals differ greatly in terms of how they define their QOL. For some, it is essential to be able to take part in sports, but for others, exercise is anathema. Furthermore, for any individual, QOL changes throughout the life span. Children are more likely than adults to emphasize the importance of physical activity. Being good at sports often conveys considerable social status. Being able to do the same as others is also important to children. Whatever they may say, they want to make good progress at reading or in other school achievements. Looking good, and wearing the "right" clothes can matter a lot. As they grow up, some of these priorities remain whereas others shift and change. For young people, QOL is intimately associated with freedom to be independent, to travel, to have their own house, and be able to have a child when it suits them.

It is not difficult to understand how cancer could compromise QOL in all sorts of ways. Treatment can affect physical appearance; most people probably know that chemotherapy makes your hair fall out. Children have a lot of time off school. This means they are unable to take part in many social activities and can also fall behind in schoolwork. They feel tired and are much less likely to be involved in after-school activities, even if they are able to keep up a reasonable attendance. So there can be no doubt that cancer and its treatment potentially has a huge and negative impact on the child's QOL. More than that, restrictions experienced during childhood can then impact on the individual's later life. Poor school attendance can mean less than optimal exam performance, and subsequently restricted work opportunities. The delayed effects of chemotherapy and radiotherapy can reduce fertility and ruin the chances of becoming a parent. Thus, it is easy to see how cancer can affect QOL both during treatment and in the longer term, and this has been recognized ever since survival rates began to improve.

However, the question of measuring QOL is much more problematic. Early attempts to measure QOL focused on simple proxy indicators such as days off school, or how far cancer affected the child's psychological adjustment, self-esteem, anxiety, depression, or IQ. More recently, measurement has become more sophisticated, and attempts to measure QOL specifically have been reported.

If the good news about childhood cancer is about survival, then the bad news is about the potential damage to QOL. A second theme of this book is therefore related to this question of how far treatment for cancer affects the child's QOL. Childhood cancer does not affect the child in isolation from the family. Parents are responsible for taking the child to hospital appointments, and for administering many treatments at home. Parents must monitor their child's health and behavior, and be vigilant in order to identify any adverse side effects of treatment. In successive chapters, therefore, the different ways that cancer can affect QOL is considered, for both the child and family. A related question is how far others, outside the immediate family, contribute to the child's QOL. Parents, teachers, friends, and medical staff can significantly help, or hinder, the process of adjustment to childhood cancer.

Research and Clinical Practice

The focus on QOL can be justified for a number of reasons. First, QOL is important for families. On diagnosis, many parents are overwhelmed and uncertain about the future. Information about how families have coped in the past can act as an example, and often an inspiration, for newly diagnosed families. Knowledge that others have been through similar experiences before is also helpful in coping with the immediate consequences of treatment. Clinically, too, there is value in describing the time course of the disease. Only by understanding the "normal" process of adjusting to cancer and its treatment can we appreciate what is abnormal, and by implication, when intervention is necessary. Thus, it should be possible to identify strategies that are conducive to good functioning. Understanding how some families are able to cope with the disease and treatment may suggest ways of coping for those who need help. Thus, in the future, it may be possible to devise new treatments that minimize the psychological implications for the family.

Second, QOL is an important consideration when comparing different treatments. Improvements in survival have partly been achieved through national and international clinical trials, which have allowed for faster evaluation of new treatments. Whereas comparison of the efficacy of new treatments was initially made in terms of survival rates, it is increasingly acknowledged that comprehensive evaluation must also take into account QOL.

Third, QOL has been considered useful when evaluating interventions. The realization that treatment compromises QOL has led to a plethora of studies documenting the problems, difficulties, and stresses experienced by children and their families. This work has also resulted in recognition that some families adopt various intuitive ways of coping with the difficulties. There is enormous potential in describing not only family problems, but also their strategies for leading a normal life, in spite of the restrictions of cancer. Furthermore, it may be helpful to communicate some of these strategies to families who are having greater difficulties. The formalization of interventions is a natural development of much descriptive research. However, justification for public expenditure involved in delivering interventions necessitates evaluation of effectiveness. Because the goal of most interventions is to improve QOL, it follows that formal methods to measure QOL are essential.

Finally, it is potentially helpful to understanding the child's point of view. Children do not share adult perspectives about the cause of disease or relationship between treatment and anticipated outcomes. It is difficult for a child to understand that the reason for this very painful treatment is in order to make them better in the future. Failing to understand the connection between treatment and future health may contribute to children's distress and sometimes their refusal to go along with medical procedures. Understanding the child's perspective with a goal to improve adult–child communication is, therefore, a legitimate aim in itself.

Implications for Multidisciplinary Work

Optimizing QOL in the child with cancer requires a multidisciplinary effort. The team typically includes consultants in hematology and oncology, to ensure medical care of the child. Pediatric nurses are vital to provide exemplary nursing care. The social worker provides advice about financial benefits, and can act as an intermediary between medical staff and the family. Thus, they can help families understand treatment plans. The psychologist provides an insight into how life-threatening illness can affect a child, and can suggest methods to cope at specific crises points. These can include situations where children refuse treatment, or become extremely fearful about treatments. The play leader is skilled in communicating with the child, and often works to reduce fear and increase understanding of what is to be expected before major surgery. Music therapists, art therapists, and others can also play a critical role.

The participation of all of these professionals underlines the fact that children are not simply cells and blood counts. The goal in treatment is not only to eradicate the disease, but also to provide a comprehensive system of care that recognizes the clinical, social, and emotional needs of the developing child. The contribution of these different professionals is vital to the provision of a holistic approach to care.

Involvement of these different professional groups can also create some problems. Differences in training and work priorities can challenge easy communication. Although all recognize the value of research in assessing current treatments and guiding new initiatives, dissemination of findings about QOL is often directed at discipline-specific journals. The result is that relevant research findings can appear in journals specializing in oncology, hematology, surgery, pediatrics, nursing, psychology, or psychiatry. It is important to try to pull together these findings in order to appreciate the impact of cancer on children and their families.

Thus, this book is written as a resource for all those involved in the care of children with cancer. The literature is diverse and growing steadily, so that it would be ambitious to include everything that has been written. Inevitably, there has been some bias in the selection of material included. The aim is not simply to regurgitate former reviews but to precipitate change. This can include changes in the type and quality of research conducted, and changes in dissemination and use of research findings.

OUTLINE OF THE BOOK

It is not as simple to describe how cancer treatment affects the child's QOL as it might seem. The real problem is in knowing how to measure QOL. Because there is no agreed way to measure QOL, a number of proxy indicators have been used. These can include children's school attendance, or their ability to socialize with others. Other proxy indicators include the child's behavior. Still others include the child's psychological functioning, especially their self-esteem, anxiety or depression, IQ, memory, and concentration. It will be seen that current understanding of QOL is largely limited to describing difficulties and problems experienced. The ultimate aim of this book is to work toward a more comprehensive understanding, of both how QOL is affected, and how to measure it. Because QOL changes throughout treatment, the organization of this book is loosely chronological, from diagnosis to long-term survival.

Part I includes three chapters that provide an essential overview to the area. Chapter 2 describes current approaches to medical care. Current views about possible causes of the disease, treatment, and prognosis are summarized for the nonmedical specialist. Pediatricians involved in the care of the child with cancer have always emphasized the needs of the whole child, and from the beginning other professionals have been brought in to complement their medical skills. In chapter 3, a brief history of psychosocial care is provided that emphasizes the interdependence between psychological and medical needs of the child. In chapter 4, the theoretical and methodological assumptions underlying applied work of this kind are discussed. It requires relatively little imagination to think how cancer might adversely affect the child, but it is much more difficult to measure the impact precisely. Accurate measurement is as important, however, as in any physical science. For many purposes, it is enough to know that the weather is mild or cold for the time of year, but if we are to be more certain about the impact of global warming, we need to measure temperature and rainfall very accurately. The same reasoning holds in the social sciences. It is important to be aware generally of how cancer affects the child, but if we are to compare the impact of new treatments, or assess the value of any intervention, then we need more accurate measurements. The aim of this chapter is to enable the reader to understand how research is conducted, and provide the skills to evaluate the findings in relation to the quality of the methods used. By placing these chapters early on, I hope to avoid much repetition and critique of methodological shortcomings. It will be clear to the reader that many studies share similar limitations. By highlighting these methodological problems, it should be possible to identify the requirements necessary for improving the quality of work in this area. Thus, the aims of Part I are essentially to set the scene. Some knowledge of the disease and treatment are essential to understand the emotional, social, and behavioral consequences for the child.

In Part II the impact of cancer is considered for the child's QOL. In chapter 5, the immediate implications of the diagnosis for the child are described. This includes dealing with the pain of treatment, and trying to understand what is happening. The way in which a family reacts will differ depending on whether the child is 3 or 13 years of age. The family of a 3-year-old may be most concerned about achieving the child's cooperation with treatment, especially where limited language makes it difficult to address the child's fears. In contrast, the 13-year-old may be well aware of the implications of the disease, and families therefore have to deal with difficult questions about life and death. The way in which children typically react depending on their age are described. In chapter 6, the focus is on what is known about children's reactions. In that the goals of treatment are to ensure quality as well as quantity of survival, children are encouraged to return to school as soon as they are well enough. Going to school is normal for the child and in chapter 7 the potential difficulties associated with return to school are described. These include relationships with other children and teachers, and dealing with questions about why you have no hair, or why you have so many days off school to go to the hospital.

For many reasons, children with cancer can experience difficulties in learning. These include the very lengthy absences experienced following the diagnosis, and continued interruptions for hospital appointments. Questions have also been raised about the possible adverse effects of some treatments. Central nervous system (CNS) radiotherapy, in particular, has been associated with learning difficulties. Additional problems are likely to be experienced for children with a brain tumor, as a result of initial damage caused before the tumor was diagnosed. Chapters 8 and 9 deal specifically with learning difficulties; first for children with leukemia, and then for those treated for a brain tumor.

Part III includes an account of the impact of the disease on parents and other members of the family, especially healthy brothers and sisters. In chapter 10, the implications of diagnosis are discussed from the parents' point of view. It should be remembered that most parents have little previous knowledge of the disease, and will often start from the assumption that cancer is inevitably fatal. The processes through which parents come to understand the disease and its treatment are described. Parents must learn rapidly, and also make a number of decisions regarding the child's treatment.

In chapter 11, parents' reactions following diagnosis are described. Mothers and fathers do not necessarily respond in the same way, and differences between them echo differences in coping between men and women more generally. The way that parents cope is critical, and has important implications for the child. Similarly, the way in which the child copes with treatment is determined very closely by how the family reacts. This is also true for brothers and sisters. Illness in a brother or sister has been recognized as one of the most stressful events that can happen to any child. Well siblings are often highly distressed, but also sufficiently aware of the seriousness of the situation to understand that they should not contribute further to their parents' concerns. In chapter 12, the consequences of cancer for well siblings are described.

Part IV focuses on the longer term consequences for those who survive treatment for childhood cancer. The experience of a life-threatening illness can have implications for adult functioning. Many children who are successfully treated for cancer (so-called "survivors") experience residual problems as a consequence of the treatment. These can include physical, social, or learning difficulties. Some may fail to grow, or have heart or fertility problems. Such physical late effects can continue to undermine normal psychological functioning, even when the cancer is "cured." General psychological issues are considered in chapters 13 and 14. Just as families are affected during the early stages of treatment, so they too can continue to experience late effects. In the final chapter of this section, the longer term issues for parents are described (chap. 15).

In Part V, attempts are made to answer the critical question about how cancer affects the QOL of the child and family. There are also implications for defining and measuring QOL more generally. We consider the implications for design and evaluation of psychosocial work. The findings are also considered for refinement in future methodology, theory, and clinical practice.

The diagnosis of childhood cancer has to be bad news. However, advances in medicine and technology have contributed toward increasingly good survival prospects. The focus on QOL is good news. Even 30 years ago poor survival rates would have made such a focus inappropriate and impossible. Despite this, there remains bad news. Improvements in prognosis can be achieved at the expense of QOL. For example, the increasing use of bone marrow transplants (BMTs) has contributed to improved survival rates, but also to compromised QOL.

As the "survival at all costs" dictum is challenged (Craft, 2000), it is important to remember that cancer affects the child's whole life and treatment is about more than controlling the physical symptoms. I hope that this book makes a timely contribution to the current debate about quantity and quality of survival, and ultimately leads to a new phase in collaboration between oncologists, families, and social scientists. The children have little to lose and much to gain.

THE HOLISTIC CARE OF THE CHILD

Cancer in children is a rare disease. Since the 1950s and 1960s when substantial gains in survival rates were first reported, much has been achieved in the medical care of children with cancer. These improvements in survival were made possible by a number of treatment innovations, including the discovery of new anticancer drugs. Over time, the cornerstone of success has been combinations of drugs, rather than any one alone. Collaboration at national and international levels has facilitated and speeded improvements in medical care. Large-scale international trials have resulted in more rapid awareness of the benefits of new treatments (and conversely termination of less successful treatments). The widespread use of antiemetic drugs, EMLA creams, Hickman lines, and Portacaths have all contributed to reductions in distress in children undergoing treatment.

In terms of survival rates, achievements over the last 50 years have been impressive. The result has been that cancer is no longer considered a life-threatening disease, but a chronic condition. This change in the qualitative nature of the disease demands an accompanying change in social and emotional care offered to the child and family. As this has been recognized, so there has been an increasing focus, not purely on survival, but on the QOL of the child, both during, and after treatment.

A number of factors have contributed to the current interest in the social and psychological implications of childhood cancer, as well as improved survival rates. These include heightened interest in child development, and awareness of the importance of early childhood experiences for subsequent psychological functioning. Disease does not simply affect the child's physical health, but has implications for social, emotional, and academic functioning. Families face a major challenge in acknowledging the potential limitations of the disease on the one hand, while also trying to maintain a normal life on the other.

Current achievements in medical progress are described in chapter 2. Treatment is long and difficult, and children experience many physical side effects. Although the aim of treatment is to cure the child, there are many potential pitfalls, and parents therefore ride an emotional rollercoaster. In chapter 3, psychosocial care of children with cancer is described from a historical perspective, emphasizing how psychosocial care has changed in response to changes in medical treatment. The purpose of chapter 4 is to provide a basic account of the theoretical and methodological challenges underlying research in this area. This will enable the reader to assess the quality of individual research studies. Research quality is vital if the aim is to enhance clinical care of these children, rather than simply being an academic exercise.

Pediatric Oncology:
A Medical Overview

Summary

Cancer is a rare disease, affecting approximately 1 in 1,400 children a year in the United Kingdom. Comparable figures from the United States suggest that 14 children in every 100,000 develop cancer each year. Although cancer was once an acute, life-threatening condition, survival rates have improved steadily since the 1960s. Depending on the cancer, some 80% of children can now expect disease-free survival 5 years after diagnosis.

Diagnosis is complex, partly because the symptoms of cancer occur in other, less serious conditions. Delay in diagnosis can also occur because of the rareness of the conditions; many nonspecialist doctors may be unfamiliar with, and not expect to diagnose such a rare condition. The principles of treatment for acute lymphoblastic leukemia (ALL), the most common form of childhood leukemia, have remained unchanged for more than 25 years. They include remission induction and intensification, CNS-directed therapy (to reduce the risk of leukemic infiltration into the CNS), and maintenance (continuation) therapy. The other main principle is the use of risk-directed therapy to achieve sustained remission, that is, individual treatment protocols depending on prognostic factors. Nearly two thirds of children with ALL are categorized as *standard risk* (aged 1–9 years, low leukocyte count). These children are considered to have the best prognosis. Adolescents and infants under 1 year are among those in the higher risk groups.

Improvements in care have been achieved by the introduction of new treatments, centralization of care, and improved supportive care. Children treated in specialist centers tend to have better survival rates than those treated elsewhere.

CHRONIC CONDITIONS AFFECTING CHILDREN

Changes in treatment and improvements in survival mean that cancer now shares characteristics with other chronic conditions that affect children, such as diabetes, asthma, cystic fibrosis, or epilepsy. Chronic conditions require regular treatment and visits to hospital, and some degree of self-care and vigilance. Diabetes is a prime example of a chronic condition. Daily insulin injections are needed and children must balance their food and energy requirements. However, most children with diabetes can and do take part in normal activities and should not experience physical symptoms or pain (assuming the disease is well managed and controlled). Chronic conditions are also characterized by periods of relatively good health and others of poorer health. They can affect children's mobility, vitality, and the way they look. In all chronic conditions, there is considerable uncertainty about the future. There is no cure. Rather, the goal of medical treatment is to control the physical symptoms, minimize the intrusion of the disease and treatment into the child's daily life, and maximize QOL.

Treatment for childhood cancer is different from other chronic conditions in at least two ways. First, cancer involves a period of intense aggressive treatment that can seriously compromise the child's ability to take part in everyday activities. Second, treatment for cancer is recommended for a defined and limited period of time. In general, longer treatment is considered undesirable, because long-term chemotherapy can also damage healthy organs. However, following the recommended treatment, it is hoped that children are cured of cancer, and many will be. Thus, treatment for cancer is shorter, but more aggressive, than for other conditions. Long-term cure is a realistic and possible aim for many.

CHARACTERISTICS OF CANCER

Incidence

Cancer is a rare disease that affects approximately 1 in 600 children under 15 years of age (Celcalupo, 1994; Stiller & Eatock, 1999). This means that approximately 1,400 new cases are diagnosed per year in the United

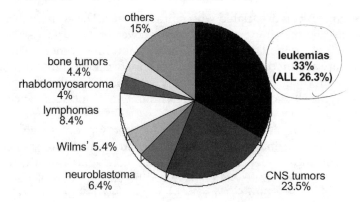

FIG. 2.1. Percentage of different childhood cancers.

Kingdom. Approximately 8,000 children are diagnosed each year in the United States (American Cancer Society, 1997). It is much less common than other conditions that affect children such as asthma, epilepsy, or diabetes. However, it remains a leading cause of death in children (C. R. Pinkerton, Cushing, & Sepion, 1994).

Approximately one third of cancers that affect children are the leukemias (C. R. Pinkerton et al., 1994). As shown in Fig. 2.1, the second most frequent cancer includes CNS tumors and the remainder include solid and rare tumors. Among the leukemias, ALL is the most common and also has the best prognosis. For both these reasons, much psychological research has tended to concentrate more on children with ALL than any other cancer. Patterns of incidence of cancer differ depending on ethnic origin. For example, Black children have an increased incidence of Wilms' tumor but almost never experience Ewing's tumor (Stiller, Bunch, & Lewis, 2000).

Causes

Childhood cancers differ from those that affect adults in several ways. First of all, childhood cancers can more often be cured. This in some ways is unexpected. Because cancer affects many more adults than children, it would be expected that more progress would be made curing the relatively more common condition. Differences in cure rates suggest that the adult disease is in some way inherently different from childhood cancer.

Children are susceptible to cancers that affect stem cells. These are relatively simple, undifferentiated cells that normally produce a range of more specialized cells in the body. Cancer is caused when a stem cell mutates, and this is thought to be the result of a genetic accident. In contrast, cancer in adults is associated with epithelial cells. These are highly differentiated cells that line body cavities or cover body surfaces. Cancer in these cells is promoted by interaction with the environment. Thus, adult cancers are acquired, often through exposure to cancer-inducing elements of the environment. Lung cancer, induced through long-term exposure to smoke, is the classic example of an environmentally induced cancer affecting adults.

In addition to these differences in cause, the superior survival in children has been attributed to the fact that children are more resilient than adults. This means they are able to tolerate more aggressive therapy than adults. Adults with cancer often have additional health problems that further reduce their ability to tolerate aggressive treatment. Thus, children's tolerance of therapy contributes to their better survival, but at the same time, leaves them at risk of long-term residual complications attributable to the aggressive therapy.

When a child is diagnosed, one of the first questions people ask is "why?" A number of hypotheses have been put forward to explain the cause of childhood cancer, but it has proved very difficult to draw firm conclusions, partly because it is a very rare disease. Early exposure to infection and the subsequent effects on the immune system has been implicated. Clusters of leukemia have been reported. Increases in childhood leukemia around power plants were initially attributed to fall-out from the nuclear plant. Other attempts have been made to determine the association between leukemia and exposure to environmental radon, proximity to power cables, and most recently, use of mobile phones. However, results have been inconsistent, and relative risks, when identified, have been small.

An alternative theory suggests that the cause may be more socially determined. Establishment of a new power plant created a need for an expanded workforce, and consequently an influx of a new population into a previously sparsely populated area. These influxes, resulting in exposure of the endogenous population to viral pathogens not previously experienced, may contribute to the pockets of cases identified. Other epidemiological work suggests that children born into households of high socioeconomic position or low density are at increased risk of developing ALL (Murray et al., 2002). The implications are that being born into an extended family may be protective and that modulation of the immune system by early exposure to infection is associated with reduced risk. Considerable work remains to be done in relation to these issues, especially in determining which infections are transmitted from adults to children.

On the basis of space–time clustering and seasonal patterns of incidence, McNally et al. (2002) concluded that there is evidence of environmental agents in the etiology of certain brain tumors. Their findings suggest either a prenatal or perinatal exposure to the onset of some brain tumors after a variable latent period, and a postnatal exposure to environmental damage before diagnosis.

A number of inherited diseases are associated with an increased risk of malignancies, suggesting some as yet not completely understood inherited component. In retinoblastoma, a family history is found in approximately one third of cases and in Wilms' tumor there may be a family history in 1% of cases. Risks to siblings are about double that for the rest of the population, but given the low incidence of childhood cancer, parents are usually reassured that risks to other children are negligible.

Most people understand cancer broadly in terms of proliferation of rogue cells. Three major molecular mechanisms have been proposed for the development of childhood cancer. These include (a) loss of a tumor suppressor gene leading to uncontrolled cell division, (b) translocation of an oncogene to a site that influences its function, and (c) mutation of a growth regulatory gene (C. R. Pinkerton et al., 1994).

Prognosis

In the days before modern treatment, childhood cancer was inevitably and rapidly fatal. The introduction of radiotherapy and chemotherapy has resulted in much more optimistic outcomes. As shown in Fig. 2.2, reductions in deaths throughout Europe have been documented (Levi, La Vecchia, Negri, & Lucchini, 2001). In the United Kingdom, overall survival increased from 26% for children treated between 1962 and 1970, to 50% for those treated between 1971 and 1985 (C. M. Robertson et al., 1994).

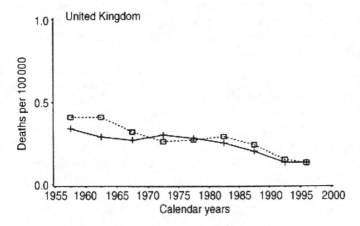

FIG. 2.2. Trends in age-standardized 0–14 years death certification rates from selected childhood cancers, 1955–1997 (+ - + boys; - - - - girls). From Levi et al. (2001). Copyright 2001 by Elsevier. Adapted by permission.

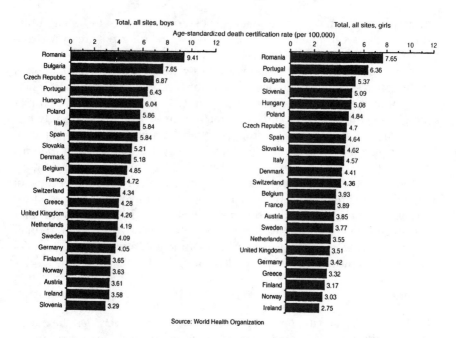

FIG. 2.3.   Age-standardized death rates for Europe. From Levi et al. (2001).
Copyright 2001 by Elsevier. Adapted by permission.

Improvements in survival rates between 1981 and 1990 were slightly
better for females compared with males (Doll, 1996). For the most common cancer (ALL), 5-year survival increased from 67% in 1980–1984 to
81% in 1990–1994. This represents a 42% reduction in risk of death over
the 5-year period (Stiller & Eatock, 1999). The majority of these children
are considered cured; that is, the risk of cancer recurrence is believed to be
small (Hawkins & Stevens, 1996).

For some cancers, survival rates are substantially greater. Rates above
90% have been reported for Hodgkin's disease, retinoblastoma, and germ
cell tumors. Unfortunately, less success has been achieved in other cases.
Survival for children with some brain tumors can be as low as 15%–20%
(Stiller, 1994). There is also considerable variability in survival depending
on country of origin. Survival rates across Europe are shown in Fig. 2.3.
For some cancers, survival rates in the United Kingdom are below a number of other European countries.

Diagnosis

Diagnosis can be very difficult. First of all, the children are very young
and therefore cannot easily explain how they feel. Second, the most common symptoms (fever, headache, vomiting, pallor and fatigue, bone pain,

limping, weight loss, and bleeding) occur in many other conditions. Consequently, there is inevitably a period of time or *time lag* between when the symptoms first occur and when the diagnosis is made. Mean time lag may be significantly longer for some tumors (e.g., CNS tumors) compared with others, and also shows some regional variation (Saha, Love, Eden, Micallef-Eynaud, & MacKinlay, 1993).

The first symptoms of childhood cancer are caused by the effects of the tumor mass on surrounding normal structures, secretion by the malignancy of a substance that disturbs normal function, or bone marrow failure (Saha et al., 1993). Clinical diagnosis takes time and is complex. Multiple procedures are required, almost all of which involve the cooperation of the child. For young children, local anesthesia and sedation may be necessary. Regular blood counts are an integral part of diagnosis and continued follow-up. Clinic visits routinely begin with a *finger-prick*. In comparison with many procedures children with cancer undergo, the finger-prick can seem rather benign. However, it can be very uncomfortable and often causes much distress. Children often identify the finger-prick as the most stressful of all procedures, partly because many other procedures are carried out under sedation. Central venous catheters, Hickman lines, or Portacaths may be inserted in the chest in order to facilitate investigative procedures. These have significantly contributed to the child's QOL by doing away with multiple injections and needles. They facilitate many investigations and diagnostic tests by enabling blood to be extracted, or chemotherapy inserted without the need for additional injections. In addition to these hematological procedures, X rays and magnetic resonance imaging (MRI) scans are important in the diagnostic procedures.

TREATMENT

Acute Lymphoblastic Leukemia

The principles of treatment for ALL, the most common form of childhood leukemia, have remained unchanged for more than 25 years. They include remission induction and intensification, CNS-directed therapy (to reduce the risk of leukemic infiltration into the CNS), and maintenance (continuation) therapy. The other main principle is the use of risk-directed therapy, that is, individual treatment protocols depending on patient's prognostic factors for sustained remission. Nearly two thirds of children with ALL are categorized as *standard risk* (aged 1–9 years, low leukocyte count). These children are considered to have the best prognosis. Adolescents, infants under 1 year, and those with high leukocyte count or with adverse cytogenetics (Philadelphia chromosome) are in the higher or the highest risk group.

The aim of treatment is first to achieve a complete remission as rapidly as possible. This typically is achieved using glucocorticoids, vincristine, and L-aspariginase, with or without anthracyclines. More than 95% of children with ALL achieve remission after 3–4 weeks of treatment. However, even in complete morphological remission, patients still have some leukemic cells. Therefore most treatment protocols include an early intensification (consolidation) therapy shortly after remission induction. Increases in survival rates of children with ALL have been achieved by a number of modifications to treatment learned through results of randomized clinical trials (RCT) all around the world. Prospective randomized trials from Europe and North America have shown that giving one or more courses of intensified chemotherapy significantly reduces the risk of relapse (Hann et al., 2000; Pui & W. E. Evans, 1998). The timing, choice, and dose of drugs in intensification blocks varies widely between protocols.

The importance of CNS-directed therapy was first demonstrated in the late 1960s (Aur et al., 1971; B. Jones et al., 1991). In many earlier protocols, CNS-directed therapy consisted of CNS irradiation and intrathecal methotrexate. This treatment was introduced to increase the chance of cure, and also reduce the morbidity resulting from CNS relapse. However, there were always concerns about side effects of CNS radiotherapy. Over time, these concerns have been realized, and it is now acknowledged that CNS irradiation is associated with a number of problems or late effects. These can include damage to almost all major organs. As a consequence, the dose of CNS irradiation was decreased from 2,400 Gy to 1,800 Gy during the 1980s. Subsequently, in recognition of the late effects experienced by children treated with radiotherapy, and no apparent differences in survival rates, CNS irradiation was dropped from treatment protocols for children of low or standard risk.

CNS irradiation is now the first choice of therapy for patients who have CNS leukemia or who are at high risk for CNS relapse (high leukocyte count at presentation, poor early response, T-cell leukemia). The dose of CNS irradiation for this group of patients varies from 1,200 to 2,400 Gy depending on the specific protocol. Most current treatment protocols for standard-risk patients include a course of intrathecal methotrexate injections during the first 3 months, followed by regular injections thereafter.

Continuing (maintenance) therapy for ALL consists of daily mercaptopurine and weekly methotrexate, with periodic steroids and vincristine. It is mainly conducted in outpatient settings and lasts for 2 to 3 years. Most attempts to shorten the duration of treatment have resulted in a high risk of relapse after the end of therapy (Childhood ALL Collaborative Group, 1996).

THE LONG TERM

In the long term, the hope is that children will get through these initial treatments to an event-free survival. As shown in Fig. 2.2, the chances of long-term survival are progressively increasing. For those who are less fortunate, the number of viable treatment options and hopes for cure deteriorate markedly.

Relapse

Relapse is the reappearance of cancer in the blood, bone marrow, or extramedullary sites (such as the CNS or testicles). Approximately 30% of children with ALL will experience a relapse in the CNS (American Cancer Society, 1997). Treatment is necessarily aggressive and involves intensification of treatment, often including CNS irradiation in addition to intrathecal chemotherapy. These more aggressive treatments have been associated with considerable declines in IQ (Mulhern et al., 1987). Relapse is clearly bad news, and at one time the chances of survival were much reduced. However, new advances in BMT have improved the prognosis considerably.

Palliative Care

Death in childhood is increasingly rare. Current figures suggest that over a 1-year period, five children are likely to die from any life-limiting illness in a health care district of 250,000 (Royal College of Paediatrics and Child Health [RCPCH], 1997). Given these figures, palliative care for children is a relatively new speciality. Depending on the disease, some children may need palliative care from infancy for many years, whereas others will need it only briefly. One of the most difficult practical questions relates to timing. In many cases, the transition from active treatment designed to promote cure to palliative care may not be clear, and both treatments may sometimes be needed in parallel (Goldman, 1998). As far as possible, it is recommended that children are cared for at home, with parents very much an integral part of the medical team. Accurate assessment of symptoms and effective pain control are essential for the child, while psychosocial support appropriate for the individual family is necessary.

IMPROVEMENTS IN TREATMENT AND SURVIVAL

Improvements in survival have been attributed to the introduction of new treatments, especially chemotherapy and radiotherapy, and more recently, BMT, centralization of care, and improved supportive care (Chessells, 2000).

Introduction of New Treatments

Depending on the cancer, children are treated by a combination of chemotherapy, radiotherapy, and surgery. Although these therapies have certainly contributed to the improved survival rates, they also have disadvantages. All have been associated with wide-ranging side effects in both the short and long term. Direct effects can occur where specific drugs are associated with late effects; for example, anthracyclines are now known to be associated with cardiac damage. Less direct effects may be experienced as a social consequence of treatment. For example, children undergoing BMT need to be nursed in germ-free environments and consequently may experience limited contacts with friends and family.

BMT has an important role in the management of ALL, particularly for children with very high risk status or those with relapsed disease. High-dose, whole-body irradiation and intensive chemotherapy are used to destroy cancer cells. Transplant with a related donor will give the highest chance of survival compared with unrelated donors (Chessells, 2000). In most patients the conditioning for BMT includes cyclophosphamide and total body irradiation between 800 and 1,400 Gy. Immunosuppressive treatments are subsequently necessary for months and even years. As these treatments suppress the body's immune function, patients must be nursed in a germ-free environment until the new marrow is successfully grafted. Late effects after BMT are common and include growth and endocrine problems, reduced fertility, and impaired cardiac and pulmonary function.

Centralization of Care

The fact that childhood cancer is such a rare disease creates a number of difficulties in terms of management. Under normal circumstances, very few clinicians come across cases of childhood cancer, and thus do not have the opportunity to develop appropriate expertise. As a consequence, centralization of care is considered important. In the United Kingdom, care of children with cancer is the responsibility of 22 designated centers. These are staffed by specialists in the care of children with cancer, and include surgeons, radiotherapists, and oncologists. Centers also have the support of specially trained nursing staff and other professionals (e.g., social workers) with specific training in care of children with cancer.

Centralization of care has also been achieved through the introduction of national and international clinical trials. As a consequence of combining experience from different centers, knowledge about the differential effectiveness of alternative treatments has accumulated faster than would be possible without such collaboration. Organization of clinical trials is managed by a number of key groups in the United Kingdom (the UKCCSG [United Kingdom Children's Cancer Study Group] and MRC [Medical Research Council]), by SIOP (Société Internationale D'Oncologie Pédiatrique) in Europe, and by COG (Children's Oncology Group) in the United States.

Early work suggested that children treated in centers have a better prognosis than those treated elsewhere, as did children treated in hospitals seeing larger numbers of cases, in both the United States (A. M. Meadows et al., 1983) and the United Kingdom (Stiller & Draper, 1989). The percentage of children with ALL referred to a UKCCSG center rose from 64% between 1977 and 1980 to 87% between 1989 and 1992 (Mott, Mann, & Stiller, 1997). There have been concerns that survival rates for children entered in national trials in the United Kingdom are lower for those from ethnic minorities compared with White children with similar prognostic features (Oakhill & Mann, 1983). An extensive study by Stiller et al. (2000) concluded that there were no differences in survival based on ethnic origin, although children from South Asian ethnic background treated on ALL trials had a slightly greater risk of death compared with Whites. This difference approached, but was not, statistically significant.

For families, the benefits of being involved in a clinical trial include the greater extent of experience accumulated, and access to the currently best available treatment. Many will also see disadvantages. These include randomization to treatment or control group, a process that families sometimes see to be arbitrary. It would be easier to feel confident if there were one tried and tested treatment. In addition, some families have to travel considerable distances for care at regional or national centers, adding to financial difficulties and creating others in terms of care of healthy brothers and sisters. Voluntary organizations have done much to ease the burden in these situations, especially by providing houses near the hospital so that families can be together.

Improved Supportive Care

Many children experience painful and unpleasant side effects during the active part of treatment. They may feel sick, have mouth ulcers, or suffer skin complaints as a result of chemotherapy. Children may have little appetite especially following the diagnosis. As steroids are introduced, children can put on a lot of weight and feel very hungry. These cycles of eating and not eating, weight loss and weight gain, can be very trying for all concerned. Changes in body image can be subtle and temporary, or may involve more permanent disfigurement (e.g., where a child undergoes amputation following a bone tumor). Chemotherapy can also have a significant effect on mood and behavior (Drigan, Spirito, & Gelber, 1992). It is common for parents to describe their child as much more emotional or aggressive during treatment.

Improved supportive care has greatly enhanced survival and QOL in children treated for cancer. The introduction of antiemetic drugs has done much to reduce the unpleasant physical side effects of therapy. The use of central venous catheters minimizes the need for venipuncture and means that it is usually possible to perform many unpleasant procedures under sedation or general anesthesia. Especially in Europe (compared with the United States), bone marrow aspirations (BMA) are routinely performed under anesthesia. In the United States, a misperception that adverse effects are associated with anesthesia has led to unwillingness to offer this treatment for fear of legal action (Hain & Campbell, 2001). Children undergoing treatment are not pain-free, but much can be done to minimize painful side effects.

DISCUSSION

This brief medical overview highlights the "good news" about childhood cancer. This condition is now curable; centralization of care has resulted in more rapid accumulation of expertise and progress in treatment; and improved supportive care means that children are spared some of the most painful and unpleasant side effects of treatment. All of this is very good news.

For families, information about statistics and innovations in treatment may be of varying comfort. Even if 80% of children survive, it follows that 20% do not, and at diagnosis, no one can say what will befall any individual child with any certainty. For families, then, there remains considerable "bad news" about childhood cancer. These include practical issues about care of other children in the family, lengthy periods in the hospital for the sick child and at least one of the parents, and financial burden associated with lost work opportunities and the increased costs associated with travel and care. Emotionally, too, there is much bad news. Families face an extended period of uncertainty. Over time, they may have to accept that life-saving treatment has left its own scars, in terms of compromised physical and psychological functioning.

In the next chapter, we see how the changes in the medical management of childhood cancer have precipitated a change in emphasis in psychological care, from the focus on caring for the dying child to one that focuses on assessment and improvement in quality, as well as quantity of survival.

A History of Psychosocial Care

Summary

Before 1970, survival was relatively poor, and this was reflected in the kind of psychosocial work conducted. The focus was on helping parents to cope with the child's likely death, and ensuring that the child was protected from information about the life-threatening nature of the disease.

As survival improved, especially from the 1970s through to 1990, there was increasing recognition of side effects associated with treatment. These included physical late effects, such as loss of fertility, reduced growth, and endocrine disorders, as well as more psychosocial late effects including compromised social skills and learning difficulties. Other changes during this time included greater recognition of the need to involve children in discussions about their disease, and where possible and appropriate, allowing them some say in decisions about treatment. The focus on defining the deficits or problems experienced by children with cancer and their families slowly gave way to an emphasis on coping or resilience, and attempts were made to identify coping strategies associated with more positive psychosocial outcomes.

During the 1990s, psychosocial work mushroomed, and was characterized by involvement of a greater range of professional (specialist nurses, social workers, dietitians, psychologists) and voluntary organizations. It is apparent that one of the key challenges is understanding why some patients overcome adversity, whereas others find it much harder to manage the undoubtedly adverse implications of the disease. The incidence of posttraumatic stress disorder (PTSD) among children and their mothers has been the subject of some research, and estimates suggest that a significant number experience clinically significant PTSD.

THEMES FROM THE PAST

As described in the previous chapter, improvements in survival have been achieved through the introduction of new treatments, changes in the organization and increasing centralization of care, and better supportive management. The changing nature of the disease, from acute and life threatening to chronic, has demanded a corresponding restructuring of psychosocial care. The early focus on providing support to the family in anticipation of the child's impending death is not appropriate in the context of improving survival rates. The need is much more for holistic psychosocial care that embraces the impact of treatment on the whole child, in both the immediate and longer term.

The reactions of children are closely bound up with those of their family, and therefore comprehensive psychological care must also address the issue of family relationships and reactions to the illness. The shift from survival at all costs, to a focus on QOL has been at the heart of a radical rethinking of psychosocial care. In this chapter, the major changes that can be identified are organized round the following periods: 1950–1970, 1970–1990, and from 1990 onward.

1950–1970

During this period, the prognosis for children with cancer was poor. Most children died within a few weeks or months of diagnosis. Treatment was not sophisticated. There were no Hickman lines or antiemetic drugs. Thus, children experienced considerable pain and distress during treatment. Consequently, the key concerns were about management of this pain and distress, and preparation of the family for the inevitable death. Classic works of this period reflected the very pessimistic outcomes expected and are captured graphically in the paper by Vernick and Karon (1965), which they titled "Who's Afraid of Death on a Leukaemia Ward?" Spinetta, Rigler, and Karon (1974) described how the terminally ill child appeared to cope by progressively withdrawing from family and friends.

The climate on the pediatric oncology ward was also very different from today. Medical opinion was that children should be protected from information about the disease, so as to limit the amount of psychological distress experienced. Doctors discussed treatment issues with parents out of the child's earshot. In a wider context, the work of Bowlby (1969) was generally very influential during this period. This emphasized the importance of mother–child attachment, for both current and future functioning. Parenting was seen to be the responsibility of mothers and much less emphasis was given to the role of other members of the family. In line with this, there was little mention of the role of the father in supporting the child and the family, or about the impact on healthy brothers or sisters.

1970–1990

With improving survival rates, especially for ALL, the "good news" began to emerge during the 1960s. These improved survival rates were attributed in part to new anticancer drugs, and also to use of CNS irradiation. In the 1970s, as the number of survivors and time since completion of treatment increased, the good news was tempered by recognition that some children experienced physical late effects as a consequence of their illness and its treatment (A. T. Meadows & Hobbie, 1986). These physical late effects included second cancers, compromised fertility, and damage to many major organs, including the heart, liver, and brain.

There was also concern about the impact of treatment on cognition and academic performance, but much less anxiety, if any, about social and emotional functioning. This focus was in large part led by parents. Increasing numbers of parents reported learning difficulties and behavioral problems in their child. The fact that their concerns were taken seriously was influenced in part by the availability of suitable measures. Acceptable and valid measures were available to measure IQ and academic achievement, though there was little consensus about how to measure social, emotional, or psychological functioning.

In order to clarify the risks associated with the treatment, attempts were made to compare cognitive and sometimes behavioral functioning between children treated for ALL by CNS radiotherapy with normal peers, healthy siblings, or occasionally children with other cancers. Together with other findings implicating CNS irradiation in retarded growth, this work contributed to decisions to change treatments and ultimately to withdraw CNS irradiation for work with children, except in special cases.

Also during this period, attempts were made to reduce the distress of children undergoing medical procedures. Anticipatory nausea and vomiting (ANV) caused much distress to children, their parents, and medical staff, and interventions for both children and parents, were reported.

Earlier decisions to protect the child from knowledge about the disease gave way to a very much more "open" family approach, and assumptions that children function better when they are informed and involved in decisions about their treatment. This arose partly through changes in clinical practice, partly from the public demand for greater accountability and involvement in decision making, and partly from the changing ethos in pediatric practice.

There were independently changes in the kind of theoretical assumptions underlying clinical and research work. Early work was dominated by the deficit-centered perspective discussed and critiqued by Drotar (1989), and focused on the problems and disadvantages experienced by children growing up in adverse circumstances. During this period, this emphasis gave way to coping models (Lazarus & Folkman, 1984). The search was on to identify demographic, social, or personality factors that characterized children and families who seemed to cope well.

It was increasingly recognized that cancer has enormous implications for the whole family, and not just the child and mother (Kupst, 1992). Furthermore, these implications varied by stage of treatment. Although the focus of attention, at least immediately after the diagnosis, is on the sick child, parents themselves face many challenges; to their parenting skills, to their relationship together, and to their work commitments. At the same time, they are likely to feel exhausted both by the physical demands of caring for a sick child, and by the emotional demands created by the awareness that the child has a life-threatening condition. Parents, perhaps more than their children, understand both the immediate and longer term implications of the disease, and can become hypervigilant about the child's health. The various tasks to be understood and implemented around the diagnosis are distinct from those involved during or after completion of treatment. In recognition of this, research efforts became more targeted, identifying the child and family experiences around diagnosis (Kupst & Schulman, 1988), during maintenance therapy (Dahlquist, Czyzewski, & C. L. Jones, 1996), and among long-term survivors (Kupst et al., 1995). Recognizing the unique demands associated with different phases of treatment is potentially more useful from a clinical perspective and should result in more appropriate interventions.

The time when the child is on active treatment is characterized by periods of wellness and attempts to resume normal living, interspersed with periods of illness and hospitalization. Parents may become increasingly confident about their own role in looking after the child, recognizing potentially adverse reactions to treatment and being confident about when to ask for professional help. At the same time, they have to ensure that the child experiences as normal a childhood as possible. When treatment is completed, it is important that the child has received as good an education as possible, and had the chance to experience a normal social life.

Although it is reasonable to assume that family QOL will be jeopardized during treatment, it is to be hoped that family relationships will return to normal afterward. However, for children themselves, there are real possibilities of physical complications as a result of either the disease or treatment. For some there are also residual psychological consequences, reflecting difficulties coming to terms with the experience of the disease and disrupted school and social life. There is now also evidence of compromised QOL for parents, especially mothers. Many mothers report continued anxiety and loneliness for many years after the diagnosis, even in cases where the child is very well (van Dongen-Melman et al., 1995). In some ways, this is not surprising. Children are expected to attend routine follow-up, partly as a precaution for early detection of relapse or second cancer, and partly to facilitate identification of late effects associated with treatment. Thus, parents continue to experience worries about children's health, and these worries are accentuated immediately before clinic appointments. In some cases, children need additional treatment (e.g., growth hormone therapy [GHT] as a consequence of growth failure). Others need special education help to compensate for learning difficulties. Thus, parents may be faced with many reminders of the disease, even in situations where clinicians would define a child as cured.

Having a chronically ill brother or sister is one of the most stressful events that can happen to a child. As parents are necessarily absorbed by the needs of the sick child, siblings can feel left out and ignored. For parents, what to do about their healthy children is a source of much anxiety. Younger siblings are often left with friends and relations and older siblings may be expected to look after themselves. Sometimes they are also expected to take on considerable responsibility for running the house or caring for younger children. Inevitably, the needs of healthy siblings can be overlooked. Parents may decide to tell them very little about the severity of the disease so as not to upset them, but this can have the effect of creating even more anxiety. Most work suggests that siblings of a child with cancer are at risk of behavioral and emotional difficulties (Carpenter & Sahler, 1991), although an increasing number of reports suggest that the experience can also have positive outcomes. Horwitz and Kazak (1990) reported that preschool siblings whose brother or sister had cancer were more helpful and considerate compared with age-matched controls who had no experience of the effects of illness on others. The implications are that children may benefit from opportunities to learn that others need help.

Typically, work has treated the experiences of children, parents, and siblings quite separately, failing to acknowledge the interactions between coping and adjustment of different family members. In part, this is as much a limitation of our methodological and statistical techniques as a failure to understand the reciprocal nature of family functioning. The way in which a child copes with the illness is probably closely related to the way in which parents cope. The way in which parents explain treatments to the child, and their own approach to dealing with the child's fear and pain during procedures, is associated with the child's ability to cope with painful procedures (Blount et al., 1989).

1990 Onward

As survival rates improved, the goal of psychosocial care continued to focus on support for the family through the very difficult and lengthy treatment, but increasingly on the assumption that a majority of children can hope to achieve a normal life. It was recognized that the diagnosis affects the whole family, and most hospitals caring for children with cancer now offer a range of professional support services, including social workers, psychologists, and play therapists as well as nursing and medical staff. The potentially adverse implications for long-term psychological health and well-being have been recognized, and childhood cancer has been likened to any other trauma (such as war or major accident). A significant minority of children and their mothers show classic symptoms of PTSD (Kazak, 1998).

Yet it has not proved possible to predict on diagnosis the characteristics of children and families who will most successfully take the stresses of treatment in their stride. In fact, we have to acknowledge the wide variation in outcomes that have been found. In the long term, it is possible to find survivors of childhood cancer who have been unable to take part in normal life and consequently lead limited and possibly unhappy lives. At the other extreme, some survivors are able to put the whole experience in a wider perspective. In many cases, their success in overcoming some of the challenges of coping with the disease seems to prepare them well for coping with subsequent, sometimes unrelated, difficulties. Following is one young woman's observation about her experience with cancer:

> It's not that I would say it was a good thing having cancer, but I'm not sorry it happened. I met lots of really nice people. When I was in hospital, I found out that I am really good with little children. When they were upset, it was often me they turned to, and I learned I could help a lot, just by playing with them, or explaining a bit more about what will happen. That's really why I decided to do nursery nursing. I feel if I hadn't had cancer, I might have done something much less worthwhile. (Jo, aged 17 years)

Thus, in parallel with work involving other chronically sick children, there has been a shift away from measuring behavior problems and toward assessment of QOL. There is an increasing awareness that some people can gain strength and are able to see life from a different perspective as a result of the illness experience. Issues of definition and measurement of QOL are considered of central importance.

At the same time, there is growing concern about the needs of children who will not survive. The introduction of home-based palliative care teams and greater involvement of parents in the day-to-day care of the dying child have been universally welcomed.

QUESTIONS FOR THE FUTURE

Medical treatments continue to evolve and change, but for the moment, they remain aggressive. Sadly, there is little indication currently that it is possible to cure childhood cancer without the use of drugs that can themselves cause damage to healthy tissue. So, for the foreseeable future, children will continue to experience adverse effects of treatment, both in the short and longer term. It is therefore important that psychosocial work remains informed about changing clinical issues, and does not continue to focus on problems that are no longer relevant. In the current era of evidence-based medicine, it is essential that we consider how best research can be commissioned and conducted so as to maximize the potential impact on practice and care of the child. Evaluation of the quality of psychosocial work must in part lie in how successfully the field can move forward and respond to changes that occur in medical treatment.

The quality of the child's life has always been an underlying theme in pediatric oncology, though the term was not formally applied until relatively recently. To a large extent, workers in the 1960s and 1970s interested in cognitive effects of treatment were concerned about the child's QOL, though this was defined rather narrowly at the time in terms of cognition and school functioning. We have become much more aware of the possible implications for the child's social and emotional, as well as cognitive development, and the ways in which cancer can affect the child into the future.

The need for psychosocial and clinical care to be complementary is now as important as ever. Identification of exactly how this can be achieved requires much closer collaboration between professionals from different backgrounds. Changes in nursing practice, or the introduction of new health technologies need to take into account the psychosocial implications for families, as well as the implications for clinic staff.

Though much has been achieved in previous decades, it is possible to point to many shortcomings, both practical and theoretical. Psychosocial research has perhaps had less measurable impact on care of children with cancer than many would like. At the same time, changes in treatments, and the possibility of offering new treatment to children with advanced and life-threatening disease, poses new questions for QOL work. New clinical issues demand new approaches to psychosocial care. A key theme in this book is the comparison of achievements in clinical and psychosocial care, and analysis of how well the two approaches are integrated. Psychosocial work should not stand alone, but must be considered an integral part of the total care and management.

As described earlier, the improvements in care of children with cancer have been achieved in large part because medical care has been centralized and coordinated, and minimum standards established. Some corresponding standards for psychosocial care have been recommended, notably in a report published by Masera et al. (1997). The authors described the kind of support needed at the level of medical services, school, and employment. The entire family requires help to understand the illness and accept the need for treatment. Parents must be helped to behave toward the affected child in the same way as to healthy siblings. Children with cancer should be helped to understand their illness and its treatment. At a wider level, health and social policies need to be developed to maximize the integration of patients and their families into society.

It is not clear how far these ideal recommendations have been met. In the remainder of this book, the current state of knowledge about psychosocial consequences of cancer for children and their families is reviewed. The ultimate aim is to set out an agenda for a more coordinated system of psychosocial care to complement modern treatment therapy.

4

Theory and Method

Summary

Children with any kind of chronic illness are more likely to experience social, emotional, or behavioral problems compared with healthy children of the same age. Statements of this type are of limited value, partly because they offer little insight into the causes of the problems. Nor do they explain the variability in outcomes; the fact that some children and their families seem to cope very well.

It is rarely possible to conduct the kind of research that is considered exemplary in more traditional scientific work. There are considerable difficulties in reconciling theoretical and basic scientific work on the one hand, with applied research on the other. It is important, however, that the quality of applied psychosocial work approaches that of more conventional scientific work. Improved theoretical and methodological rigor is vital.

A theory is an attempt to explain why and under what circumstances certain phenomena occur. Theory-driven research is essential to guide research programs and build knowledge. In this chapter, key theoretical assumptions underlying research are described.

Related to this are questions about the most appropriate ways to measure the impact of cancer on children. In the absence of formal QOL measures, a number of proxy indicators are often used. These can include measures of depression, anxiety, self-esteem, or body image.

QUALITY OF SURVIVAL

Children with any kind of chronic condition are more likely to experience social, emotional, or behavioral problems compared with healthy children of the same age (Pless & P. Pinkerton, 1975). The risks to normal adjustment are consistently found to be greater for children with diseases that involve the CNS compared with diseases that are not associated with CNS involvement (Breslau & Marshall, 1985). Furthermore, the risks are not confined to childhood but can continue into adulthood (Pless, Power, & Peckham, 1993). Thus, the child with a chronic illness is potentially a vulnerable adult.

For children with any chronic illness, questions have to be asked about the quality as well as quantity of survival. We may point to success in terms of improved survival statistics, but the reality is that statistics are less relevant to families if their child is unable to take part in normal childhood activities. True success, therefore, needs to include not only the clinical control of the disease, but also the promotion of optimal physical, emotional, social, and family functioning.

As part of everyday life, all children must learn to deal with a number of stressful events. From the earliest ages, children can experience stress when they are unable to reach a desired object, or when a brother or sister has something that they very much want themselves. When they go to school, children are confronted by a greater number of situations that are potentially stressful. How children learn to deal with these situations is important for both their immediate and longer term well-being. Indeed, early experiences are thought to be critical, laying the foundation for how well children are able to cope with stress as adults. Such early experience may have an impact on later life by altering an individual's sensitivity to stress or modifying styles of coping. In this way, the experience of stress may, on the one hand, predispose, or, on the other hand, protect, the child when confronted with subsequent threatening events. Rutter (1981) argued that, in all our lives, stress is inevitable, but individuals learn to protect themselves in different ways. As a general rule, individuals can protect themselves either by altering the meaning of the risk or by changing exposure to risk. Higher self-esteem or self-efficacy may also be protective.

This quality of survival was originally measured in terms of *adjustment*. Yet from the earliest investigations, it was clear that the concept of adjustment to a chronic disease is complex (Pless & P. Pinkerton, 1975). Children who are ill or have a disability are expected to function in two worlds. These include the world of the normal or healthy, as experienced at school, and the world of the sick, as experienced on routine visits to hospitals and clinics. This almost schizophrenic kind of life can be distressing. On the one hand, children are confronted with information that they are expected to do as well in school as anyone else. On the other hand, there are messages that they need to be more careful than others, and their activities may be restricted. In attempting to cope with these dual worlds, they may choose to withdraw from the situation. Children with physical problems may withdraw from any situation that accentuates the difficulties they have with sporting activities. An alternative strategy might be to deny the potential limitations, and make every effort to succeed. Many children do adopt this latter approach very successfully. Thus, denial may be every bit as good a strategy for adjustment as acceptance. For some children in some circumstances, it may be ideal.

In that a central goal of childhood experience is the attainment of an autonomous, healthy, and well-functioning adult, adjustment has often been defined in developmental normative terms: "Good adjustment, then, is reflected as behavior that is age-appropriate, normative and healthy, and that follows a trajectory toward positive adult functioning. Maladjustment is mainly evidenced in behavior that is inappropriate for the particular age, especially when this behavior is qualitatively pathological or clinical in nature" (Wallander & R. J. Thompson, 1995, pp. 125–126).

Thus, when considering the quality of survival, early work focused on measurement of adjustment to chronic disease. In practice, the focus was on maladjustment rather than adjustment, on quantity rather than quality of life. Information was collected from parents (but mostly mothers) rather than children. With time, questions were asked about the appropriateness of this bias to maladjustment rather than adjustment and the almost exclusive reliance on information from mothers rather than children. The shift to measures of QOL reflects attempts to deal with both these criticisms. The emphasis is on quality rather than deficit, and on the child's, rather than the parent's perspective.

THEORY

A theory represents a tentative explanation about why and under what circumstances certain phenomena occur. A theory must be clearly stated, bring together or organize known facts, relate information that may seem unrelated, and enable us to make predictions. Critical is the role of predictions, because these can guide research programs. A theory provides an articulated rationale for choices about participant selection, study design, and strategies for analyzing data. Theory-driven research results in a systematic process and suggests specific research programs to address gaps in knowledge. Theory-driven research is a cumulative process that can involve multiple investigators in order to build knowledge.

Common to many current theoretical approaches is the notion that chronic illness is a specific stressor. New cognitive and emotional strategies are necessary to deal with the stressor. Approaches that acknowledge the unique challenges when a child is ill, rather than an adult, also emphasize the role of the family and the relationship between child and parental functioning.

The *noncategorical* approach is based on the assumption that whatever the specific condition, children with chronic disease and their families face similar adverse experiences that are based on generic dimensions of their condition (Stein & Jessop, 1984). These generic aspects may include the regular demands for treatment and the intrusion this creates into daily life, or the uncertainty that is an integral part of most illness.

The noncategorical approach contrasts with the more traditional medical model, which is based on the assumption that the consequences are disease-specific. In practice, there are likely to be disease-specific and generic processes that are involved in determining adaptation to chronic disease.

In the absence of any comprehensive theory, researchers have assumed that survivors of cancer will show deficits in relation to the normal population. It is further assumed that these psychological problems will decrease with time since diagnosis. This deficit-centered approach dominated early work. Typically, studies involved comparisons of children with cancer with normal peers or siblings, with the hypothesis that those with cancer would compare poorly with normal healthy children. Whereas some studies reported no differences between children with cancer and healthy controls (Anholt, Fritz, & Keener, 1993; Goertzel & Goertzel, 1991), others provided supporting evidence for the deficit-centered approach. Occasionally, and without satisfactory explanation, some reported better adjustment in those with cancer compared with healthy controls (Anholt et al., 1993). In other cases, children with cancer did not rate themselves differently from controls, but parents or teachers did identify deficits.

The Disability-Stress-Coping Model

In acknowledging the variability in outcomes, it has become clear that any approach that is based on the assumption that children with a disease or illness will show deficits in relation to peers is limited. More sophisticated models are necessary to account for the different ways in which children adjust to, and cope with cancer. One of the most influential is the disability-stress-coping model (Wallander & Varni, 1992). These authors hypothesized that a number of variables were potentially involved in good adaptation, and further that these could be explained using a risk-resistance framework. They defined adaptation broadly to include mental health and social and physical functioning, and predicted that the main cause of psychosocial maladjustment was stress. With any disease, there are a number of different types of stress. These can include the functional limitations associated with the condition, those associated with children's everyday lives such as daily hassles, and other stressors associated with daily living such as school transitions. Thus, stress can be unique, involving the specific implications of the disease for the child (and family), and also more generic. Children with cancer still need to go to school, worry about their homework, and take exams. These stresses are shared with other children, and may be made more difficult to achieve given the disease and treatment.

In coping with stress, Wallander and Varni (1992) suggested that individuals have access to three resources. *Intrapersonal* factors include relatively stable individual variables such as temperament, competence, or problem-solving ability. *Stress-processing* factors include cognitive appraisal and coping behaviors. These include the meaning of the illness to the individual, and idiosyncratic approaches to management of stress. *Social ecological* factors include family resources. They can include family economic and financial resources, as well as family resilience and robustness to deal with the problem.

The overall model has precipitated considerable research. Consistent with the noncategorical approach, there has been little evidence to suggest that either condition or severity are important in determining adjustment. Instead, more generic variables such as daily hassles, and characteristics of the child and family, have been shown to be involved.

Appraisal Models

Ireys, Werthamer-Larsson, Koloner, and Gross (1994) suggested that individuals differ in the extent to which they perceive their condition to be responsible for ongoing difficulties and handicaps, regardless of more objective indicators of disease. This "perceived impact" mediates the relationship between condition characteristics and psychological symptoms. Some support for this perceived impact model was obtained in a study involving 600 young people born between 1966 and 1970 who had been diagnosed with a range of conditions. Of the total sample, 286 young adults and their parents ($n = 138$) agreed to take part. In addition to collecting information about the severity and course of the illness and any impairments still experienced, the authors developed a four-item scale to assess perceived impact.

Young-adult survivors reported a high incidence of physical symptoms (relative to figures for population norms). The risk of psychological symptoms was greater for those with restricted activity days, unpredictable physical health, poor prognosis, presence of more than one condition, and presence of speech and hearing problems. Thus, as we might expect, there is a positive relationship between physical and psychological health. However, the effect of these risk factors was moderated by the young adult's perception of the impact of the disease. The more the individual perceived a problem associated with the illness, the more psychological symptoms were reported.

The shift away from deficit-centered approaches was hastened by the increasing recognition that children with serious illness were often adept at identifying gains or benefits associated with the condition. Usually these benefits centered on greater empathy or sensitivity. The experience of illness can change lives, but not inevitably for the worst. For example, Greenberg and A. T. Meadows (1991) interviewed 118 children aged 8–16 years and 120 of their parents. Seventy-one stressed the negative impact of cancer. Negative responses included worries about health, problems with late effects, anger at having been ill, and problems with family interaction. However, 47 were able to identify positive gains about surviving cancer. Results such as these should not be interpreted to suggest that there are real benefits to having cancer, or that anyone would want to have had the disease. However, the point is that things are not necessarily all bad. Individuals vary in how far their family or personal resources help or hinder them overcome the disadvantages associated with illness.

It follows that the long-term impact of cancer might vary depending on the individual interpretation or appraisal of the whole experience. The way in which the individual rationalizes the experience, and integrates the meaning of the disease into a wider life experience may be as critical as the physical experience of the disease. One of the merits of these *appraisal* models is that they provide an additional reason for emphasizing the interdependence between physical and psychological consequences of illness.

Monitoring–Blunting Models

Adjustment to cancer involves striking a fine balance between taking into account the real risks associated with the disease with the need to adopt as normal a lifestyle as possible. Treatment with anthracyclines can increase the risk of cardiac malfunction, and consequently the survivor of childhood cancer may be advised to avoid sudden strenuous and unnecessary exercise. On the other hand, QOL would be severely and pointlessly compromised if the individual took no exercise at all, and stayed in bed all day. Survivors need to be realistic about the risks but at the same time lead as normal a life as possible.

A framework that is concerned specifically with how individuals respond to threatening information was proposed by Miller (1995), and was used by Eiser, Cool, Grimer, Cotter, Carter et al. (1997) to assess psychological outcome among survivors. According to Miller, individuals differ in their responses to aversive events. The styles of monitoring and blunting have been used to determine and predict how individuals cope under threat (Miller, 1995). *Monitors* seek out high levels of information, whereas *blunters* will distract themselves from information and are more likely to suppress or avoid both cognitive and emotional threats.

Monitors are, on the whole, seen to be a population at risk. Their approach to information gathering leaves them vulnerable to stress. Monitoring can be associated with chronic worry that perpetuates negative thoughts and interferes with effective problem solving. Monitors typically show slower recovery from illness, more treatment side effects, and greater self-reported physiological and behavioral dysfunction (Miller, 1995).

Monitoring seems to increase stress through overattention to the potential severity of the situation. Monitors are well tuned-in to what might go wrong. Implicit in the original definition is the notion that monitors typically focus on information and exaggerate the threats cognitively and emotionally (Miller, Rodoletz, Schroeder, Mangan, & Sedlacek, 1996). Miller (1995) also raised the possibility that subtypes of monitors may be identified. Some monitors may be basically "negativistic." These people not only scan for and amplify their health threats, but also expect the worse and have little confidence in their ability to cope effectively. Adverse effects result when "attention to threat serves to repeatedly expose individuals to threatening cues and restokes the fires of fear" (p. 23). In these cases, monitoring is associated with extreme distress and feelings of lack of control. In the study by Eiser et al. (1997) involving survivors of bone tumors, such an approach resulted in extreme preoccupation with worries that things might go wrong, or that cancer will recur. This negativistic approach may be contrasted with a more "adaptive" monitoring in which patients are able to process the information they monitor so that they are able to accommodate the demands of the situation without undue limitations on their QOL.

Although the model has some appeal, the measurement of monitoring–blunting poses some problems. Miller (1987) developed a Monitoring–Blunting Style Scale (MBSS). This is an objective self-report measure that describes four hypothetical situations (e.g., you are scared of flying but have to go somewhere by plane). Each scenario is followed by eight ways of coping, half of which represent monitoring (listen for engine noises) and half blunting responses (watch the movie). Scores are normally calculated to reflect the choice of monitoring over blunting options.

The measure has been criticized for its focus on hypothetical situations (Steptoe, 1989), and lack of internal consistency within the two subscales of monitoring and blunting (Muris, van Zuuren, de Jong, De Beurs, & Hanewald, 1994). Little agreement was found between individuals' own accounts of their behavior in threatening situations and scores on the MBSS (van Zuuren & Wolfs, 1991). In real-life situations (decision making in women undergoing prenatal diagnostic tests), van Zuuren (1994) found that the MBSS failed to tap the full range of coping responses typically employed. In addition, the MBSS was felt to lack sensitivity in a real-world context, and van Zuuren suggested that at the least the scale should be modified to include a 5-point scale instead of a simple yes/no dichotomy, in order to account for grades of response.

Cognitive Processing Theories

Cognitive processing theories have had some success in accounting for how individuals adjust following the experience of traumatic events such as environmental disaster and victimization. Work in this tradition has very much enhanced our understanding of the cognitive, behavioral, emotional, and physiological sequelae of trauma. The central theme in these theories of stress response is that of successfully integrating the trauma into a schematic representation that restores feelings of security and invulnerability (Janoff-Bulman & Frieze, 1983).

The experience of a traumatic event confronts individuals with information that is inconsistent with that included in preexisting schemas. Typically, these preexisting schemas emphasize safety and invulnerability. For recovery to occur, new information inherent in the traumatic experience must be processed until it can be brought into accord with inner models (Horowitz, Wilner, & Alvarez, 1979) and modification of preexisting schemas has to take place to accommodate the new information. Attempts to assimilate threat-related information require exposure to aversive stimuli, resulting in increased arousal and a desire to avoid or escape thoughts and reminders of the trauma. Until a traumatic event can be assimilated and integrated into existing schemas, it is stored in active memory and the psychological elements continue to produce intrusive and emotionally upsetting recollections. The numbing that occurs in PTSD is seen to be a defense against the breakthrough of these images.

Horowitz (1976) proposed two general types of response to stress. The first involves intrusive repetitions of the trauma in thought, imagery, emotion, or behavior. As states of intrusion are inherently painful, a second response mode develops that involves attempts to suppress intrusions, using mechanisms such as denial, emotional numbing, and deliberate avoidance of reminders. Recovery from trauma is thought to result either from cognitive assimilation of the traumatic memory or by revision of existing schemas to accommodate new information.

Cognitive processing theories raise issues concerning the links between intrusive cognitions, reappraisals, and psychosocial adaptation to trauma. Intrusive cognitions are seen to be a normal and necessary part of the cognitive integration process and reappraisal as uniformly adaptive. This adaptive view of intrusions stands in contrast to the designation of persistent intrusive reexperiencing as symptomatic of PTSD. Thus, in common with other contemporary theories, is the idea that adjustment involves active cognitive and emotional work to redefine the threat and direct approaches to coping.

DISTINCTIONS BETWEEN THEORETICAL
AND APPLIED RESEARCH

In considering the value of theory, it is important to emphasize the differences between basic or theoretical work, and more applied or clinical work. In applied work, it is rarely possible to aspire to the levels of precision of data collection and management that is expected in more theoretically orientated work. As a consequence, theoretical work can be criticized or dismissed as lacking generalizability. At the same time, others feel uncomfortable with the lack of control characteristic of applied work.

Researchers are often trained in the experimental method and aspire to these ideals. An experiment is a controlled study in which a researcher manipulates one variable to study its effect on another. In a well-designed experiment, or clinical trial in health-related work, other variables are controlled or held constant. Based on the experimental method, we might wish to test different predictions based on our chosen theory. Thus, the simple prediction in much early work was that children with cancer (or any chronic disease) would have worse psychosocial outcomes compared with healthy children.

There is an immediate problem here in slavishly following the demands of the experimental method. Ideally, children would be randomly assigned to experimental or control groups. In applied work this clearly is not possible. The result may be that our two groups, the experimental (children with cancer) and controls (healthy children), differ on dimensions other than illness. These other dimensions may cloud distinctions between the two groups and reduce our ability to draw definitive conclusions about the impact of cancer on the child's development.

In health-related work, therefore, it is more common to conduct quasi-experimental studies. In this approach, it is not possible to draw firm conclusions about the nature of relationships between variables, because the data are often correlational. Thus, it is not possible to conclude that one variable *causes* another, but rather that there is an association between two variables. It is also possible that the association is mediated by a third, perhaps unidentified variable.

There are a number of variants of the basic quasi-experimental design including the distinction between retrospective and prospective research. The retrospective design looks back at the histories of patients in order to determine commonalities in histories that might account for current health status. The prospective approach looks forward in individuals' lives by studying variables over a period of time. A prospective approach might be used to look at the effects of school absence on children's learning, based on a hypothesis that more absence would be associated with poorer educational outcomes. This would involve recruiting a large number of children on diagnosis, and then assessing their school attendance and educational achievement over a number of years. The advantages over the retrospective approach is that the data are considered more reliable; we don't need to rely on parents' recall of their child's school absences.

It was argued in chapter 3 that the age when children become ill may be an important determinant of how they react to the diagnosis and adjust over time. Studies to look at the effects of age are essentially quasi-experimental studies. It is not possible to assign children randomly according to their age, but we can create different groups of approximately similar ages. It is then possible to compare these different age groups on key variables of interest. Again it is possible to identify two basic approaches. The cross-sectional approach involves comparing groups of children of different ages at the same time. In the longitudinal approach, groups of children are followed up over time, which enables us to determine how individuals change over a period of time.

MEASURING QUALITY OF SURVIVAL

The information in chapters 2 and 3 was presented to give a preliminary account of the many ways in which diagnosis of cancer imposes a major challenge to the child's adjustment and well-being. In many situations, we may want to have formal methods to document the degree of distress. What do we mean by adjustment and how can it be measured? Standardized ways of measuring adjustment are potentially useful. These allow us to compare findings across studies, or over time. Clinically, such measures would provide standards against which we could determine if a child was improving, or deteriorating with time. As with other work in the social sciences, measurement of adjustment has proved more difficult than measuring concepts in the physical sciences, such as height or weight.

In the final section of this chapter, some of the most frequently used measures are described. It is important to be familiar with how aspects of adjustment have been measured. A major problem is that most measures in common use were developed for general purposes, and may not be so appropriate for work involving children with cancer. The measures reviewed include those most commonly assumed to be affected by cancer: adjustment, depression, anxiety, self-concept, and body image. In all cases, the assumption is that the experience of cancer will leave an individual vulnerable, and this will be demonstrated in worse scores compared with the normal healthy population. As can be seen in later chapters, other concepts have been assessed, but there has been a real bias to use of the following limited number of measures. Appreciating the problems inherent in measurement of psychological concepts is essential in order to appraise critically the resulting research literature.

Psychosocial Adjustment

As already described, quality of survival has traditionally been measured in terms of adjustment. In turn, this has often been based on parents' reports and most commonly involved use of the Child Behavior Checklist (CBCL; Achenbach, 1991). This was developed for use by parents of children aged between 4 and 18 years. Parents are asked to rate their child's behavior over the past 6 months on a series of scales. The measure yields a *Social Competence* subscale that includes 40 items about the child's activities, social involvement, and school performance, and a total social competence score. There is also a *Behavior Problems* subscale that includes 113 items that assess behavioral syndromes (Internalizing, Externalizing, and Total Behavior Problems). The scale was initially standardized on a large sample (2,368 recruited children from the general population and mental health services). The measure has traditionally been considered to be exemplary of its kind. The CBCL was subsequently modified for teacher reports and a further measure is suitable for self-completion by adolescents (Achenbach & Edelbrock, 1987).

Nevertheless, it has come under some criticism as a measure of adjustment in sick children (Perrin, Stein, & Drotar, 1991). First, many of the items refer to somatic symptoms. As a consequence, it has to be expected that children with cancer (or any physical illness) would show more problems than healthy children. Cursory examination of total scores might therefore be taken to indicate that sick children had more behavior problems than healthy children, though these figures may be artificially inflated as sick children would inevitably have more somatic symptoms than healthy peers. Second, given that the measure was originally designed to assess psychopathology, it is unlikely to be sensitive enough to detect the mild behavior problems that might be expected in sick children. Third, the items used to assess social competence tend to measure accomplishment and participation in activities rather than competence in social interaction: "Several items assess outcomes such as the level of activity in sports and clubs that may be limited by illness, physical handicap, transportation requirements, doctors' appointments and medication needs. The fact that some children with chronic illness are unable to participate in certain social activities solely because of their condition does not mean that they are socially less competent" (Perrin et al., 1991, p. 416).

Depression

A number of paper-and-pencil measures are available to assess depression. Although there is overlap between the measures, there is also considerable difference in emphasis. Measures such as the Children's Depression Inventory (CDI; Kovacs, 1983) assess the frequency of depressive symptoms whereas interview measures tend to focus on the presence or absence of a clinical syndrome.

The CDI (Kovacs, 1983) is a self-report measure for children between 8 and 15 years of age that includes 27 items to assess appetite, sleep, fatigue, and school performance. The scale has good internal consistency and significant item–total correlations. Paralleling the objections raised about the CBCL, questions about the appropriateness of the scale for work with children with cancer were raised by Worchel et al. (1988). These authors compared depression scores for children with cancer with a sample of children referred for psychiatric assessment and healthy schoolchildren. As would be expected, the psychiatric group reported more depression than the other two groups. Unexpectedly, however, healthy children tended to report more, rather than less, depression than those with cancer. As an explanation for these findings, the authors suggested that children with cancer are less depressed than would be expected because they use denial as a means of coping with their cancer. This was further supported by findings that children with cancer reported that they were getting better. The problem may be in differences in interpretation of "getting better." Although the authors felt the children were being unrealistic, it is possible that they did feel much better compared with when they were diagnosed. Within the group of children with cancer there was considerable variability, with some children indeed showing significant amounts of depression, and others much less. This created an additional problem in that some items did not distinguish between these depressed and nondepressed children with cancer. In particular, somatic items and those thought to measure low self-concept (feeling that one does things wrong, hates oneself, feels not as good as other kids) did not discriminate between the two groups.

As with the CBCL, it is possible that depression scores for sick children are inflated, given that they are likely to miss school or experience disturbances in appetite as a result of their illness rather than because they feel depressed. At the least, it is recommended that separate scores are derived for depression and psychological symptoms. Given the apparent ambiguities in their study, Worchel et al. (1988) recommended the use of multiple measures of depression for work involving children with cancer.

Use of depression measures may have limited value in general assessments of children with cancer. The kinds of behaviors assessed (withdrawal, sadness) may reflect a normal response to hospitalization and children's attempts to protect themselves from the threats involved. Depression inventories, by including somatic items along with those more typically associated with depression, may result in artificially inflated estimates of depression in physically sick children. The focus on negative behaviors must be questioned and there is a concern among some that asking children to complete such negative questions may be demoralizing in itself.

Anxiety

Anxiety in children is usually assessed by one of three scales: the State–Trait Anxiety Inventory (STAIC; Spielberger, 1973), the Revised Children's Manifest Anxiety Scale (RCMAS; C. R. Reynolds & Richmond, 1985), and the Social Anxiety Scale for Children (La Greca, Dandes, Wick, Shaw, & Stone, 1988).

The STAIC measures two concepts of anxiety. These include state or situational anxiety and trait or personality anxiety. Children of 8 years and above should be able to complete the scale for themselves. The anxiety subscale includes 20 items that are each rated on 3-point scales. Internal consistency based on ratings made by 246 children was between .82 and .87 for children aged between 8 and 13 years of age.

The RCMAS is a 37-item self-report inventory of trait anxiety in children. Items are scored true or false. Subsequently, three factors have been identified underlying the scale (W. M. Reynolds, 1985). These were labeled physiological anxiety, worry and oversensitivity, and concentration anxiety. The scale has been reported to have good internal consistency, test–retest reliability and construct and discriminative validity.

The Social Anxiety Scale for Children assesses fear of negative evaluation, social avoidance, and social distress.

Self-Esteem

The Self-Perception Profile for Children (SPPC; Harter, 1985) was designed to assess personal competence across a number of domains (global self-worth, scholastic competence, social acceptance, athletic competence, physical appearance, and behavioral competence). An adolescent version (Harter, 1988) includes additional items to measure romantic appeal, close friendships, and job competence. In the child version, each domain is assessed with six items. Children are asked to choose between two statements that best describe themselves and then rate whether the statement is "really true for me" or "sort of true for me." Good internal reliability for the whole scale and domains has been reported. There is also a pictorial scale for work with younger children (Harter & Pike, 1984).

The Piers–Harris Self-Concept Scale (PHSCS; Piers & D. Harris, 1969) was developed for children between 10 and 18 years and includes 80 items that were adapted from a pool of items collected from children who were asked to describe what they liked and did not like about themselves. Responses are made on a yes/no basis. The scale was originally conceived to be unidimensional but subsequently six domains were added. These include behavior, intellectual and school status, physical appearance, anxiety, popularity, and happiness/satisfaction.

Body Image

Work attempting to clarify the factors that affect body image in individuals with chronic conditions has been slowed by the lack of a comprehensive and standardized measure (Ben-Tovim & M. K. Walker, 1995; Hopwood, 1992; Vamos, 1993). In the absence of a cancer-specific scale, most research has relied on measures developed to study body image in normal children and adolescents, or for groups with special needs such as those with eating disorders. Again, these measures have met with some criticism when used with the chronically ill. For example, the Body Cathexis Scale (Secord & Jourard, 1953), which attempts to assess satisfaction with body parts and body processes, has been criticized for lacking accuracy and being too lengthy for use in clinical settings (Hopwood, 1992).

Measures developed within the field of eating disorders are not ideal for children with cancer, as they often include questions about body size distortion. Individuals who score in the range typically indicative of distortion may simply be demonstrating heightened awareness or distress related to body parts affected by the illness or treatment. Children with cancer can experience eating fads and fancies, but these are often associated with learned aversive reactions to specific foods during chemotherapy.

Moreover, instruments measuring individual's feelings about their physical appearance, typically focusing on weight-related appearance, are not ideal because they do not touch on all of the areas relevant to chronic illness. These include patient's feelings about specific body parts affected by treatment, reactions of others to visible marks of illness, and feelings about how the condition affects body functioning. In addition, many of these scales were validated on samples predominantly composed of females (J. K. Thompson, Penner, & Altabe, 1990). Consequently, they may have less face validity for work with males, especially males who are ill rather than having weight problems.

Body image scales most commonly used with children include:

1. The Self-Image Questionnaire for Young Adolescents (Petersen, Schulenberg, Abramowitz, Offer, & Jarcho, 1984) is an 11-item measure designed to assess the positive and negative feelings toward general aspects of body among normal adolescents. Items are rated on 6-point scales with responses ranging from "describes me very well" to "does not describe me at all." Good internal consistency has been reported and the measure correlates as predicted with general measures of self-esteem.

2. The SPPC (Harter, 1985) as described previously. Both the versions for children and adolescents include a subscale to measure physical appearance.

3. The Body Image Avoidance Questionnaire (BIAQ; J. C. Rosen, Srebnik, Saltzberg, & Wendt, 1991) includes 19 items that are thought to reflect body image disturbance (avoid looking in the mirror, don't go out socially). Again the scale has been reported to have adequate internal consistency and significantly correlates with attitudes about shape and distortion of body size.

4. The Body Image Instrument (Kopel, Eiser, Cool, Grimer, & Carter, 1998) was developed specifically for work with adolescents with cancer and is suitable for both males and females. Unlike previous measures described, it was developed specifically to assess the impact of cancer on body image in children and adolescents. Items were elicited from previous interviews with children in the defined age range undergoing treatment for a number of different cancers. The scale includes 28 items rated on a series of 5-point scales. Psychometric data were reported based on the responses of 40 males and 27 females. Five subscales were identified. These included *general appearance, body competence, others' reaction to appearance, value of appearance,* and *body parts.* Adequate internal reliability for the subscales and the total body image score were reported. Predicted correlations between these subscales and measures of QOL (Eiser, Havermans, Craft, & Kernahan, 1995) were also reported.

Coping

Four approaches to measuring coping have been identified (Compas et al., 2001). These include self-report questionnaires, semistructured interviews, observations, and reports from others including parents or teachers. The Kidcope (Spirito, Stark, & C. Williams, 1988) is probably the most widely used measure for children with a chronic illness. This is a 10-item self-report measure for adolescents aged 12–18 years. Although there are no subscales, individual items are designed to tap different approaches to coping, such as seeking social support, wishful thinking, distraction, or blaming others.

CONCLUSIONS

In developing theories of adjustment to childhood cancer, it is possible to draw on expertise from two different areas. The choice is between extending adult theories of adjustment to illness, or borrowing ideas from theories of normal child development. To the extent that children coping with cancer are more similar to other children than adults, the most appropriate approach may be one that takes into account normal cognitive and social development.

Similar reasoning must underlie choice of measures. Again, measures in most frequent use have often been developed by "downward extension" and simplification of adult measures. As such, they may fail to capture fully the unique ways in which cancer affects a child compared with an adult. Understanding the unique ways in which children perceive their illness may require a different approach, and one that routinely involves children in development and evaluation of new measures. The involvement of children may lead to not only more sensitive measures but also a greater range of measures. If we listen to children, the limited focus (on behavior, self-esteem, and body image) may need to be reappraised.

II

CHILDREN ON TREATMENT

The aims of Part I were first to introduce the reader to important medical information about cancer and second to show how psychosocial work has developed in response to changes in medical treatment and changes in prognosis. The need for regular and often painful treatment, the intrusiveness of medical care into everyday life, and the degree of stress experienced by the whole family contribute to concerns about how cancer and its treatment might affect the child's normal development. In measuring the success of treatment, therefore, it is important not only to control the disease, but also to try and ensure that the child grows into a socially integrated and autonomous young adult. The ultimate goal of treatment is to ensure quality, as well as quantity, of survival.

It is clear that for the most part researchers have measured QOL in a variety of ways. At different times, QOL has been inferred from information about the child's emotional functioning, cognitive functioning, or social relationships. At other times, school attendance and participation in school activities have been taken as proxy indicators of adjustment and QOL. The problem with much of this work is that the emphasis has been more on describing deficits rather than competencies, school absence rather than attendance, and problems rather than coping. This bias is only slowly giving way to interest in children's coping, resilience, and QOL.

In chapter 5, we consider how a diagnosis of cancer affects children in different ways, depending on their age. We have learned that the child's response is unique and different from that of adults facing chronic illness. Drawing on much work in child development, it has been recognized that children and adolescents experience and perceive illness and treatment differently from adults, and furthermore, that children's reactions differ predictably depending on chronological age. The restrictions of cancer that most upset the 3-year-old are different from those that upset the 12-year-old. Younger children may be most upset by the interruptions to their daily routines, older children by the restrictions that illness places on their social lives.

Whatever their age, a big question that faces parents and medical staff concerns how to explain the illness to the child. Medical opinion is that informed children cope better and are more likely to comply with medical treatment. Although there is only limited evidence in support of this idea, current practice is to be as honest with children as possible. We have learned that it is impossible to shield children from information about the possible consequences of cancer, and that open and honest communication may be most helpful.

In chapter 6, the effect of cancer on the child's behavior and adjustment is considered. This chapter is organized around five commonly used outcome measures: depression, anxiety, self-esteem, body image, and coping. Much of this work is based on parents' views about the child's emotional and behavioral adjustment. As can be seen in chapter 11, parents' views can be biased, perhaps because of parents' own distress.

Though children may be "patients" at home, they are expected to lead a more normal life in school. Teachers and classmates may be less inclined to excuse tantrums and bad behavior compared with parents and grandparents. It is important for children with cancer to go to school so that they have the same opportunities to learn as other children, and also to be with friends. In the short term, school offers the opportunity to do well and consequently the potentially damaging effects of illness on self-esteem can partly be mitigated. In the longer term, school success is critical for success in life. In chapter 7, the focus is on school behavior and social relationships. This chapter concludes with a description of some interventions that have been used especially to ease the child's reintegration to school after diagnosis. The subsequent chapters focus more on academic achievement, first for those with ALL (chapter 8) and second for those with a CNS tumor (chapter 9).

Effects of Chronic Illness
on the Child

Summary

Diagnosis of any illness is a challenge to the attainment of tasks character-istic of the child's development. The schema originally described by Erikson (1959) is described and appropriately modified to account for the challenges of a cancer diagnosis.

As described in chapter 3, there has been a major shift in attitudes to communication about illness, from protecting children from knowledge of the disease and its implications, to recognition that more open and hon-est communication might be associated with better outcomes. It is as-sumed that children who understand more about the disease will accept treatment better and be more cooperative with medical procedures. All the evidence suggests that informed children do accept the illness and treatment better, but many questions remain about how, and when, it is best to tell them. Very little is known about how children below 8 years of age understand their illness or its implications for their future health.

CHILDREN ARE NOT LITTLE ADULTS ✕

In this chapter, the emphasis is on the experience of diagnosis from the child's point of view. Following diagnosis, many decisions need to be made, and in the case of younger children, these are of course made by parents. Even for older children, the fact that they are invariably so ill on diagnosis means that parents make most of the crucial first decisions. Other issues, such as telling other friends and relations about the illness, also affect parents much more than children. Even so, the child's life is turned upside down, often in a very brief period of time, and so it is important to try to understand the experience from the child's point of view.

Whenever we are miserable or upset, or feeling ill, a natural reaction is to behave as younger than we really are. So the student, ill for the first time away from home, takes one of her childhood books to bed with a cup of hot chocolate. Children are exactly the same. When they are ill, they can behave as if they were much younger. So the 3-year-old who used to feed herself and go to bed at night without a fuss suddenly demands to be fed and to sleep in her parents' bed. The child may well have achieved a good deal of independence in terms of feeding herself or cleaning her teeth, but now expects help with all of these things. She may have previously been positive about going to preschool, but now cries when she is left. The previously placid child throws a tantrum for the slightest reason. For parents, dealing with a 3- or 4-year-old who behaves like a baby again is an added difficulty in coping with the cancer.

Older children can also react by behaving in younger ways. They too can become more dependent on parents and withdraw into themselves. Adolescents are typically poor communicators, and it is difficult to tell if refusing to talk about things is a depressive reaction to treatment or part of normal behavior.

The preceding examples are based on observations and there is surprisingly little formal literature attempting to describe how children typically react following diagnosis. It is, of course, very difficult to collect these kinds of data. Very sick children may be unable to describe their feelings, and whatever their age, most children feel too ill on diagnosis. So research is quite limited in that it is necessary to rely on parents' reports about how children reacted in the past, or to ask children what they remember after all treatment has been completed.

The diagnosis of any chronic illness during childhood or adolescence is particularly difficult because it is so unexpected and out of time. As individuals grow older, it is inevitable that they succumb to a greater number of illnesses, but at least in developed countries, it is expected that children lead very healthy and disease-free lives. Thus, illness at any time during childhood poses special problems for all concerned.

More than this, the way in which a disease affects the family may depend on the child's age. "The mechanism by which a child's physical illness may modify the expected developmental progression can be seen in the same light: the illness affects the child's interaction with the physical and social environment in which he or she lives, and aspects of the child's environment such as parents, peers, or school systems, are altered as a result of the illness" (Perrin & Gerrity, 1984, p. 19).

Thus, the extent to which any illness affects QOL is in large part dependent on the child's developmental stage at the time. This has been recognized with respect to physical illness generally (Perrin & Gerrity, 1981) and diabetes specifically (B. J. Anderson, 1990), but can also be applied to childhood cancer. Early work suggested that children diagnosed during middle childhood or adolescence are more at risk of psychosocial difficulties compared with those diagnosed in infancy (Koocher, O'Malley, Gogan, & Foster, 1980). By way of explanation, Koocher et al. proposed that the developmental tasks of infancy may be less disrupted by illness than those of adolescence. In practice, many variables contribute to the normative attainment of developmental tasks, and there is unlikely to be a linear relationship between disease onset and subsequent adjustment. Even so, it is important to recognize that the impact of illness may have a differential impact depending on developmental level.

According to Erikson (1959), development in childhood proceeds through a series of stages. Erikson identified eight developmental phases, each characterized by a specific psychosocial crisis needing to be resolved. These include (a) trust versus mistrust, (b) autonomy versus shame and doubt, (c) initiative versus guilt, (d) industry versus inferiority, (e) identity and reputation versus identity diffusion, (f) intimacy and solidarity versus isolation, (g) generativity versus self-absorption, and (h) integrity versus despair.

It is assumed that certain developmental tasks need to be attained within a given age range. Attainment of these tasks is considered to be the hallmark of healthy growth and development. Maturation and experience interact to enable the child to achieve particular tasks and proceed to the next developmental stage. Physical, psychological, and environmental processes may interfere with the normal sequence of attainments. Chronic illness generally and cancer particularly pose one such potential threat.

Infants

According to Erikson (1959), it is important for the young child to acquire a sense of trust in adults. Small children may be adversely affected by periods of separation from their parents. Clearly, diagnosis and hospitalization challenge the child's attainment of a basic sense of trust. Although many hospitals offer accommodation for parents, it is inevitable that children experience some enforced separations, either because parents must spend some time at home with their other children or because hospital policies do not encourage parents to be present during medical procedures. Far from providing a safe and nurturing environment, the child may come to view adults as people who cause pain and distress. Parents may feel particularly helpless because it is not possible to explain what is happening to the child or prepare them in advance for painful procedures. The threat to the infant's development centers therefore on the challenge to attaining a sense of trust in others.

Children

Key developmental tasks in childhood involve the attainment of autonomy and establishment of relationships with friends. Like infants, school-age children experience many separations from parents. Critical for the school-age child, however, is the fact that cancer makes them feel different from others. Differences may arise partly because they are less able to keep up with friends and take part in normal activities (Spirito, De-Lawyer, & Stark, 1991), and partly because they look different. Children with leukemia can be teased when they return to school (Ross & Ross, 1984), especially when they have no hair after chemotherapy. For some children, teasing can be more upsetting than the physical pain experienced from the disease or diagnostic procedures.

Cancer can also make a child feel lonely or isolated and create difficulties establishing and maintaining friendships (Noll, LeRoy, Bukowski, Rogosch, & Kulkarni, 1991). Difficult relationships with friends can have negative implications for many aspects of school life. Children may have to cope with teasing, and comments from peers, as well as deal with their own concerns about feeling different and unattractive (La Greca, 1990). Although hospital policy is generally to encourage children to return to school as soon as possible after diagnosis, many experience difficulties. Children with cancer experience more absences than do healthy friends or those with other chronic conditions (A. Charlton et al., 1991). Occasionally, children become so upset about how cancer has affected the way they look, or become so afraid of being teased or laughed at, that they simply refuse to go to school. However, documented incidences of school phobia are very rare (S. B. Lansky, Lowman, Vats, & Gyulay, 1975). School absence also has implications for cognitive development and normal academic achievement. Teachers are often uncertain about how to handle sick children, especially in knowing how far they can be treated the same as other members of the class (Eiser & Town, 1987). Teachers' lack of knowledge about childhood cancer and their own fears about the disease can further compromise the child's successful integration in school, as teachers' response to their own uncertainty may be to make allowances and expect lower achievements. Thus, cancer may challenge attainment of autonomy, initiative, and industry.

Adolescents

The key developmental tasks of adolescence are attainment of independence from the nuclear family, development of a supportive peer group, and identity formation through adoption of appropriate work and career choices. The task requires differentiation from the family, while still maintaining warmth and closeness (Grotevant & Cooper, 1985). Peers make a significant contribution to the achievement of identity formation, with adolescents typically oscillating between family and peers for support and encouragement. Cancer, like any other serious illness, potentially compromises the individual's ability to achieve these goals (Hauser, DiPlacido, Jacobson, Willett, & Cole, 1993). Adolescents may be forced into a position of dependence on parents while also being less able to participate in a normal social life. Treatment can be especially disruptive for education during adolescence, and many are forced to interrupt their studies or delay taking major examinations.

Adolescents, often more than younger children, are concerned about changes in their physical appearance as a result of cancer. Some changes are temporary. Newly diagnosed patients, for example, may lose their hair or put on weight. Later, there can be more permanent changes in appearance. Many children, particularly those treated by CNS irradiation, have growth problems. At the extreme, some patients may have had an amputation to remove an affected limb. Clearly such drastic surgery may pose considerable challenges to the attainment of normal body image, as well as restrict work and social opportunities. Adolescents face risks to the attainment of identity and intimacy.

Young Adults

According to Erikson (1959), one of the key tasks of this period is the achievement of a close, loving relationship with a romantic partner. There is some evidence that young adults who experienced cancer as children have particular difficulties in this regard (Mackie, J. Hill, Kondryn, & McNally, 2000). Whether this is because they have closer and more dependent relationships with parents compared with children with no history of illness, or whether they are fearful of making close interpersonal relationships is not clear. Anxieties about treatment-induced infertility have been suggested as a reason why some young adults delay establishing close relationships. Again, the attainment of intimacy is under threat.

Thus, there may be some specific implications of diagnosis of cancer depending on the child's age. However, the implications are unlikely to be as specific as described initially; the attainment of a sense of industry may be challenged by illness whenever it occurs. Like any schema, these ideas are tentative, and many other variables, including gender or family circumstances, will also affect the way the child reacts. However, the underlying message remains important. We cannot assume that chronological age will be the only, or even the most important, variable in determining how the child and family adjust to cancer. However, in many cases, age may prove a good general indicator. It is crucial to consider children with cancer separately from adults with cancer, but furthermore, we must recognize the enormous changes in development that take place throughout childhood. Limiting the negative impact of cancer for a 3-year-old requires a different approach compared with working with the adolescent.

TELLING THE CHILD

Following the diagnosis, parents are faced with many difficult decisions, not least of which concerns what to tell the child. Some intuitively want to talk things through. These parents rationalize their decisions on the grounds that "the child is bright and will find out anyway." Others opt for a more protective approach, believing that too much information can only lead to distress. There are no "right" answers.

When questions were first raised about whether children should be told if they had a life-threatening illness, the popular view was that children should be protected from information that could be distressing (Share, 1972). This view needs to be seen in the context of public attitudes at the time. It was widely accepted that patients, both children and adults, did not need to know details of their illness. Patient groups were less organized and less vociferous, and patients themselves were more likely to accept the absolute decisions of the doctor. These decisions, about not involving children, were often justified given the relatively poor survival rates. If children had a short time to live, there was less need to burden them with details of the condition.

Many events have occurred to change these views and the result is a more open approach to information giving between patients and their doctor. First, patients want and expect much more detail about their illness. Patient groups have pressed for a role in decision making. The Internet has made information more widely available, and means that families are not dependent on their doctor as the only source of information. They can use the Internet to find out more than they were told in clinic or to check out the accuracy of information they were given. They will want to satisfy themselves whether or not alternative treatments are available, and that they are being offered the most up-to-date information.

Second, modern medicine requires patients to take a more active role in their own care. Thus, children with diabetes have to learn to balance their food and energy requirements and self-inject insulin. Children with cystic fibrosis need to integrate a regimen of medication and physiotherapy into their daily routine. There are fewer demands made of children and families in the context of self-management of childhood cancer, but treatment can still take time and cause family friction. Families must manage a complex medication program. Children may be advised to take special care of their teeth and use a mouthwash regularly. In addition, especially in the early stages of treatment, care has to be taken to avoid infection and any early signs of high temperature need to be responded to urgently. Parents have to be especially vigilant about the child's health and daily activities.

As soon as treatment programs required patients (and their families) to take on responsibility for some aspects of their care, greater information was essential. How can patients be expected to implement home care routines if they do not understand the reasons? One of the arguments put forward to justify improving explanations to children was based on an assumption that informed children would comply better with treatment than would noninformed children.

Third, the whole approach to information giving had to change as life expectancy improved. As the goals shifted from preserving life at all costs to promoting the overall quality of the child's life, both during and after treatment, finding better ways to communicate with children became paramount. Doctors have to find ways to establish a working relationship with families so as to facilitate collaboration over many years.

Fourth, it was increasingly acknowledged that children really wanted to know about their illness. If they were not given the information that they wanted, they would set about finding out in other ways. Restricting the child's information is rarely successful. Children can piece together information given them by other children; they are exposed to information in magazines, on television, and through the Internet. It is only a matter of time before they know they have cancer, and therefore it is better that they have accurate information, rather than pick up fragments or inaccuracies.

Children's Knowledge of Cancer

Thus, the current climate in pediatric oncology is for open, honest communication between children, their parents, and doctors. This is based on the assumption that well-informed children will cope better, follow the doctor's advice, and generally adopt a more positive approach to managing their illness. Consequently, informed children will have a better QOL. In contrast, it is argued that poorly informed children may believe their illness is more serious than it really is and worry more. The rationale for involving children in decisions about their treatment and its implications are now widely accepted, at least in the United States and many European countries.

Despite all the arguments about involving children in decisions about their own care, very little is known formally about what children know, how they come to gain their knowledge, and how far they understand the implications. Almost without exception, research has been restricted to asking parents what they have told the child or what they think the child understands. However, there are real limitations in relying on parents for information about what the child understands about the disease. Parents may assume that the child knows more than they do or that they would ask if they wanted to know. A further limitation of work in this area is that parents are asked to recall what they told their child, often many years after the initial diagnosis. Although there is no reason to suppose that parents would deliberately report incorrectly, their views will inevitably be colored by subsequent events. Their memories will also be blurred as a result of their own emotional states at the time of diagnosis; we may remember less well during times of emotional crisis.

Chesler, Paris, and Barbarin (1986) interviewed parents about their views concerning what and how children should be told, and how they themselves had set about it. Parents reported that what the child was told was influenced by the child's age, whether or not there were other children in the family, their own religious beliefs, and their access to information and support. As would be expected, parents of younger children shared less information with their child compared with parents of older children. In the study by Eiser, Parkyn, Havermans, and McNinch (1994), all the children were told about the illness on diagnosis, though in a number of cases this was very much on the recommendation of the consultants. Left to themselves, a number of parents would have preferred to wait and see before telling the child.

The assumption that any information is better than no information has been supported by a limited amount of empirical work. Claflin and Barbarin (1991) asked 43 children about what they knew about the illness. Children below 9 years of age had been told less than older children. However, children's stress was unrelated to age or level of information. Thus, if the goal in not telling children was to protect them in some way, it does not appear to have been successful. Moreover, it seems that the sooner children are told the better. Children who were told about the illness on diagnosis, or within 1 year if they were under 6 years on diagnosis, were better adjusted compared with those who were not told until later (Slavin, O'Malley, Koocher, & Foster, 1982).

Similar conclusions about the importance of early and accurate communications were reached by Last and van Veldhuizen (1995). Fifty-six children aged between 8 and 16 years of age completed self-report measures of anxiety and depression. Their parents were interviewed about how much information had been given to the child. Children who had been given more information about the diagnosis and prognosis of their disease were significantly less anxious and depressed than those who were given less information. The majority of children expressed the view that it was better to be told about the disease.

These studies suggesting that children who are told about the illness have better emotional health than those who don't know are slightly difficult to interpret. It is not explicitly stated exactly what children know, so it is not clear that they "know" the worst, in terms of the potential life-threatening nature of the disease. Parents may prefer to tell them that they are seriously ill and will need treatment for a long time, while skirting around some of the more difficult aspects such as the potential life-threatening nature of the disease or possibility of long-term side effects. (However, parents may genuinely have difficulties understanding some of these issues themselves.) Also, it is not clear if it is important that children know the facts about their disease or simply that they trust adults to be honest with them.

Certainly there are few systematic accounts about how children find out about their disease. The focus is on knowledge rather than how information is given. It can be assumed that children of 3 or 4 years of age cannot be expected to understand much about the disease but even at this age it is likely that children do adopt aspects of parental attitudes.

To date, all the studies identified have relied on retrospective reports. Much less is known about the implications of children's knowledge for their adjustment and coping with cancer over time. From this perspective, prospective studies, attempting to link how children find out about the illness with their subsequent coping, would be useful.

A Working Committee of SIOP reported in 1997 about the "best ways" of informing families and children about the diagnosis. Based on the experiences reported in 10 specialist centers throughout the world, many practical recommendations were made. With regard to children, the Committee recommended that "attention . . . should be . . . paid to variations in the child's age and developmental level. Communicating with the child should focus on explaining the disease and its treatments, realistic discussion of potential side-effects as well as long-term cure, and various interpersonal and social issues" (Masera et al., 1997, p. 384).

So how should "variations in the child's age and developmental level" guide our discussions with them? In the next section, the focus is on children's understanding of illness and treatment, and how far this has influenced, or should influence, communication on a pediatric oncology ward.

CHILDREN'S UNDERSTANDING OF ILLNESS

In order to make rational decisions about a child's need for information in clinical contexts it is first important to understand how children's views about illness, its cause, and treatment differ from those of adults.

The Psychoanalytic Approach

The very earliest efforts to account for children's understanding of illness were developed from the principles of psychoanalytic theory. Thus, it was argued that children would blame themselves for their illness. This idea of blame may then be reinforced in that treatments are often painful. Thus, children might think they are being punished for wrongdoing.

Early work provided some support for the hypothesis that sick children would blame themselves for their illness (Brodie, 1974; Cook, 1975). Langford (1948) described how adults may unwittingly communicate these ideas to children:

> Parental admonitions intensify any latent fear that the child may have that illness comes as a punishment. Colds come because the child disobeys and does not wear his rubbers. A leg is broken because the child does not heed his mothers cautioning advice not to roller skate in the street. Upset stomach could be avoided if the child would only eat what he is supposed to. Eyes are ruined by fine print or reading in poor light or from too assiduous attention to comics. The warnings about what will happen are often supplemented with an "I told you so" when something does happen to the child. These are common statements by almost all parents and contribute to the child's idea that when he is sick he is being punished. The all too common practice of threatening the child with the doctor or an operation if he continues to be bad (which to many parents means disobedience) lends further reality to the child's fears when he becomes sick and is taken for medical advice. (p. 244)

A number of workers have tried to determine how far children with cancer do blame themselves. Ross and Ross (1984) interviewed 32 children with leukemia aged between 5 and 12 years. They were a very well-informed group, with 88% understanding that leukemia resulted from a proliferation of blood cells and 81% understanding why different procedures were necessary. None of the children blamed themselves for the illness.

Springer (1994) reasoned that if children blamed themselves for cancer, they might expect to be blamed for other activities as well. Children with cancer and healthy children were asked how likely it was they would get sick after eating a stolen apple. Most children in both groups rejected the idea that it was possible to become sick through eating stolen food. However, children with cancer were slightly more likely to say that they would get sick after eating a stolen apple compared with healthy children. Perhaps, though, they were not thinking in terms of blame. Children undergoing chemotherapy are likely to be sick a lot anyway, and perhaps they simply were stating what to them was quite obvious—they got sick a lot more than before they had cancer.

So although there is little to suggest that today's children blame themselves, those who do may have a hard time. Bearison, Sadow, Granowetter, and Winkel (1993) found that children who thought they were to blame for their cancer were coping less well than those who accepted explanations in terms of other causes (e.g., environmental).

Cognitive Approaches

By far the most popular approach has been guided by a perspective linking development of understanding of illness to the different stages of cognitive development (Piaget, 1952). This suggests that children progress through a series of stages in their understanding of illness that parallel those described by Piaget to account for changes in understanding of physical concepts. Children's understanding of physical concepts, such as space or time, change throughout development, so it is reasonable to suppose that similar changes occur in understanding of illness.

Bibace and Walsh (1979, 1981) built on these accounts of development put forward by Piaget. They developed a semistructured interview to probe children's understanding of illness. This included questions about the cause, treatment, and consequences of illness. Children's responses were coded and the results interpreted to suggest that children's understanding of illness followed a similar pattern as described to account for understanding of physical concepts. They proposed that in the preoperational stage (between 2 and 6 years) children use immediate temporal or physical cues to account for the onset of illness. Thus, in the interviews they conducted, children might say that colds were caused by magic, or from trees, or by God. Disease was typically described in terms of single events linked with their own experience. At a later concrete-operational stage (7–11 years), children become aware of the contagious nature of illness. At least initially children believe that, for a disease to be contagious, some physical touching or proximity is necessary. Finally in a formal operational stage, children from 11 years of age understand the difference between internal and external causes of disease, can accept that illness can have multiple causes, and ultimately understand the connection between physical and psychological well-being. Thus, a heart attack can happen as a result of physical ill health but also because of a particular psychological approach to life. In the same way, recovery can be aided by an individual's mind-set. As Piaget emphasized, not all individuals reached the most sophisticated level of understanding of physical concepts, so too Bibace and Walsh suggested that not all individuals understand these more sophisticated views about understanding illness.

This broad schema has been taken up by others to account for children's understanding of the body (Crider, 1981), where babies come from (Bernstein & Cowan, 1981), and the role of the doctor (Steward & Steward, 1981). Bibace and Walsh (1981) also went on to work with healthy children and used the schema to describe children's understanding of the dangers of smoking.

The Role of Experience. In contrast to the emphasis on chronological age, the impact of direct experience has received less attention, with findings being inconsistent. On the face of it, experience in any domain would be expected to relate to improved knowledge. On the other hand, illness is potentially distressing, and therefore children may not be able to benefit from such a learning experience.

Neff and Beardslee (1990) found that children with cancer undergoing treatment as outpatients had more knowledge about body functioning than did children with orthopedic illness or healthy children. In two separate studies, Crisp, Ungerer, and Goodnow (1996) studied differences in children's understanding of illness depending on their experience. Both studies made comparisons of children with a major illness (cystic fibrosis in Study 1 and cancer in Study 2) with children whose experience was mild or acute illness. The measure of understanding of illness was adapted from Bibace and Walsh (1981) in which children are asked nine questions about the common cold. Both age and experience were found to relate to understanding.

Applications to Children with Cancer. A number of studies have pointed to inadequacies in this cognitive model to account for children's understanding of cancer. Evidence that preschoolers are interested in finding out about their illness was reported by Kendrick, Culling, Oakhill, and Mott (1986). Furthermore, these children were unlikely to assume personal responsibility or blame. The wish for information has also been shown among school-age children (R. Ellis & Leventhal, 1993). These authors asked 50 children aged between 8 and 17 years to complete questionnaires about their information needs and decision-making preferences. Parallel questionnaires were completed by their parents. Some 76% of children wanted more information about their illness, but only 36% felt this would be appropriate. Children understood that decisions involving the initiation of treatment would be made by their parents, but wanted more say themselves about changes in treatment. Only 10% of children as against 44% of parents felt it was appropriate for children to make decisions about their own care. Sixteen percent of children and 39% of parents felt they had no say in treatment decisions because they were made without consultation by medical staff. Fewer children (37%) compared with parents (75%) believed their illness to be serious. Thus, children may say they would like to be better informed, but often accept that practically, decisions will have to be made by their parents or doctors.

Implicit within this cognitive model has been the notion that more effective communication can be achieved by "matching" the complexity of information to the child's cognitive level. Thus, children in the concrete-operational stage who may overgeneralize ideas about contagion to all diseases would benefit most from information that addressed this issue. Similarly, detailed information about the biological bases underlying disease progression would only be helpful for children in the formal-operational stage (Bibace & Walsh, 1981). Potter and Roberts (1984) provided some support for these ideas. Information about a child with either diabetes or epilepsy was given to healthy schoolchildren, with the explanation that a child with a similar illness would be joining their class. Information was either *descriptive* and limited to a simple account of the illness, or *explanatory* and involved details about how the illness might affect the child. Children's comprehension was affected by both the kind of information and their own stage of cognitive development. That is, children who were given explanatory accounts, especially those in concrete rather than preoperational stages of thought, showed greater understanding than those given simple descriptive accounts.

Criticisms of the Cognitive Stage Approach. The cognitive stage approach remained unchallenged for some time, especially as applied to the issue of children's understanding of illness. The earliest criticisms were directed at the methodology employed in much of the work. Most studies used unstructured interviews to elicit the child's view. There are substantial difficulties in coding these interviews. Such an approach might lead to biased conclusions about the child's knowledge for at least two reasons. First, in interviews, children may infer that adults who ask the questions know the answers anyway. Therefore they are confused about the purpose of the questioning and give restricted answers. Second, the traditional focus of much work was to define what children do *not* know. If the emphasis shifts to describing what children do know, a very different picture emerges.

Bearison and Pacifici (1989) used a script approach to assess children's understanding of procedures and treatments. Children aged between 4 and 17 years of age were asked to describe "everything that happens when you come to clinic." A number of errors did occur, particularly in their accounts of BMAs and chemotherapy procedures. However, children from 7 years of age were able to give well-structured and ordered accounts of many procedures experienced in clinic.

Thus, a body of work developed that more than anything else suggested that (a) children knew much more than was originally supposed and (b) there was much greater heterogeneity in what children understood than was implied by the cognitive stage model. Carey (1985) argued that this heterogeneity reflects reasoning that is not specific to domains of knowledge. Thus, it was argued that explanations were not dependent on general stages of cognitive development.

Intuitive Theories

Carey (1985) proposed that two phases underlie children's acquisition of knowledge of biology. From the preschool period to approximately 6 years, children learn facts. Thus, they learn that eating dirty food makes them ill, that animals are alive, that babies come from inside their mothers. She argued that acquisition of all this biological knowledge is impressive, but is not the same as having a "framework theory" of biology.

Intuitive theories are the conceptual structures that determine a person's ontological commitments and causal schemas. They include abstract concepts from which are derived predictions, inferences, and explanations concerning the phenomena in the domains. A huge body of experimental evidence suggests that children by 4 years of age have developed an intuitive theory of mind (Wellman, 1990).

In this tradition two assumptions are made. First, knowledge about the world is divided into distinct content domains, each of which is organized and structured according to a different intuitive framework. Second, it is assumed that the process of knowledge acquisition can best be described as a process of theory elaboration and theory change within domains. It is claimed that individuals' knowledge in various content domains exhibits properties of theories including coherent structures, unique causal principles, and characteristic patterns of change.

One of the most important concepts is conceptual coherence. Theoretically, it becomes impossible to consider a single concept in isolation because its meaning and significance are determined by its role in an interrelated web of other constructs (Wellman, 1990). Because each concept gains meaning from others, when one changes so do the others. The implications are that it is not useful to study children's understanding of illness separately from their understanding of nutrition, pain, or death as has been done in the past. Rather, to the extent that these are all interrelated (it is not possible to understand nutrition and the need for food without understanding the relationship between food and life or death) then it follows that the child's theory of life and illness are interrelated.

Evidence is accumulating that around 6 years of age children construct a vitalistic biology, that is, an intuitive theory of biology organized around a core belief in a vital or life force. Before this, children lack the biological concept of life, cannot unite animals and plants under a single category of "living thing," cannot conceive of animals in terms of a life cycle, and cannot understand the role of bodily functioning in maintaining life.

The Concept of Life. This is most commonly studied using the "animism" interview (Piaget, 1929). Children are typically asked to name "things that are alive" and "things that are not alive." They are then presented with a list of items and asked whether each is alive and why. Young children overattribute life to some inanimate objects perhaps on the basis of motion (clouds are alive because they move), usefulness (a table is alive because you can eat on it), or activity (a clock is alive because it goes tick-tock). Based on these findings, it has been suggested that it may not be until 10 years of age that children restrict their attributions of life to animals and plants by reference to biological criteria such as the need for food or water.

However, it is possible that some preschoolers do have a concept of life, but this is limited to animals and does not include plants (Carey, 1985). Jaakkola (1997) in fact argued that children construct a biological theory of life between 4 and 6 years of age. Children were asked to choose between three types of causal explanations. With regard to a question about why we eat, explanations could be intentional (because we want to eat tasty food), vitalistic (because our stomachs take in vital power from food), and mechanistic (because we take food into our body after it is changed inside us). Whereas 4-year-olds showed no preferences for these different explanations, 6-year-olds preferred vitalistic and mechanistic explanations. In the same study, Jaakkola asked a series of questions about functions of different organs in the body and what would happen if a part were missing. Between 4 and 6 years of age there was a significant increase in explanations involving life (so you can live; so you don't die) compared with nonlife responses (to eat; to think). Children were subsequently categorized as "life-theorizers" if they mentioned the goal of maintaining life for more than one body organ. Whereas only one third of 4-year-olds were categorized as life-theorists, virtually all the 6- to 10-year-olds were. Thus between 4 and 6 years of age, children begin to use the abstract concept of life to predict and explain biological phenomena.

DOES KNOWLEDGE HELP THE CHILD COPE WITH CANCER?

Theories about developmental changes in children's understanding of illness have most often been assumed of relevance to questions about how much, and when, it may be appropriate to tell children about their illness.

The stage approach described first by Piaget has been by far the most influential. The admittedly loose implications from the theory have been that children have limited understanding of biology, and that explanations are unlikely to be of value until the stage of formal operations. Despite the criticisms that have been made of this model, it has remained very influential in the context of communications with sick children. The implications of more contemporary theory for illness communication, such as Carey (1985), have been largely unexplored.

Knowledge of the illness may be important in understanding children's behavior. Thus, it might be thought that children who are unaware about the seriousness of their disease will be more difficult patients and less inclined to be responsible for their own care. If they do not understand why they have to take medication, they are likely to be less adherent. It may be different for adolescents. Not knowing the implications of the illness may serve a protective factor in these cases. Understanding that you have a potentially life-threatening condition may prove more challenging to adolescents than at any other stage in the life cycle.

Parents are as likely to be worried when children refuse medication, are aggressive toward their siblings, or refuse to eat, as they are about explaining the illness. Surprisingly, perhaps, the relationship between knowledge and behavior problems is relatively unexplored.

Children undergoing treatment must undergo many painful procedures. What do children understand about why treatments are conducted, and how if at all does this understanding affect their attitude toward treatment? Parents may hope that children will forget details of procedures (because they are young) although evidence from other sources suggests that young children do have good recall of details of procedures and other traumatic events. For example, Howe, Courage, and Peterson (1995) showed that children have accurate memories for events and accuracy increase with age.

In terms of studying children's memory for painful events, we can draw on much related work looking at children's recall of abuse or natural disasters (Howe, 1997). Children with cancer are required to undergo traumatic procedures throughout the course of their treatment, and therefore it may be especially important to understand how they perceive and recall traumatic treatments. Furthermore, the way in which the child handles future diagnostic procedures may well depend on their initial experiences. Although this relationship has not been frequently addressed for children, research with adults suggests that memory can influence future behavior. Adults who remember a painful dental procedure are more likely to report high anxiety before subsequent dental procedures than those who do not recall past dental experiences as painful (Davey, 1989). Similarly, J. Katz and Melzack (1990) found that painful memories associated with a missing limb affect current perceptions of pain.

A study by Chen, Zeltzer, Craske, and E. R. Katz (2000) set out first of all to describe the accuracy of children's memory for events during lumbar puncture (LP) procedures and any differences between recall for factual versus emotional details. In addition, the authors predicted that children who were more distressed during procedures would subsequently show greater distress than those who did not report being so distressed initially. Children were assessed on two occasions at 1-week intervals. They completed measures of anxiety and pain ratings and a memory interview (Merritt, Ornstein, & Spicker, 1994). Children's distress during procedures was rated in terms of 10 behaviors. These included screaming, crying, or verbalizations of anxiety.

As would be expected, older children reported more accurate memories for factual events than younger ones. However, this was not affected by the number of previous LPs experienced. Neither were there differences between their recall of factual or emotional events. Children with cancer recalled fewer details of procedures than reported previously for those who had experienced a traumatic injury (Peterson & Bell, 1996).

Critically, the study explored the relationship between recall of a *past* LP with subsequent anxiety. Children who were more distressed on the first LP remembered fewer details before their next LP. Greater distress at first LP was associated with more exaggerated negative memories 1 week later. The findings were independent of age; children with greater exaggerations in negative memory reported and showed greater distress at future LPs. Although the reasons for this relationship remain speculative, the implications for intervention may be considerable. Interventions that aim to reduce exaggerations in memory about procedures may prove as effective as interventions aimed at changing the child's coping *during* such procedures.

6

Measuring Outcomes: Children Adjusting to Cancer

Summary

Children with any chronic condition are known to be at higher risk of compromised QOL compared with healthy children. In the absence of comprehensive measures of QOL, a number of proxy indicators have been used, including depression, anxiety, self-esteem, and body image.

Despite all their disadvantages, there is little consistent evidence to suggest that children with cancer routinely compare poorly with healthy children. Although parents of children with cancer often report worse adjustment for their children compared with parents of healthy children, such differences are not found when children rate themselves.

A distinction needs to be made between coping with cancer-related stressors (taking medication) and everyday stressors (going to school or taking exams). Different coping strategies are used depending on the nature of the stressor, and children's ability to use more appropriate strategies appears to increase with age.

A major limitation of much of this work is the focus on single outcomes and failure to acknowledge the relationship between different outcome variables. Thus, cancer may directly affect physical appearance, but how far this matters depends on the child's self-esteem and coping strategies. This work has considerable potential for rehabilitation programs, but this has not been acknowledged.

BEHAVIOR AND ADJUSTMENT

In previous chapters, it has been shown that children with any chronic illness are at risk of compromised psychological adjustment. However, research findings have sometimes been difficult to interpret. Variations in findings have been attributed to differences between conditions. Diseases vary in how far they restrict the child's mobility or the amount of self-care required. There is also considerable difference in methodological rigor between different studies. Critical differences may include the size of the sample of children studied, how representative the sample is of children generally, or the exact measure of adjustment used.

In an attempt to pull together some of the early literature, Lavigne and Faier-Routman (1992) conducted a meta-analysis involving 87 separate studies, which included children with different chronic conditions as well as cancer. They concluded that children with any chronic condition were more vulnerable to adjustment problems compared with normal controls. Compared with healthy children, sick children were more vulnerable to internalizing problems such as depression or anxiety rather than externalizing problems such as acting out or aggression. In addition, Lavigne and Faier-Routman noted that conclusions were dependent on the method of the study. In general, adjustment problems were greater where comparisons were made against published norms rather than against specific age- and gender-matched controls. The implications are that many studies are limited by poor matching of children with chronic disease and healthy control groups. No differences in vulnerability were found depending on the condition.

The most prevalent approach to determining child adjustment has been based on the disability-stress-coping model described by Wallander and Varni (1992). As discussed in chapter 4, chronic illness can be viewed as a chronic stress both for children and their families. According to Wallander and Varni, child adjustment is potentially modifiable through a series of risk (disease/disability parameters, functional independence, and psychosocial stress) and resistance variables (intrapersonal, socio-ecological and stress-producing factors). In an effort to determine the value of the model, Varni, E. R. Katz, Colegrove, and Dolgin (1996) assessed the potential role of socio-ecological factors, especially family functioning, in determining child adjustment. This was measured on diagnosis and at 6 and 9 months later. At 9 months, child adjustment was better predicted from family functioning than adjustment on diagnosis. The rather complex set of results point to the role of family functioning in moderating child adjustment, and also to the need for multiple measures of adjustment and family functioning. It was concluded that no single measure can capture the full range of behaviors associated with adjustment and coping to the disease.

Sawyer, Streiner, Antoniou, Toogood, and Rice (1998) reported a related study in which they attempted to determine how parents' mental health on diagnosis was related to the child's adjustment 2 years later. Somewhat differently from the study by Varni et al. (1996) described earlier, both mothers' mental health and family adjustment on diagnosis were predictive of child adjustment later. This study points clearly to the vulnerability of children whose mothers are especially distressed following the diagnosis. In contrast, fathers' mental health was not related to the child's later adjustment.

Thus, the way in which parents react to information about the diagnosis may have some implications for the child's longer term outcomes. However, clearly many other intervening variables are also important. It has not yet proved possible to identify families on diagnosis who might benefit from professional help more than others. Together these studies point to the huge methodological difficulties in determining the processes underlying adjustment over time. The potentially large number of relevant variables is daunting.

Depression

Depression has often been used as a proxy indicator of QOL. There are at least two reasons to suppose that children with cancer may be more depressed than others. First, depression has been reported to be common in children with any chronic illness. Second, depression is also a common response to cancer in adults.

Bennett (1994) conducted a meta-analysis of 60 studies involving children and young people (aged 4 to 28 years) with chronic medical problems, including cancer. This meta-analysis suggested that children with any physical illness were slightly more at risk for depressive symptoms compared with controls, but there was little evidence of clinical depression. There was no obvious relationship between depression and time since diagnosis, gender, or age. Parents reported that their child was more depressed than children did themselves. Parents' ratings suggested their sick children were more depressed when the results were compared with parents of community controls than if comparisons were made with population norms. Few studies were identified that involved comparisons of children with different chronic conditions. However, Bennett concluded that children with asthma, recurrent abdominal pain, and sickle cell anemia had higher rates of depression than children with cancer or diabetes. It is hard to explain this result, which may partly be dependent on differences in methodological quality between different studies.

There is an extensive literature concerned with the responses of adults to a diagnosis of cancer, with much suggesting that depression is a common reaction. Given these findings, it is perhaps to be expected that attempts were made to determine whether or not children also become depressed following diagnosis. It was initially expected that the incidence of depression would be higher among children with cancer than healthy peers, and this was supported by some early findings (G. D. Armstrong, Wirt, Nesbit, & Martinson, 1982; Kashani & Hakami, 1982; Sanger, Copeland, & Davidson, 1991; van Dongen-Melman & Sanders-Woudstra, 1986). Other reports suggested that depressive symptoms are no more common among children with cancer than healthy children (Greenberg, Kazak, & A. T. Meadows, 1989; Radcliffe et al., 1994; Tebbi, Bromberg, & Mallon, 1988; Worchel et al., 1988). Canning, Canning, and Boyce (1992) reported that adolescents with cancer adopt a repressive coping style (low anxiety and high defensiveness). Thus, they argued, adolescents adopt a policy of self-deception and consequently appear less depressed than peers.

Varni, E. R. Katz, Colegrove, and Dolgin (1993) studied 30 of 41 children aged 8–13 years who were relatively newly diagnosed with cancer (9 months after diagnosis). They completed a battery of paper-and-pencil measures to determine perceived social support, depression, anxiety, social anxiety, and self-esteem. Parents completed the CBCL (Achenbach & Edelbroch, 1979).

Considerable variability in the incidence of depression and other psychological outcomes was noted. Varni et al. (1993) did not report comparisons with population norms, but attempted to identify predictors of psychosocial status. Children who believed they had little classmate support reported higher levels of depression and anxiety. They were also described by their parents as having more internalizing and externalizing problems than might be expected. These results suggest that classmates have an important role to play. The less they offer practical and emotional support, the greater the likelihood of depression and other emotional problems in the child with cancer.

Allen, Newman, and Souhami (1997) assessed anxiety and depression in newly diagnosed patients (and their parents). Of 47 families approached, 42 adolescents (12–20 years) completed measures of depression and anxiety on diagnosis (median = 3 weeks). These data were compared with responses of 173 age- and gender-matched adolescents recruited from local schools. There were no differences between adolescents diagnosed with cancer and controls in terms of state anxiety although the control group had higher trait anxiety scores. There were no differences in depression scores. For both groups, girls were more depressed than boys.

The authors concluded that as a group, newly diagnosed patients were not more anxious or depressed than healthy controls. This is an exceptional study to the extent that anxiety and depression were investigated in very newly diagnosed adolescents. However, the findings need to be interpreted with caution. There was no assessment of how well adolescents understood their situation or the severity of their condition. Nevertheless, the findings may support those of Canning et al. (1992), that adolescents with cancer are less depressed than normal controls. The question of repression as a style of coping with threat needs also to be considered. In addition, the control group included a number of young people with above-average levels of depression. They may have contributed to a higher mean score for the healthy group than might be expected.

As always, studies that rely on comparisons of mean differences between groups can mask the underlying fact that whereas some children with cancer are more anxious and depressed than healthy children, many others show no such reactions. Consequently, attempts have been made to identify subgroups of children who may be especially vulnerable. A number of demographic and clinical variables have been investigated, including age and clinical status.

It may well be that children who are more seriously ill will also be more depressed, and some support for this hypothesis was provided by Mulhern, Fairclough, Smith, and Douglas (1992). Children with cancer who were hospitalized were more depressed than those who were not hospitalized. There was also a tendency for children who had been hospitalized for longer to report more depression.

Siegel and Graham-Pole (1991) also reported a relationship between clinical status and depression. They investigated the relationship between a number of psychological measures and the child's immune status. Sixty-three patients with ALL were followed over an 18-month period from diagnosis. Measures of immune function and details of relapse or infections were taken from medical records. Children who had relapsed and those with a greater number of infections reported more anxiety, depression, hopelessness, and daily hassles. Given the correlational nature of the study, it is not possible to be certain whether the occurrence of a setback in the form of relapse or infection precipitates depression and hopelessness, or whether a negative outlook on life precipitates the medical setback.

Anxiety and Posttraumatic Stress Disorder

In the 1980s, it was assumed that children exposed to frightening events responded with transient distress. These early studies may well have led to underreporting the incidence of distress in children, because they relied heavily on information from parents and teachers, rather than children themselves (Yule, 1999). PTSD was first recognized by the American Psychiatric Association in 1980. It was described as an anxiety disorder characterized by three types of symptom. These included distressing and recurring recollections of the traumatic event, avoidance of stimuli associated with the trauma, and increased physiological arousal. By definition, PTSD is restricted to the presence of symptoms in response to extreme stress more than 4 weeks after the event.

PTSD may be viewed as a nonadaptive adjustment reaction. When children face very frightening situations, they become distressed. This can take the form of crying, clinging, or becoming very fearful. Normal reactions can also include going into shock and becoming unresponsive to outside stimulation. This is a normal adaptive reaction that can serve as a protective factor. Withdrawal allows the individual to concentrate on the threat and not be side-tracked by trivia. When the danger passes, return to normal can occur. After a time, extended periods of withdrawal are no longer functional. What was a normal reaction becomes disabling; PTSD is present. Dissociation (subjective sense of numbing, detachment; reduction in awareness of surroundings; de-realization; depersonalization; dissociative amnesia or inability to recall an important aspect of the event) at the time of the event seems to predict PTSD (Koopman, Classen, & Spiegel, 1994). In the *Diagnostic and Statistical Manual of Mental Disorders* (*DSM–IV*; American Psychiatric Association, 1994), a new diagnostic category was introduced to account for these early reactions. *Acute stress disorder* (ASD) is used to describe symptoms in the first 4 weeks following the traumatic event. Symptoms of ASD are similar to those for PTSD but include the criterion that there must be at least three symptoms of dissociation.

Following a traumatic event, many children become very "clingy." They can regress and need reassurance. Children can also experience intrusive images of the event. The child "sees" the event again and again. On occasions, these are so vivid that the child believes the event is reoccurring. These dissociative experiences are called flashbacks. As flashbacks are most likely to occur at night, children will resist going to sleep. Consequently, they become tired, irritable, and angry.

Early reports suggested that children undergoing treatment for cancer did show symptoms characteristic of PTSD (Nir, 1985), as did those undergoing BMT (Pot-Mees, 1989). However, in the 1980s, medical illness was not considered an event outside the realm of human experience, and therefore not considered sufficient to lead to a diagnosis of PTSD.

Is there any evidence that children do experience ASD or PTSD after diagnosis and treatment? Although children often show some symptoms of PTSD, are these sufficient to justify a diagnosis of PTSD? Certainly children can withdraw, and perhaps part of the reason children do not ask questions about the illness is because they do not want to reexperience the events of diagnosis and hospitalization.

In one of the few studies to involve newly diagnosed children, Butler, Rizzi, and Handwerger (1996) compared PTSD among children on treatment (*n* = 30; aged 3–16 years) and a group of survivors (*n* = 42). Of the children on treatment, 14 were being prepared for a BMT and 10 had previously been treated for BMT following relapse.

PTSD was high for the whole group. Fifteen (21%) met the criterion for PTSD. (This compares with estimates of 1%–14% of the general population and 3%–58% for other at-risk groups.) Children with more symptoms of PTSD had more severe disease, were more likely to be on treatment, and were more likely to be waiting for a BMT. In contrast, the survivors showed little evidence of PTSD.

Body Image

Physical attractiveness is highly prized in our society. Cancer treatment potentially compromises an individual's perceived attractiveness in a number of ways. There are physical changes associated with treatment; loss of hair is perhaps the most often discussed. In addition, children can lose (or gain) large amounts of weight; they may have skin problems. Body image can be adversely influenced by other less visible changes. Mouth ulcers may not be visible, but can nevertheless leave the child feeling uncomfortable and miserable about their body. Massive insults such as limb amputation are likely to be devastating at any time but perhaps especially during adolescence.

Adolescence is often described as an important and sometimes vulnerable period in the development of body image because of the rapid and dramatic physical growth and maturation that occurs. The development of secondary sex characteristics, heightened awareness of sexuality, and physical and social relationships make adolescents acutely aware of their appearance. A diagnosis of cancer during this time, and the changes in body appearance brought about by cancer treatment, are likely to challenge the normal development of body image (La Greca, 1990; B. Price, 1992; Susman et al., 1982). Workers in the field of cancer (B. Price, 1992) and other chronic conditions suggest that patients whose conditions emerge during adolescence may feel more negatively about their bodies than those who do not experience illness onset at this time. Evidence for this comes from Ben-Tovim and M. K. Walker (1995), who studied body image in young women with a variety of physical conditions considered to be disfiguring, disabling, or both. Those who experienced illness onset during adolescence were more distressed than those with earlier or later onset.

Painful and invasive procedures and the large number of medical staff involved in treatment can cause acute feelings of distress and loss of privacy. Such changes in physical appearance and body experience can have a marked effect on body image. Young people with cancer and other chronic conditions may be at increased risk for developing eating disorders (Rodin, Daneman, & deGroot, 1993). Weight gain, interference with normal growth and development, scars, and other marks left by treatment may degrade the patients' feelings about their bodies as well as their self-esteem. Even where there are no obvious physical effects from treatment, the experience of having an illness that seemingly comes from nowhere, has no known cause, and may recur, can precipitate anxiety that revolves around the body.

Many conditions in addition to cancer can affect children's body image. Perhaps more than any other concept, body image is highly dependent on subjective opinions about the nature of beauty. Thus, how individuals think about their physical appearance is more important than any objective evaluation of attractiveness. Varni and Setoguchi (1991) showed how psychosocial factors can moderate the impact of treatment on body image. Perceived physical appearance among children with congenital or acquired limb deficiencies was predicted from peer acceptance and the child's perceptions of their competence in school and athletics. Once again, it seems that the child's adjustment in school and the way other children react are both crucial in predicting outcomes.

Pendley, Dahlquist, and Dreyer (1997) compared body image in 21 adolescent survivors and matched controls. Although described as a survivor study, the time since diagnosis was relatively short ($M = 17$ months). Adolescents with obvious physical deformities (e.g., amputations) were excluded. Data were collected from 9 females and 12 males aged 11–21 years. (This is a small sample but represents 91% of those eligible and known to follow up at the time.) Controls were recruited from advertisements in local newspapers and were paid $25 for participation. A number of measures of body image were used, including the Self-Image Questionnaire for Young Adolescents (Petersen et al., 1984); the Body Cathexis Scale (Secord & Jourard, 1953), self-report Likert ratings of body image, the physical appearance subscale of the Self-Perception Profile for Adolescents (Harter, 1988), the Body Image Avoidance Questionnaire (J. C. Rosen et al., 1991) and Body Image Distress (Cash, 1991). In addition, objective ratings of attractiveness were made by undergraduate observers based on videotapes of participants. The relationship between the various measures of body image and psychosocial adjustment was investigated. Psychosocial adjustment was measured in terms of peer activities: loneliness (Asher, Hymel, & Renshaw, 1984), social anxiety (La Greca, 1992), and self-perception (Harter, 1988). Mothers were asked for information about the child's school attendance. No differences were found between those with cancer and controls on measures of body image; nor were there any differences in terms of objective ratings of attractiveness made by independent observers. There were no differences in terms of loneliness, social anxiety, or school absenteeism, but survivors participated in fewer activities.

It is important to consider some of the potential difficulties in this study before accepting the findings of no differences between the groups. The study involved a relatively small number of children. It is possible that the numbers involved were too small to allow for statistically significant differences. In addition, children with obvious body image problems were excluded. Although there were no differences on a number of measures of body image, the worry would be that the generic scales used were not sufficiently sensitive to pick up body image concerns in children with cancer.

Self-Esteem

Diagnosis of cancer may well compromise children's self-esteem. They become dependent on others for help to complete everyday tasks. They may not be able to take part in sports, and may fall behind in schoolwork. Initially at least, the diagnosis of cancer may be a blow to maintaining satisfactory self-esteem. Things may change with time. Children with cancer spend a lot of time with adults, and have to learn to express their opinions in front of clinic and nursing staff. They may find themselves being used as role models for more recently diagnosed children. It is not therefore inevitable that self-esteem is compromised indefinitely. Disappointingly, there has been less attention to issues of self-esteem compared with other outcomes such as depression.

Hockenberry-Eaton, Dilorio, and Kemp (1995) studied 44 children aged between 6½ and 13½ years. Fifteen of the children had experienced a relapse. In addition to a measure of self-esteem (Harter, 1985) children also completed measures of anxiety, coping strategies, and perceived stressors. Nevertheless, self-esteem scores correlated negatively with number of months since diagnosis; that is, children who had been longer on treatment had lower self-esteem. Self-esteem was also lower for children who had experienced a relapse compared with those who had not. Children who had relapsed also reported more trait anxiety.

Coping

The work reviewed so far is grounded in the traditional deficit-centered model, with the assumption that children with cancer show a range of problems compared with normal healthy controls. However, as has been shown, there is considerable diversity in how children cope with the consequences of cancer treatment, and it is therefore important to document how it is that many children seem to cope very well despite the illness and its implications.

It is important first to distinguish between different types of stressors. In practice, a wide range of stressors can be identified (Chesler & Barbarin, 1986). These include: (a) understanding the diagnosis, prognosis, and treatment, (b) adapting to treatment and side effects, (c) relating to medical staff, (d) relating to family and peers, and (e) dealing with two worlds, illness and health, being special and normal both at the same time.

Thus, it is possible to make a major distinction between stressors involved in coping with medical interventions and those needed to cope with everyday home and school activities that may be aggravated by cancer. All children have to learn to manage the stress associated with taking exams, or take the consequences for not doing their homework on time. These everyday stressors can be an additional burden for those who must also remember to take their medication or fit in hospital appointments.

Regardless of the nature of the stressor, research concerned with coping has frequently drawn on the theoretical distinction between *problem-focused* and *emotion-focused* coping defined by Lazarus and Folkman (1984). Problem-focused coping includes strategies directed at changing the environment or personal behavior; emotion-focused coping is defined as efforts to regulate emotional states that are caused by, or related to, the stressful event.

In one of the first studies to pursue this distinction between cancer-specific and everyday stressors, Bull and Drotar (1991) studied 39 children with cancer aged 7–17 years. Nineteen had survived at least 5 years from diagnosis and the rest were well and in remission. Children completed measures of general stress (Wertlieb, Weigel, & Feldstein, 1987) and cancer-specific stress and coping (M. McCabe & Weisz, 1988). They identified many more non-cancer-related stressors ($n = 161$) compared with cancer-related stressors ($n = 27$). Of the non-cancer-related stressors, 24% were concerned with school, 24% with family, and 19% with friends and social situations. Among cancer-related stressors, 30% were concerned with physical handicap associated with the disease and 22% with treatment.

Different coping strategies were identified depending on whether or not the stressor was cancer related. For cancer-related stressors, adolescents were more likely than children to report emotion- rather than problem-focused coping. (This is to be expected because cancer-related stressors, such as hair loss, cannot be changed; children can deal with this only by focusing on the emotional issues.) This study suggests that children are able to distinguish normal everyday stressors from cancer- and treatment-related stressors, that they adopt different approaches to managing cancer- and non-cancer-related stress, and that adolescents may have developed more successful patterns of responding than children.

Phipps, Fairclough, and Mulhern (1995) compared coping strategies in 66 children treated for cancer and a control group of 414 healthy children. They drew on Monitoring–Blunting theory (see chap. 4) and argued that individuals differ in their willingness to confront or withdraw from threatening information. Children completed the Child Behavioral Style Scale (CBSS; Miller, Sherman, Caputo, Kruus & Combs, 1993). The CBSS includes four stress-invoking scenarios (imagine you are in school and a teacher wants to see you at break), followed by six alternative responses. Three of these are thought to reflect a "monitoring" bias (think about what the teacher might do to you) and three reflect a blunting orientation (think about other things to get your mind off the teacher). The measure thus yields two scores, one reflecting the number of monitoring items endorsed and the other reflecting the number of blunting items endorsed.

Children from three age groups (6–8, 9–11, and 12–15 years) completed the measure and a parallel version was completed by parents. Compared with healthy children, those with cancer endorsed more blunting items, but there was no difference in the number of monitoring items endorsed. Parents reported that their children adopted more avoidant coping compared with the children themselves. This provides further support for the idea that children should be asked to rate their own behavior wherever possible. Phipps et al. (1995) suggested that their findings support other work showing that children with cancer are more likely to adopt avoidant or blunting styles of coping to deal with stress compared with healthy children (Canning et al., 1992). Again, the possibility that denial serves an adaptive purpose is raised.

In further work, Phipps and Srivastava (1997) recruited 107 children with cancer from oncology clinics. They were compared with a control group of healthy children attending a summer camp. All children completed questionnaires to assess anxiety (Spielberger, 1973), depression (Kovacs, 1983), approach or avoidant coping style (Miller & Mangan, 1983), and social desirability (Crandall, 1966). In addition, for children with cancer, ratings of child depression and anxiety were obtained from a parent and clinician.

Children with cancer rated themselves to be less depressed and less anxious compared with the healthy children. Comparison with previously published norms suggested that the healthy children were functioning within normal levels, but the children with cancer were reporting significantly less depression and anxiety than might be expected. However, children with cancer scored higher than controls in terms of social desirability and on the blunting dimension of the Coping Style Scale. Again, these data appear to suggest that children with cancer adopt a defensive bias toward minimization of stress, and this accounts for the unexpected findings that they have lower levels of depression and anxiety than other children. This bias is assumed to serve a protective function. There were no significant correlations between child, parent, and physician ratings of depression and anxiety, again emphasizing the importance of obtaining information from children wherever possible.

Hockenberry-Eaton, Kemp, and Dilorio (1994) reported one of the few studies that attempted to relate psychological measures of stress and coping with physiological indicators. Forty-four children aged between 6 and 14 years took part. The children who participated included those who were still on chemotherapy and others who had completed treatment. They completed measures of self-esteem, social support, anxiety, and family relationships. The physiological measures included norepinephrine, epinephrine, and cortisol levels.

Children were assessed during two routine clinic visits. Mean epinephrine levels were higher than expected for children in this age range at both visits. However, norepinephrine and cortisol levels, though increased, were not above normal levels. Anxiety levels were comparable with published norms. Hockenberry-Eaton et al. (1994) suggested that children with cancer show increased physiological responses compared with those expected for normal children perhaps indicating that they were experiencing a degree of chronic stress. There was no relationship between physiological and psychological indicators of stress.

CONCLUSIONS

This literature challenges any theoretical model that emphasizes the "deficits" associated with dealing with an illness. It is clear that children respond in many other, often more optimistic and resilient ways.

In terms of adequacy of measures, the dependence on general indicators of anxiety and depression is frequently justified on the grounds of comparability with previous work and the availability of population norms. Yet these measures may be far from satisfactory in terms of determining the way in which children are affected by the cancer diagnosis. Most measures of depression include a number of somatization items, which mean that physically ill children may score higher than healthy children because of a bias in the nature of items included in the questionnaire (Bennett, 1994). Similar criticisms about the use of the CBCL have been made by Perrin et al. (1991).

Second, conclusions are related to the type of method adopted. Results tend to suggest a higher incidence of depression where comparisons are made against population norms rather than matched controls.

Third, results vary depending on the specific measure used. Results that are based on standardized measures of adjustment, including depression, anxiety, or body image, have yielded inconsistent results, but tend to conclude that children with cancer have relatively few, if any, problems compared with either healthy children or population norms. This tends to contrast with findings based on more clinically orientated studies, involving specially developed, rather than standardized interviews. This is illustrated clearly in work concerned with assessment of body image in survivors of childhood leukemia compared with a control group of healthy adolescents attending a dental clinic. Puukko, Sammallahti, Siimes, and Aalberg (1997) used both a standardized measure of body image (Offer, Ostrov, & Howard, 1982) and a semistructured open-ended interview to explore body image concerns. Mean scores on the standardized measure were almost identical between the two groups. However, based on the interview, it was felt that the leukemia patients had more concerns and were more evasive about answering questions about their body image. The advantages and disadvantages of using standardized or nonstandardized measures runs through all work in this area. The trade-off is between obtaining data quickly compared with the time taken to collect interview responses, and between numerical data that seem easy to interpret compared with more complex information that does not easily convert to numerical form.

Fourth, different results have also been reported depending on the informant. Most commonly, parents rate their child's depression or adjustment to be worse than children themselves. Perhaps parents are more realistic about how cancer may affect the child in the longer term. They also have a greater experience of life, which may mean that they are more aware of the potential difficulties that may occur in the future. However, studies that rely on parents for information about their child's psychosocial function may be limited to the extent that parents themselves may feel depressed as a consequence of the child's illness and project their own feelings on to the child. Although the evidence is somewhat equivocal, depressed parents are more likely to report behavior problems among their children than nondepressed parents (Mulhern, Fairclough et al., 1992). Similarly, we need to consider how well clinicians are able to diagnose depression in children and whether or not they are confusing depression with some other behavior. Realistically, clinicians should not be expected to judge the child's mental health on the basis of brief clinic appointments. It may help to know more about how clinicians rate children's behavior and the kind of problems they regard as indicative of depression. As with parents, the questions are about how well adults, whether parents or clinicians, are able to judge the child's feelings.

Fifth, questions about the most appropriate respondent follow from the aforementioned. If neither parents nor clinicians have access to the child's innermost thoughts, it follows that the most acceptable data is that provided by the child. In the past, there have been a number of objections to relying on children to provide information. They have been considered unreliable informants. It used to be thought that children could not be depressed because they were unable to conceptualize the future. It is now clear that this is not so. It is much more accepted that it is possible to diagnose clinical depression in children (Kovacs, 1983) and measures to assess depressive symptoms in children at least from age 8 years have been reported. The question as to whether even younger children can become depressed remains for the future.

Sixth, to a large extent, issues about the incidence of depression (or psychological adjustment more generally) have been conducted without taking into account the child's physical health. In the future, clinicians and behavioral scientists need to work together more closely in order to understand the relationship between psychological and physical measures.

Finally, the practice of explaining inconsistencies in the research literature in terms of methodological problems is inherently limited. In any applied work, it is not possible to control characteristics of the sample and other aspects of method in the same way that it is possible in more experimental areas. Thus, methodological inconsistencies are an integral part of all work in this area. Explanations must therefore be more theoretically based, because it is only by clarifying the processes underlying adjustment that we will be able to account for differences in our findings. Thus, a number of studies suggest that children with cancer report less depression than would be expected. The findings may simply reflect the limitations of currently available measures. More interesting explanations have focused on whether children cope by denial or repression of emotions.

Treatment for cancer inevitably is associated with changes in physical appearance. The extent to which children are able to accept these changes may well have consequences in many other situations. Changes in physical appearance leave a child vulnerable to teasing. The focus on physical appearance as distinct from social acceptance and athletic competence has been unhelpful. Recognizing the interdependence between concepts is vital, especially if the results of research are to be used as the basis for comprehensive rehabilitation programs.

Attempts to explain the variability in outcomes have focused on determining variables that protect the child from emotional problems, such as family or social support. There is consistent evidence that the child's perception of support, from family or friends, is critical. Children who believe others are helpful function better than those who perceive themselves to be less well supported. Further support for this hypothesis can be found in chapter 7, focusing on the child's reintegration in school.

7

Back to Normal; Impact on Schooling

Summary

Return to school after diagnosis is encouraged to give children opportunities to mix with friends. Return to school also symbolizes that life is returning to normal and allows parents time to work and keep up with everyday tasks. Children with cancer have poorer school attendance compared with healthy children and those with other chronic conditions. Although this is inevitable, especially immediately after the diagnosis, it is not clear how far absences subsequently affect the child's academic, behavioral, or social functioning.

According to teachers, children with cancer are more socially withdrawn and isolated compared with others in the class. These findings have not been corroborated by children's ratings of their own behavior. They tend not to see themselves as different from others.

Teachers report many concerns about having a child with cancer in the class. These include worries about what the child can be expected to do, and how far they should be integrated in all school activities. Intervention programs to increase teacher knowledge and confidence have been reported, but are difficult to evaluate. Increases in knowledge have been reported, but it is not clear that this affects the teacher's actual management of the child in the classroom. Inevitably, teachers tend to be self-selected for intervention programs, and therefore are highly motivated or personally interested prior to attendance.

Evaluations of the relative merits, efficacy, or cost-benefit of different interventions are needed, as is improved communication between home, hospital, and school.

BACK TO SCHOOL

More Than the ABCs

School is not just about learning the ABCs. School is an opportunity for young people to make friends, learn new things, achieve success, and please their parents. When asked why they wanted to go to school, children who were experiencing long absences said they wanted, first, to make or be with friends and, second, to be like everyone else. Relatively few children were concerned about the possible implications for their work, but they did worry more about how much effort would be required later to "catch up" (Bolton, 1997; Closs & Norris, 1997).

For many children, school is first of all a place to meet and make friends. In their turn, friends are frequently seen to be an important and hopefully constructive influence on children. "It is becoming clear how children's friendship networks help facilitate processes of cultural reproduction, for it is largely with their peers that children play, tell jokes and swap ideas" (A. James, 1993). Friendships are important not only to children's immediate enjoyment of school and recreational activities, but also to many aspects of their physical, cognitive, emotional, and social development (Ramsey, 1991). Positive peer relationships in school have other implications for out-of-school activities and also for adult life (S. Asher & Coie, 1990). The popularity of Web sites established simply to put old school friends back in touch attests to the relatively enduring nature of friendships formed during this period.

However much children enjoyed school before they were ill, the return after the diagnosis of cancer can present them with a unique challenge. Depending on the specific cancer and the timing of the illness in the school year, children inevitably experience lengthy absences before the diagnosis. As described in chapter 2, these are partly due to difficulties in diagnosing cancer. Absences can remain common throughout treatment. These may be for routine hospital visits. In addition, as chemotherapy suppresses the immune system, children are at risk of acute infections. Consequently, outbreaks of infectious disease, especially chicken pox, can be especially harmful and everyone, including teachers and parents, needs to be vigilant. Some parents may judge that the risk of infection is too great, and keep their child away from school until chemotherapy is complete and the child's immune system returned to normal. Additional school absences may occur because the child is unwell or tired.

Even when children do attend school, they may not necessarily be as involved with activities as they might have been. Those who are being treated with radiotherapy or chemotherapy are unlikely to be functioning at their optimum. Some of the commonly used agents have acute side effects that can be associated with psychological or behavioral problems. Prednisone, for example, is associated with mood swings and irritability. Vincristine can adversely effect fine motor coordination and speed. In practice, this means that teachers find the children very difficult to deal with. It is hard to manage chemotherapy-related tantrums at home, but harder still in a classroom of other children. Problems with fine motor coordination create difficulties for the child in writing, as well as limiting the opportunities to take part in physical education and sports activities.

In the longer term, many children are at significant risk of learning problems. These may be partly a consequence of long absences following the diagnosis. However, many factors affect learning as well as school attendance. These include attitudes of teachers, the family, and friends. No child will do well in school if they feel different, left out, or bullied. Any evaluation of the child's school experience therefore needs to include assessment of the child's absence, achievement, and social integration. Consideration needs to be given to all these potential barriers to achievement. Over and above these general issues, learning problems may also be a consequence of the specific treatments or combination of treatments required. Concern about learning difficulties has most frequently been addressed in relation to children with ALL (see chap. 8). Children with a CNS tumor experience additional disadvantages associated with the site of the original tumor as well as the specific treatment involved (see chap. 9).

Attendance

In encouraging school attendance after diagnosis, doctors hope that families will benefit from a return to normal life. The child's reintegration in school also allows for the resumption of a more normal relationship between mother and child. This is important as mothers and their children spend so much time together in hospital following diagnosis. For children, the benefits of school attendance include opportunities to mix with other children, in addition to hoped-for examination success. For mothers, the return to school after diagnosis can be difficult. There are anxieties that children may be teased because of the way they look. They may need extra help to get around the school. Mothers will also worry that no one will know exactly what to do if the child is unwell. Understandably, some school absence is probably the result of mothers' anxieties.

Regular attendance at school is important. It is conducive to the child's long-term academic achievement, and it is important for friendships. All the research that has been reported suggests that children with cancer experience frequent and long absences. A. Charlton et al. (1991), for example, compared the school experiences of children with cancer with those with other chronic conditions and a group with orthopedic problems. Information was obtained from school records and interviews with parents and teachers. All the children experienced some difficulties on return to school but these were greatest for those with cancer and least for those with orthopedic problems. Although it is not clear why, girls were absent more often than boys.

High absence rates were also reported by Noll, Bukowski, Rogosch, LeRoy, and Kulkarni (1990). Those with cancer missed 25.6 days during the school year, compared with 6.5 days for gender-matched classroom controls. Koch, Harter, Jakob, and Siegrist (1996) obtained data from a postal survey of 1,168 parents of children with cancer. Among those who responded (39%), parents reported that children missed 80 days during a school year, equivalent to half their school time. One third had to repeat a school year. Survivors of a brain tumor had twice as many absences as the rest of the class (Vannatta, Gartstein, Short, & Noll, 1998). In most cases, reasons for absences were quite legitimate, associated with general illness or hospital visits. Occasionally, more serious cases of school refusal have been reported. School phobia has been defined as refusal to attend school, fear of separation from the mother, and somatic complaints. A higher incidence of school phobia was reported among children treated for cancer (10%) compared with the general population (1.7%) (Lansky et al., 1975). The authors concluded that prompt return to school is essential to reduce the risk of school phobia, and that counseling should be offered to children and parents.

Especially for older children, there are concerns about the effect of school absence on examination performance. At least for healthy children there is a link between higher absence rates and poorer examination performance (Malcolm, Thorpe, & Lowden, 1996). However, the same relationship may not necessarily hold for children with chronic illness, or cancer specifically. In fact, research in the United States (Fowler, Johnson, & Atkinson, 1985) found no statistically significant link between poor national achievement tests results and absence in children with chronic health conditions, except for those with conditions involving impaired cognition such as epilepsy or spina bifida. Pless, Cripps, H. A. Davies, and Wadsworth (1989) reported significantly lower examination results for those who had been chronically ill compared with the general population, but only for those from manual social class backgrounds. Thus, other variables may moderate the relationship between school absence and chronic illness on educational attainments.

Children's Behavior

The suggestion that children with cancer have difficulties in school was raised almost as soon as substantial numbers began to survive treatment. Deasy-Spinetta and Spinetta (1980) asked teachers to rate the behavior and achievements of a child with cancer in comparison with a "typical" child. Children with cancer were not rated differently from healthy peers in terms of their willingness to attend school, how much they were teased by classmates, or the extent to which they showed age-inappropriate dependent behaviors. However, they were judged to have less energy than a typical child and had more difficulty concentrating and completing tasks. Those with cancer were also seen to be more socially and emotionally inhibited. The questionnaire devised by Deasy-Spinetta and Spinetta in this study was later used as a "gold standard" in much other work.

It was used, for example, by Adamoli et al. (1997) to determine teachers' assessments of behavior in children treated for leukemia. Questionnaires were sent to teachers of all children treated during the period 1988–1994 and responses were compared with matched controls chosen by the teacher. Of 350 questionnaires sent out, 291 were returned. Significant differences were noted in terms of learning, socialization, and emotionality. However, a small number of children contributed disproportionately to these findings. Particularly in the context of learning, children below 6 years of age at diagnosis and those treated with CNS irradiation were most likely to be having difficulty.

Gregory, Parker, and Craft (1994) also used the questionnaire to compare the behavior of 14 children returning to primary school after treatment with their 11 siblings. Forty-four children from the same classes were selected as controls. There were no differences between the groups. Although teachers reported that they anticipated problems before the child's return to school, few were experienced. The authors speculated that the good outcomes were the result of a well-developed system of community liaison nursing that had been introduced at the hospital.

Thus, in terms of behavior, these three studies yield contradictory findings. Deasy-Spinetta and Spinetta (1980) reported a number of difficulties; Adamoli et al. (1997) reported difficulties for some children; and Gregory et al. (1994) reported none. The contradiction in findings may reflect methodological differences between the studies. There are big differences in the size of samples studied, choice of control groups, and cultural backgrounds against which the work was conducted. Perhaps also, some of the specific items in the measure by Deasy-Spinetta and Spinetta apply less well in cultures outside the United States.

Teachers have other worries in addition to those concerning the child's behavior. They also report anxieties and lack of knowledge about how to deal with medical emergencies and the effects of school absences and fatigue on the child's learning (A. M. McCarthy, J. K. Williams, & Eidahl, 1996). Teachers in this study reported that the school nurse and the child's parents were their most helpful sources of information, with very few attempting to locate any written information themselves.

Mothers, teachers, and children with cancer have different concerns about the child in school (A. M. McCarthy, J. M. Williams, & Plumer, 1998). Mothers' main concerns were about safety and teasing by other children, although they had very few worries about the child's academic progress or attainments. Teachers were more concerned about their own lack of knowledge and how other children might react. Their concerns were not focused on the child with cancer but were spread across the whole class. The children, in contrast to their mothers, were anxious about their own academic progress and general standing in the classroom. They were concerned about "not fitting in," that they looked different, and what to do if they felt ill in school. Some were worried about damage to their Hickman line. These results, emphasizing the differences in concerns between parents, teachers, and children with cancer, should not be surprising, but do serve to highlight the various perspectives. The inference is that interventions may need to be directed at all three groups (parents, teachers, and children), and that targeting any individual member of the triad may have more limited success.

Social Behavior

On return to school after diagnosis and initial treatment, the child can be confronted with a very different situation compared with before they were diagnosed. It can happen that the child returns to a new class and new teacher, depending exactly on how much time has been missed. Some classmates will have left, and others arrived. Friendships will have evolved and changed. The task of reintegration can be challenging, especially if the child with cancer is set apart by changes in appearance, or has difficulties physically getting around the building. The hospital experience may also change the child. Extended periods in the company of parents or other adults can lead to accelerated maturity. Children can look different, feel different, and simply be different, compared with how they used to be. So there are a number of reasons to be concerned about the return to school and social relationships in the classroom. Measuring social relationships in the classroom, however, is quite a task.

A novel method to assess social functioning was pioneered by Noll and his collaborators (1990) who used a version of the Revised Class Play assessment task (Masten, Morison, & Pellegrini, 1985). In this activity, teachers are asked to imagine that they are the "director" of a school play. The "job" of the director is to cast members of the class into appropriate roles. Three dimensions (confirmed through factor analysis) have been reported to underlie teachers' choices of children for specific roles: (a) sociability-leadership (someone who has good ideas; someone everyone listens to), (b) aggressive-disruptive (someone who disrupts others' activities), and (c) sensitive-isolated (someone who can't get things going; someone who can't get others to listen; and someone who plays alone).

Using this method, Noll et al. (1990) asked teachers to assign 24 children with cancer (8–18 years) and healthy controls to different roles. In addition to the generic roles just described, nine additional roles relevant to understanding the adjustment of children with cancer were defined. Three of these were related directly to the illness (someone who misses a lot of school); two to the possible impact of cancer on appearance (someone who is very good looking); two were concerned with academic competence (someone who has trouble with work); and two with athletic competence (someone who is very good at sports). Children were given scores for each role according to the number of times they were nominated for that role. For younger children, ratings were made by the class teacher and for those in middle or high school by the English teacher.

Children with cancer were less often selected for roles requiring sociability-leadership and more often for those involving sensitive-isolated characteristics. These findings were taken to suggest that (at least according to teachers), children with cancer differ from healthy children in key areas of social functioning and have restricted leadership and social skills.

In a separate study (but apparently based on the same sample of children as just discussed), Noll et al. (1991) again compared the sociability of children with cancer and gender-matched classroom controls. This time ratings were made by children rather than teachers. Children completed the Revised Class Play assessment twice, once for their same-gender classmates and once for themselves. In addition, they completed a sociometric questionnaire. In this they were asked to name their three best friends and then rate them on a series of rating scales. On a subsequent assessment at their home, children completed a measure of loneliness (Asher et al., 1984) and self-esteem (Harter, 1985, 1988).

The healthy children were more likely to nominate children with cancer for sensitive-isolated roles than they were to nominate other healthy classmates. There were no differences between the groups on measures of self-reported loneliness or self-esteem. Thus, these findings suggest that, like teachers, healthy children regard the child with cancer as a more appropriate choice for certain types of role than others. Interestingly, the children with cancer did not see themselves as better suited to certain roles than others. The work raises some interesting questions. Are teachers stereotyping the child with cancer into certain roles and activities? Or are teachers making quite accurate judgments about the behavior of the child with cancer? Either way, teachers' views do not seem to be shared by the child with cancer.

The aforementioned studies included children with different cancers. In practice, there may be some differences in behavior depending on the type of cancer and its treatment. Children with diseases involving the CNS generally show more behavioral and emotional problems compared with healthy children, or those with diseases not involving the CNS (Breslau & Marshall, 1985). Given the nature and treatment of a CNS tumor, it is possible that children with these conditions are more likely to experience significant social and emotional problems, compared with those with leukemia. Social and emotional difficulties may be a direct result of the tumor, or exacerbated by educational difficulties.

In recognizing this, Noll, Ris, W. H. Davies, Bukowski, and Koontz (1992) compared 15 children aged 8–18 years with a CNS tumor, 26 with a malignancy not primarily involving the CNS, and 33 with sickle cell disease (SCD). As before, teachers were asked to complete the Revised Class Play task for each child (Masten et al., 1985). Teachers reported significantly higher levels of social isolation for survivors of a CNS tumor compared with classmates. To the extent that children with malignancies were nominated for a variety of roles, the authors concluded that the experience of the cancer did not have an adverse impact on their social adjustment. However, children treated for a CNS tumor were more often nominated for social-isolated roles compared with either of the other two groups, including those with malignancies not involving the CNS. Children with SCD were not seen to be significantly different from peers, suggesting that the critical variable is cancer rather than a chronic disease.

Vannatta, Gartstein et al. (1998) used similar procedures to assess social functioning among children successfully treated for a CNS tumor. Twenty-eight survivors aged 8–18 years were compared with a matched control group of healthy children. According to teachers, peers, and self-report, survivors of a CNS tumor were more often chosen for the sensitive-isolated roles than healthy children, but were not more likely to be chosen for roles involving sociability-leadership or aggressive-disruptive behavior. Survivors of a CNS tumor were less likely to be nominated as a "best friend" by healthy peers.

Vannatta, Zeller, Noll, and Koontz (1998) used the Revised Class Play task to compare social functioning in 48 children (8–16 years of age) following BMT with that of same-classroom, gender-matched peers. Time since BMT varied from 9 months to 8 years. Nine children, almost 20% of the sample, were excluded because they attended special schools, and is important when considering the results.

Peers selected BMT survivors significantly more often than others for passive-anxious and sensitive-isolation roles. Teachers nominated BMT survivors significantly less often for aggressive-disruptive roles. However, self-reports did not differ between the BMT survivors and normal controls. Thus, support for the idea that BMT survivors would be chosen for social-isolation and withdrawal roles were obtained from peer reports but not from self-reports. BMT survivors were chosen by peers significantly less often as a best friend and were less likely to have their best-friend choices reciprocated, partly supporting the idea that BMT survivors would be less accepted by friends. BMT survivors were significantly more likely than peers to be nominated for roles related to illness and missing school. There was little indication that choices were affected by time since diagnosis, except that peer nominations for roles involving "sick a lot" and "misses a lot of school" were reduced with increasing time since treatment.

These data suggest that peers describe BMT survivors as more isolated or socially withdrawn than others. Lack of correlation with time since diagnosis is potentially worrying, because there are no suggestions that social problems during treatment remit with time. This may be exacerbated by continuing absences and illness episodes. Peers described BMT survivors as less attractive and less athletically competent. (There were no independent ratings of attractiveness against which to compare these judgments).

METHODOLOGICAL LIMITATIONS

As has been seen, there are inconsistent findings about the impact of cancer on the child's behavior in school. These findings are often based on teacher ratings using the measure developed by Deasey-Spinetta and Spinetta (1980). This has recently come under some criticism. Findings appear to be sensitive to the exact way in which instructions are given. In particular, van Dongen-Melman, De Groot, Hahlen, and Verhulst (1996) questioned the practice of allowing teachers to select one other child as "typical" against which to judge the behavior of the child with cancer. These authors showed that different results could be obtained depending on whether teachers rated the sick child against such a "typical" child, or against a child randomly chosen by the researchers. The implication is that results based on this measure may overestimate the extent of school-related problems for the child with cancer. School attendance and school behavior will also be very much influenced by family attitudes and behavior, but these are not routinely measured.

In terms of social behavior, the Revised Class Play task (Masten et al., 1985) is frequently used for both teacher and child ratings. The measure was initially developed for use by children, and it is not clear that it is appropriate as a measure of social functioning when used by teachers. Differences between children with cancer and controls have consistently been found for one of the subscales (sociability-isolation), but no differences have reliably been found for the other subscales.

Current research in this area remains of mixed quality. Samples are generally small and include children with a range of cancers. The specific needs of children with different cancers, especially those with learning difficulties associated with treatment, needs to be recognized. The practice of excluding children with special educational needs is likely to distort findings, to the extent that these children may well experience worse attendance and poorer behavioral and educational attainments.

Attention has focused on a small and restricted range of variables including school attendance and children's social or behavioral functioning. Choice of these variables has been made on grounds of availability of measures, rather than any theoretical or clinical need. Consideration needs to be given to the child's whole school experience. This may include involvement in extracurricular activities, especially physical sports and school outings. Social relationships and friendships are important to the child and deserve greater attention. Measures with greater sensitivity compared with the Revised Class Play (Masten et al., 1985) need to be explored.

INTERVENTIONS

For Children

In School.   For many children, return to school is a potentially difficult and challenging task. In recognizing this, many hospitals employ specialist nurses or social workers who liaise with the school and prepare the staff and pupils for the child's return. This can involve a relatively informal visit by someone from the hospital to the school, with the aim of providing some basic information about what to expect. Others offer a class discussion of the issue, led by a specialist nurse (Deasy-Spinetta, 1993). A more formal program was described by Katz and colleagues (E. Katz,

Rubenstein, Hubert, & Blew, 1988). This program involves four components: (a) preliminary intervention, assessing the child's school behavior and parental involvement with an aim to arrange appropriate remedial help through the diagnostic period, (b) conferences with school personnel to help them plan for the child's return, (c) classroom presentations, in the child's presence, to provide peers with age-appropriate information, and (d) follow-up contact after the child's return to provide any further help.

Evaluation of this intervention was based on responses of 37 children with cancer aged 5–17 years. Children completed measures of self-esteem and depression before the intervention and again at follow-up, some 8 months later. Data were also collected from parents, teachers, school records, and physicians. Comparisons were made against a group of 36 age-matched controls, who had had cancer diagnosed within 3 years of the start of the project (but had not taken part in the intervention). Children in the intervention group showed improvements in self-esteem and reductions in depression, but did not differ in terms of school grades or attendance.

E. Katz, Varni, Rubenstein, Blew, and Hubert (1992) evaluated a program for children aged 5–17 years. The program included supportive counseling, educational presentations, systematic liaison between hospital and school, and periodic follow-up. Thirty-four children, 30 parents, and 33 teachers rated their perceptions of the utility of the intervention. All evaluations were positive.

Other programs have been directed more specifically at helping the child with cancer acquire the social skills to cope with school life. It is inevitable that the child with cancer may have to answer questions about what has happened to their hair, why they go to the hospital so often, or why they do not have to do physical education or games. Varni, E. R. Katz, Colegrove, and Dolgin (1993) developed a social-skills-training program to provide the child with the necessary skills to deal with these questions. The program consisted of three modules, each of 1-hour duration. A *social-cognitive* problem-solving module taught children to identify problems, consider their cause, and explore alternative ways of resolution. The *assertiveness-training* module taught children how to express their thoughts and concerns to others. The *handling-teasing-and-name-calling* module taught children how to cope with verbal and physical teasing associated with changes in physical appearance. Children also took part in two follow-up sessions at 3 and 6 weeks following their return to school.

Evaluation of the program was conducted at 6 and 9 months and was based on child self-reports of depression (Kovacs, 1983), anxiety (Spielberger, 1973), self-esteem (Harter, 1985), and social support (Harter, 1985). Parents rated their child's behavior (Achenbach, 1991). Children enrolled in the social skills program reported that classmates and teachers were more supportive than children not enrolled in the program. Children in the program also reported better self-esteem at 9 months compared with those not in the program. Parents reported fewer behavior problems and greater school competence for children who went through the problem-solving skills training compared with parents of a group who received standard return to school instruction at 9 months follow-up.

Out of School. "Activity weeks" or summer camps for children with chronic conditions have been described. The goals of such camps have been variously defined, but include provision of a variety of experiences for children outside of the regular school environment, opportunities to mix with others and develop more positive social skills (Swenson, 1988). They also offer opportunities for time away from the family. Children can become more independent, or simply have time away from being a "child with cancer." The assumption is that children are likely to benefit simply from opportunities to have a good time and feel "normal" (Smith, Gotlieb, Gurwitch, & Blotcky, 1987).

There is evidence from work with children with other chronic conditions that regardless of the specific aim, both parents and children report positive experiences associated with attendance at camp. After attending a camp, parents of a child with asthma reported that their child had become more self-sufficient, more knowledgeable about their condition, and more positive about their illness (Punnett & Thurber, 1993). Briery and Rabian (1999) also reported positive experiences, this time based on reports of children with asthma or diabetes. Their camp offered a very outdoor-oriented activities week, supported by educational sessions about the child's illness (asthma or diabetes). At the end of the week, children held more positive attitudes toward their illness coupled with a decrease in anxiety.

Unlike other authors who emphasize the need for the child at camp to feel "normal," Bluebond-Langner, Perkel, Goertzel, Nelson, and McGeary (1990) recognized that camp can provide an opportunity to help children understand more about their disease and its treatment. They reported that children knew much more about cancer by the end of their camp stay, especially those who were more recently diagnosed. Much of the knowledge acquisition took place informally; that is, children learned from other children rather than any formal adult interventions. The authors argued that gains in knowledge were likely to be important to increase the child's self-esteem and improve adjustment.

Regardless of the specific goal of camp, it is hoped that the experience will be a positive one for children. Disappointingly, then, not all children want to attend. Concerned that nonattenders might be exactly those who might benefit most, Balen, Fielding, and Lewis (1996) surveyed families about how they made the decision about whether or not the child should attend camp.

Parents of children aged 9–16 years were sent a questionnaire with an invitation for the child to attend camp. The questionnaire included requests for information thought relevant to the decision (preference for different activities; concerns or fears about the week). Forty-six children (20%) applied for a place on the activity week. There were a number of differences between applicants and nonapplicants. Those who did not want to attend had been diagnosed for longer and preferred sedentary activities compared with those who did wish to attend. Parents of applicants hoped their child would gain new experiences from the week, gain in independence, make new friends, and mix with others.

For children who have lost confidence in their physical skills or have limited coordination and mobility as a consequence of treatment, or simply those who enjoy sporting activities, the invitation to take part in a week of physical activity supervised by medical staff may offer an excellent opportunity. For others, the need may be more for a quiet week to be themselves away from parents. There is therefore room for different kinds of camp, offering children a range of activities. Evaluating such camps may be considered essential to justify funding, but, as with any evaluation, choosing an appropriate methodology is very difficult. Realistically, attendance at a camp for 1 week can only have short-term implications for the child's emotional adjustment.

It is also important to remember that many who might benefit from camp attendance are exactly those who are most anxious about going somewhere without a parent and where they may know none of the other children. Camps need to be seen as an integral part of a social rehabilitation program and not just a 1-week experience. Children who are highly anxious need to be prepared over the preceding year. There need to be opportunities for brief periods away from home, perhaps initially for just an hour. Without such preparation, many children may remain unable to benefit from a camp experience. Parents too need reassurance that appropriate medical support will be available, and may benefit, as much as their children, from opportunities to "practice" leaving the child in the care of others.

For Teachers

A number of studies report the results of questionnaire surveys to assess teachers' knowledge of and attitudes toward children with cancer. Many teachers have no experience of sick children and know very little about treatment or prognosis (Eiser & Town, 1987). Many teachers reported being uncertain about the academic potential and physical capabilities of children with cancer (Larcombe et al., 1990). This reduces their confidence.

According to teachers, there are a number of things that could be done to ease the child's integration back in school (Gregory et al. 1994). Teachers should be informed as soon as possible about the child's illness, siblings of the ill child should be identified, interventions should begin at diagnosis, and links need to be established between the school and the ill child. Teachers wanted information about the name of the hospital teacher and the possibility of visits by either the teacher or other pupils. This should reduce the child's feelings of isolation.

School nurses have also been used to provide interventions, usually focusing on increasing knowledge and competence of schoolteachers to manage the child with cancer in the classroom. Workers in the United States have concluded that the most successful of these seem to focus on the needs of a specific child, rather than improving the general education of groups of teachers (Baysinger, Heiney, Creed, & Ettinger, 1993).

When a child with cancer returns to school following diagnosis, the simplest interventions involve provision of information. Stevens, Kaye, Kenwood, and Mann (1988) surveyed 18 regional oncology centers in the United Kingdom to determine contact with teachers and if any written information was provided for schools. Replies were received from 13 (72%) of the centers. Six of the 13 centers sent written information to schools covering general issues but not specifically written for teachers. One sent information written for children, and all emphasized a need for personal contact with schools. All the written material provided an overview of childhood cancer, including incidence and treatment, and stressed the importance for the child of a rapid return to school. Stevens et al. pointed out that fewer mentioned issues that were likely to be particularly important to teachers: that children were usually aware of their diagnosis or that medical problems were unlikely to arise while the child was at school.

Workers in the United Kingdom have reported study days for teachers, aimed at increasing general awareness rather than focusing on the issues for a specific child. Larcombe and A. Charlton (1996) organized study days for teachers involving informal presentations from the hospital team and involvement in workshops to share information. Improved knowledge of childhood cancer and confidence to manage typical problem situations were reported.

An alternative intervention focusing on teacher education was reported by Cleave and A. Charlton (1997). This program involved identifying and exploring elements involved in effective listening, how children cope with cancer, and cognitive and affective issues about cancer. The course covered 2 days and included opportunities to practice skills and feedback discussions. Evaluations were reported in two separate studies, the first involving experienced teachers and the second newly qualified teachers. Participants reported increased confidence to cope with children with cancer and other life crises, with experienced teachers reporting most benefit.

Teachers are invariably anxious about having a child with cancer in the classroom, and therefore programs to inform and alleviate their worries may be expected to have beneficial effects for both the teacher as well as the child. There is, however, little evidence that increases in knowledge affect the teacher's actual management of children with cancer in the classroom. Evaluation of interventions aimed at increasing teachers' knowledge of cancer or empathy with the children is subject to many difficulties. Participants tend to be self-selected and are often highly motivated or personally interested prior to attendance at a course. In addition, evaluations typically focus on a specific type of intervention, rather than compare the relative merits of different interventions. As a result, it is not clear whether any intervention is better than nothing. Evaluations of the relative merits, efficacy, or cost-benefit of different interventions are needed.

An interview with a teacher closely involved with the schooling of two children, both with a CNS tumor, is summarized next. This raises questions about the hospital–school liaison and the need for schools to have up-to-date information about a child beyond the initial diagnosis period. The lack of liaison can exacerbate difficulties between school and family. Although this teacher was initially very sympathetic toward the child, she was losing patience after a year or so. The school is set to clash with the parents as they consider a more heavy-handed approach to improving the child's attendance. More accurate information from the hospital about the likely course of the disease and realistic assessment of the longer term accounts could do much to offset these problems:

> Of course, yes, I am concerned about the children with cancer in the school. In this school, something like 18% have special educational needs. Since there are 400 children altogether, it means there are 80 with special educational needs. My main concern is with those with behaviour problems. These children can cause trouble for themselves and other children. Those with cancer are not trouble in the same sense. It is easy to forget about them. Their problems are not so much "in your face."
>
> One of my main problems has been getting any information about the children. The parents do come in occasionally, but I find it difficult to ask them questions I really want answered. When the child was diagnosed, we did get a letter from the hospital consultant, but it was only by chance I found out later that this person is no longer looking after her. I don't know when but at some time another doctor became involved. This makes it difficult for us to know where to go if we want more information.

But our feelings in the school are that these children should be attending more than they do. There is no reason that we can see why they do not attend more regularly. We know that the parents are worried something might happen in school especially that they might get knocked over. We understand that, but we have a legal obligation to provide an education and we are going to look into what can be done.

CONCLUSIONS

Realistically, we have to expect that cancer can have a significant negative impact on the child's schooling. All the evidence suggests that school absences are considerably higher for children with cancer compared with both healthy children and those with other chronic conditions. Exactly how far these absences have any detrimental impact on academic achievement or social adjustment is much less clear.

Guidelines for the schooling and education of children with cancer have been published by SIOP (Masera et al., 1993). According to their report:

- School integration is critical, and children must not only be entitled to attend school, but also be stimulated to obtain a full recovery.
- The management of children with cancer requires a multidisciplinary team and some appropriate schooling should be provided while the child is in the hospital.
- When the child is ready to return to normal school, a program must be developed subject to parental approval.
- Communication between school and hospital is essential. Hospital personnel must explain the disease to teachers and be prepared to explain it also to other children in the class.
- A manual for teachers should be prepared. Suggestions should be given to teachers about how to help the child adjust and reduce any anxiety about school. The proposed program should support teaching methods that help the child to keep up with classmates even when at home (fax, two-way telephone, video or audio lessons).
- It is incumbent on the hospital/school team to determine the specific educational competence and needs of the child and to establish a personalized program if the child requires extra help.
- The school–hospital liaison is critical to the child's total care and needs to be considered from diagnosis, through treatment, and after completion of therapy.

It is far from clear the extent to which these recommendations are followed in practice. Parents of ill children are often preoccupied emotionally and physically with their child's condition and have little time or energy to spare for campaigning in relation to education. The links between poor health and lower socioeconomic status (Acheson Report, 1998) may mean that some parents already feel disempowered. Parents may collude willingly or unwillingly with their ill children and encourage school absence.

Many education authorities do not believe that it is the responsibility of schools to stay in touch socially or educationally with pupils absent on the grounds of health, although some do so voluntarily (Closs & Norris, 1997). There is often little realization on the part of schools that absent children who "lose touch" could become fearful of returning. Enabling learning, by sending and marking homework or collaborating with outreach teachers, has been seen as an aspect of benevolence, not a school duty (Closs, 2000). In relation to attendance there is a need to understand that, for many children, their state of health is not dichotomously either "fine" or "ill"—it is somewhere in between, a state that teachers found hard to understand (Closs & Norris, 1997).

Linked to this conceptual difficulty is a practical one. Many schools also lack what they feel is adequate medical and paramedical support. In some areas there are no school nurses, and auxiliaries may not provide support that would enable a child with a health difficulty to attend school rather than be absent. School doctors under time pressures may not be able to contribute to staff development. National guidance on issues such as medication and medical treatment in school is needed. However teachers unions are resistant to teachers being involved in such practices without training and legal indemnification.

School support for the child with cancer does require a multidisciplinary approach, which includes school and hospital teaching staff, educational psychologists, nursing and medical staff, and school and community nurses. However, many interventions are not evaluated, either in terms of their benefits to the children or in terms of their cost-effectiveness with regard to treatment delivery. Such evaluation is crucial if services are to be supported in an era of financial restraint.

Although many children with cancer return to school successfully and experience few difficulties, it must be recognized that some children are at special risk. Those treated for a CNS tumor remain particularly vulnerable. Future research needs to distinguish between children who are more or less vulnerable, and focus on educational provision and appropriateness of remedial education offered to those in special need.

A number of changes in medical care have probably contributed to better school attendance for children treated more recently (compared with the children included in the original studies reported by Deasey-Spinetta & Spinetta, 1980). Community nurses can provide school- or home-based care that reduces the need for hospital visits. Awareness of risks of infectious disease such as chicken pox and availability of suitable vaccines may have reduced parental anxiety in this regard and also contributed to better attendance. Against this, increasingly aggressive modern protocols may unwittingly contribute to poorer attendance.

The incidence of significant ill health and medical conditions in children has been shown to be underestimated by education staff who suggested, in a national survey of education authorities, figures as low as 1% (Closs & Norris, 1997). Low levels of knowledge, understanding, and personal experience of education staff, teachers, and policymakers about medical matters and their implications for educational practice is widespread (Closs, 2000; Eiser, 1993; Larcombe, 1995). Lack of empathy and interest results from this and the motivation to include children with medical conditions may be low as a result. One of the difficulties experienced in negotiating extra help or special support for children returning to school after cancer is the fact that many other children also have special needs. Some 10%–15% of the school-age population has a chronic illness (Hobbs & Perrin, 1985). Learning problems are associated with many of these (epilepsy, diabetes, AIDS). From this perspective, it seems that the most useful strategy would be to marshal appropriate resources for all children and not make unrealistic demands for any single group (Closs, 2000).

As described in chapter 5, the key developmental tasks during middle childhood include the development of a work ethic, establishment of a supportive peer group, and some independence from parents. Chronic illness during this time might be expected to have particularly negative effects for the child's school functioning, both in terms of academic achievement and in compromising the move to independence and relationship with friends. However, the studies described previously provide only partial support for the notion that social relationships are severely compromised.

The concern about children's social relationships following cancer can partly be attributed to other work showing that children who have problems in their social relationships grow up to have similar difficulties as adults (Rubin, Chen, McDougall, Bowker, & McKinnon, 1995). However, just as there is a suggestion that the negative effects of school absence on attainment found in healthy children may not be the same for those with a chronic illness, so we cannot necessarily extrapolate findings about social development from well children to those with cancer. It might be hoped that any social difficulties experienced by the child with cancer would dissipate with increasing time since diagnosis and treatment. The limited information about this is reviewed in chapters 13 and 14.

8

Learning Difficulties in Children Treated for Leukemia

Summary

Children with a chronic disease are more likely to do poorly at school, have lower IQ scores, and have more difficulties learning than healthy children. For example, this has been shown for children with diabetes (Ryan, 1990) and epilepsy (Hiemenz, Hynd, & Jimenez, 1999). Children who are younger when they were diagnosed are also at greater risk of subsequent learning difficulties compared with those who are older on diagnosis. Although the situation may be more complex than it first seems, the broad conclusions of this chapter support these general findings for children treated for leukemia. Many children do have learning difficulties in school, and the likelihood of this happening is greater for children who are less than 5 years of age on diagnosis. In this chapter, a number of reasons why children may experience learning difficulties are identified and then currently available empirical work reviewed. Although the first studies suggested that CNS irradiation was the most likely explanation for learning difficulties, later work has challenged this view. Over time there has also been a change in the kind of tests used to assess children's learning. For a number of reasons, IQ tests are no longer considered entirely appropriate, and need to be supplemented by tests of specific functioning, such as memory, attention, or concentration. Changes in treatment protocols over time, use of different tests in different studies, and difficulties establishing the contribution of treatment over more general social and family variables, has limited the theoretical and clinical relevance of this work. However, in drawing the work together, consideration is given to the implications for remedial help and interventions for the children.

BACKGROUND

Treatment for childhood cancer was always, and remains, highly aggressive. It is therefore not surprising that children's behavior and school progress can deteriorate during treatment. Short-term effects, including poor academic progress during the course of treatment, have to be expected. The most important question therefore concerns the extent to which children who have been treated for leukemia show longer term problems. In addition, we might ask whether longer term problems are the direct result of iatrogenic effects of treatment or occur as a more general effect of illness or reduced schooling. Thus, are learning difficulties shown by children with leukemia similar to those found for children with chronic disease generally or are they more sinister?

There are also questions about the vulnerability of children at different ages. According to current theories about the development of the human CNS, it has been suggested that the child's vulnerability is dependent on the specific stage when damage occurred. This has led to an assumption that vulnerability is greater for children diagnosed and treated at a younger age. There is also the question of permanence of any damage. How well is the CNS able to compensate for any damage incurred? All of these questions have implications for advancing theoretical knowledge about the development of the human brain. More important for families, evaluation of the degree and extent of learning difficulties should provide a basis for education and rehabilitation for children.

The material in this chapter focuses on children's learning following treatment for leukemia and should be considered separately from that in chapter 9 concerned with the consequences of treatment for CNS tumors. There are some overlapping issues. Regardless of whether the child has leukemia or a CNS tumor, the consequences for the family are traumatic. In either case, families have to balance the needs of the sick child with the goals of promoting as normal and healthy a lifestyle as possible. School absence and restricted opportunities to engage in a range of activities are also likely to limit school progress.

In practice, the two situations are quite different. The child with a CNS tumor experiences a much greater number of difficulties. Some damage might have been caused before the diagnosis. The developing tumor may infiltrate healthy areas of the brain and the tumor itself can cause pressure and damage. Depending on the location of the tumor, treatment may re-quire surgery, and sometimes this can be associated with damage to healthy tissue. In many cases, it is not possible to remove the whole tu-mor. Thus, the child with a CNS tumor is subject to greater risk compared with the child with leukemia.

Deficits in IQ and cognitive functioning are assumed to result from vas-cular and biochemical abnormalities associated with radiotherapy and chemotherapy, though there are many confounding factors. Cell damage caused by treatment is thought to underlie subsequent cognitive deficits. At least three hypotheses regarding the nature of cell damage have been put forward. The first involves damage to the capillary endothelial cells, the structural basis of the blood–brain barrier. Radiation damage results in cell death or endothelial hyperplasia. The second proposed mechanism involves damage to glial cells. White matter changes without vascular al-terations are thought to be consistent with this hypothesis. The third hy-pothesis is that CNS damage is a form of allergic response to antigens released from impaired glial cells (Packer, A. T. Meadows, Rorke, Gold-wein, & D'Angio, 1987). Among drugs routinely administered as part of cancer treatment, methotrexate is thought to be the most likely cause of subsequent cognitive dysfunction (Boogerd, 1995). Methotrexate may cause direct damage to endothelial cells (Phillips et al., 1987) resulting in secondary demyelination and possible loss of cells.

Historically, there have been extensive concerns about the functioning of children with ALL. In part this arose initially from parents' reports that children showed marked difficulties following treatment, difficulties that seemed more substantial than might be expected. Difficulties in motor functioning or loss of hearing sensitivity will contribute further to the child's learning difficulties.

In the 1960s, when questions about learning difficulties first arose, CNS irradiation was considered the most likely cause. Consequently, changes to protocols were made for several reasons. First, CNS radiation was asso-ciated with a number of adverse physical outcomes. Second, there was considerable evidence to suggest that intellectual and behavior problems were associated with CNS radiation therapy, or combined CNS radiation and chemotherapy. Radiation is particularly toxic to cells that are migrat-ing or multiplying (Hicks & D'Amato, 1966), and even more so in combi-nation with methotrexate (Bleyer, 1988). Finally, there were indications that survival was as good for children treated by chemotherapy alone compared with chemotherapy and CNS irradiation. Given that questions about the toxicity (and efficacy) of this treatment were raised, efforts were made to reduce the amount of radiation. In later work, therefore, the ques-tion shifted from determining the effects of CNS radiation therapy to assessing outcomes for children who (a) received reduced doses of CNS irradiation and (b) were treated by chemotherapy alone.

The Assessment of Intelligence—IQ Tests Revisited

Interest in the assessment of intelligence can be traced to the beginnings of the 20th century and was driven by the need to establish appropriate learning environments for brain-damaged children. Given their long and apparently successful history, IQ tests were thought to yield highly reliable and validated estimates of ability. In practice, few alternatives were available.

In the review that follows, it is clear that assessment of children following treatment for ALL has relied heavily on a small number of IQ measures. The most frequently cited are the series of scales developed by Wechsler (1991), which include versions for children aged 4–7 years, 7–16 years, and adults. All yield measures of Full Scale Intelligence Quotient (FSIQ), Verbal Intelligence Quotient (VIQ), and Performance Intelligence Quotient (PIQ). The advantages of these measures include the availability of population norms, possibility of relating the child's score at one age to a comparable score at a later age, and the accumulated expertise related to use of the measures.

However, none of the versions are suitable for children below 4.5 years. This is a particular problem for work with children with ALL, because many are below 5 years of age on diagnosis. For these reasons, work with younger children has often involved the scales developed by D. McCarthy (1970) and the British Abilities Scales (Elliott, D. Murray, & Pearson, 1978).

With time, there have been objections to the extensive use of IQ tests. Criticisms have been based on the view that the concept of intelligence, at least as measured by these tests, is relatively narrow. Some have argued that IQ tests represent what an individual has learned in the past, rather than their future potential (Herrnstein & C. Murray, 1994). Indeed, Sparrow, Carter, and Cicchetti (2000) suggested that IQ tests are inadequate as comprehensive developmental assessments.

Researchers increasingly acknowledge the problems with relying on IQ tests and explore the impact of treatment on more specific skills. The field of neuropsychology, or the study of brain–behavior relationships, has received more recent attention. In contrast to traditional IQ tests that make a distinction between verbal and nonverbal skills, most neuropsychological work requires independent evaluation of attention; auditory, visual, and tactile perception; verbal and language functions; spatial processing; memory; learning; and executive function (conceptual reasoning, problem solving, planning, flexibility, and implementation of cognitive plans).

Evidence for Long-Term Difficulties in Learning

Suggestions of learning difficulties among children treated for ALL treated by CNS irradiation were reported almost as soon as survival rates began to improve (A. T. Meadows & A. E. Evans, 1976). As a consequence, a number of studies were published in the 1980s to try to establish whether or not learning difficulties were an inevitable consequence of cancer treatment. This literature has subsequently been the subject of many reviews (Brouwers, 1987; Cousens, 1997; Cousens, Ungerer, Crawford, & Stevens, 1991; Eiser, 1991; Fletcher & Copeland, 1988; Mulhern, 1994; Packer et al., 1987; Stehbens et al., 1991; J. M. Williams & Davis, 1986). These reviews inevitably focused on different literatures and different areas of interest. With time, the number of studies for review has mushroomed, and conclusions have become increasingly complex with the expansion of the number of treatment protocols. Thus, whereas early reviews focused simply on the effects of CNS irradiation, later reviews tried to distinguish between treatments differing in radiation dose and chemotherapy. In addition, the studies included in early reviews tended to be based exclusively on results from children's IQ tests. Later reviews, reflecting the shift away from IQ tests, assessed a wider range of abilities. It is difficult therefore to draw any overarching conclusions. Perhaps, though, it is true to say that whereas the first reviews were inconclusive about the association between irradiation and learning deficits, subsequent reviews have become increasingly decisive in their conclusions that some children are vulnerable.

J. M. Williams and Davis (1986) reviewed 28 articles and concluded there was no evidence that CNS irradiation was associated with neuropsychological impairment. A short time later, both Brouwers (1987) and Packer et al. (1987) suggested that some neuropsychological impairment was likely. These reviews laid the foundations of much of what was to follow.

Fletcher and Copeland (1988) reviewed 41 studies and also concluded that some impairment was likely, especially among younger children. They distinguished between three types of study:

1. In-treatment: These involve children undergoing treatment by CNS irradiation. Based on the review of literature until this time, Fletcher and Copeland suggested that these children show average performance on tests of cognitive function.
2. Survivor studies: These include evaluations of children after completion of therapy and suggest that survivors show deterioration following CNS irradiation.
3. Longitudinal studies: These include evaluations from diagnosis and throughout treatment and tend to support the aforementioned find-

ings, as well as suggesting deterioration with time since treatment. It was suggested that deficits were most likely in the areas of nonverbal abilities, attention, concentration, and arithmetic.

Cousens, Waters, Said, and Stevens (1988) conducted a meta-analysis of 30 studies. Their findings suggested that children treated by CNS irradiation had FSIQ scores approximately 10 points below those expected from population norms. Children treated by CNS irradiation have lower IQ scores than siblings (Jannoun, 1983; Twaddle, Britton, Craft, Noble, & Kernahan, 1983), matched normal controls (Eiser, 1980; Eiser & Lansdown, 1977), and children with other cancers not involving CNS irradiation (Eiser, 1980; Soni, Marten, Pitner, Duenas, & Powazek, 1975; Stehbens, Ford, Kisker, Clarke, & Strayer, 1981; Stehbens, Kisker, & Wilson, 1983). Based on two longitudinal studies available at the time (Goff, H. R. Anderson, & Cooper, 1980; Verzosa, Aur, Simone, Hustu, & Pinkel, 1976), Cousens et al. also concluded that deficits increase with time since treatment. This is a significant finding, suggesting that learning difficulties are not simply related to school absence. It suggests that damage caused by irradiation may have *cumulative* effects, limiting the child's ability to learn.

Madan-Swain and R. T. Brown (1991) extended the focus of their review to include academic and psychosocial functioning as well as IQ scores. They pointed to many methodological problems in interpretation of findings, but in particular emphasized that future work needs to take more account of age at diagnosis and background family variables that contribute to social and cognitive development.

Stehbens et al. (1991) concluded that children treated by CNS irradiation and intrathecal methotrexate experience a variety of learning problems especially when treated before 5 years of age. They reviewed 24 studies focusing on neuropsychological functioning, including visuospatial skills, attention and concentration, fine motor skill, nonverbal and verbal memory. Positive and negative findings were reported for each area, suggesting no simple pattern of deficits. However, 73% of studies reported deficits in fine-motor skills, compared with only 14% in receptive language.

Mulhern (1994) reviewed and tabulated results from 24 studies. He concluded that patients treated by CNS irradiation had lower IQ scores than those treated by protocols not including this treatment. No conclusions were made about changes in IQ over time. There were two unusual findings. First, in contrast to most other work, Mulhern concluded that there was no evidence that younger children were more vulnerable following CNS treatment. Second, Mulhern was able to identify four studies that included subsamples of children who had relapsed. Because increasingly aggressive protocols are used to treat recurrence of the disease, these children must be considered to be at even greater risk of neuropsychological problems. As expected, significant loss in IQ following treatment for relapse (Kun et al., 1984; Mulhern et al., 1987) and in relation to those who did not relapse (Longeway et al., 1990; Ochs et al., 1985) was found, perhaps suggesting a cumulative effect of irradiation.

Cousens (1997) reviewed the literature, focusing especially on comparisons between children treated by CNS irradiation and alternative protocols that were thought to be less toxic. She reported little evidence to suggest that reduced levels of CNS irradiation or treatment by intrathecal methotrexate alone are conclusively associated with better learning outcomes compared with CNS irradiation of 2,400 Gy. She argued further that studies should focus more on the nature of the learning deficit than simply attempting to demonstrate its existence. Cousens argued that memory, attention, and some visual processes need to be assessed more than general IQ. To account for her findings, Cousens proposed a model that links CNS irradiation with a general slowing of processing and/or a reduction in attention.

In most published work, *some* intellectual difficulties have been reported for *some* children at *some* time during the course of treatment. However, in drawing together the findings from these early reviews, it must be emphasized that a small number of studies have found no effects of treatment on cognitive function. These included research by Soni et al. (1975); Verzosa et al. (1976); Mulhern, Fairclough, and Ochs (1991); Mulhern, Wasserman, Fairclough, and Ochs (1988); and Ochs et al. (1991). It is easy to identify some methodological problems post hoc with each of these and consequently dismiss the findings, but in practice, similar methodological problems can be identified in most published research.

K. S. Williams, Ochs, J. M. Williams, and Mulhern (1991) argued that the real issue is not about IQ scores but how far children are able to function in terms of everyday tasks and achievements. In their study, ratings of everyday function were made by parents of 51 children with ALL and 24 children with learning disabilities (aged 6–16 years). Children with ALL were at least 2 years since completion of treatment and none had experienced a relapse. Parents of 203 healthy children responded to advertisements and were matched in terms of age, gender, race, and social class with a child with leukemia. As a result, a control group of 51 normal children was identified. Parents' views about their child were assessed using a 112-item questionnaire specifically developed for the study. Four areas of functioning were assessed: cognitive problems (difficulty remembering names), academic skills (arithmetic), school history (absence and grade average), and demographics. Children with leukemia had a grade point average midway between the normal children and those with a learning disability. They also had higher school absence than either of the other groups. Academic skills were rated as poorest for the leukemia group. Although as a group the children with ALL were performing poorly in comparison with a healthy group, there were no differences in the four areas depending on whether or not children were treated by CNS irradiation.

Specific Neuropsychological Functioning

Criticisms of studies based on IQ measures led to an increasing focus on specific neuropsychological outcomes. The theory is that because different regions of the brain may be differentially vulnerable to radio- or chemotherapy, localized brain injuries reflecting specific patterns of deficits might be expected.

The most frequently reported cognitive deficits include those associated with attention and planning, memory, and motor skills (Brouwers, Riccardi, Fedio, & Poplack, 1985; Mulhern et al., 1988; Pfefferbaum-Levine et al., 1984).

Attention and Planning. Attention deficits were first reported by Peckham, A. T. Meadows, Bartel, and Marrero (1988). Brouwers and Poplack (1990) suggested that survivors show symptoms similar to those identified among children with attention deficit hyperactivity disorder (ADHD). Both groups of children are often described as distractible and have difficulty sustaining attention. Difficulties in attention may then contribute to lower performance on other measures.

In one of the most comprehensive assessments of attention in survivors of ALL, Lockwood, Bell, and Colegrove (1999) assessed 56 patients aged between 8 and 29 years of age. Survivors were grouped by type of CNS treatment (CNS irradiation vs. no irradiation) and by age on diagnosis (above or below 54 months). The authors cited a contemporary model of attention (J. Cohen, 1993) and selected their outcome measures on this basis. According to Cohen, four aspects of attention need to be considered. These include: (a) *sensory selection*—basic information processing and automatic shifting of attention; (b) *response selection*—the capacity to inhibit or control oneself during goal-directed activity and involves attention, focusing, and automatic shifting of attention; (c) *attentional capacity*—mediated by processing speed and subfactors of arousal and motivation; and (d) *sustained attention*—the maintenance of attention over time.

A battery of neuropsychological tests was used to assess these different aspects of attention. The results suggested that CNS irradiation has a significant impact on sensory selection particularly for children diagnosed at younger ages. Consequently, even the simplest of tasks such as focusing and shifting of attention may be compromised, especially in children treated when very young. There were also some impairments in the response selection domain. The deficits seemed to reflect problems with mental flexibility and ability to learn from feedback but not necessarily perseveration or impulsiveness. Thus there are suggestions that CNS irradiation may lead to deleterious effects on the ability to carry out goal-directed behavior due to problems in set shifting. Significant deficits on almost all tasks of attentional capacity were found for those treated by irradiation. Again these effects were more pronounced for those treated when younger. Finally, the results suggested an association between radiation and sustained attention over time, especially vigilance and persistence. Overall the suggestion is that global impairment in attention is found among children irradiated at younger ages, whereas milder and more isolated deficits characterize those irradiated when older.

Memory.   Cousens et al. (1991) reported more problems in short- compared with long-term memory, but this may partly reflect the greater practical difficulty in assessing long-term memory. The publication of new memory tests that include standardized assessment of long-term memory may help to clarify these findings (e.g., Children's Memory Scale: M. J. Cohen, 1997).

D. E. Hill, Ciesielski, Sethre-Hofstad, Duncan, and Lorenzi (1997) studied 10 survivors of ALL. Children were assessed at least 3 years after completion of treatment. All had been treated with intrathecal methotrexate but without any CNS irradiation. Comparisons were made against a control group matched on a number of criteria, including age, handedness, school grade, socioeconomic status, and gender. (However, inspection of individual data suggests that some matching may be less precise than was hoped. In two pairs, for example, chronological ages were reported to be 8 and 10 years, with one case favoring the cancer group and the other the control. Although this would not be expected to affect mean scores, it may not be very satisfactory from an individual perspective.) All children completed a battery of neuropsychological assessments including the Wide Range Assessment of Memory and Learning (WRAML; Sheslow & Adams, 1990) and the Wechsler Intelligence Scale for Children (WISC; Wechsler, 1991).

Children's scores were compared with population norms and also with the scores of the control group. Children treated for ALL scored significantly worse than controls on measures of verbal memory, visual memory and learning, and on the Verbal, Performance, and Full Scale scores of the WISC. Children with ALL also had lower scores than would be expected from population norms on all tests except for learning memory.

This study seems to suggest that significant negative effects on learning and memory can be identified in children treated by chemotherapy without CNS irradiation. The size of the discrepancies was substantial, some 10–20 points lower on the WISC. However, this study did include children treated before 5 years of age, a group that has consistently shown to be more vulnerable to cognitive deficits compared with children undergoing similar treatment at later ages.

Language. Treatment of the CNS with radiation and/or chemotherapy has been particularly implicated in terms of deficits in processing speed, visual–motor integration, fine-motor coordination, sequential memory, and arithmetic. These functions are typically associated with the frontal cortex, basal ganglia, and periventricular areas of the brain, especially those in the right hemisphere. It has been suggested that deficits are most typically in these nonverbal functions whereas language and verbal abilities seem more resistant to damage (Fletcher & Copeland, 1988). It has often been concluded that mathematical skills are more likely to be affected by irradiation than are language skills (Brouwers et al., 1985; Copeland, Dowell, Fletcher, Bordeaux et al., 1988a; Eiser, 1980). However, these conclusions were usually based on relatively poor scores on the arithmetic subtest of the WISC in comparison with subtests measuring language (e.g., vocabulary or comprehension). More comprehensive assessments of language are needed before we can conclude that language is more likely to be spared than mathematical skill.

Only a limited number of studies have been concerned with language function in children treated for leukemia. Buttsworth, Murdoch, and Ozanne (1993) compared the performance of 22 children treated for leukemia with age- and gender-matched healthy controls. Children completed tests of language development, comprehension, naming, and semantic skills, including word retrieval. Differences in favor of the control group were reported. Children with leukemia performed considerably worse than controls on measures of expressive language, grammar, and writing. Older children with leukemia were notably worse than controls in their ability to follow spoken commands but this difference was not found for younger children. Among 23 case studies reported by Murdoch, Boon, and Ozanne (1994), 13 had language abilities within the normal range, 9 showed mild or moderate deficits, and 1 child had severe impairments.

In their extensive review of language difficulties following treatment for leukemia, Murdoch and Boon (1999) concluded that there was little evidence to suggest that language abilities were routinely compromised by treatment for leukemia. However, given the importance of language for cognitive function generally, speech and language pathologists need to be aware of the difficulties experienced by some children.

MODERATING VARIABLES

Age and Gender

As has been shown, children who are diagnosed when younger tend to have poorer cognitive function compared with children diagnosed with the same problem when they are older. This applies, for example, in diabetes (Rovet & Fernandes, 1999) or epilepsy (Hiemenz et al., 1999). Children who were diagnosed earlier with liver disease also show poorer intellectual functioning compared with those diagnosed when older (Bannister et al., 1995). Conversely, for children with heart disease, corrective surgery conducted at younger ages is associated with better outcomes than when surgery is conducted with older children (Newburger, Silbert, Buckley, & Fyler, 1984).

Early studies pointed relatively consistently to the fact that age at treatment is a predictor of deficits (Eiser & Lansdown, 1977; Fletcher & Copeland, 1988). The exact age above which children become less vulnerable tends to vary between 3 and 5 years of age. The confusion must lie partly in the specific samples included and also the measures used to assess functioning.

Mulhern, Kovnar et al. (1992) specifically examined neuropsychological status in children treated for ALL before 2 years of age. Of these children, six had received no radiation, five received 18 Gy, seven received 20 Gy, and five received 24 Gy. Three children received additional treatment following CNS relapse. Comparisons were made with 26 children treated at a similar age for Wilms' tumor (and therefore not treated by CNS irradiation). Mean times since completion of treatment were 7.3 and 9.8 years respectively. All children completed measures of neuropsychological functioning including age-appropriate subscales of the WISC and school achievement. Measures of immediate, short-, and long-term memory were also made. Ratings of cosmetic and functional impairment were made by clinic staff and cranial CT scans were conducted on the children treated for ALL.

There were no differences between the groups in staff ratings of cosmetic or functional impairment. No problems were reported for 85% of the leukemia children and 92% of those treated for Wilms' tumor. However, children treated for ALL had lower IQ scores than those treated for a Wilms' tumor (IQ = 87 and 96, respectively). Two of the 26 children treated for ALL functioned in the mentally retarded range. Although there were no differences in reading or spelling scores, children treated for ALL scored significantly lower in arithmetic. Correlations between IQ scores and time since diagnosis were not significant for the Wilms' tumor group, but longer time since diagnosis was associated with poorer scores for the leukemia group. Contrary to expectations, there was no significant association between IQ score and age at diagnosis for both groups. The results from this study were taken as contradicting previous views that the effects of CNS treatment were associated with chronological age (Mulhern, 1994).

There is also some evidence that girls are more vulnerable than boys (Bleyer et al., 1990; Christie, Leiper, Chessells, & Vargha-Khadem, 1995; Jannoun, 1983; Robison et al., 1984; Waber, Gioia et al., 1990; Waber, Urion et al., 1990). These findings are especially challenging given the higher incidence of learning disorder among boys compared with girls in the general population.

Waber, Gioia et al. (1990) reported that 89% of girls and 54% of boys showed some degree of learning difficulty based on measures derived from the WISC and tests of reading comprehension. These gender differences were most pronounced for the arithmetic and digit span subtests of the WISC, the Wide Range Achievement Test (WRAT) for arithmetic, and a comprehension task. Girls on average had IQ scores 8.5 points lower than boys.

Waber, Urion et al. (1990) specifically evaluated gender differences in cognitive processing among 51 children (27 female, 24 male, aged 8–16 years) treated for ALL by CNS irradiation and intrathecal methotrexate, and diagnosed between 2 and 10 years. On assessment, ALL children had been disease-free for 5–12 years. A control group of 15 children treated for Wilms' tumor was also assessed. A number of outcome measures were included to assess aspects of free-recall, story recall, and reaction time as well as subtests of the WISC. Relative to the Wilms' tumor group, the ALL group showed deficits on tasks involving organization of complex visuospatial material and alertness, with females more seriously affected than males.

Christie et al. (1995) attempted to distinguish the effects of both age and gender on the incidence of cognitive deficits in children treated for ALL. The study included 35 girls and 47 boys, all in first remission following treatment (range = 3–12 years after diagnosis). Twenty girls and 26 boys were diagnosed before 4 years of age. Age at testing was 6–19 years. All children completed age-appropriate versions of the Wechsler IQ scales. Mean Verbal, Performance, and Full Scale IQ scores for the total group were lower than published population norms. Girls scored lower than boys on verbal IQ and three of the six verbal subtests. However, there were no significant differences in terms of Performance or Full Scale IQ. The effect of age at diagnosis was more pronounced on the Performance scale subtests. The results suggest that there was a selective impairment for girls in terms of verbal ability and that children treated before 4 years of age were more likely to show impairments in nonverbal ability. The study also demonstrated no effects of time since diagnosis or number of methotrexate injections on any outcome measure.

Explanations for the increased vulnerability of girls have included the hypothesis that girls are more sensitive or responsive to one or more of the treatment regimes. Waber, Urion et al. (1990) also speculated that two processes may be at work. The first is a generalizable deficit that affects all treated children and the second is a developmentally determined factor that only affects the nervous system at a specific stage of development. These conclusions are supported by a complementary series of experiments conducted at the same institution suggesting that similar processes operate in irradiated animals.

CAN COGNITIVE DEFICITS BE REDUCED WITHOUT COMPROMISING SURVIVAL?

Attempts to reduce the incidence of neurological problems have included reducing the total dose of radiotherapy, increasing the number of fractionations in which the total CNS radiotherapy is given and eliminating radiotherapy in children below 2 years of age altogether. Attempts to replace radiotherapy wholly or in part with chemotherapy have also been reported. None of these modifications has had any effect, detrimental or otherwise, on survival. Neither is it clear that there are any significant effects on the incidence or severity of learning problems. The relevant literature is reviewed first in relation to changes in radiation dose and second in terms of chemotherapy.

Reducing the Dose: 2,400 Versus 1,800 Gy

During the 1990s, there was increasing concern about the use of CNS therapy in treatment of children with ALL. At least, there were concerns that CNS therapy of 2,400 Gy was associated with late adverse effects resulting in neuroendocrine and neuropsychological abnormalities, and supported by brain imaging. Recommendations were made for treatment protocols to involve a reduced dose of 1,800 Gy. Initial studies suggested that this reduced dose eliminated the neuropsychological problems characteristic of groups of children treated with 2,400 Gy (Said, Waters, Cousens, & Stevens, 1989). However, children in this study were still on treatment and follow-up of children over longer periods of time raised questions about the long-term efficacy of the reduced treatment (Cousens et al., 1991; Mulhern, Kavner et al., 1992; Rubenstein, Varni, & E. R. Katz, 1990).

Similar reservations were made by Rodgers, Britton, Kernahan, and Craft (1991) in comparisons involving healthy siblings. Twenty-three children were treated with 2,400 Gy and 41 children with 1,800 Gy. At diagnosis children were aged between 10 and 162 months, and at testing between 55 and 253 months. This study includes a number of unique features. First, rather than rely on the WISC as an outcome measure, age-appropriate subtests from the British Ability Scale were used (Elliott et al., 1978). Second, a pretreatment estimate of intelligence was derived. This was based on the assumption that the child with ALL would have an IQ score halfway between that of a sibling and a population mean of 100 (McNemar, 1962). Based on this estimate, the 2,400-Gy and 1,800-Gy groups were calculated to show losses of 12.4 and 12.5 points respectively over the course of treatment. Both groups therefore appear to show significant losses in IQ but the effects are comparable regardless of the treatment dose.

An exception to these findings was made by Moore, Kramer, Wara, Halberg, and Ablin (1991). In their study IQ scores were approximately 9 points higher for those receiving 1,800 Gy compared with those receiving 2,400 Gy. Survivors treated by the reduced dose were also reported to have better achievement scores on reading, spelling, and arithmetic tests.

Irradiation Versus No Irradiation Therapy

Jankovic et al. (1994) reported a collaborative European study involving patients from 14 different centers in five countries. The aim was to compare the effects of 1,800 Gy against no irradiation and treatment by methotrexate alone. The study included 203 children (aged 6–17 years) in continuous first remission and who remained in remission at least 18 months after completion of therapy. Patients had all been treated for low-risk ALL between 1979 and 1988 and those with known CNS involvement were excluded.

Comparisons were made between children treated by CNS irradiation up to 1,800 Gy in 10–12 sessions ($n = 129$) and a group who received high-dose methotrexate and no radiotherapy ($n = 74$). Although assignment to each group was not random, the groups were relatively well matched in terms of age, time since diagnosis, age at diagnosis, and age at assessment. All patients were individually assessed using the WISC. The results suggested an interaction between time since diagnosis and CNS irradiation, so that the radiated group showed a significant decline in Full Scale IQ with longer time from diagnosis. A similar pattern was observed for the Verbal and Performance scales of the WISC. There was also a significant relationship between age at diagnosis and radiation therapy. Radiated patients who were younger on diagnosis had lower IQ scores. This relationship with age was found even though 80% of patients were between 4 and 8½ years of age, that is, considerably older than children previously thought to be vulnerable. This may suggest that the age effects typically found in patients treated by 2,400 Gy remain even when the dose is reduced to 1,800 Gy.

V. Anderson, Smibert, Ekert, and Godber (1994) compared three groups: children diagnosed with ALL and treated by CNS irradiation (n = 100); those diagnosed with ALL or other cancers and treated by chemotherapy and no CNS irradiation (n = 50); and a group of healthy control children (n = 100). Children were aged 7–16 years on assessment and had completed treatment at least 2 years earlier. The complete cohort of children eligible for inclusion was contacted and the first children to consent were included (no information was given about refusal rates). All children completed the WISC and Achievement tests. Parents completed the CBCL (Achenbach & Edelbrock, 1983).

Verbal and Performance scale scores were lower for the group treated by CNS irradiation compared with the other two groups. The irradiated group also had lower scores on all the achievement measures (reading, spelling, and arithmetic) compared with the other two groups. These findings are supported by data from parents, with the irradiated children reported to have poorer school performance compared with the other two groups. There were no differences in parents' reports about the children's behavior (based on internalizing and externalizing scales of the CBCL). However, compared with the other two groups, the irradiated group was described as having more specific symptoms or problem behaviors (being withdrawn, anxious/depressed, or having social and attention problems). This study points clearly to deficits for children treated by CNS radiation compared with healthy controls and children treated with chemotherapy but no radiotherapy. Those treated for cancer without CNS therapy did not differ from a normal sample.

R. T. Brown et al. (1996) compared 38 children with leukemia treated with CNS prophylactic chemotherapy with 25 children who did not receive this therapy. All children were aged 2–15 years on diagnosis and were followed over a 3-year period. Those who received CNS therapy showed more adverse effects in terms of academic functioning than children who did not. The groups did not differ on any of the measures immediately after diagnosis, but the CNS group scored more poorly on tests of reading, spelling, and arithmetic at 3 years postdiagnosis.

Butler, J. M. Hill, Steinherz, Meyers, and Finlay (1994) studied four groups differing in diagnosis and extent of prophylactic treatment. The first group included children treated for Hodgkin's disease or leukemia who received both CNS radiotherapy and intrathecal methotrexate (n = 38), the second group were leukemic patients treated by intrathecal methotrexate without CNS radiotherapy (n = 22), the third group included brain tumors (n = 34), and the fourth group had cancers not normally associated with CNS involvement or treatment (n = 26). These groups were identified to allow for comparisons of CNS irradiation, intrathecal, and systemic chemotherapy. A comprehensive battery of measures was included to assess general functioning (Wechsler scales appropriate for chronological age) and memory (WRAML); learning (Rey, 1964); language (B. M. Kaplan, Goodglass, & Weintraub, 1983), visuospatial judgment (Benton, Varney, & Hamsher, 1978), and mental flexibility and achievement (Heaton, 1981).

There was evidence that children treated by CNS irradiation had lower IQ scores compared with the other groups. Irradiation in combination with intrathecal chemotherapy was potentially most harmful. However, the effect of radiation was not dose dependent and the authors suggested an all-or-none effect of irradiation. There were no systematic effects associated with intrathecal or systemic chemotherapy. Performance on intelligence, achievement, and neuropsychological function was related to social class, age, and amount of schooling missed.

J. Hill et al. (1998) traced 110 survivors of ALL (mean age = 20.8 years) who had been disease-free for at least 1 year. All had previously been randomized to receive 2,400 Gy and intrathecal methotrexate, or intermediate dose systemic methotrexate with intrathecal methotrexate. Twelve-year follow-up of these patients suggested that both treatments were associated with similar outcomes in terms of survival (Freeman et al., 1997). Of 202 survivors who were eligible for the study, 60% were located and most of these agreed to take part. Nonparticipants differed from those who agreed to take part in terms of age at diagnosis, with those who took part being older on diagnosis than those who did not.

Survivors took part in a telephone interview to assess their psychological, sexual, vocational, and social functioning. Survivors who were treated by CNS irradiation had poorer body image, lower school achievement, and a tendency to poorer overall adjustment than the other group.

Separate analyses were conducted to compare adolescents (under 18 years of age) and adults. There was a trend for adolescents treated without CNS irradiation to have better adjustment than those treated by irradiation. Significantly worse school achievement and greater psychological distress was found for those treated by CNS irradiation. Lower school achievement was found to be a significant predictor of psychological distress. For the total group, only 9% reported moderate distress and 13% reported continued conditioned nausea.

In addition to CNS irradiation and poor school achievement, greater psychological distress was predicted for those from poorer family environments. Better adjustment was associated with feeling less personal responsibility for their illness. There were also some issues of specific concern to young adults as opposed to adolescent survivors. Young adults treated by CNS irradiation had poorer body image than adolescents.

This study is based on a large group of survivors, followed for a longer time than most previous work (up to 15 years). It appears to point to differences between treatment groups, with poorer outcome for those treated by CNS irradiation. The finding of better adjustment among those expressing less personal control is difficult to explain. Given that there were no differences in survival, the study clearly points to the advantages of treatments not involving CNS irradiation. Methodologically, the very extensive test battery, delivered by telephone, might be seen by many to be an inappropriate way to collect data. Although some efforts were made to control for the large number of comparisons made, it should be recognized that differences between the two treatment groups were not identified on the majority of measures.

Dibenedetto et al. (1997) compared 22 children treated with CNS irradiation (1,800 Gy) with 24 children treated by chemotherapy alone. Significant differences between the two groups were found for Full Scale, Verbal, and Performance IQ. However subgroup analyses showed that these differences occurred exclusively in children below 3 years of age. Thus they suggest that treatment without radiotherapy is to be preferred for children below 3 years of age, but that there is little evidence (from their data) regarding any beneficial effects for older children.

Changes in Function Over Time

Initially, it was hoped that any deleterious effects on cognitive function would be short-lived, and that on return to school and completion of treatment, no long-term effects would be observed. Such a pattern was reported by Copeland, Dowell, Fletcher, Sullivan et al. (1988) and R. T. Brown et al. (1992), who both reported improved functioning 1 year after radiotherapy. However, other work suggests that declines in performance continue throughout treatment and may still be observed after completion of therapy. Significant declines in IQ were reported by A. T. Meadows et al. (1981) and Rubenstein et al. (1990). Mulhern (1994) reported that declines in function were most likely to occur 2 to 4 years from diagnosis and initiation of treatment.

Understanding how IQ changes over time is limited in that most studies have involved relatively short follow-ups. An exception is work reported by Kato et al. (1993), who followed survivors for 10 years. Many of their findings mirrored those of earlier studies; lower IQ scores were reported for children diagnosed and treated when less than 5 years of age, and outcomes were worse for girls compared with boys. A subsidiary finding was that 27% of girls and 2% of boys showed precocious puberty. Again, these findings point to the greater vulnerability of females compared with males to the effects of radiation. IQ scores continued to decline over the 10-year period, raising practical questions about the education of these children and theoretical issues regarding the ability of the young brain to recover from early insult.

The trend of deficits observed, coupled with observations concerning the timing of function loss, suggests that the processes involved parallel normal brain development. Most structures of the brain are developed by birth, although myelinization continues for a number of years. Normal development from 3 to 4 years typically involves improvements in fine-motor coordination, more rapid processing of information, improved visuospatial abilities, and decreased distraction and impulsivity. Abnormalities in the frontal cortex where most myelinization after birth occurs have been noted as the most frequent neuroradiographic findings in children treated with radiotherapy or intrathecal methotrexate. These findings suggest that treatment has a greater effect on later neural development than on brain structures that are already developed. Because the underlying structures of the brain are developed before treatment, there should be no significant deficit immediately following therapy. However, if treatment interferes with neurological development of the frontal cortex, then functions that would have emerged as part of normal development will either fail in some way, or be delayed.

Relationship Between Neuropsychological Functioning and Imaging

Computerized tomography (CT) scans and autopsy suggest that CNS irradiation is associated with white matter necrosis and alterations in arterial function. The greatest concentration of intracerebral calcifications have been found in the basal ganglia (Brouwers et al., 1985). In some instances, but not all, there was a high association between the results of CT imaging and neuropsychological abnormalities. Children in the ALL group who had evidence of calcification of the basal ganglia or white/gray matter junctions had a significantly lower IQ and memory performance than children who had no calcifications. IQ was inversely correlated with total radiation dose, with those not receiving radiation having the highest scores.

METHODOLOGICAL ISSUES

It is important to acknowledge the limitations of current work. Not least this is critical in order to evaluate the conflicting findings and draw some conclusions from the relatively large database available. Before being very critical of the current literature, it is important to acknowledge that this research is difficult to conduct.

As noted, earlier studies relied heavily on IQ measures. Notwithstanding the criticisms of IQ tests, they are often not administered in an appropriate way. Researchers may rely on shortened versions, or include a selection of subscales chosen on an *ad hoc* basis. Decisions to use a short form are invariably taken on the grounds of time, that of either the child or the tester. From the child's point of view, lengthy tests can be exhausting. From the tester's point of view, lengthy tests are expensive in time and money. However, shortened forms show reduced reliability and validity compared with the complete scales (Sattler, 1988).

In response to criticisms about the appropriateness of IQ tests, more recent work has included assessment of specific neuropsychological skills. IQ measures were developed to assess school performance rather than brain–behavior relationships and may therefore lack sensitivity to deficits in neuropsychological function. Comprehensive neuropsychological testing should include general intellectual functioning, language, memory and learning, visual perception, visual memory and visual–motor functioning, behavior competence, academic achievement, and neurological status.

Although not systematically assessed, there appears to be poor correspondence between neuropsychological test results and results of brain-imaging techniques. Few studies have explored the relationship between IQ or cognitive functioning and structural changes in the brain. Studies that have explored this relationship have failed to establish that there is any simple relationship between the presence of brain anomalies and cognitive functioning.

Comparisons between different studies can be limited because of inadequate description of samples, methods, and procedures generally. This criticism is easily remedied. Information about the representativeness of the group assessed compared with the total population is needed, as is information about social class of parents, children who refuse to be involved, or children who are unable to complete assessments.

Mulhern et al. (1992) made the point that family and environmental factors can be more influential than treatment factors in some cases and emphasized the need to consider family variables more systematically in this kind of work. There is other evidence that social class is an important mediator of treatment effects (Butler et al., 1994; J. Hill et al., 1998). Given these findings, it is important to control for social variables such as socioeconomic class or school attendance when attempting to determine the toxicities of different treatment protocols.

Though longitudinal data would help resolve some problems, there are practical difficulties, particularly in that IQ tests are age specific. Although there is some comparability between different versions of the Wechsler scales, different items may add to difficulties in interpretation, and assessments at the extremes of the scales are less reliable. Children are too ill on diagnosis to complete lengthy test batteries. Consequently, we have limited evidence about children's functioning prediagnosis and treatment. It is also impossible to separate out the contributing effects of cancer, its treatment, school absence, or responses of school or the family.

The relationship between learning difficulties and behavior problems has rarely been explored, although there is some evidence that survivors with learning difficulties are especially vulnerable to long-term adjustment problems (Kazak, Christakis, Alderfer, & Coiro, 1994). When this work first began, the question was relatively simple, involving a straightforward evaluation of the impact of CNS irradiation versus no irradiation. The increasing number of protocols now in use makes comparisons much more problematic. Subtle distinctions between protocols are almost impossible to detect especially given the very small numbers of children involved. Small sample sizes are the norm, possibly resulting in type II errors (failure to identify a significant effect where one exists). To control for potential statistical errors especially family-wise error rates (where a number of statistical tests are conducted on a single data set), appropriate corrections need to be made. Calculations of statistical power have rarely been reported. The bottom line however is that understanding the relationship between treatment protocol and cognitive functioning is only possible with an increasingly sophisticated and multicenter approach.

Difficulties in conducting truly randomized trials in this area are quite formidable and the ideal requirements of assignment to a clinical trial are often not met. Unexpected responses to treatment, and infections mean that children assigned to a specific treatment have to be removed from the trial, with the associated reduction in number of participants.

The most consistent findings point to deficits for children treated below 3 years of age. Given our understanding of brain development, it is easy to understand why this group might be most at risk. It is also true that children of this age are difficult to assess, partly because there are fewer reliable and valid measures compared with those available for older children. There is therefore some possibility that at least part of their problem might relate to difficulties in measurement issues, rather than reflect genuine problems for those treated at younger ages.

The timing of testing is crucial. It is not clear if neuropsychological functioning improves or deteriorates with time since diagnosis. The development of appropriate interventions rests on better understanding of the process of neuropsychological development following irradiation.

Published work has tended to focus on IQ scores as indicators of cognitive function, with much less attention given to everyday learning difficulties. Yet it is precisely this aspect of functioning that tends to cause most distress for parents and teachers. Frustration and exasperation are common, as children seem to experience difficulties in concentrating or understanding simple instructions. They may need patience and repeated teaching in order to understand relatively simple tasks. Despite established work, we still have little precise information (apart from broad indicators such as age at treatment or gender) about the characteristics of children who are vulnerable to learning problems following treatment.

Though it is important to acknowledge these methodological limitations, it is also imperative to recognize the clinical implications of this work. Children who experience learning difficulties following treatment deserve timely assessments and thoughtful decisions about remedial help. Parents who have spent several years negotiating with clinic staff while the child is on treatment often have few resources to battle with educational services.

IMPLICATIONS

There remain arguments about the exact mechanisms whereby learning is compromised in these children. What is not in dispute, however, is that some compromise to the child's potential is possible. Having established that a proportion of these children have learning and memory deficits in the long term, it is incumbent on us to develop and assess methods to ameliorate these problems, if at all possible. The question of exactly how the deficits arise, whether they are mediated by treatment or social and family attitudes, is of importance, precisely because the kind of intervention that may be most likely to be successful may differ depending on the cause of the deficit.

Given the accumulated findings, it seems appropriate that attention should now be paid to developing interventions to reduce these problems. Intervention research is, of course, notoriously difficult, and consequently very few studies can be identified. However, there are some exceptions. With respect to academic progress, School Hospital Services and home teaching can play a part, though few children are well enough on diagnosis to benefit academically. Even brief visits from a home teacher can do much to provide some continuity for the child, as well as offering mothers some, very brief, respite. Home teachers can often be instrumental in encouraging the child to return to school after extended absence. Favrot, Frappaz, Saltel, and Cochat (1992) described efforts to introduce a two-way teleconferencing system to link children in hospital with a secondary school. To date, no evaluations of the procedure have been reported.

A proportion of children treated for cancer experience more substantial learning difficulties that are not easy to correct on return to school. Such children will need remedial tuition. However, placement in a special-needs class is not always successful, because the kind of learning difficulties these children have are not the same as their classmates. More specialized provision, aimed directly at the deficits most usually resulting from treatment (e.g., concentration and memory), would seem to be necessary.

What is missing in all this work is any real emphasis on developing compensating education packages for the child. Although there has been little interest in developing remedial packages, much can perhaps be learned from other areas. Work with children with other learning problems, for example, dyslexia and the like, may contribute to our understanding of the type of programs that work in developing home- or school-based interventions and the type of skills needed to be addressed. We should be poised for a new generation of studies that provide scientific evaluations of theory-driven interventions for these children. Such an approach requires also collaboration with parents, schools, and youth workers.

In one of the few papers to attempt to improve learning in children with identified learning problems, S. J. Thompson et al. (2001) explored the benefits associated with methylphenidate (MPH). Long-term survivors of ALL or a CNS tumor were selected based on preliminary screening of learning problems. The sample included 32 children with an IQ score above 50, and academic achievement in the 16th percentile or lower in reading, math, or spelling. Children also were required to show an ability to sustain attention in the 16th percentile or lower for their age and gender. Children were prescribed either a placebo or MPH (0.6 mg/kg; 20-mg maximum). They then repeated parts of the screening battery after an interval of 90 minutes.

Differences between the two groups suggested there were some benefits following MPH. These children showed some improvements in sustained attention over the control group. There were improvements in sustained attention and overall scores, though no differences in terms of errors of commission (indicative of impulsiveness) or in reaction times. There were no differences on either a verbal memory or word association task. The authors were optimistic, however, and concluded that there were some improvements that could not be attributed to placebo or practice effects.

Though not a conventional intervention, Elkin, Whelan, Meyers, Phipps, and Glaser (1998) attempted to explore some of the factors that might contribute to poor school achievements. They suggested that children may be at higher risk of receiving failure feedback than others, and may therefore benefit from interventions that help them interpret their failure experiences in more productive and goal-oriented ways. Children were asked to complete a simple task and then given either *effort orientation* ("do the best you can") or *outcome orientation* information ("do better than anyone else"). Children were then given the opportunity to practice the behavior associated with the assigned orientation. Children were then given success or failure feedback. Seventy-nine children with cancer were included in the study and compared with a sample of healthy children matched in terms of age, gender, and race. Regardless of achievement orientation, children with cancer wanted to engage in more difficult problems in the future compared with healthy children. They also persisted less with tasks. More important, *effort orientation* did not protect children from failure feedback. This applied to both children with cancer and healthy controls. Children who received *outcome orientation* and success feedback chose more difficult tasks than children in the other three conditions.

Parents frequently describe intellectual problems and these reports can be the impetus for referral and educational assessment. Parents have a keener insight into their child's problems and may be more able to identify problems than formal IQ tests. "Whatever the methodological limitations of the studies, individual children continue to have difficulties in the academic environment, often detected only by their parents" (F. D. Armstrong & Horn, 1995, p. 295). Reservations are nevertheless sometimes expressed that parents report problems that typically occur in all children and attribute these to cancer rather than normal developmental issues.

The problems of individual children should not be trivialized, but it would be inappropriate to conclude that the consequences of treatment are inevitably damaging. Many children do recover and are able to perform academically as well as their peers or normal siblings; some make outstanding achievements. There remains an enigma about the relative contributions of treatment regimens, family functioning, and disease process in the etiology of learning difficulties. Ethical issues that might be raised in creating sound experimental designs may preempt further clarification of the questions, and attention should shift toward identification of appropriate and achievable educational remediation.

Findings of deficits in mathematical or language skills raise questions about how results of this kind should be communicated, especially to families. In a clinical context, children with leukemia often do report difficulties with number skills. It is not unknown for them to add, "The doctor told mum I wouldn't be able to do maths after my treatment." In practice, evidence for number difficulties is based on a relatively small number of studies. Furthermore, these studies have relied on a limited number of tests of number and language. More systematic and comprehensive assessments of both are probably needed.

Most of the work reviewed points to considerable risks of learning disabilities for children treated with CNS irradiation. These findings are important for a generation of children treated routinely for ALL with irradiation. Many continue to struggle academically, often with little educational support. The findings do need to be put in perspective, however. Such treatment is no longer part of routine care except for those children with high-risk disease. We may therefore hope that, in the future, the incidence of learning difficulties may decline substantially among this group. Even so, we must recognize that these children remain at some risk, albeit reduced. Current protocols may not include CNS irradiation, but do include an aggressive cocktail of chemotherapy drugs. As a result, extensive school absence remains the norm for children undergoing treatment. Children treated for ALL remain at risk of learning problems as a consequence of school absence and compromised social opportunities. For these reasons, there remains considerable interest in learning following treatment for ALL. It may not be possible to isolate a single cause, but the vulnerability is real.

The Impact of a CNS Tumor on Children's Learning and Quality of Life

Summary

CNS tumors in children are very different from those seen in adults. In adults, CNS tumors frequently occur as a result of spread from tumors from other sites. In children, nearly all CNS tumors are primary or develop in the brain itself. CNS tumors are the second most frequently occurring cancers among children, accounting for approximately 20% (Stiller & Bunch, 1992). Survival rates remain below other cancers. Although they have improved in recent years, these tumors have proved resilient to treatment and mortality rates remain high. The location of these neoplasms and risk to cerebral integrity put children at risk of suboptimal behavioral, emotional, and cognitive outcomes.

Children with a CNS tumor can experience neuropsychological, behavioral, and intellectual problems consequent on the disease and its treatment. Children who are younger on diagnosis are especially vulnerable. Outcomes are also dependent on the site of the tumor and specifics of the treatment regimen. Those who experience a greater number of treatment modalities (radiotherapy, surgery, chemotherapy) have poorer outcomes.

In many cases, the extent to which cognitive functioning is compromised is not apparent until some years after treatment. Findings based on group IQ scores offer little to the family or clinician working with an individual child.

INCIDENCE AND CLASSIFICATION
OF CNS TUMORS

Cancers of the CNS account for nearly 20% of all cancers in children (Gurney, Severson, Davis, & Robinson, 1995). Nearly 80% of these affect children below 10 years of age (Leviton, 1994). This relatively young age at onset, coupled with the high prevalence of physical and learning problems consequent on the disease and treatment, means that, in many cases, children must live with the adverse consequences of these tumors for most of their lives. Despite advances in treatment, these tumors have proved relatively resistant and mortality remains high (Wingo, Tong, & Bolden, 1995).

Nearly 100 different brain tumors have been identified in children and a number of different schemas exist for their classification. Most use a combination of pathology and tumor location. Most CNS tumors can therefore be categorized into one of two major types. The most common are the astrocytomas and gliomas, or glial cell tumors. These account for some 60% of all tumors and affect boys and girls equally. Survival rates depend on the grade of severity and location in the brain. Thus, survival rates for children with low-grade astrocytomas is approximately 50%–80% after 5 years, but is reduced to 35% or less at 2 years for those with high-grade astrocytomas. Ependymomas account for 10%–15% of CNS tumors and are significantly more prevalent in children below 5 years of age.

The second type are the embryonal tumors. These occur almost exclusively in children rather than adults and are most common in the cerebellum. The PNETs (Primitive neuroectodermal tumors) of the cerebellum account for 20%–25% of CNS tumors and occur more frequently in males than females (Gurney et al., 1995). Survival rates in these tumors are approximately 50%. These three CNS tumors (astrocytomas/gliomas, ependymonas, and PNETs) together account for 97% of brain tumors affecting children (Gurney et al., 1995).

Treatment

Current treatment protocols include a combination of chemotherapy, radiotherapy, and neurosurgery. In general, children who experience a greater number of treatment modalities subsequently have more compromised QOL, although this is likely to be the result of a combination of factors including the more aggressive tumor and increased number of treatment modalities.

In many cases, it is important to reduce intracranial pressure before proceeding with more major surgery. This can be achieved by insertion of a ventriculoperitoneal shunt. Removal of the tumor, where possible, can be performed with microsurgery techniques and computer-guided instrumentation. These techniques afford considerable accuracy, and the aims of surgery are to remove as much tumor as possible without damage to critical brain functions.

Radiation is associated with considerable negative consequences, especially for the developing brain. As a result, radiation therapy is not used for children below 2 or 3 years of age. In these children, radiation therapy is delayed as long as possible. In older children, external-beam radiation therapy is used to deliver 2,000–7,000 Gy to the tumor, whole brain, or spinal chord. These doses are significantly higher than those described in the previous chapter to treat children with ALL. Given these considerable doses, it is common practice for children to receive radiation in fractionated doses over a number of weeks. As with other cancers, chemotherapy remains an important arsenal in the treatment of CNS tumors. Current protocols tend to rely on 6–12 months of chemotherapy, often in addition to surgery or radiation treatment.

LEARNING AND OTHER OUTCOMES

There has been much less follow-up of children treated for CNS tumors compared with other cancers, especially leukemia. In part this reflects the poorer survival rate following CNS tumors. Clinicians are reluctant to refer children with poor prognosis into longitudinal studies, and poor survival rates means that it takes a long time to accrue a meaningful sample. In addition, CNS tumors tend to be diagnosed in very young children, creating practical problems in terms of assessment. There are fewer reliable tests available to assess younger children. These routine problems involved in assessment are compounded where the condition is associated with learning and memory deficits. In addition, children with CNS tumors are not a homogeneous group, in either clinical presentation or underlying neuropathology (Taylor & Fletcher, 1995). Concern that the impact of the tumor will be site dependent, and that it is not possible to attribute the cause of any problem specifically to surgery, chemotherapy, or radiotherapy, have all acted to deter research in this area.

Even so, it is recognized that children with CNS tumors experience unique problems compared with those with other cancers. The extent of morbidity can be high. Neurological, physical, endocrine, and psychological problems have been identified. These frequently co-occur, meaning that children can experience extremely compromised QOL.

At least mild processing problems have been identified in many survivors (F. D. Armstrong & Horn, 1995). The most frequently replicated findings are that younger children have more deficits than older children, although no consistent associations with tumor site have been found. Despite the hope that recovery can be achieved with increasing time since diagnosis, this has not been established, and much work suggests that declines in functioning continue beyond the immediate treatment phase (Hoppe-Hirsch et al., 1990). However, there are inconsistencies in findings. A number of moderating variables have been identified, including demographic (e.g., age at diagnosis), clinical (e.g., tumor site, treatment), social (e.g., family), and psychological factors.

In assessing the effects of a CNS tumor on children, at least two major types of behavior have been assessed. These include: (a) academic and cognitive function, and (b) behavioral, social, and emotional adjustment.

Academic and Cognitive Function

In determining the impact of a CNS tumor on the child's development, much more research has focused on IQ and cognitive outcomes compared with behavioral, emotional, or social functioning. This emphasis is a reflection of the relatively greater importance attributed to cognitive compared with social outcomes by doctors, parents, and teachers, as well as the belief that IQ can be measured more objectively than social or emotional concepts. The most common research paradigm involves comparison of IQ scores between children with a CNS tumor and population norms, healthy siblings, or children with other cancers that do not involve CNS function. The findings of this work have been relatively predictable: For the most part, children with a CNS tumor have lower IQ scores in comparison with any of these groups.

A recent review of studies evaluating long-term outcome suggests that the type of treatment a child undergoes is more important in predicting outcome than is tumor location (Ris & Noll, 1994). More recently, Dennis, Hetherington, and Speigler (1998) found that tumor location alone was not a predictor of attention or memory. CNS radiation therapy has been implicated as a causal factor (Ris & Noll, 1994).

It has been shown consistently that children younger than 3 years of age at the time of diagnosis are at significantly greater risk for severe cognitive impairment than children older on diagnosis (Ellenberg, McComb, Siegel, & Stowe, 1987; Packer et al., 1989). Mulhern et al. (1992) reported that younger children treated with whole-brain radiation showed a 14-point deficit in IQ compared with older children undergoing the same treatment. Reports by Packer et al. and Ellenberg et al. suggest that children who are under 7 years on diagnosis show greater loss in function over time compared with those who are more than 7 years.

However, it must be remembered that the effects of age at assessment and length of time since diagnosis are interrelated, with several studies showing that intellectual functioning decreases with time since treatment (Dennis, Spiegler, Hetherington, & Greenberg, 1996; Kun, Mulhern, & Crisco, 1983; Packer et al., 1989). In a series of studies, Radcliffe and colleagues reported changes in IQ scores up to 4 years after diagnosis. Two years after diagnosis, they reported losses in IQ scores for children treated with CNS irradiation, but no comparable loss was shown by children who were not treated with this therapy (Packer et al., 1989). Follow-up of the same sample at 4 years from diagnosis suggested that IQ scores had not declined significantly further (Radcliffe et al., 1992). The authors suggested that the impact of a tumor and its treatment on intellectual functioning was most damaging in the initial 2 years, and that there was less evidence than might be expected for declines beyond this time.

Other work is less optimistic. Hoppe-Hirsch et al. (1990) reported declines in IQ for 10 years after treatment, with the extent of decline dependent on age on diagnosis.

Limitations of IQ Assessments

Reliance on IQ tests is increasingly criticized. IQ scores in themselves say little about the child's learning capacity. Deficits in memory, sequential processing, fine-motor coordination, and physical stamina have been reported, often in children with apparently normal IQ scores (Dennis et al., 1991; Radcliffe et al., 1992).

Dennis et al. (1998) demonstrated that poor attention and memory can occur in children with otherwise preserved intelligence. Significant impairments in memory, manual dexterity, verbal fluency, and mathematical ability were reported in a group of survivors of medulloblastoma, all of whom had apparently normal IQ scores (Packer et al., 1989). Similar problems were reported by Johnson et al. (1994), although they found that verbal memory and verbal fluency tasks were unimpaired relative to nonverbal tasks.

Behavioral, Social, and Emotional Adjustment

The behavioral adjustment of children treated for CNS tumors has been less frequently addressed (cf. Carpentieri, Mulhern, Douglas, Hanna, & Fairclough, 1993; Mulhern, Hancock, Fairclough, & Kun, 1992). However, significant behavioral problems have been reported (Danoff, Cowchock, Marquette, Mulgrew, & Kramer, 1982; Kun, Mulhern, & Crisco, 1983; Lannering, Marky, Lundberg, & Olssom, 1990; Lebaron, Zeltzer, Lebaron, Scott, & Zeltzer, 1988; Mulhern, Kovnar, Kun, Crisco, & Williams, 1988;

Slavc, 1994). Most of this work relies on parents' reports about the child's behavior (Achenbach, 1991). A more innovative approach was reported by Vannatta et al. (1998) based on the work developed by Noll and colleagues described in chapter 7. Using a similar methodology, they reported that survivors of a CNS tumor were described as socially isolated by peers, teachers, and self-report. Peers perceived survivors to be ill, more easily tired, and to have more school absence than the rest of the class.

However, it is not clear that children with a CNS tumor have worse behavioral problems compared with those with other cancers, especially during the acute phase of treatment (Carpentieri et al., 1993). In attempting to explain this finding, Mulhern, Carpentieri, Shema, Stone, and Fairclough (1993) argued that the neuropsychological consequences of treatment for a CNS tumor are delayed, so that children with any cancer are equally vulnerable to adjustment problems during the acute phase of therapy. The effects of CNS irradiation on IQ may not be manifested for 2 to 4 years following completion of therapy (Ellenberg et al., 1987; Kun et al., 1983). It is therefore likely that the adjustment of children with brain tumors will deteriorate over time relative to that of children having cancer without CNS involvement.

An important question concerns how far the child has awareness of the often extensive changes in learning and school achievement that can affect them following diagnosis of a brain tumor. Many children may also have to accept additional changes in their physical appearance, their energy and competence to take part in sports, or even their ability to get around school. The extent to which children have insight into their disabilities may further affect their self-esteem and QOL.

Moderating Variables

Moderating variables include those related to characteristics of the tumor, as well as demographic variables including age and gender. Carpentieri et al. (1993) reported that tumor location and increase in abnormal brain volume, functional and cosmetic status, gender, and age were significant predictors of long-term maladjustment.

Family variables are also important. Mulhern et al. (1993) reported that children from single-parent families showed an increased frequency of social deficits and externalizing problems. They were more likely to show undercontrolled, antisocial, and aggressive behaviors compared with those from intact families. Parenting a child with a CNS tumor is especially challenging, and presumably the presence of two adults to share the load is beneficial. Carlson-Green, Morris, and Krawiecki (1995) reported that higher intellectual functioning was associated with fewer treatment modalities, a two-parent family, higher socioeconomic status (SES), a shorter period postdiagnosis, and mothers' coping resources. Findings suggest that children from families experiencing high levels of stress around the time of diagnosis may be specially at risk for subsequent child behavior difficulties.

METHODOLOGICAL LIMITATIONS

A number of methodological limitations can be identified in this literature. First, there is an emphasis on cross-sectional work. This has been useful in describing the extent of treatment-related sequelae, but has not contributed to an understanding of the processes underlying recovery or deterioration. Where longitudinal studies have been conducted, they have focused on brief follow-up and a narrow range of outcome variables, notably IQ. Longitudinal work that contributes to an understanding of the interaction between clinical, social, and family variables in determining outcomes is essential.

Second, almost all of the work has been based on general IQ assessment. Though individual subtests in IQ tests can yield useful information, overall mean scores often reported are less helpful, because they hide areas of specific problems. Critically, global IQ scores do not suggest appropriate interventions. Test batteries that are currently in use tend to be extremely lengthy and involve numerous assessments. In addition, reliance on measures developed at different times and for different purposes may result in a rather cumbersome battery. The drawings and content of many established tests can appear old-fashioned to modern children. The result is that there are few measures available that can be used in clinical practice (as opposed to research). Techniques that can realistically contribute to the assessment of children on a clinic basis are badly needed. There have therefore been calls for more extensive and sensitive batteries of neuropsychological function (Mulhern, Armstrong, & Thompson, 1998).

Third, it is virtually impossible to obtain estimates of children's functioning separately from the effects of the tumor and treatment. Initial assessments are invariably conducted after some form of therapy and may therefore underestimate the child's premorbid skill.

Fourth, family and social resources can affect outcomes. This is a critical finding, to the extent that it suggests that improvements in function can be achieved, given appropriate resources.

Finally, despite all the studies suggesting cognitive and neuropsychological problems, there has been very little attempt to develop interventions. As a consequence, very little is known about recovery following a CNS tumor. Yet this information is vital for teachers and parents in their efforts to guide children to attain their optimal performance.

INTERVENTION WORK

Following diagnosis and treatment, many children have special educational needs (SENs). Duffner et al. (1983) reported that more than 40% of their sample had SENs. Radcliffe et al. (1996) reported that all children in their study under 7 years of age had SENs and half of those over 7 years. These needs may be further compounded where the child also experiences sensory loss or motor disturbance associated with the tumor or its treatment. Learning and behavioral problems have been reported for children both in the acute phase following treatment (Mulhern et al., 1988) and among long-term survivors (Lannering et al., 1990; Mostow et al., 1991). Survivors of a CNS tumor differ from normal children in other ways as well. Radcliffe et al. reported they were less athletically competent, more difficult to parent, and were viewed by parents as having social problems.

The special needs of this population have been recognized for a long time and yet there has been no national program developed to rehabilitate survivors or provide educational support. The reasons for this are partly historical—survival was once the only goal and "quality of survival" secondary—and partly financial—there are limited educational resources available and children with a potentially life-threatening condition do not necessarily qualify. Perhaps the reasons are also to do with medical training and the organization of the health service, geared to heroic medicine and not to long-term rehabilitation. Whatever the reason, the result is that many families of children with a CNS tumor lack support, from the hospital (who is concerned with "new" patients) and from schools, who lack the knowledge or understanding necessary to provide appropriate education.

In the United Kingdom, a five-stage approach to identifying and supporting children with SENs has been identified. Initially it is the school's responsibility to identify children who may have special needs (Stage 1). If an initial support plan does not lead to significant progress, the school's SEN coordinator should then construct an individual education plan (IEP) for the child (Stage 2). The IEP typically prescribes a structured, targeted, support program, including provision of external help (Stage 3). If this still fails to lead to significant progress after at least 6 months, the child should be referred for a Statutory Assessment of SEN (Stage 4). The Assessment may then lead to a Statement of SEN for the child (Stage 5). This in turn leads to the development of an ongoing support and monitoring program.

In principle, survivors of CNS tumors should be included automatically within their school's SEN support system. In practice, however, this is not always the case. Many teachers are reluctant to complete the lengthy form filling required to initiate the procedures (possibly because they fail to distinguish between CNS tumor and other serious illness, and thus assume that intellectual recovery will occur in time). Even if a teacher does decide to take action, it is likely that the standard literacy-related support methods are poorly tuned to the needs of CNS tumor survivors. These children may have missed several years of schooling. Consequently, they lack the foundation skills necessary for achievement throughout the school. Despite the obvious fact that children who miss years of school will lack basic skills, many are expected to function in age-appropriate classrooms. Any child who misses so much school will flounder, and even more so those who have poor attention and memory skills, perhaps have visual loss as a consequence of the tumor, and may also be unhappy at school and unpopular with other children. Parents repeatedly complain about lack of school support and teachers' resistance to acknowledge the special needs of this population. Many resort to paying for extra help after school or taking on considerable responsibility themselves for helping the child after school. Such efforts are often helpful, but can put additional strains on the parent–child relationship. The child is tired after school and must struggle to complete required homework assignments. Little time is left to go over the basic skills that are so important for the child's continuing progress. As children become aware of their problems, they may increasingly switch off and fall further behind. The child who loses confidence in their ability becomes even harder to help.

It is likely that, in addition to their education-related problems, survivors of a CNS tumor may also suffer from a range of other problems. They are often lethargic and lack energy. They may be clumsy and have poorly developed physical and social skills. This range of problems requires a broad-based approach to intervention, with standard literacy work augmented with motor skills and motivational work. Furthermore, given the crucial role both of home and school (Nutbrown & Hannon, 1997) a dual support scheme would be optimal, in which parents, child, and school work in concert. In the course of work with children with SENs, a range of interventions can be identified that may be adapted to these requirements.

Much can be learned from the model of care described by Sherwin and O'Shanick (2000). They discussed rehabilitation of children and adolescents who experienced traumatic brain injury. In practice there are a number of ways in which the implications of traumatic injury parallel those of a CNS tumor. In both cases, onset is sudden and affects children and adolescents who were previously well. In both cases, families have to come to terms rapidly with the immediate and long-term consequences for the child.

In assessing the literature concerned with pediatric brain injury, Sherwin and O'Shanick (2000) made the point that "the literature is largely frozen in time, focusing on a facet of the injury (e.g. decreased awareness, cognitive impairment) or a specific need (e.g. family therapy, school re-entry). . . . the longitudinal perspective, the temporal implications of deficits and the evolution of needs, has not been addressed" (p. 267).

The greatest contribution of this work may be to families, who often have to deal with children with SENs without support or understanding from local education authorities. Delineation of the children's problems can bring enormous relief to parents who may be imprecisely aware of subtle difficulties, but have faced denial from the school that anything was wrong (Middleton, 2001). Moderate to severe disability may be exacerbated if resources for physical and educational rehabilitation are inadequate or inappropriately directed (Glaser, Rashid, Chin Lyn, & Walker, 1997).

Given the importance of school achievements for the child's social status in the classroom, it is not surprising that many report that the impact of the tumor on intellectual and emotional functioning is more stressful than some of the more physical consequences (Lannering et al., 1990). Children in this study reported that intellectual problems were more damaging to their QOL compared with visual or hearing impairments, hormonal deficiencies, or disfigurement.

DISCUSSION

The current literature has traditionally focused on IQ scores as outcome measures, and these remain important as indicators of general achievement. For many families, IQ scores may be less important than limitations in ability to function independently and at an age-appropriate level. Our clinical work suggests that many survivors of a CNS tumor lack basic skills to care for themselves at home. They do not regularly make a cup of tea or piece of toast, go out independently, or are able to be left unsupervised in the house. Survivors may be unable to handle money or make decisions.

Most families cope with these problems alone. For many parents, there is a sharp and unexplained distinction between the care and money lavished on these patients on diagnosis compared with the frugality afforded to support and intervention in the long term. Most survivors lack opportunities to mix with their peers, whether these are healthy classmates or other children with a tumor. There may well be benefits in providing opportunities for these children to mix with other survivors of a CNS tumor, with the aim to gain social skills and self-confidence. Special educational support is essential to overcome the problem that children have missed so much basic schooling. Beyond this, most require teaching in small classes, or one-to-one support to compensate for their difficulties working in situations where there are many distractions. Finally, it must be remembered that families have experienced long periods of chronic stress associated with caring for the child during treatment and the continued demands associated with caring for a child with multiple physical and sensory problems. Their instinct to protect the child may have been entirely appropriate during the early stages of the disease, but may become maladaptive with time. Whatever the child's limitations, the ultimate goal must be to promote optimal physical, cognitive, and social functioning, both for the immediate and long-term future (Holmes-Bernstein, 2000). Achievement of this may require families to reappraise the child's strengths and weaknesses. Thus, interventions must not be restricted to the classroom, but must also focus on redefinition of family relationships.

III

THE WIDER FAMILY

As has been shown, childhood cancer challenges the attainment of QOL in children in many ways. The burden of care falls heavily on parents, especially in the period following diagnosis. At this time, they have to work hard to understand the implications of the disease and learn about the child's medical care, both in the hospital and at home. They must also make difficult decisions about treatment options, at a time when they are stressed and highly emotional.

Beyond the initial diagnosis period, parents are confronted with many difficult situations. The goal is to find a way to balance the demands of the illness with the needs of the developing child. In many ways, this balancing act is not unique to families of a child with cancer, but is shared with families of children with other chronic conditions. Statistics suggest that approximately 15% of children have a chronic illness. These include, for example, children with asthma, diabetes, cystic fibrosis, or muscular dystrophy. All are dependent on medical treatment and cannot be offered any magic cure for their illness.

Parents are expected to be responsible for many aspects of the child's treatment. So parents of a child with diabetes need to think about diet, test blood sugar, and inject insulin. Parents of a child with cystic fibrosis have many demands on their time, including daily physiotherapy to clear the child's lungs. In addition to these practical disease-specific tasks, parents are naturally more vigilant with a sick child.

In chapter 10, the emphasis is on how parents respond in the period immediately following the diagnosis. In a very short period of time, parents have to become knowledgeable about the disease and its treatment, make difficult decisions about different treatment options, including clinical trials, and also facilitate the child's experience on the ward. These demands place a huge burden on parents' mental health. In many cases, mothers are uniquely responsible for daily treatments. In chapter 11, differences in responsibilities between parents, and differences between men and women in how they deal with stress are described, showing that mothers and fathers typically differ in their emotional responses. In chapter 12, the focus is on how all of this affects parents' emotional well-being and how this in turn has implications for the child's adjustment.

10

The Diagnosis—Parents' Perspectives

Summary

Following diagnosis and admission to a specialist pediatric oncology unit, events move fast. The aim of this chapter is to describe parents' experiences following the child's diagnosis, focusing on the acquisition of information and decisions needing to be made.

Parents must first come to terms with the fact that the child has a potentially life-threatening condition. This involves learning about the disease, its prognosis, and treatment implications.

Second, despite limited information, parents are confronted with a number of decisions that need to be made about the child's treatment. Of these, treatment decisions involving randomized clinical trials (RCTs) may be the most difficult. Though current guidelines emphasize the need for informed consent, parents are required to make decisions at a time of great stress and often when they have had little time to assimilate the information.

Third, parents act as a go-between between the child and medical staff. Parents are encouraged to stay with the child in hospital, and this can provide an opportunity for parents to learn about treatment and become more confident about managing the disease at home. At the same time, the need to be with the sick child in hospital creates many difficulties for themselves and for any other children at home.

It is appropriate that the focus of this book has so far been on the implications of cancer for the child, but inevitably all members of a family are affected. In this chapter, consideration is given primarily to parents, from the time when they first wonder if something is wrong with the child through to when they learn the diagnosis.

For some parents, the time between when they first realize that something is wrong with their child until a diagnosis is made is very quick. For others, there is a long period of uncertainty and frustration. In either case, parents often are overwhelmed by the speed with which things happen as soon as the diagnosis is suspected. Within a very brief period of time, parents need to accept and understand the implications of the disease and its treatment, master new tasks to care for their child, and take on new responsibilities.

The period following diagnosis is a steep *learning* curve. In the hours following diagnosis, parents are given, and expected to assimilate, a huge amount of information. First, there is the need to accept that the child has a life-threatening illness. It is natural to question whether or not the diagnosis is correct and to seek out other opinions. As it is so rare, many adults have no real understanding of childhood cancer or, more important, of the progress that has been made in improving survival. It can be very unhelpful if parents have previously known a child with cancer. Treatments have changed radically over the years and prognosis varies depending on the specific cancer. Ideas that childhood cancer is inevitably fatal therefore need to be relearned and put into perspective. Parents hear many words for the first time: chemotherapy, vincristine, maintenance therapy, lymph cells, T cells. The list is almost endless. There is a whole new vocabulary to learn.

Second, there is a period of *decision making*. In addition to understanding the diagnosis and its implications, there are many other tasks to master and decisions to make. With limited understanding, and under great emotional pressure, many will be asked to consent for the child to be recruited to a clinical trial. They need to understand concepts such as "randomization" and accept that survival rates have improved in large part because families in the past have been prepared to be involved in a clinical trial. The choice is most usually between two treatments, where both are assumed associated with similar quantity of survival but differ in anticipated side effects. Thus, they need to balance the relative merits of different treatments and accept that no treatment guarantees a cure. In many current treatment protocols, parents have no time to "come to terms" with the illness, but are immediately plunged into understanding the need for clinical trials and making decisions about the treatment to be followed.

Third, parents need to act as mediators between the child and the medical staff. Parents know their child better than anyone else and will often need to make staff aware of special difficulties. They must also assume responsibility for many day-to-day aspects of the child's health. Treatment protocols are quite complex, and parents must learn about and become responsible for giving the child medication, liasing with medical and nursing staff, and monitoring any adverse reactions in their child.

The aim of this chapter is to try to bring to life the experience of parents. For most families, information about childhood cancer, its treatment, and prognosis is all very new and unfamiliar. Decisions have to be made on the basis of insufficient information, because it takes time for test results to become available. It may be necessary to give the child and other relatives some information about the illness before details of treatment have been decided. Parents are thrown into a frenzy of activity, involving learning about the illness, making decisions about treatment, and reorganizing every aspect of their lives.

Learning the Diagnosis

As discussed in chapter 2, diagnosis of childhood cancer can be difficult. The symptoms are not specific and can often be confused with more common, less life-threatening conditions. Although some children become seriously ill very quickly, others can show more general symptoms over a long period of time.

Especially where the child has been ill for some time, the diagnosis can be a relief, because any diagnosis is associated with some course of action. In other cases, the diagnosis brings guilt, and anxieties that parents should have acted sooner.

Telling parents that their child has a potentially life-threatening disease is very difficult. Parents are upset, often the news is very unexpected, and information about treatment is necessarily complex. For all these reasons, much has been written about how to give parents information about the diagnosis. Masera et al. (1997) recommended that discussions with parents should be conducted in a private room where there is unlikely to be interruptions. Every effort should be made to involve both parents, or to make sure that single parents have a friend or close relative with them. Information needs to be truthful and offer positive support, but not to be unrealistic. In recognizing the considerable and complex nature of information being given, Masera et al. suggested that it can be helpful for parents to have written information to take home. The presence of a nurse or other member of staff who will be available for follow-up discussions can also be helpful.

In practice, it is not always possible for these recommendations to be met. It may be necessary to inform one parent at a time when the other is not available. Parents also differ in their preferences for information.

Whereas some welcome specific news, others are not interested in practical details. Some parents can be critical of doctors who, in their opinion, painted too bleak a picture. Others prefer very pessimistic news, on the grounds that "things could only get better" (Eiser et al., 1994).

Making an accurate diagnosis is complex and takes time. In some cases, consultants may be certain the child has cancer, but less certain about the specific type. Complications also arise depending on where the child was initially diagnosed. If the referral is made through a nonspecialist hospital, staff there may be reluctant, or unable, to give parents specific information. In these cases, parents must wait for referral to a specialist center. Inevitably, then, the process of learning the details of the disease and treatment takes time.

For many parents, the trauma of the diagnosis remains a vivid memory for a very long time. The way in which the information is given is often thought to be critical, because it may color the reactions of the family in both the immediate and longer term (C. R. Pinkerton et al., 1994).

Early theorists suggested that emotional reactions to any physical illness or trauma followed a series of stages, including anger, shock, guilt, depression, and disbelief (Futterman & Hoffman, 1973). It is natural to question whether or not the illness could have been avoided, or critically, would the prognosis be better if the illness had been recognized and diagnosed sooner? Parents are likely also to search for explanations about the cause of the disease. Especially if one or both parents smoke, or previously worked in an industrial environment, they will need to be reassured that they are not to blame for the child's illness.

Many parents experience anticipatory mourning, meaning that the shock of the diagnosis is so great that for a time at least they cannot imagine that anything is likely except that the child will die (van Dongen-Melman & Sanders-Woudstra, 1986). Eiser et al. (1994) interviewed 28 mothers and 23 fathers about their recall of the time immediately before their child's diagnosis. The mean time between when they first took the child to a doctor and when a diagnosis was made was 17 weeks. The longer the time between initial suspicions and actual diagnosis, the more parents blamed their general practitioner. Although parents remembered being told the diagnosis and some details of the proposed treatment, they were much less likely to remember whether or not they were told about side effects, complications, or the cause of the cancer.

Decision Making

Parental agreement has formally to be sought for all diagnostic and therapeutic procedures. For legal reasons, parents must agree that invasive diagnostic procedures can be conducted, that tissue is taken for analysis, and that surgical procedures are undertaken. These are for both diagnostic and treatment purposes. Parents may also be asked to agree that spare tissue be stored for research purposes. Parents of older children, and the children themselves, may be asked to agree to "sperm banking" as a precaution against later loss of fertility.

In addition to requests for the child to be treated on an RCT, parents may be asked to agree to be involved with other research projects. These can range from requests for blood or other samples for clinical research, to projects of a more psychological nature. Especially in specialist centers, the number of requests can seem quite overwhelming. Centers may be participating in national or international research projects, local initiatives, and student projects. In all cases, researchers are required to explain and give families written information, and families are expected to give signed consent to be involved. However much care is taken, families may find it difficult to understand the reason for the project, or feel obligated to take part. The issues are complex and, for this reason, attempts have been made to assess family understanding of the informed consent process.

Acceptability of Randomized Controlled Trials

Many parents assume that there is a single tried-and-tested treatment for childhood cancer and are shocked to learn that there is still a degree of experimentation in current protocols. As discussed in chapter 2, improvements in survival of childhood cancers have been attributed in large part to the introduction of national and international RCTs.

The basic and most simple choice is between standard or the best currently available care and a new treatment. The assumption is that the new treatment will be beneficial in some way, perhaps by reducing physical side effects associated with treatment or, in the longer term, by improving survival rates. In many current trials, differences in survival between the two treatments are not expected, but it is hoped that the new treatment will have a positive impact on the child's QOL. Despite the emphasis on QOL as an outcome in evaluating a clinical trial, the measurement has largely been restricted to physical symptoms.

RCTs allow for more rapid assessments of the impact of different treatment protocols than would be possible without such collaboration. However, accurate assessment of the comparative merits of different treatments requires that all eligible patients are treated according to the prescribed protocol. (Exclusion of some groups of children could possibly lead to biased results.) It is important then, that parents (and children where appropriate) understand the reason for clinical trials and agree to randomization. In contrast to trials involving adults with cancer, pediatricians generally have a much better record in recruiting children into clinical trials. Nevertheless, the way in which the purpose of a trial is explained to patients is critical, and clinicians may sometimes be reluctant to be involved, partly because explanations to patients and families can be time consuming.

The process of obtaining informed consent has been identified as potentially problematic by both clinicians and parents. One of the main reasons why pediatricians are more successful than adult oncologists in recruiting patients to trials may be that pediatricians tend to be more involved with the family anyway. Pediatricians often develop close contacts with the family and trusting relationships are likely to promote good communication. Where there is time between diagnosis and need for decision, then there are opportunities for good relationships to develop between clinic staff and families, and these are likely to facilitate satisfactory decision making. Some treatment protocols present more difficulties. In some trials, requests for randomization must be made almost immediately following the diagnosis, before any rapport has been established with families. With this kind of protocol, it may be much more difficult for pediatricians to broach the subject with families.

Objections to recruiting children into RCTs have been made by both clinicians and parents. Clinicians who are reluctant to enter patients into clinical trials often cite the lengthy explanations needed to obtain informed consent as a major obstacle. Clinicians may also feel reluctant if they are not themselves convinced about the value of the trial or feel that one or more of the treatment options is too aggressive for the child.

Parents can find the process of consenting for their child to be treated on a clinical trial to be distressing, especially where they feel the child is being treated as a "guinea pig." They are effectively being asked to make a major decision at a time when they are extremely emotional and their understanding of the issue is necessarily limited. In situations like this, especially when a child is seriously ill, parents expect doctors to have the answers. The idea of an RCT, with the implications that there are no definite answers or guaranteed outcomes, can add to parents' distress. The idea of randomization conjures up pictures of treatment decisions being taken by clinicians with whom the family have no contact, or worse by inhuman computers, and is therefore difficult to accept. Other parents, accepting the rationale for national or international trials, then question whether local provision of care can be very good. (In practice, the converse is likely to be true. Centralization of care as occurs in the organization of clinical trials ensures expertise to all participants.) There is evidence that agreement to participate is influenced by perceptions of disease severity. In an experimental study investigating healthy adults' views about a sham RCT, Gallo, Perrone, De Placido, and Giusti (1995) found that the worse an individual's perception of the outlook, the less likely they were to refuse a hypothetical trial.

Evaluation of the informed consent process is difficult. Outcome measures may include recall of information or evaluation of the consent document. Health care professionals may be asked for their perceptions of how well parents understood and assimilated the information. Typically researchers have relied heavily on the use of questionnaires to collect data about parent attitudes.

In practice, little empirical work has been conducted, especially in pediatric oncology. An exception was reported by Lesko, Dermatis, Penman, and Holland (1989), who studied parental consent to BMT. Although they concluded that parents in this study understood the nature of the disease and reasons for BMT, many experienced difficulty making a decision (68%). They saw clinicians as very persuasive about the need for treatment (98%) and relied heavily on them for help in decision making (95%). Not surprisingly, then, parents reported that information from the clinician was more helpful than information provided in consent forms. Of 17 potential risks identified in the consent form, parents accurately recalled about 8. A comparison of adult patients making a comparable decision for themselves revealed that twice as many adult patients felt able to make an autonomous decision compared with parents, suggesting perhaps that parents felt inhibited about making such a decision for their child.

Decisions may anyway be more complex for a child because the implications of any side effects may become important over a number of years. Parents of a 7-year-old may be prepared to accept that treatment may compromise fertility and see this to be an acceptable risk compared with no treatment and certain death. The consequences may seem less acceptable to the child in later years. This example highlights the special difficulties involved in making treatment decisions for a child. It is essentially a different decision compared with making it for oneself. The difficulties experienced by parents in the study by Lesko et al. (1989) have to be considered in relation to the fact that they were asked to make decisions about BMT, some time after diagnosis of the child's condition. This contrasts with parents who are asked following diagnosis to make decisions about the child's treatment, at a time when they are likely to be less informed generally and unprepared.

Ruccione, Kramer, Moore, and Perrin (1991) studied 28 parents of children entered on one of four protocols for the treatment of newly diagnosed ALL. Parents completed two questionnaires 48 hours after consenting to treatment. These included measures of anxiety and a specially developed questionnaire to assess understanding of the informed consent process. Although most parents reported being satisfied with the informed consent procedures, they did not understand key aspects of the information.

Harth and Thong (1995) also concluded that parents do not understand key information concerning the aims and purpose of clinical trials. Most believed that trials conducted by hospitals were of "little" or "no" risk. A "significant minority" felt that strict informed consent procedures were not necessary, as they would do whatever the doctor advised. Generally they did not understand that trials were to assess drug safety as well as efficacy. Only one third understood that they could withdraw their child at any time from a trial. Thus there may be significant attitudinal barriers preventing parents fully understanding the implications of involvement in clinical trials, not least their basic trust in the doctor.

Being asked to make such a decision is hard enough, but is made more difficult where children are of an age that they also require explanations. Many chronic conditions can involve long and painful treatment, and in the case of young children there is no question but that parents must make treatment decisions. With older children, however, the question arises as to how far they should be able to make decisions about their own treatment. Despite the importance of this issue, there is little work concerned with how children and adolescents come to understand treatment alternatives and make reasoned decisions. One exception is the work by Weithorn and Campbell (1982), who developed a series of scenarios involving either psychological or medical treatment decisions for four different problems: diabetes, epilepsy, depression, and enuresis. The study compared the performance and decisions made by healthy children aged 9, 14, 18, and 21 years. Young adults aged 14 years or more demonstrated a level of competence equivalent to that of adults. Nine-year-olds were less competent in terms of understanding or giving rational reasons for the research, but did not differ from adults in understanding treatment choices or reasonable outcome alternatives. The authors concluded that the majority of adolescents are able to make competent decisions about their own welfare before the currently accepted age of 18 years. However, the way in which children and adolescents make decisions in hypothetical situations may be very different from the choices they make when faced by real-life treatment dilemmas. Unfortunately moral and ethical objections mean that real-life decision making is particularly difficult to study, and evidence as to how well children are able to understand the concept of a clinical trial or make rational decisions about their own treatment is scarce. Accurate measures that reflect the impact of treatment from the child's perspective are urgently needed and should be seen to be an integral part of the evaluation of new treatments.

A number of studies have reviewed the general principles involved in children's decision making in this context. Some emphasize the child's cognitive maturity (Broome & Stieglitz, 1992); others the emotional issues (Dorn, Susman, & Fletcher, 1995). McCabe (1996) outlined the issues involved in informed consent decisions and made recommendations about how to assess the appropriateness of the child's involvement.

Dorn et al. (1995) studied 44 children aged 7–20 years who were admitted for the first time to pediatric departments. Twenty patients were being treated for cancer and the rest for obesity. Children were interviewed to assess 12 elements of knowledge involved in participation in research. Children also completed a measure of anxiety and tasks to assess cognitive development. Children who were more knowledgeable about participation in research reported greater feelings of global control. Emotional factors, such as anxiety, were more critical in determining the degree of understanding than were cognitive variables.

In a follow-up study involving the same children, Susman, Dorn, and Fletcher (1992) tried to be more specific about children's understanding of the reasons for research. Children were most knowledgeable about concrete information (freedom to ask questions, length of time involved to take part in the study, and possible benefits of participation). They were least knowledgeable about abstract information (scientific vs. therapeutic benefits of the study and alternative treatments).

Postlethwaite et al. (1995) considered the psychological consequences of involving children in decisions about whether or not to undergo GHT to counteract retarded growth as a consequence of renal disease. The choice did not involve any life-threatening decision, but did come after the children had gone through many years of treatment. Thus, the choice was to refuse more treatment and remain small, or accept further treatment in order to attain a more normal adult height.

Decisions about whether or not to agree to the treatment were difficult for both parents and child. The majority of parents were able to understand the issues involved, but ease of decision making was not related to understanding. Thus, understanding more about what was involved made the decision more difficult. Surprisingly, decisions were less likely to be made on the basis of physical variables, such as the child's height deficit, or on concern about growth or understanding of the risks of treatment. However, parents' decisions were influenced by the views of pediatricians and by their own emotional states. The children (aged 9–14 years) had much more difficulty understanding the information than did their parents. Even so, most felt that they had been involved in decision making. The authors highlighted the need to provide children with age-appropriate information, but were not very specific about what this might entail.

One of the main problems in this area is the lack of reliable methods to determine the views about treatment options for younger children with limited language and reading skills. In order to begin to understand more clearly what children know about their illness, child-centered instruments need to be developed that are less dependent on language than the traditional semistructured interview approach, and that can be used with sick or handicapped as well as healthy children.

Mediating Between Children and Hospital Staff

Some of the more significant changes in the care of sick children in the United Kingdom followed publication of the Platt Report (Platt Committee, 1959). This allowed for more child-centered hospital care, encouraging provision of play and educational facilities for children, and requiring hospitals to allow parents to stay in the hospital with their child. Participation of parents in the hospital care of their child was believed important for the well-being of the sick child. However, it may also provide an opportunity for parents to learn about the disease, and crucially to gain confidence to look after the child on return home. Parental involvement in care of the child is hoped to be beneficial for the child, but also provides an opportunity for learning more about the condition.

For parents the time spent in the hospital with their child can be very stressful. This is, of course, partly because of the uncertainty regarding the child's treatment. The life-threatening nature of cancer means that periods in the hospital are especially threatening and worrying. Parents also have practical concerns when they are staying in the hospital. Some react by wanting to be fully involved with the care of their child; others prefer to leave it to the professional staff. Some parents wish for clear guidelines from staff about what they should do on the ward. Parents are better able to recognize symptoms in their child than staff (Callery, 1997). As the time spent on the ward increases, parents can become highly knowledgeable about procedures and may feel that new staff are failing to administer medications appropriately. In these cases, some conflict between parent and staff is inevitable.

Nursing children with cancer is highly stressful, and the presence of parents on the ward can add to the tension for the nursing staff. Nurses too are not necessarily skilled at sharing tasks and responsibilities with parents. They may have been trained to have certain expectations regarding the parents' role, believing that parents should take charge of routine mothering tasks but leave technical care to the professionals. Nurses use implicit strategies to invite parents to be involved in care of the child. These have been labeled "inform and leave" (showing parents that they can feed their child if they wish but leaving the decision open-ended) or "do-as-if-at-home" (telling parents they are free to care for the child as they wish). This latter strategy is often impossible because of explicit or implicit rules on the ward. Such instructions can therefore add to parents' concerns about what is expected of them (Darbyshire, 1994).

Especially in caring for children with cancer, nurses, like parents, can experience strong emotions. The work is hard and stressful, and many people marvel at how medical and nursing staff can protect themselves from their work stress. Grootenhuis (1996) suggested that staff want to see children and their parents as strong and able to cope with treatment. In doing this, they aim partly to protect themselves. By convincing themselves that families are special and resilient, they can continue to care for the children while also acknowledging the burden of care. Thus, this strategy of "double protection" enables nursing staff to deal emotionally with complex situations where they are forced to question the benefits and risks to children.

Although Grootenhuis (1996) reported only limited support for these arguments, the tendency for staff to overestimate family coping and adjustment may potentially aggravate conflict between staff and parents. Staff need to assess the burden for families accurately if they are to provide appropriate care.

As parents become familiar with techniques and procedures necessary for their child's care, they can become increasingly vigilant and sometimes critical about treatment received in the hospital, especially nursing care. Lozowski, Chesler, and Chesney (1993) reported that 56% of their sample of 116 parents felt obliged to intervene at some point on their child's behalf. These interventions were predominantly intended to (a) prevent or correct erroneous administration of drugs, (b) remind staff of correct or incorrect procedures, (c) alter intravenous procedures, and (d) mediate the staff's approach to the ill child.

Parents with higher incomes, better education and who were more active in local self-help support groups were more likely to intervene. Important to note, parents who reported less satisfaction with the emotional support received from staff were also those who were most likely to intervene.

Having a child in the hospital for any reason is very difficult for parents. They must balance the needs of the sick child with the needs of their other children, routine work, and employment demands. Parents who are used to the comfort and privacy of their own home may find it especially difficult that, at a time when they most want privacy, it is impossible to find. Consequently, the hospital stay may not always provide the best opportunity for learning.

Caring for a child with cancer is emotive and can involve highly technical skills (e.g., administering chemotherapy) as well as very sensitive recognition of the emotional needs of parents and children. Nowadays, with the escalating demands upon health services, parents are expected to do more and more. Whereas many parents welcome this, the potential burden is huge. Parents are responsible for administering complex treatment regimens to their child, in the knowledge that failure may have life-threatening implications. Diagnosis of childhood cancer and the subsequent treatment imposes a huge demand on parents' physical and mental health. In the next chapter, the focus is on how parents themselves adapt to the situation.

11

Beyond the Diagnosis:
The Impact on Parents

Summary

Compared with parents of healthy children, those with a child with cancer show higher levels of psychological distress. The differences are especially pronounced in the months immediately after the diagnosis. Commonly reported symptoms include anxiety, depression, and marital distress. Mothers tend to report more mental health problems (anxiety, distress, and depression) compared with fathers. These have been attributed to differences between mothers and fathers in responsibility and in the experience and management of stress.

Parents' mental health has implications for the child, to the extent that parents who are anxious tend to have children who are anxious. A process of "emotional contagion" has been proposed to account for the relationship between child and parent mental health.

In this chapter, the way in which parents influence their child's adjustment is considered first in relation to behavior when the child undergoes treatment-related procedures, and second in relation to everyday activities. In the clinic, parents who adopt punitive or inconsistent styles of behavior have children who show more distress, but this relationship between parent and child behavior is most pronounced for children under 8 years of age.

THE IMPACT ON PARENTS

Understanding parents' emotional and behavioral reactions to diagnosis and treatment is important. First, the way in which parents react is likely to shape the behavior and emotional response of the child. In situations of uncertainty, children model the behavior of others. If parents are frightened of needles and highly anxious, they can easily communicate this to the child. Second, the more that is understood about how parents and children manage their lives during the course of treatment the more we will be able to provide information that will help families in the future. "Forewarned is forearmed" and knowing what to expect may be essential information for many families. Third, it is important not simply to describe parent reactions, but to relate or predict initial reactions on diagnosis to later adjustment and coping. In this way, it may be possible to direct the limited support services available in most hospitals to those most in need.

As noted in previous chapters, cancer shares many characteristics with other chronic diseases. For this reason, considering parents' reactions when their child is diagnosed with any serious illness can help us understand reactions to cancer. R. J. Thompson and Gustafson (1996) described a number of approaches that have been adopted to understand parental reactions in these situations.

The first involves determining the incidence of psychological stress. When a child is diagnosed with any illness, parents naturally experience increased psychological distress. Parents of a sick child have a much greater number of practical and emotional problems to deal with compared with parents of healthy children. Practically, these include the additional caretaking demands associated with medical care that have to be given at home. Emotionally, there are considerable unknowns, and the future is often uncertain. Given these increased practical and emotional demands, considerable research has focused on determining how far parents report higher levels of psychological distress, physical symptoms, or psychiatric disorder compared with parents of healthy children.

Second, there are questions about differences between mothers and fathers in their experience and management of stress. Men and women typically differ in concerns about their own health, their preparedness to use health services, and the way in which they react to stressful situations (Hoekstra-Weebers, Littlewood, Boon, & Postma, 1991). These gender differences are likely to be associated with different patterns of behavior between mothers and fathers following the child's illness.

Third, it is clear that parents, like their children, do not all react in the same way. The identification of personality or demographic variables that characterize different ways of coping is potentially useful from a clinical perspective. If it can be established that parents with certain characteristics or family resources cope better than others, then clinic and social work staff could direct more attention to those families in greater need.

Fourth, most of the work conducted in this area has focused on the immediate effects of illness following diagnosis, with much less being known about how families adjust over time. There is an assumption that most help is needed following diagnosis, and that with time, parents become more able to accept the situation and return to normal. Because relatively little work has looked at parents' reaction more than 2 or 3 years beyond the diagnosis, the long-term consequences are not known.

The Incidence of Psychological Distress

Much of our knowledge about parent reactions to the diagnosis is based on retrospective reports often conducted many years later. Parents may feel angry and guilty, and question whether the diagnosis should have been made earlier. Families with a child with cancer experience more stress (Thoma, Hockenberry-Eaton, & Kemp, 1993) and report more conflict and less cohesion than do families with a healthy child (Morris et al., 1997). Even long after the diagnosis, parents report many worries concerning their child's illness and ongoing financial difficulties. In terms of their own health, many parents recall experiencing both more minor and more serious physical illnesses. However, these experiences are not universal and can coexist with more positive outcomes. Some parents focus more on how they have reappraised their values and reoriented life goals (Koch et al., 1996).

Distress can take many forms and this is reflected in the type of outcome assessed. Some work has focused on the occurrence of psychiatric symptoms, depression, or anxiety, whereas others have concentrated on marital distress. As reviewed in the following, most published studies suggest that between 25% and 40% of parents show higher than expected levels of distress.

Approximately 25% of mothers and 28% of fathers reported significant marital distress in the period immediately following diagnosis, but there was no evidence that mothers experienced more distress than fathers (Dahlquist et al., 1993). Manne et al. (1995) reported that, compared with population statistics, parents were depressed after diagnosis. However, there was wide variability, with 42% of parents rated as nondepressed, 34% as mildly depressed, 15% as moderately depressed, and 9% as severely depressed. Three months later the mean depression scores remained in the mildly depressed range for 32% of parents. Forty-nine percent were classed as nondepressed, 12% were moderately depressed, and 7% severely depressed. These means were higher than reported in other cancer studies (e.g., Dahlquist et al., 1993) and higher than expected from population norms.

In a 6-month follow-up of the same families, Manne et al. (1996) found that symptoms of depression remained present in a significant subset of parents, especially those who had scored within the moderate-to-severe range when assessed on diagnosis. However, there was considerable stability over time in parents' reactions. The majority had either remained nondepressed or became less depressed (e.g., moved from moderate to mild) with just three parents reporting increased levels of depression. Parents who reported more support from their partner had fewer depressive symptoms.

P. Sloper (1996) interviewed the main caregiver in 98 families with a child with cancer 6 months after diagnosis. The incidence of psychological distress was high. Some 55% of mothers and 41% of fathers showed high levels of emotional distress. More distress was reported where parents also experienced additional problems, such as difficulties at work, financial strain, or poor social support outside the family. Sloper also noted considerable distress about possible delays in diagnosis. Families themselves felt that some distress could be alleviated by provision of appropriate counseling.

Allen et al. (1997) investigated depression and anxiety immediately after diagnosis in a prospective study involving 42 adolescents, 34 of their mothers, and 27 of their fathers. Although there were no differences between mothers and fathers in depression, mothers were more anxious than either fathers or adolescents.

An extensive review conducted by Grootenhuis and Last (1997) based on a computerized literature search from 1985 until 1995 summarizes many of these findings. They concluded that there was substantial evidence of increased levels of depression and anxiety among parents immediately after the diagnosis of cancer in their child. However, although marital distress was high after diagnosis, divorce rates did not differ from the general population.

Differences Between Mothers and Fathers

Mothers tend to report more stress than fathers, including higher levels of depression, anxiety, and obsessive-compulsive behaviors (Hauser, Jacobsen, Benes, & B. J. Anderson, 1997; Kovacs et al., 1990; Larson, Wittrock, & Sandgren, 1994). At least three reasons have been put forward to account for this. First, mothers and fathers differ in *responsibility*. Mothers tend to be more involved in the day-to-day care of the sick child than do fathers. Mothers tend to take greater responsibility for caregiving, whereas fathers are more concerned to keep up outside work commitments and maintain financial resources (Koocher & O'Malley, 1981). The convention is that fathers go off to earn money, know little about the child's illness, and their role is limited to supporting the mother's efforts. Although this might seem undemocratic, it may work well for many families. In a situation where there is a lot to do, it makes sense to divide up the tasks, and especially if men have greater earning power, the simplest solution may be for them to keep working. Whereas some mothers do resent being left to manage all the illness tasks, others prefer to be with their child and would not want anything else. Given the extensive social changes that have occurred since publication of the work by Koocher and his colleagues, it would be interesting to see if this was reflected in a similar division of labor among modern parents.

Second, different stresses follow from the responsibilities for child care compared with outside work. Consequently, mothers and fathers differ in their *experience* of stress. Mothers tend to spend more time in the hospital, speak to medical staff, and be around when procedures take place. In contrast, working fathers are much more preoccupied with work-related stress, issues about meeting workplace deadlines, and attempting to lead a "normal" life, while knowing that their child is seriously ill. Fathers do, of course, feel distressed, but perhaps for different reasons. Spinetta and Deasy-Spinetta (1981) reported that fathers are more likely to feel isolated from the child especially where the mother is not working and spends more time in hospital.

Fathers also know less about the child's illness compared with mothers (Hanson, Henggeler, M. A. Harris, Burghen, & Moore, 1989). Cayse (1994) raised concern that fathers are commonly excluded from studies that recruit mothers as the primary caregiver. Thus, we know more about what mothers *think* about their own and their partners' roles in caring for the child, but different conclusions might be drawn if fathers contributed more directly. Cayse showed that fathers are distressed by information about the diagnosis and need to be included in many more studies. Even if he makes minimal contribution to care, the presence of the father is critical to the extent that he is able to provide emotional support to the mother (Nagy & Ungerer, 1990).

Third, men and women differ in their *management* of stress. Typically, women are more likely to seek social support as a means of handling distress compared with men. This reflects the conventional view that women gain comfort through talking with others whereas men adopt a stiff-upper-lip approach.

Many of these assumptions are based on stereotype, of course, and ignore the increasing literature that points to the critical role that fathers play in the child's development under normal circumstances. From birth through to adolescence, fathers play a unique role in shaping and facilitating child development. Compared with mothers, fathers spend more time in play and leisure-time activities, and are especially important in encouraging demanding physical activity, self-reliance, and accentuating gender roles (Russell & Saebel, 1997). The process of encouraging independence is especially important during adolescence. Although fathers spend less time with adolescents than do mothers, a greater proportion of adolescent–father time is spent in leisure activities or play (Youniss & Smollar, 1985). Typically, fathers may be better at acknowledging their child's independence, expressing support, and showing a greater interest in children's suggestions compared with mothers (Hauser et al., 1987). Fathers are also more sensitive about physical changes experienced by adolescents. Thus, in promoting independence, fostering autonomy, and facilitating sport and leisure activities, the father's role is crucial.

Responsibility.   As discussed previously, it is generally assumed that mothers are more responsible for everyday aspects of care compared with fathers, though surprisingly little research has been concerned with the ways in which mothers and fathers divide care of the child. K. A. Brown and Barbarin (1996) confirmed these assumptions about the different roles played by mothers and fathers. Mothers tended to take on a more direct caregiver role with regard to the illness. This included handling medical aspects of the illness, doing housework, keeping family and friends informed about changes in the child's illness, spending more time with other family members than fathers, taking the child to and from appointments, and staying with the child in the hospital. Fathers reported feeling more stress and spending more time on earning money for the household and medical expenses than on general "fathering."

The Experience of Stress.   Mothers of children with cancer showed significantly more distress than mothers of healthy children and reported more anxiety and difficulties sleeping. Fathers with a child with cancer showed higher levels of anxiety and insomnia compared with fathers of healthy children, though the differences were less than for mothers. Differences between mothers and fathers were attributed to differential involvement in child care, although this was not measured directly (Sawyer, Antoniou, Toogood, Rice, & Baghurst, 1993).

Management of Stress.   Men and women typically differ in how they manage stress, and consequently we may expect to find differences between mothers and fathers in how they attempt to handle the stresses associated with diagnosis. As might be expected in this situation, mothers tend to report greater use of strategies involving problem solving, seeking information, expressing emotions, and seeking social supports as ways of coping compared with fathers (Larson et al., 1994).

Personality or Demographic Differences in Coping

Wittrock, Larson, and Sandgren (1994) studied parents who had a child with either cancer or the flu. They identified two types of coping: *engaged* coping (offering medicinal, physical, or emotional comfort to the child) and *disengaged* coping (withdrawal, denial, and lack of emotional expression). In both groups, parents who were more anxious reported greater use of disengaged coping. Parents of children with flu used more engaged coping strategies, were less anxious and depressed, and were more satisfied with their marriage, than were parents of children with cancer. The implication is that some parents may need help to put their own concerns into perspective and adopt more engaged coping styles regardless of the specific illness.

However, parents of a child with cancer typically rely on some denial (Hardy, F. D. Armstrong, Routh, & Albrecht, 1994). They found that parents of children with life-threatening conditions (AIDS or cancer) used more "wishful thinking" strategies than other parents. Such a strategy may fulfill a very important function in situations where treatments are not currently available to cure the child.

Grootenhuis, Last, De Graaf-Nukerk, and Van Der Wel (1996) studied secondary control strategies used by parents of children with cancer. They based their work on previous studies by Rothbaum, Weisz, and Snyder (1982). These authors distinguished between *secondary* coping skills, referring to attempts to modify oneself (e.g., by changing one's hopes or expectations), and *primary* coping skills, directed toward modifying objective conditions (e.g., changing treatment schedules, appointments, etc). The authors defined four types of control: predictive (e.g., anticipate disappointments), vicarious (associate with powerful others), illusory (e.g., associate with chance), and interpretative (e.g., derive meaning from problems and accept them). Mothers tended to rely more on interpretative and illusory control than fathers, and parents of children in remission relied more on predictive and vicarious control. In addition, parents who had a lower educational level were found to rely more on predictive, illusory, and vicarious control. Interpretative control was the only strategy not to be associated with education level.

Individuals differ in their understanding of cancer, and this in turn can affect their coping behavior (Bearison et al., 1993). Parents and children who made external attributions about cancer (e.g., believed it was caused by environmental factors, fate, or physical trauma) coped significantly better than those who held internal attributions (e.g., believed that the disease was inherited or caused by personal wrongdoing) or no attributions at all. Parents coped better when their attributions matched those of their children. These results were found even though all of the parents reported that medical staff had made it clear that the cause of the child's cancer was unknown. Despite this, 70% of parents and approximately 50% of patients had constructed their own views about cause, some appearing rather irrational, others seeming very realistic and rational.

The importance of social support as a protective factor in both physical and psychological health has been recognized for some time (Cobb, 1976; S. Cohen & Wills, 1985). Although Noll et al. (1995) found no differences in perceived social support between parents of children with cancer and healthy families, lack of social support and number of times the child was hospitalized were the best predictors of depression (Mulhern, Fairclough et al., 1992). It is not clear how social support moderates stress, but two main models have been proposed. The *main effect* model suggests that social support exerts a beneficial influence regardless of an individual's level of stress. The *buffer model* predicts an interaction between stress and social support, so that individuals with a high level of social support who have well-developed, satisfying social relationships will be protected from much of the negative effects of stress (S. Cohen & Wills, 1985). In a third *moderator model,* social support is perceived to be an intervening variable between stressor and outcome.

Changes in Coping With Time

That parents experience considerable anxiety and depression at the time of diagnosis is hardly surprising. As described earlier, parents' mental health can be poor following the diagnosis. Over time, however, we might expect that things "return to normal" at least to some extent. It is important to understand the coping trajectory: the normal course of events and when families begin to feel that life is improving or getting back to normal. Efforts have been made to determine changes in parents' mental health over time, on the expectation that this will improve with the longer time since diagnosis. In other studies, comparisons are made between families on treatment and those where the child is well and off-treatment. Again the assumption is that parents' mental health and family functioning will be better in families when active treatment is finished. These very simple assumptions have received a degree of empirical support, but more interesting may be differences between families at the same stage of treatment. In practice, the way a family copes will be determined by many factors in addition to the disease. Many events can occur during the course of treatment: episodes of neutropenia requiring unexpected hospitalization; occurrence of chicken pox in school requiring the child to have extended periods at home. So family experiences can vary substantially depending on the child's specific experience. In addition, families have to deal with many other events that can help, or compromise, their ability to cope with the medical situation.

Despite these reservations, the overall incidence of depression and anxiety in parents decreases with time. This was demonstrated in a series of studies reported by Sawyer and colleagues in Australia. Families were compared with a control group of normal families on diagnosis and 1 year later (Sawyer et al., 1993) and again 2 years later (Sawyer, Antoniou, Toogood, & Rice, 1997). Although parents' stress was higher than controls on diagnosis, there were no differences at the 2-year follow-up. Similar results were reported by Kazak et al. (1994). One year after diagnosis, levels of parental distress, family functioning, social support, and perceived self-competence were shown to be comparable with values expected for a normal population.

Brown, Kaslow et al. (1992) examined levels of parental functioning at three time points: just after diagnosis, 1 year after diagnosis, and 1 year after chemotherapy was completed. This was not a conventional longitudinal study, as the authors did not follow the same group over time, but studied similar groups of individuals at different time points in the illness trajectory. Both children and parents reported low levels of psychopathology. However, parents reported more family cohesiveness and marital satisfaction at the third time point (when chemotherapy was completed). One year after diagnosis mothers reported more anxiety than mothers of children in the other two groups, suggesting that anxiety increases throughout the first year before falling after treatment ends. In contrast, mothers reported less depression after treatment ended compared with any of the earlier time points. A similar pattern in depression was observed for fathers. For both parents, better functioning correlated with good problem-solving skills, good communication, and having a positive outlook on the illness.

Using a more conventional prospective design, Nelson, Miles, Reed, Davis, and Cooper (1994) measured depressive symptoms in parents of children with cancer shortly after diagnosis, at 6 months postdiagnosis and 12 months later. Almost half the parents reported some degree of depressive symptoms during the early diagnostic and treatment period and more than one third (all mothers) did so on the second testing. Mean scores for mothers at both times were above the critical point assumed to indicate risk for major depression. At 12 months postdiagnosis, mothers continued to score high, but fathers' scores were lower. Symptoms that were most worrying included sleep disturbances, changes in eating patterns, weight fluctuations, difficulty completing tasks and concentrating, sadness, loneliness, and a very quiet demeanor. Depression was not related to perceived severity of the child's illness or social support.

Dahlquist et al. (1996) followed up the 42 families reported in their earlier study (Dahlquist et al., 1993). Of the original 67 mother–father dyads, 42 were included in the follow-up 20 months later. Mothers' mean state and trait anxiety scores had decreased to nearly normal by this time although there were no changes in fathers' scores. Marital adjustment was relatively unchanged for both mothers and fathers and was best predicted from depression and partner marital satisfaction. Marital adjustment in fathers but not mothers was related to child health.

INTERVENTIONS

Given the relatively high levels of anxiety and depression reported by parents, it is important to consider what can be done to reduce distress. One of the first and still the most extensive study is the "Coping Project" reported by Kupst and her colleagues (Kupst & Schulman, 1988). This is exceptional in providing follow-up data over many years. The study was set up to determine the relationships between key variables (e.g., social support, quality of marriage) and subsequent coping, and the effectiveness of a psychosocial intervention to promote coping with childhood leukemia: On diagnosis, families were randomly assigned to a total, moderate, or no-intervention control group. The intervention, delivered by a social worker or counselor, was aimed to establish rapport with the families, clarify information concerning the illness, and help the family to strengthen their support system and anticipate treatment problems.

Sixty-four families of children with ALL (mean age = 6 years) were initially enrolled. Coping was defined to include both what people did in their attempts to master the situation and in terms of the adequacy of their coping. Adequacy of coping referred to the ability to understand the meaning of the illness and treatment, to manage emotional reactions, to take necessary care of the child and other responsibilities, and to provide support to one another.

At their 2-year follow-up (Kupst et al., 1984), 60 families were located (93.7% of the initial sample). Although coping took many different forms (e.g., denial, anger, etc), medical personnel judged that most of the families were coping well. Families scored in the normal range on the standardized tests. Variables that correlated with good coping included lack of concurrent stress, how well other family members coped, and a good marriage. Following the acute phase of the illness, most families had achieved a level of stability in which the intervention was necessary only if there were complications or relapses.

In the 10-year follow-up (Kupst et al., 1995), the remaining families ($N =$ 28 patients and their parents) were found to be coping adequately. Long-term survivors were found to recall details of their illness easily and were able to discuss how they coped with different aspects of their lives. They viewed their illness as a thing of the past and were more concerned with looking forward to the future. Kupst et al. concluded that although approximately 25%–33% of families had developed problems in coping at some time, most did not require intensive and lengthy intervention.

In a more recent intervention study in the Netherlands, Hoekstra-Weebers, Heuvel, Jaspers, Kamps, and Klip (1998) invited all parents of children diagnosed over a 2-year period to take part in an intervention study, and 62.5% agreed. The children (mean age = 6.4 years) had all been diagnosed with leukemia. Parents in the control group received standard care. During the first 6 months following diagnosis, the intervention group received standard care plus a manual-guided program of eight 90-minute sessions. The intervention involved cognitive-behavioral techniques, with attention given to emotions, the identification and challenging of negative thoughts, encouragement of problem-focused coping, communication and assertiveness, and information about the possible psychosocial consequences of the treatment for the child and family. Sessions involved the therapist and parents. Evaluations were made soon after diagnosis, and at 6 and 12 months postdiagnosis. There were no differences between parents in terms of their mental health, symptoms, anxiety, and social support. The only significant finding was that all parents became less distressed with time.

It is disappointing when interventions fail to achieve their objectives. In discussing this, Hoekstra-Weebers et al. (1998) suggested a number of potential problems with the study. First, it was a relatively brief intervention. Second, the very general outcome measures used may lack sensitivity. Third, the intervention was quite general and consequently may have failed to address specific areas of parental concern. Fourth, the intervention focused on issues around the diagnosis and did not necessarily give parents the tools to cope with the changes in treatment demands that occur with time.

The lack of success associated with these general interventions raises questions about both the content of interventions and issues of evaluation. With regard to content, it is not clear that parents were involved in developing the content of intervention programs. Consequently issues of central concern may not be addressed.

With regard to evaluation, researchers fail to specify exactly what the intervention is designed to achieve. Interventions may impact on knowledge, self-confidence to handle the daily aspects of care, or relationships between parents and their children. Both the content of programs and evaluation need to be tailored accordingly. In practice, evaluations often rely simply on measures of parent mental health.

Kupst and her colleagues identified a range of coping strategies employed by families, but did not conclude that any one was necessarily the most appropriate. However, it is important to define "good" coping, not least because otherwise there are no standards against which to judge the success of an intervention. Recognizing this, Kupst suggested that good coping involves working toward a cognitive understanding of the realities and implications of treatment, managing the emotional aspects of the disease, coping behaviorally through participating in medical care of the child, dealing with other family responsibilities, and providing support and communication within the family.

IMPLICATIONS OF PARENTS' BEHAVIOR FOR CHILDREN'S ADJUSTMENT

So far, we have considered how the diagnosis of cancer in the child can affect mothers' and fathers' mental health, well-being, and coping. Although this is important in itself, parents' mental health can have far-reaching implications for the child. A broad consensus has emerged over the past few decades that parenting practices have a substantial impact on child development (Darling & Steinberg, 1993) and that, over time, parental influence leads to generalized and stable behavior tendencies (e.g., Holden & Miller, 1999; Maccoby, 1984). Parenting has been linked to child behavior problems (e.g., Lamborn, Mounts, Steinberg, & Dornbusch, 1991), school performance (e.g., Glasgow, Dornbusch, Troyer, & Steinberg, 1997), and aggression (e.g., Deater-Deckard, Dodge, Bates, & Pettit, 1996).

Parents undoubtedly do influence their child's attitudes and behavior. Where a parent has a chronic or ongoing health problem, children are more likely to present with unexplained pediatric pain (L. S. Walker, Garber, & Greene, 1991). The most parsimonious explanation for this centers on a social learning model; children model their own illness behavior on that of key adults in their lives.

In the context of childhood cancer, the relationship between parents' coping and the child's adjustment and behavior has been considered in two contexts, reflecting the distinction between disease-specific and everyday normal activities. In terms of disease-specific situations, researchers have looked at parents' behavior during medical procedures in the hospital and also during home-based procedures.

Disease-Specific Activities

Medical Procedures.   Children undergo many painful procedures as part of their diagnosis and treatment. The most distressing procedures include BMAs and LPs. Newly diagnosed children may undergo BMAs and LPs frequently, and these continue to be a source of distress throughout treatment. Younger children, particularly, react to distress by kicking or screaming. Dealing with children who are so distressed is upsetting for staff and parents. In addition, the risks associated with treatment increase where children behave in this way. Children who move unpredictably make it more difficult for staff to perform the procedures. This results in longer time for completion and increases the risk of accidental injury.

Although it is easy to empathize with the distressed child, such fear and anxiety is not inevitable. Many children are able to tolerate the procedures with minimal fuss. This raises the question about what exactly characterizes children who tolerate procedures from those who do not. Parents' anxiety and behavior is thought to be critical. Some parents are extremely anxious about medical procedures themselves and may communicate this to their child. This concept of "emotional contagion" has been considered, both for children undergoing hospital procedures generally and more specifically in the context of children with cancer.

Melamed (1992) published some of the first work linking parents' and children's behavior. She showed that some parents are so distressed themselves that they are unable to help their child. The importance of parents' behavior can begin even before the child enters the treatment room. Hospital treatment always involves lengthy waits, and children's (and parents') distress can increase during this time. Parents are routinely confronted with questions about how to deal with the child who is anxious while waiting to see the doctor.

Melamed (1992) showed that parents differ in how they deal with this situation. Some recognize the potential problem and are prepared to adopt a variety of strategies to distract the child's attention. In her study, children who were less disruptive during procedures had parents who read to them in the waiting room. Children who were more disruptive had parents who showed highly anxious behavior themselves. These parents appeared agitated and uneasy, and unresponsive to the child's concerns. These findings suggest that some parents may inadvertently cue and reinforce their child's distress and subsequently affect treatment outcome.

A series of studies have been reported involving observations of children undergoing BMAs and LPs and their parents. In one of the first, Cox, Dahlquist, and Fernbach (1987) reported that parents' behavior was a more important determinant of distress and anxiety among younger children, compared with those over 8 years of age. Parents who were anxious were less consistent in their discipline and used more punishment than parents who were less anxious. They also rated their child to be more anxious. Thus, these authors suggested that anxious parents had anxious children and were more likely to ignore their child or use physical punishment while waiting for procedures. The effects were especially clear for parents of children below 8 years of age. The behavior of parents of older children had less direct influence on their responses.

R. I. Blount, Landolf-Fritsche, Powers, and Sturges (1991) classified children into high- and low-coping groups. Parents of high-coping children engaged in more coping-promoting behaviors, such as talking about other things rather than the procedures, using humor to distract the child, and actively suggesting ways the child could cope (such as directions to breathe deeply). Children showed more distress behaviors (e.g., crying, screaming, verbal resistance) where parents were critical or kept apologizing.

Jacobsen et al. (1990) examined the effect of demographic, medical, and psychological variables on child distress during invasive procedures. They were interested in the relationship between individual parent behaviors and child distress across different phases of the procedures. Seventy 3- to 10-year-olds undergoing venipuncture and their parents took part. Overall distress was greater in younger children who had experienced fewer previous procedures, who had poor venous access, and whose parents rated them prior to the procedures as less likely to be cooperative. Child distress was less where parents provided explanations about the procedure. However, the success of parents' explanations depended on when the explanation was given and the child's level of distress at the time. It is difficult to console a child who is distressed, and successful parents anticipate this by preparing the child for what will happen.

In a later study, Manne et al. (1992) videotaped adult–child interactions during venipuncture procedure. Again, the use of distraction techniques by parents resulted in better child coping and specifically reduced the amount of distress and crying. There was no relationship between child behaviors and whether or not children had been given explanations about what would happen. However, children who were given more control (e.g., allowed to make decisions about some aspect of the routine) were less distressed.

Dahlquist, Power, Cox, and Fernbach (1994) replicated their earlier finding showing that children under 8 years of age were more distressed during routine procedures. These children showed more distress where parents ignored them or were themselves very agitated before the procedure, and where they tried to give information during the procedure. In contrast to previous research (Zabin & Melamed, 1980), highly anxious parents did not necessarily have children who showed the greatest distress during the medical procedure.

Interestingly, parents and clinicians affect childrens' behavior differently (Dahlquist, Power, & Carlson, 1995). Clinicians were less verbally interactive than parents both before and during procedures, and generally have much less influence on children's behavior.

Several studies indicate that child distress can be effectively targeted by training parents (R. L. Blount et al., 1989; Powers, R. L. Blount, Bachanas, Cotter, & Swan, 1993). Jay and Elliott (1990) compared a stress inoculation program (parents merely observed their child's participation in a cognitive behavior therapy program) with a child-focused intervention designed to help parents cope with their children's procedures. Parents were assessed during a baseline procedure and then randomly assigned to either program. Parents in the stress inoculation program reported lower anxiety scores than parents in the child-focused condition.

Manne, Redd, Jacobsen, Gorfinkle, and Schorr (1990) developed a behavioral intervention for parents whose child routinely required physical restraint during venipuncture. This involved coaching parents to use attentional distraction and positive reinforcement to control child distress during invasive treatment. After the intervention, observed child distress, parent-rated child distress, and parent ratings of their own distress were significantly reduced and remained so across three intervention trials. There was also a significant reduction in the amount of physical restraint necessary to manage child behavior. Disappointingly, children's self-reports of pain and nurse ratings of child distress were not significantly affected.

Manne, Bakeman, Jacobsen, Gorfinkle, and Redd (1994) tried to disentangle the effectiveness of different components of a behavioral intervention. Parental use of distraction was associated with less crying, but involvement from a health professional did not enhance the effectiveness of the intervention. Older children and those who were less distressed were more positive about the intervention. Children coped better when their parents gave them direct and specific coping commands, as opposed to more general encouragement.

Powers et al. (1993) studied four preschool children with leukemia whose parents were taught coping behaviors for use before and during painful injections. Prior to the intervention, the children and parents were unable to manage the fear, pain, and distress associated with repeated, invasive medical procedures. Children were taught to engage in distraction activities such as interactive play or conversation prior to the medical procedure and active breathing or counting strategies during the injections procedures. Parents were taught to engage in the distraction activities before and to coach the child's use of breathing and counting strategies during the procedures. Toys, coloring books, dolls, puzzles, and party blowers for the child and parents were placed in the treatment room for training purposes and used during the procedures.

After intervention parents demonstrated interactive distraction behaviors and children responded to the strategies. The level of child behavioral distress was reduced after training, and these findings suggest that using parents can facilitate children's acquisition of coping strategies during routine invasive procedures. Other work is necessary to see if the results are generalizable for older children as well as preschoolers.

Broome, Lillis, McGahee, and Bates (1992) looked at the value of relaxation, distraction, and imagery techniques with children during LPs. The study examined the children's pain experience during cancer treatment, as well as their parents' anxiety and behavioral stress. Fourteen children, 11 boys and 3 girls, aged 3 to 15 years (mean age = 6.6 years) with ALL were videotaped while undergoing LPs over an 18-month period. Self-ratings of child fear and parent anxiety, videotaped observations of both child and parent behavior, and child pain ratings were obtained.

The children's behavioral responses to the procedure varied considerably. Children's fear scores remained stable although there was considerable variation in their behavioral distress. Their reports of pain decreased over time. In this study, there was no relationship between age and child distress. However, parents in the study were very supportive during the procedures.

In much of the work reported in the preceding discussion, it is clear that although procedural distress is a problem for some children, others are not so affected. The study of these "natural" copers might help to determine the variables that mediate successful coping.

In evaluating this literature, it is important to point to differences in health care between clinics in the United States compared with the United Kingdom. In the United Kingdom, children who are distressed by procedures are routinely offered sedation. As sedation is associated with a small risk to the child's health, it is less routinely offered in the United States for fear of litigation. This is not to say that children in the United Kingdom are free from all treatment-related pain, but it is considerably reduced.

The choice between use of nonpharmacological or pharmacological strategies is an issue that deserves further attention. The ideal situation would be to have both treatment modalities available, so that choices could be made based on the age and preference of the child and family. The fact that children of around 7 years are better able to articulate their fears and communicate their need for support and control could be used as a guideline for introducing the concept of choice to the child. The best possible outcome for children who must undergo painful medical procedures will probably be achieved with a mixture of pharmacologic and behavioral support. Research indicates that reliance on either alone will probably not meet the needs of all children.

Home-Based Care. In line with pediatric practice generally, children with cancer spend as little time as possible in the hospital, putting the onus on parents to provide home-based care. In comparison with other chronic or life-threatening conditions that can affect children (e.g., diabetes, cystic fibrosis), home-based care of the child with cancer is relatively straightforward. For the most part, home-based care in cancer includes giving the child medication (although treatment protocols can be quite complex). In addition, parents may have to be especially vigilant with regard to oral hygiene (children are prone to mouth ulcers and sores). They may also have to care for the child's central catheter line. They must also be attentive to changes in the child's condition; they must report any potentially adverse reactions to treatment to clinic staff and decide whether or not it is necessary to consult clinic staff at different times. Parents are also the link between the child and the outside world. They must inform extended family about the child's progress, liase with the school about attendance and participation in school activities, and be alert to outbreaks of infectious disease such as chicken pox, which might be particularly dangerous for the child. Thus, they need to be vigilant and confident about when they can look after the child at home and when it is appropriate to call on professional care.

Manne, Jacobsen, Gorfinkle, Gerstein, and Redd (1993) found that difficulties with compliance with home-based care were related to the child's age, functional status, medical condition, and parenting styles. Satisfactory appointment keeping, prompt reporting of adverse symptoms, and competent implementation of home-based treatments were used as indicators of compliance. The authors focused specifically on compliance with mouth and central-line care.

Parents of younger children reported greater difficulties implementing mouth and central-line care compared with parents of older children. For all ages, however, better compliance (in terms of appointment keeping and prompt reporting of symptoms) was related to parenting style. Parents who were more sensitive, less restrictive, and more nurturant were rated to be more compliant by clinic staff.

Everyday Situations

In families of healthy children, parenting stress, marital distress, and disagreements between parents about childrearing have been associated with emotional and behavioral problems in the children (Abidin, Jenkins, & McGaughey, 1992; Creasey & Jarvis, 1994). In families with a child with a chronic illness, the risks may be magnified. Given that parents of sick children are under increased stress and show elevated levels of anxiety and depression at least at certain crisis points, there needs to be special concern about how these stresses impact on the way in which the child reacts to illness and treatment. The inverse is also true, in that children with chronic illness are at greater risk of emotional and behavioral problems compared with healthy children (Cadman, Boyle, Szatmari, & Offord, 1987). Thus both parents and children are under greater stress than in healthy families.

As has already been described, there is a high incidence of mental health problems in mothers and fathers of children with cancer. The children, in their turn, also are more vulnerable to mental health problems. Given these findings, it might be expected that the parent–child relationship itself is also at risk. A first question therefore concerns whether parent–child relationships in the context of cancer are different from healthy dyads. As a result of the illness, parents and children may spend more time together. Children may "model" their own behavior on that of their parents.

There is some evidence that parents and children do respond similarly or that over time their ways of reacting become related. In a very early study, Blotcky, Raczynski, Gurwitch, and Smith (1985) reported significant correlations between parental distress and the child's feelings of hopelessness. Varni and Setoguchi (1993) reported that parental anxiety and depression predicts the child's anxiety and depression. Research has not always focused on the transmission of negative attitudes and emotions. Positive ways of coping are also linked. Thus, parents who maintain family integration have children who express a more optimistic definition of their illness and report fewer psychological difficulties (Sanger et al., 1991). On the other hand, parents with higher levels of trait anxiety had children with more externalizing behavioral symptoms, suggesting that the more anxiety reported by parents the more acting out and behavioral problems shown by children (Frank, R. L. Blount, & R. T. Brown, 1997).

R. T. Brown et al. (1993) assessed 61 children with ALL (2–17 years) and their mothers. Based on a structured clinical interview, 34% of mothers met recognized criteria for at least one psychiatric disorder. Mothers who reported more anxiety and maladaptive attributional style reported by their children were more depressed and showed a range of internalizing behavioral symptoms.

Again, one of the major criticisms of this work is the lack of concern about the timing of assessments or consideration about how parent–child relationships change with time. Not only is this important with regard to the progression of the illness, but also with regard to the developmental status of the child. We know little about how normative changes in parent–child relationships are affected by the occurrence of a major disease.

In addition to providing home-based medical care, parents must also continue to attend to the mundane and everyday issues concerning child care. Parents are warned of the dire consequences of spoiling the child and are encouraged to "treat the child as normal." How this is to be achieved is rarely made explicit. How do parents cope with the normal aspects of parenting when everything around them is abnormal?

Parenting a child with cancer is difficult. As more and more children are surviving cancer, it is essential that parents are given clear, realistic guidelines concerning how to continue with "normal" parenting amid all the confusion and upset caused by cancer. Parents face a difficult task in providing a balance between the demands of the illness and creating a family environment conducive to the development of a "normal" and unspoiled child (Kazak & Nachman, 1991).

In attempting to establish how parenting is affected when a child has cancer, Hillman (1997) compared parenting used by parents of children with cancer ($n = 58$) and healthy children ($n = 58$). Children with cancer were between 2 and 17 years old, were currently on treatment, and had been diagnosed at least 1 month before participation in the study. Parenting was assessed using the measure described by Block (1965). In this task, parents are shown 91 cards describing different ways of dealing with childrearing and asked to sort them on different dimensions. Parents of children with cancer were significantly different from parents of healthy children on 11 of these dimensions. These included parental expectations, discipline, emotional expression, parental concern/worry, and overprotectiveness. Parents of children with cancer expressed most concern about discipline and overprotectiveness. Parents of children who had been diagnosed for more than a year were less likely to spoil their children and more likely to have established rules than were parents of newly diagnosed children.

Jelalian, Stark, and Miller (1997) compared self-reported discipline strategies in 22 mothers of children on treatment (aged between 3 and 10 years) with a normal control group (Zabin & Melamed, 1980). They found that there were no differences in parenting strategies between the groups. However, mothers of children with cancer reported more conflict about discipline and felt less in control in situations requiring discipline than did control mothers.

LIMITATIONS OF METHODS

Much of the work reviewed in this chapter about parents' coping can be criticized on similar grounds as was described for work involving children with cancer. Retrospective reports about parents' coping with specific time points are of limited value compared with prospective research. Disappointingly, very few attempts to document such changes over time have been reported. In the study by Kupst et al. (1984), much of the data was based on ratings made by clinic staff. Clearly, clinic staff can see only one aspect of parental coping and are unable to make judgments about behavior outside the hospital setting. It is not clear that clinic staff and parents share each other's views about what constitutes good coping. Indeed, we know that clinic staff and parents do differ in their perceptions of the impact of treatment (W. H. Davies, Noll, DeStefano, Bukowski, & Kulkarni, 1991).

Interpretation of longitudinal data is also limited as a result of changes in the treatment or prognosis of the disease across time. Certainly survival improved greatly during the course of the study by Kupst and her colleagues. There were also changes in philosophy about psychosocial care. As a result, the kind of behavior measured was perhaps less appropriate at the end of the study than it was at the beginning.

Subject loss, or attrition, is another problem characteristic of longitudinal studies, and this can become more acute as the length of follow-up increases. Differences between those who remain in the study compared with those who drop out may be critical. Families who drop out of a study may do so because they are doing well and are happy and do not have time to fit it into their agenda. Equally, they may drop out because they feel overburdened by the illness or for other reasons.

In selecting outcome measures, there needs to be a balance between the use of standardized measures (e.g., anxiety or depression), which allow comparisons with other studies and more sensitive, but not well-validated assessments of the specific demands made on parents looking after a child with cancer. Standardized measures are often justified on the grounds that considerable psychometric data are available. However, psychometric data are often reported for a specific group or population and cannot necessarily be assumed to be relevant to other groups. Further work is needed with other cultures, socioeconomic groups, and ethnic minorities.

It is difficult to compare studies as different measures are used. The concepts of "coping" and "adjustment" are used interchangeably, which adds to difficulties when interpreting results (Grootenhuis & Last, 1997b).

The literature attests to the considerable problems faced by families and consequently the potential need for interventions to improve knowledge and alleviate distress. However, in a cost-effective health service, it is not enough to provide some well-meaning intervention, but it is essential that work is formally evaluated and justified. In designing, implementing, and evaluating interventions, many issues need to be considered. In many published papers, small sample sizes makes drawing conclusions difficult. Larger samples, achieved through multisite collaboration, will improve the power of a study and make within-group comparisons possible.

IMPLICATIONS

As expected, parents' reports about their initial reactions to the diagnosis of cancer in their child is overwhelming, and higher levels of anxiety and depression have been observed compared with parents of healthy children. However, at some time parents learn to accept the diagnosis and become highly skilled in managing both hospital- and home-based treatment procedures. In describing how parents react to the diagnosis of cancer in their child, there has been a focus on the experiences of mothers compared with fathers. Although some differences between mothers and fathers have been identified, there have been fewer attempts to explain how differences between mothers and fathers arise. This would require inclusion of different kinds of questions concerned with details of how parents divide up care or gender differences in preferences for coping strategies. The studies reviewed here point to a limited number of variables that appear to be associated with coping. Attributions, particularly about the causes of cancer, and availability of social support have been identified.

Although these ideas have generated considerable interest and contributed to an understanding of differences between mothers and fathers in coping with the child's illness, much less attention has been given to the implications for family functioning. On the one hand, gender differences may be problematic, where one parent is very optimistic, for example, and the other is the opposite. Such differences in viewpoints may create tension and arguments and limit parents' abilities to communicate together. On the other hand, gender differences may have more positive implications. One partner who feels very pessimistic can take heart from the other, and the result might be a more balanced way of looking at the child's illness and prognosis.

Despite these criticisms, the findings have been useful in providing some insight into how parents' thoughts and behaviors change during the course of treatment. The focus has, however, been on parents in relatively traditional families where both parents are available. There is a dearth of work looking at how other families cope, especially where there is only one parent. Similarly, little is known about how families of different ethnic or religious backgrounds manage.

The focus too has been on how parents' mental health and well-being impacts on the child's behavior during treatments. The responsibilities for parents are enormous, and for this reason more work is needed to examine the effect of caregiving tasks on parents' QOL, satisfaction as a parent, or perceived competence.

Despite the potential clinical value, very few studies have addressed the question of the relationship between parent and child coping. Only one study has linked parenting style with treatment compliance (Manne et al., 1993). A number of studies suggest that specific parenting behaviors are associated with better tolerance in children undergoing painful procedures.

The relationship between parent and child behavior is especially important for children below 8 years of age. These findings suggest that interventions must target the parent–child dyad and that attempts to change behavior in either one alone will be of limited value. In addition, certain parenting styles seem particularly inappropriate. Parents who are highly anxious or adopt punitive or overly permissive parenting styles tend to have children who show more distress during procedures. Again, this points to the need for interventions to focus on changing parent behaviors in line with those adopted by parents who appear to be more successful in helping their child manage treatment-related pain.

12

Brothers and Sisters

Summary

The relationship between brothers and sisters is one of the most enduring of all human relationships, usually outlasting that between children and parents. Although there are elements of rivalry and competition between siblings, there is also a close bond, with older siblings often playing a crucial role in educating and socializing younger children. In their turn, younger children potentially learn a lot from older siblings.

In the event of one child becoming seriously ill, it is inevitable that healthy siblings experience sadness, loss, and fear. They are confronted by illness in a previously healthy playmate and confidante, in turn raising questions about their own health and vulnerability. In addition, they experience loss of normal family life and parents' time and attention. It is impossible to be in the hospital with a sick child and at home with other children at the same time. It is not surprising that many healthy children develop behavioral problems at home and school. Somatic, sleeping, and eating problems as well as emotional difficulties have all been identified.

Less expected are findings that siblings can show enhanced maturity as a consequence of cancer in their brother or sister. They may become more mature, compassionate, and independent. Sometimes, the experience of helping care for a sick child can direct siblings to future work in the caring professions.

We have so far concentrated on the QOL of children with cancer and, to a lesser extent, their parents. The impact goes further, and brothers and sisters are also affected. It is impossible for parents to be in the hospital with the ill child and at home at the same time, and so they are faced with difficult decisions about their other children. If they are old enough, siblings can be left to fend for themselves at home, perhaps with help from a neighbor or relation. Where they are at school during the day, this can work well, especially when one parent can come home for the night. With younger children, it is much more difficult. Healthy siblings may have to be left with friends and neighbors. Although this protects them from the hospital environment, they can be very distressed by the interruptions to their routines and lack of contact with their parents. Worry about their other children is one of parents' main concerns. In practice, it is almost inevitable that siblings experience some compromised QOL themselves.

The fact that healthy brothers and sisters experience compromised QOL should not be surprising. The relationship between siblings is very special. It probably lasts longer than any other relationship, outlasting that with parents and predating that with partners. Siblings spend a good deal of time together and can learn a huge amount from each other. At different times, brothers and sisters are playmates, teachers, and confidantes.

As they grow up, siblings spend more time together than with peers. This proximity can make them aware of each other's strengths and weaknesses. It is also through play with siblings that children learn strategies for resolving interpersonal conflict (Youniss, 1980). Typically, younger children learn by observing and imitating older siblings whereas older siblings teach games and physical skills. Older siblings may be more influential than parents in socializing young children. Older siblings are also potential teachers. Cicirelli (1972) found that siblings gave more detailed explanations and descriptions to a brother or sister than they gave to peers.

Sibling closeness can change during middle childhood, as friends become increasingly influential and children spend more time outside their families. Consequently, some of the affection between siblings can decrease during adolescence compared with earlier in childhood (Buhrmester & Furman, 1990).

There is also a competitive edge to the sibling relationship. From the beginning, brothers and sisters compete for parent attention and for resources in the family. From a young age, children monitor their parents' behavior in an effort to determine any inequalities in treatment (Dunn & Stocker, 1989). In their turn, parents do not treat all their children in the same way. Older children may be given less affection and more is demanded of them compared with younger children. Dunn, Stocker, and

Plomin (1990) found that mothers showed less warmth and were more controlling toward older children. These behaviors seemed in turn to be associated with more internalizing problems. Thus, differences in the way children perceive that they are treated by parents have implications for their own adjustment (Daniels, Dunn, Furstenberg, & Plomin, 1985).

In all families, siblings argue and fight, and typically children complain that life is "not fair." The "baby" typically gets away with a lot more and perhaps is allowed independence at a younger age than older siblings. Younger children may contribute less to household chores than older ones. Parents may be more lenient with younger children and impose less strict rules than they did with older children. Differences in the way siblings think they are treated can be real or imaginary.

Everyday issues like these can become much more of a problem in families with a chronically sick or disabled child. The sick child may need much more parental time and attention. First, the sick child may need medications at home or have to be taken to clinics and the hospital. All of this means more parental attention. Second, where one child is ill, parents may expect others in the family to help more around the house. Thus, differential treatment can occur because the well child *has to help* while the sick child has *to be helped*. Third, in conflicts between siblings, parents may favor the sick child. Excuses are made for sick children. They may be irritable or horrid, but perhaps it is the drugs. Boisterous play may be a normal part of growing up, but parents of a child with cancer worry that the Hickman line may be pulled out. With some justification, parents may be more anxious that the child does not come to any physical harm. Even a minor accident for a sick child might have sinister repercussions.

Despite the many ways in which the presence of a sick child can change family relationships and valid reasons why parents should make allowances for the sick child, they usually try to treat all children "the same." The question is how successful are they? Horwitz and Kazak (1990) identified two-child families including one with cancer, and compared them with similar families where both children were well. Parents first rated each of their children on a series of scales (e.g., neat–messy). Parents of healthy children were happy to acknowledge differences between their children. In contrast, parents were much more likely to focus on the similarities between their children where one had cancer. The implication is that mothers of healthy children may be more tolerant of differences between their children than mothers of a child with cancer. It is less clear how far this is a dysfunctional strategy. Perhaps the strategy serves a purpose for parents (so Jo has cancer but really she is not so different from Emma; neither of them are any good at sports). These attributions may have a different implication for the sibling, of course. The fact that parents are less likely to recognize differences between their children may restrict the experiences of siblings. It may also add to siblings' concerns that they too will get sick.

Previous Reviews

Confronted by the diagnosis of cancer in their child, parents find that virtually all their time is taken up by managing treatment demands, both at home and in the hospital. Emotionally too, they invest a huge amount of time thinking about the sick child. Other children in the family will have to take a back seat, perhaps being cared for by friends or grandparents, and for a time at least they have very restricted access to their parents. Alternatively, parents can arrange that one of them stays at home with the well child, attempting to keep life as normal as possible. Whatever they do, parents are likely to feel that they should have done something else. Certainly, the question about how best to care for other children in the family poses parents with a significant problem.

Many psychosocial reviews are primarily concerned with the experience of children with cancer, but some (Chang, 1991; Kazak, 1992; Kazak & Christakis, 1996; van Dongen-Melman & Sanders-Woudstra, 1986) make limited attempts to address the issue of siblings. However, much of what is currently known about the adjustment of siblings is based on reports made by parents and health care professionals. Attempts to involve siblings directly are few and far between. Though siblings are sometimes involved in research, it is often as "controls" for their sick brother or sister, rather than in terms of how their own well-being is affected by the disease.

Van Dongen-Melman and Sanders-Woudstra (1986) reviewed the literature concerning psychosocial aspects of childhood illness from the 1970s to mid-1980. Siblings of chronically ill children, including those with cancer, were reported to experience a range of problems: irritability, social withdrawal, jealousy, guilt, academic underachievement, enuresis, acting-out behavior, and were highly vulnerable to illness and injury. They also were found to have low self-esteem. The list of problems was long and very negative. At the time of the review, the main difficulties for siblings were put down to disruptions in their interpersonal relationships, especially with parents.

During the 1990s, an increasing number of reports suggested that there was much greater variability in how brothers and sisters reacted. Yes, there was anger, disappointment, and sometimes fear, but there was also empathy, understanding, and warmth. Increasingly it was suggested that all was not bad news.

The way a family reacts, and especially how parents talk to and involve the sibling in information about the illness and the day-to-day care of the sick child, is clearly going to be crucial. But it is not simply that some families get it right and others get it wrong. Where there is more than one sibling in the family, there can be very different responses. One child may become very mature and take on a responsible role toward younger siblings and domestic chores, whereas another copes by going out as much as possible. Some siblings report that the whole experience has made them reappraise their lives. In some cases, looking after their sick brother or sister can make siblings realize that they are very good at caring, and consequently the experience directs their choice of career. Others maintain it has had no affect on them at all.

Continuing the same deficit-centered tradition that was applied to work with children with cancer, Chang (1991) concluded that siblings experience guilt and jealousy toward the ill child, anger, acting-out behavior, fear of abandonment, and concerns about their own health. Compared with healthy children, siblings of the ill child are more likely to become socially withdrawn, irritable, and anxious, and to experience psychosomatic illnesses. Older male siblings of leukemia patients were thought to be more vulnerable than females. However, Chang noted that despite these problems, siblings appear to adjust remarkably well over time. Jealousy and worries about being "left out" tend to be resolved and normal sibling relationships were restored in most families.

Kazak and Christakis (1996) also emphasized how much variability there can be in the way in which brothers and sisters react. Although many studies document the difficulties siblings experience, Kazak and Christakis suggested that this might be attributed in part to the bias in the kind of questions asked. In the study described previously, Horwitz and Kazak (1990) collected data on family adaptability and cohesion as well as that concerning parental perceptions of similarities and differences between ill and well siblings. They identified positive prosocial behaviors in preschool siblings of children with cancer, suggesting that at least during the preschool period, siblings may learn empathic and altruistic behavior in a way that would not be possible in families with healthy children.

Carpenter and Levant (1994) reported a comprehensive review focusing solely on the consequences of childhood cancer for healthy siblings. The review was based on selected studies from 1956 to 1992. Taken together the work suggested that approximately 50% of siblings experience adjustment problems at some time during the course of the disease and treatment, including emotional, behavioral, and somatic symptoms. Feelings of guilt, loneliness, rejection, sadness, and depression, declines in school performance, increased acting out at home and school, headaches, stomachaches, and changes in sleeping and eating habits were all reported. Precipitating factors associated with poor adaptation were related to communication problems between siblings and their parents about the illness. Siblings who had few opportunities to help with the treatment or care of the sick child or felt isolated from parents, especially their mothers, were especially vulnerable.

Similar suggestions were put forward by Kazak (1992), who recommended a focus on vulnerability rather than "deficits" in understanding the experience of families of handicapped and chronically ill children. Awareness of developmental and ethnic diversity, attention to perceptions of normalcy within families, investigation of disease-specific or general variables in assessing adaptation, and the need to consider different perspectives (e.g., child and parent) were all emphasized as issues in need of consideration.

THE PSYCHOLOGICAL IMPACT ON SIBLINGS

Adjustment

The literature concerned with sibling adjustment very much parallels the methods adopted in work with children with cancer. Thus, there has been a tendency to rely on parents' reports rather than ask siblings themselves, and emphasis on problems rather than strengths or coping resources. The results, too, parallel the findings reported for children with cancer. Parents typically describe the negative implications, with siblings themselves reporting a greater range of consequences. Siblings are often more aware of the seriousness of the disease than their parents realize and actively try not to add to their parents' worries. Parents themselves do not often seem to be aware, or report, these aspects of sibling understanding and behavior.

Based on parents' reports, Carpenter and Sahler (1991) concluded that emotional lability, poorer school performance, and withdrawn behavior are among the most frequently reported problems for siblings. Somatic complaints, changes in sleeping or eating patterns, bed-wetting, or other evidence of regression were mentioned less frequently. Of the 112 siblings whose brother or sister was alive at the time of study, parents reported that 59% had shown changes in behavioral/emotional functioning since diagnosis.

Chesler, Allswede, and Barbarin (1991) interviewed 21 siblings (aged 10–21 years) of children with cancer. Siblings generally expressed a wish to care for the ill child and often seemed to be aware of the stresses their parents experienced. Well siblings almost universally expressed worry and distress about the illness, that their home life was disrupted, and that there was more sadness than before. However, some siblings also reported that they had attained a greater level of maturity and coping ability. Comparable findings were reported by Havermans and Eiser (1994).

P. Sloper and While (1996) reported that 24 of 99 siblings showed negative changes in behavior following the diagnosis. Both mothers and siblings identified behavior changes after the diagnosis (95.2% of mothers; 85.7% of well siblings). Positive behavioral changes included greater sensitivity, greater sociability, and more thoughtful behavior. More negative changes identified were trouble sleeping, headaches, stomachaches, aggressiveness, fighting, mood swings, irritability, attention-seeking behaviors, and thoughts of running away or hiding. At 6 months postdiagnosis, these same 24 siblings had scores in the borderline or clinical range on both parent- and teacher-completed measures of behavioral adjustment.

The aforementioned studies focused simply on reports from siblings about how they thought they had been affected by the illness. Where comparisons of adjustment have been made between siblings of a child with cancer and healthy controls, few differences have been reported (Dolgin et al., 1997; C. A. Evans, Stevens, Cushway, & Houghton, 1992).

The Sibling Adaptation to Childhood Cancer Collaborative Study Group. The most comprehensive series of studies in this area have been reported by The Sibling Adaptation to Childhood Cancer Collaborative Study Group. This represents a collaborative work involving seven pediatric oncology centers in the United States. A series of studies have been reported, variously focusing on sibling or parent reactions (e.g., Barbarin, Sargent, Sahler, & Carpenter, 1995; Sahler, Roghman, Carpenter, & Mulhern, 1994; Zeltzer et al., 1996).

Sargent et al. (1995) interviewed 254 siblings of children with cancer, aged 4–18 years. The most common emotional problems included distress about family separations and disruptions to normal activities. Siblings also found it difficult to deal with the focus of the family on the ill child rather than themselves and their own negative feelings and worries about cancer treatments. Siblings also worried that their brother or sister might die. However, siblings reported that their families became closer because of their shared experiences and they themselves had learned more compassion. These positive experiences were more likely to be reported by older siblings.

Barbarin et al. (1995) interviewed 179 of the parents involved in the aforementioned study. Parents reported that fewer than 12% of siblings had shown behavioral or affective symptoms before the diagnosis. However, after the diagnosis, 26% showed some of these symptoms. The type of problem was unrelated to gender, birth order, or severity of the illness. Parents also reported positive behavioral and emotional changes such as increased maturity, supportiveness, and independence. Positive effects were more likely to occur among adolescent and first-born siblings and when the patient's prognosis was poorer.

Zeltzer et al. (1996) assessed health status, health care utilization, somatization, and health-risk behaviors of siblings and compared the data with matched controls or population norms. Although siblings experienced significant problems in terms of disturbed sleeping and eating, they were moderately healthy overall. However, parents consistently underreported health-related issues for siblings. The implication is that parents are so concerned with the sick child that they are less aware of the concerns of other siblings.

Long-Term Effects

The research reviewed so far has been concerned with sibling functioning at or near the time of diagnosis. We must expect that during this period, siblings may present with many problems reflecting the suddenness and trauma of the diagnosis. However, time does heal, and as noted by Chang (1991) there seems to be a reduction in problems with time. It is to be hoped that the situation for siblings of survivors would be very different, perhaps even "back to normal." Reflecting the increase in numbers of survivors, attention has recently turned to the longer term repercussions for siblings of survivors.

Van Dongen-Melman, De Groot, Hahlen, and Verhulst (1995b) examined the longer term experiences of 60 siblings of children who were well and had completed treatment. There were no major differences in self-concept, personality, or depression compared with healthy controls or population norms. On all measures of emotional and behavioral problems, siblings scored the same or better than controls. Siblings' adjustment was not affected by any demographic, family, and disease-related factors that could be identified.

Thus, parents tend to report an increase in behavioral problems in siblings from before to after diagnosis. However, problems are reported to diminish with time. As always, reliance on parent reports is unlikely to tell the whole story, and work involving siblings themselves can provide an additional dimension to our understanding.

Predictors of Sibling Adjustment

The findings described previously suggest that siblings do not routinely and inevitably react by showing behavioral or emotional problems. The fact that some siblings appear to cope or even rise above the potential stress suggests that it may be valuable to identify characteristics of those who do well. Such an approach was initially described by Carpenter and Sahler (1991). They distinguished between well- and poorly adjusted siblings according to parents' reports. Difficulties between well- and poorly adjusted siblings were not related to the severity of the disease, concerns about becoming ill themselves, or fears that they might "catch" cancer. However, siblings who were less well adjusted perceived themselves to be ignored, unwanted, and misunderstood, and at the same time they did not want to bother their parents with their worries.

Thus, as with children with cancer, the implication is that adjustment of siblings is dependent on family attitudes and behavior. Madan-Swain, Sexson, R. T. Brown, and Ragab (1993) reported that family size affected sibling adjustment to cancer in a brother or sister. Sibling adjustment was better in larger and more cohesive families (D. S. Cohen, Friedrich, Jaworski, & Copeland, 1994) and where parents reported better interpersonal support (Dolgin et al., 1997).

In a similar study, P. Sloper and While (1996) found that siblings who were poorly adjusted were more likely to come from manual social class backgrounds, from families reporting financial problems due to the illness, and from families who did not have a car. Neither family composition nor sibling age, gender, or birth order were related to adjustment. In contrast to the work reported by Carpenter and Sahler (1991), siblings who were poorly adjusted were also those with a brother or sister who had spent more nights in the hospital and had a poorer prognosis. Thus, adjustment problems were related to disruption in family life occasioned by the illness, the resources available to the family to cope with the effects of such disruption on siblings, and siblings' perceptions of negative interpersonal effects on their lives.

In acknowledging the close relationship between the way different family members might respond, Sahler, Roghman, Mulhern, and Carpenter (1997) were concerned with the relationship between behavioral and emotional adaptation among siblings and maternal well-being. In general, mothers of children with cancer reported significantly worse well-being compared with mothers of healthy controls. Mothers of siblings who showed the worst behavioral or emotional adaptation reported poorer well-being themselves and were more likely to have sought professional help than mothers of better adjusted siblings. They also reported little informal social support. Thus, there is a relationship between maternal well-being and sibling adjustment that is similar to that reported between mothers' well-being and adjustment of the child with cancer in chapter 11.

Communication.   The aforementioned studies suggest that adjustment in siblings is dependent on family relationships. Perhaps one variable that may contribute most to family adjustment is communication. Good adjustment may be dependent on open and honest communication between siblings and parents, as has been shown for children with cancer and their parents. Yet a number of studies suggest that some siblings are given little or very inadequate information from their parents (C. A. Evans et al., 1992; Stallard, Mastroyannopoulou, Lewis, & Lenton, 1997; S. C. Taylor, 1980). Certainly for parents, talking about the child's illness may be very stressful. They may not themselves feel informed about the illness and its implications, and therefore talking to other siblings is difficult because they do not understand the issues themselves (Stallard et al., 1997). At other times, talking may result in such overwhelming feelings of anxiety or sorrow that parents avoid it as much as possible (Gallo, Breitmayer, Knafl, & Zoeller, 1992).

It is therefore possible that siblings may be aware that the illness is serious but lack any opportunity to talk to their parents about it (Altschuler, 1997). As a consequence, siblings do not have the opportunity to develop their own story about the illness, a process some consider essential in establishing psychological resilience. In support of this, Gallo et al. (1992) reported that positive parenting enabled well siblings to mobilize their own internal resources and construct a meaningful story about their experiences. This can provide a basis on which development can proceed.

Helping Siblings: Therapies and Interventions

A number of hospital-based programs to promote positive adaptation and QOL in siblings have been reported. These include "Sibshops" (Meyer, Vadasy, & Lassen, 1994). This is an illustrated practical guide to the organization of a workshop to bring together 8- to 13-year-old siblings of children with a variety of special needs, including cancer. The workshop can be used by teachers, psychologists, social workers, parents, and other professionals. It aims to bring together siblings with similar experiences in a recreational setting; facilitates open discussion with other siblings about common joys and concerns; offers insight into how to handle difficult situations through the experiences of others; explores the implications of a child's special needs; and increases parents' and service professionals' awareness of sibling concerns.

Sourkes (1991) assessed three structured art-therapy techniques used to facilitate emotional expression of children with cancer and their well siblings: the mandala (color-feeling-wheel), the change-in-family drawing, and the "scariest" drawing. Other techniques, including letter writing, have been described. Sourkes suggested that the structured aspect of these methods allows "focused" questioning by the therapist and permits interpretation within the context of the child's reality. Useful properties of this type of therapy are that the techniques can be adapted for individuals from 3 years of age through to adulthood and can be used in individual, family, or group therapy.

Dolgin, Somer, Zaidel, and Zaizov (1997) described the development and evaluation of a structured group intervention for school-age and adolescent siblings of childhood cancer patients. In a 6-week program, 23 siblings participated in one of two parallel age-appropriate groups: younger siblings (aged 7–11 years) or older siblings (aged 12–17 years). The topics to be discussed were decided prior to the intervention and were selected on the basis of the available clinical and research literature and a pre-intervention survey. Facilitated group discussion, art therapy techniques, role playing, and social interaction were employed. Pre- and postmeasures focused on cancer-related knowledge, feelings and attitudes toward cancer, and overall mood state. Results indicated statistically and clinically significant improvements in interpersonal problems, disease-related communication, mood, and cancer-related knowledge.

Haberle, Schwarz, and Mathes (1997) described an intervention that lasted for 4 weeks and was designed to address physical, psychological, and social rehabilitation in the whole family. An evaluation based on 104 families showed significant reductions in the severity of physical and psychological symptoms of patients, parents, and siblings. Moreover, the rehabilitation offered all family members opportunity to build important and supportive resources.

The evaluation of interventions is critical. Without evaluation, it is not clear what works, why it works, or what are the limitations of any method. Almost all published papers conclude that siblings find interventions to be beneficial. True evaluation requires more than superficial comments by siblings that the intervention was "OK" or that they might be prepared to attend again in the future. Disappointingly, none of these papers identified offer more than cursory evidence of the efficacy of the intervention.

CONCLUSIONS

The Importance of Sibling Relationships

There can be no doubt about the importance of sibling relationships for their own and for each other's development. The occurrence of a serious or life-threatening disease in one child in the family will inevitably have enormous ramifications for each child and for the wider family. It follows that if a child is ill, there is less opportunity for learning through sibling play, interaction, and communication.

Although early work pointed to problems for all siblings, later work more consistently suggested considerable variability in sibling reactions. This led to the search for moderators of sibling reactions. If there is a single variable identified most frequently it is the presence of open and "honest" communication within the family. Many clinicians feel this is such a well-established finding that they advise parents to adopt an open approach in talks with their children (e.g., Lansdown & Goldman, 1988). In point of fact, we know very little about exactly what is communicated within families.

Methodological Issues

The majority of work has adopted a traditional pseudoexperimental design. The pressure has been to compare siblings against a "gold" standard, whether this involves siblings of healthy children, or even more cursorily, population norms. Based on a deficit-centered approach, the hypothesis is that siblings of children with cancer will have lower scores or compare unfavorably with population norms. The flaws in this argument are clear. First, cancer is but one of a number of adversities that can potentially affect young children, and it is therefore possible that the gold-standard group itself includes children who also have experienced unpleasant events during the course of their childhood. Second, taking the experimental design further, the impetus has been to select measures of functioning for their psychometric properties, rather than their suitability for the task in hand. Consequently, there is a body of work that focuses on comparisons between groups in terms of behavioral adjustment, depression, anxiety, or self-esteem. None of this is informative when it comes to understanding how siblings understand what is happening in their families, how their own cognitive and social development is affected, and critically, how it is that as far as we can tell with currently available measures, the majority do not grow up with major behavioral or emotional problems.

The number of studies in this area remains small although their findings are significant. The work by Horwitz and Kazak (1990), for example, raises interesting questions about both sibling development and the way mothers respond differentially to their children when one is sick. The authors showed that even preschoolers can empathize with their sick sibling. Interesting, too, is the finding that mothers of a child with cancer perceive their children more similarly compared with mothers of healthy children. The implication is that mothers of healthy children can tolerate differences between their children, perhaps even foster such differences. In contrast, mothers of sick children, perhaps knowing that the sick child has many disadvantages, have to play down the significance and possible implications. It is uncomfortable to have to acknowledge that treatment that is vital for the child's life is, at the same time, undermining the child's development and future QOL.

The reliance on parents' reports is very limiting. Although parents often say they treat their children similarly, observation studies involving parents and children with other chronic conditions suggests that this may be difficult to achieve (Quittner et al., 1996). More direct monitoring of parental behavior as reported by Quittner and her colleagues may provide much greater insight into how parents attempt to provide a "normal" family environment for all their children.

Based on their reviews, several authors have drawn up recommendations for conducting research with siblings. For example, Carpenter and Sahler (1991) suggested that:

- Research should be conducted from a family-centered framework.
- Individual differences in response to chronic stress should be recognized.
- The emphasis should be on competencies rather than deficits.
- Strategies that families and children use to cope with various illness-related demands need to be described.
- The role of illness and treatment-related variables needs to be considered.
- Longitudinal, within-subject designs should be used in preference to cross-sectional, between-group designs that compare a chronic illness group with a non-chronic-illness "control" group.
- Measures that assess the interrelationships among specific characteristics and developmental processes of individuals and families and those stressors that alter the day-to-day functioning are needed in preference to measures that assess psychopathology.

In general, research on siblings has focused more on preschool or young children compared with adolescents. Given that cancer often affects preschool children, this bias may be appropriate, but especially as children survive longer, there is a need for a more comprehensive understanding of the impact of the illness on siblings across the age range. The schema described in chapter 3 outlining the critical ways in which illness may affect a child depending on their age can also be applied to siblings. Separations from parents, emotional upset, and disruptions to everyday routines will have a different effect on children depending on their developmental level. Those with less developed linguistic skills may be specially challenged by the unexpected events, whereas older children may be more aware of the emotional implications. Adolescents have a support system outside the family and spend less time with their siblings compared with peers anyway. Even so, the occurrence of serious illness in a sibling will not be without considerable impact on the older child. This group may prove especially difficult to work with; adolescents may be reluctant to share their innermost feelings with strangers. For all these reasons, it is important to develop a more thorough and age-appropriate approach to work with siblings. There needs to be a more comprehensive approach to examining the impact on siblings and greater sensitivity to developing methods that are acceptable to older children and adolescents.

In addition to the developmental effects, greater attention needs to be given to demographic differences between healthy siblings that may contribute to the overall impact on the family. Gender, birth order, or spacing may be critical. Unraveling the implications of these numerous variables requires a collaborative orientation to work in the future.

The focus on cross-sectional work also has its limitations. Although prospective work has many advantages, the theoretical and practical difficulties should not be underestimated. By the nature of longitudinal studies, developmental change and change associated with the phenomenon under study occur together. Research should distinguish or at least be aware of differences between the two.

Increasing the Link Between Research and Provision of Support for Siblings

The impact of cancer on siblings' psychological development needs to be explored further. How do healthy siblings compensate, if they do, for the nonavailability of a previously healthy active playmate? Do the limited opportunities for interaction between siblings following diagnosis of cancer have any detrimental effect on the cognitive development of either? Does the apparent development of altruistic behavior that can occur in healthy siblings have any impact outside the immediate family? Do healthy siblings really select jobs in the caring professions as a consequence of their childhood experiences? Does it affect their relationship with their own children? How does it affect their views of their own health?

All of these questions raise concerns about the *interaction* between well and ill siblings. Furthermore, the bidirectional influence of siblings on one another must be taken into account (Dunn, 1988; Dunn & McGuire, 1992). Where a family member has a chronic illness, children are more likely to present with unexplained pain (L. S. Walker et al., 1991). It has to be expected that siblings will at first be anxious about their own health. Again, this issue has received no attention. To date, one of the few studies to consider these issues (Zeltzer et al., 1996) suggests that parents underestimate the impact of cancer on the physical health of healthy siblings (compared to what siblings say). This is often confirmed in conversations with parents. They suddenly become aware that a healthy sibling is having considerable difficulties at school and realize that they would have picked up cues much quicker under normal circumstances.

There is a growing awareness of the possible impact of cancer on the development of healthy siblings. This has come about through research documenting potential needs of siblings, the changing awareness of the family and the impact of cancer on everyone, not only mother and child, and the emergence of charities specifically or partially vociferous in their support of siblings. Charities in particular have done much to raise the profile of sibling needs and emphasize that more intervention programs and other resources for helping this group need to be available. In the United Kingdom, Siblinks has been established as a charitable organization to bring together siblings. This aims to provide social and support events for siblings aged 15–25 years, with an agenda of fun and also sharing of experiences.

A number of Web sites are now available, offering information and support to siblings (http://www.cafamily.org.uk/siblings.html). Although a number of leaflets and booklets are also available for siblings, few are reported in the research literature. An exception is a booklet for parents of survivors reported by van Dongen-Melman (1997). One section addresses possible late effects on brothers and sisters after the ill sibling has survived. The booklet acknowledges the difficulties of coping with healthy children alongside an ill sibling, and describes how healthy siblings can sometimes feel left out of the family during and after the illness experience. The booklet addresses how parents may help siblings express and cope with their feelings, suggesting among other things that parents take the initiative in bringing about siblings' expression of their experiences. The assumption is that by helping parents, the booklet can enhance open communication with siblings, but no evaluation is reported.

IV

SURVIVING CHILDHOOD CANCER

Each year approximately 800 children in the United Kingdom become new "survivors" of childhood cancer (Wallace et al., 2001). As we have seen, they are survivors of a disease that was previously life threatening. They have endured extensive and aggressive treatments, and many carry the scars of this treatment in the form of residual physical and psychological problems. Yet the extent to which the experience subsequently defines the individual's life varies enormously. For some, it is something that happened in the distant past, about which they remember very little, and has few consequence for their everyday lives. At the other extreme, it is possible to meet survivors whose lives have been massively compromised by the experience. For these people, there may be daily reminders of cancer, perhaps because they have motor or other problems as a legacy of treatment. Others may be very concerned about second cancers or relapse, sometimes much more than they need to be. This dichotomy, and every reaction between, raise a huge question: How is it that some are able to shrug it off as a trifle whereas other lives are destroyed by cancer?

In the 1960s, there was considerable optimism about the prognosis for children with cancer. Survival rates were improving dramatically, but at the same time there was little real evidence of physical complications. This initial optimism was rapidly tempered by reports about late effects. As

more children were treated "successfully," it became clear that an unwanted legacy was the frequency and severity of physical late effects. Although concerns were first based on individual cases, questions began to
be raised about the QOL of survivors generally. Increasingly it was argued that cure should not be seen purely in terms of physical survival.
Van Eys (1991) famously distinguished three components of cure. These
included the biological (eradication of the disease), psychological (the acceptance of having had cancer as a past event without interference with
normal development and schooling), and social (incorporation of the person cured of cancer into society, without consideration of past history of
cancer and its therapy).

A seminal paper by Holmes and Holmes (1975) attempted to determine
the QOL of survivors. They were able to identify 124 survivors of childhood cancer, treated between 1944 and 1963 and registered with the Tumor Registry at the University of Kansas. All had survived at least 10
years from diagnosis. Their work raised questions that are still pertinent
today:

> Little is known or has been written about the fate or rehabilitation of long-
> term survivors of childhood cancer. Obviously, the ultimate justification for
> dangerous and drastic therapy (mutilating surgery, irradiation, and
> cytotoxic drugs) is survival affording normal, near normal, or at least an ac-
> ceptable life style and quality of life for some of the children treated....
> Some very basic questions remain to be answered. Is the life saved worth
> living? Do survivors achieve educational and economic status commensu-
> rate with their premorbid expectations? Is the development of a secondary
> primary malignancy likely? Do survivors marry and beget children? Do sur-
> vivors' children get cancer? Do some childhood cancers recur after ten
> years? (p. 819)

The results of their survey suggested the following:

> Most survivors have made excellent adjustments and have matured to live
> essentially normal lives. A few with serious mental disability have not en-
> tered the mainstream of life, yet the majority has achieved premorbid expec-
> tations, or a bit more, and a few have been true overachievers. Thus, it
> would appear that the drastic, dangerous, and often mutilating approaches
> utilised in the modern treatments for cancer are justifiable. These afford per-
> manent cure of those surviving longer than ten years after diagnosis, and
> enable the overwhelming majority to enjoy a normal or nearly normal life
> style. (Holmes & Holmes, 1975, p. 823)

Much has been achieved in the intervening years to reduce the likelihood of late effects. Increased understanding of the potential side effects
of surgery and radiotherapy have led to changes in practice that have

minimized the incidence of "mutilating" surgery. In the treatment of Hodgkin's disease, for example, radiotherapy to the affected area resulted in limited growth and face and neck asymmetry. Recognition of this resulted in radiation to both sides.

Despite the improvements in treatment and care, survivors remain a population at considerable psychological risk. Follow-up of children who have experienced different kinds of trauma, whether child abuse, other serious illness, or traumatic events, suggests that many experience long-term psychological difficulties. These studies suggest that we should be sensitive to psychological effects of childhood cancer for adult adjustment and QOL.

In chapters 13 and 14, emotional, behavioral, and interpersonal functioning is considered among young-adult survivors of childhood cancer. Caring for the child takes its toll on parents, and this is considered in chapter 15.

13

Long-Term Consequences
of Surviving Childhood Cancer

Summary

Many survivors experience late effects associated with treatment. Depending on the specific therapy experienced, a wide range of physical problems has been identified. Psychological late effects may be associated with having to live with these physical consequences and/or reflect a more direct result of experiencing a life-threatening disease.

Early research focused on identifying psychological "deficits" in survivors of childhood cancer compared with healthy controls. However, research findings were mixed, with relatively few studies suggesting a significant incidence of problems. Unexpectedly, a small number of studies suggested that survivors had fewer problems than healthy controls. There was also evidence that children who were younger on diagnosis were more at risk than those who were older on diagnosis. However, these results need to be tempered by a consideration of the methodological problems inherent in much research.

Other evidence points to an association between childhood cancer and PTSD at least among a subgroup of children. Approximately 12% of survivors and 35% of parents may be affected. Among survivors, psychological and family variables seem to be predictive of PTSD more than medical variables.

"The Child Is Father of the Man"—Wordsworth (1888)

Early experience is believed to play a critical part in later psychological functioning. Follow-up studies of both medically vulnerable and normal children offer plenty of evidence to suggest that early experiences are critical. The implications are that early adverse experiences are associated with increased risks to social, behavioral, and educational outcomes.

Evidence linking experiences during childhood with vulnerability to emotional difficulties in adult life comes from a number of sources. These include studies of healthy children growing up in adverse situations (Masten, Best, & Garmezy, 1990). Those who do not experience regular opportunities to mix with children of their own age can have difficulties establishing interpersonal relationships as adults (Hymel, Rubin, Rowden, & LeMare, 1990). Involvement in deviant peer groups and school-age aggression are associated with later aggression, antisocial behavior, and substance abuse in adolescence (Dobkin, Tremblay, Masse, & Vitaro, 1995; Rubin, Chen, McDougall, Bowkder, & McKinnon, 1995). Early aggressive behavior has also been linked with early onset of alcohol and drug abuse (Boyle et al., 1992). There is, therefore, considerable evidence that the child is "father of the man."

Children who experience chronic physical illness or other medical emergencies subsequently show compromised psychological, learning, and social functioning. Children who experience repeated hospitalizations or periods away from primary caregivers are at risk of long-term psychological difficulties (Rutter, 1981). Large-scale epidemiological studies point consistently to the risk of maladjustment among children with chronic illness (Cadman, Boyle, Szatmari, & Offord, 1987; Gortmaker, D. K. Walker, Weitzman, & Sobol, 1990; Rutter, Graham, & Yule, 1970). Children with chronic disease and physical disability were three times as likely to suffer from psychiatric disorder and were considerably more at risk of social maladjustment compared with healthy children (Cadman et al., 1987). The risks for those with chronic disease without physical problems were less but remained higher than in the general population.

Thus, there is every reason to be concerned about the long-term adjustment of children who experience extensive medical treatment in early childhood. There is good evidence that children brought up in adverse circumstances, or who experience traumatic illness or injury, are at risk of psychological problems in adult life. Added to this, we know that survivors of childhood cancer experience physical problems as a result of illness. The presence of ongoing physical problems may further aggravate psychological vulnerability. In this chapter, the type and extent of physical problems experienced by survivors are summarized before considering the long-term psychological implications.

LATE PHYSICAL EFFECTS

Type and Prevalence

Concern about the social and psychological implications following child-hood cancer fit in with the view that early adverse experiences have nega-tive implications for adult functioning. The child with cancer may well ex-perience repeated admissions to the hospital, time away from home and parents, and care from a number of different people. This may challenge attainment of a basic trust in others, and school absence can contribute to compromised academic achievement. In addition to these childhood ex-periences, survivors may be left with residual physical problems associ-ated with their disease or its treatment. Comprehensive reviews of physi-cal late effects can be found in Hawkins and Stevens (1996) and Schwartz (1995).

Discussion of late effects was initially restricted to those occurring within 5 years of diagnosis, but as longer survival times became more common, it has become clear that the type of late effects changes with time (Hawkins & Stevens, 1996). Neglia and Nesbit (1993) described a three-way classification of late effects depending on time of onset. *Early* or *Stage 1* are those seen in the first 5 years following completion of therapy; *inter-mediate* or *Stage 2* occur 5–20 years from completion, and *very late* or *Stage 3* occur more than 20 years after completion of therapy. A continuum of late effects has been identified from the relatively minor associated with little morbidity, through to those that are extremely severe and cause a high rate of morbidity and mortality (Robison, 1993). Almost all organ systems are vulnerable, with the degree of abnormality related to the type and to-tal dose of therapy.

Second Cancers

For many survivors, fear of relapse, or a second cancer, is a major concern. In practice, the risk of recurrence of the original cancer, or diagnosis of a secondary cancer, is small but real. Within 25 years of diagnosis, about 4% of survivors in the United Kingdom develop a second primary cancer, about six times the expected number (Hawkins, Draper, & Kingston, 1987). This excess risk among survivors is attributable to both the carcino-genic effects of anticancer therapies used to treat the original cancer and genetic predisposition. The risks are very different depending on the ini-tial cancer. For example, among children with hereditary retinoblastoma approximately 30% experience a second cancer in adolescence or adult life (Tucker et al., 1987). In contrast, only 2%–8% of children treated for ALL experience a second cancer (Neglia et al., 1991).

Musculoskeletal System

Bones. Children treated for cancer show reduced bone mineral density (Nysom, Colan, & Lipshultz, 1998). The worry is that this reduced bone mineral density will increase the risk of fractures in later life, although this has not yet been demonstrated.

Eyes, Ears, and Teeth. Hearing loss is relatively common following treatment with cisplatin and may be further aggravated by radiation. Consequently, hearing loss is commonly found following treatment for a brain tumor. As with any hearing loss, the consequences may be most profound for children treated before speech is fully developed.

Evidence of cataracts in the eye may emerge 2–3 years after total-body irradiation. Dry eye is a consequence of damage to tear production and the cornea, and artificial tear drops may be prescribed.

Short and longer-term effects of cancer treatment on dentition have been documented. These complications can in themselves be painful, but also interfere with proper nutrition. Children who had cancer had a higher incidence of dental caries (tooth decay) compared with a control group (Dens, Boute, Otten, Vinckier, & Declerk, 1995).

Cardiopulmonary System

Heart. Anthracyclines have been linked with an increased incidence (1%–10%) of death and clinically symptomatic heart disease (Nysom et al., 1998). The risk factors include cumulative dose, as well as young age, length of follow-up, and gender, with females at greater risk than males.

Lungs. Chemotherapy, especially bleomycin, as well as chest irradiation can both affect the lungs. Treatments can cause scarring that reduces lung capacity, restricts breathing, and reduces exchange of oxygen and carbon dioxide.

Genito-Urinary

Kidneys. Damage to kidneys may cause wasting of salts such as magnesium and potassium. Long-term use of some chemotherapeutic agents, especially ifosamide and cisplatin, can lead to kidney failure. Children who are younger at treatment again appear more vulnerable.

Bladder. Cycophosphamide and ifosamide can cause bladder irritation and bleeding both during and after treatment. Patients treated with pelvic irradiation are further at risk of urinary tract infections.

Endocrine System

Growth is adversely affected in both boys and girls. However, precocious puberty following childhood ALL is more common among girls (Shalet, Clayton, & D. A. Price, 1988). Children treated for ALL can become obese during treatment and remain obese at final height (H. A. Davies et al., 1995). There are many potential contributing factors including growth hormone insufficiency (GHI) secondary to CNS irradiation, steroids, chemotherapy, and reduced physical activity.

GHT will be required for the majority of children treated for a brain tumor with high-dose CNS radiotherapy. The growth response is attenuated in those children who received additional spinal radiotherapy. Again, the younger the child at treatment the greater is the potential problem (Sulmont, Brauner, Fontura, & Rappaport, 1990). Thyroid dysfunction is common following total-body and cranio-spinal irradiation.

Fertility

The impact of combination cytotoxic chemotherapy on gonadal function is dependent on gender and age of the child undergoing treatment and the nature and dose of the drugs received. Both the testis and ovary are vulnerable to radiation damage (Waring & Wallace, 2000), and survivors need to be assessed for infertility. Depending on the specific damage, it may be necessary for some children to be treated with life-long sex hormone replacement therapy to induce secondary sexual characteristics.

Nervous System

Radiation to the brain and chemotherapy have been associated with learning deficits in children. As discussed in chapter 8, the risk of damage seems greater for younger children. Children who receive more than one course of radiotherapy (e.g., following relapse) are at greater risk. High-dose cisplatin is associated with nonreversible hearing loss. The eyes can also be affected, although cataracts may not appear for many years after the end of treatment.

Peripheral neuropathy can also occur. This results in numbness, tingling, pain, and muscle weakness. These symptoms often resolve at the end of treatment.

THE IMPORTANCE OF IDENTIFYING LATE EFFECTS

Physical

Identification of physical late effects is important for a number of reasons. First of all, there are issues for the individual patient in terms of information, counseling, and advice. Clear information about *lack* of risk can be as important for one individual as identification of risk is to another. Fertility is an excellent example. The possible link between radiotherapy, chemotherapy, and loss of fertility is often highlighted in the popular press, with the result that some survivors can worry unnecessarily. Yet information that fertility is not compromised is important so that individuals adopt appropriate behavior if they do not want a child. At the same time, individuals who may have fertility problems have a right to sensitive counseling and advice about any available treatments. Early identification gives time for individuals to make rational decisions about alternative courses of action. Currently, these can include egg or sperm donation. Where these options are unsuccessful, individuals may wish to look into adopting a child.

Second, and of greater interest to clinicians, if certain treatments can be linked to specific physical late effects, then future treatments can be planned, as far as possible, to use treatments less frequently associated with side effects. Thus, identification of physical late effects is important as part of the development and evolution of new treatments. This rationale lies at the heart of large-scale epidemiological studies aimed at linking different treatment protocols with subsequent physical late effects. Thus, awareness of possible long-term complications is not only important for optimizing the health care for current survivors but also for modifying future protocols to reduce unacceptable treatment related morbidity or mortality in the future.

Third, there are implications for the organization of health, social, and education services. Early estimates suggested that 1 in every 1,000 adults aged 20 years would be a long-term survivor of childhood cancer by the year 1990 (A. T. Meadows, Krejmas, & Belasco, 1980). These figures are likely to have increased substantially, and suggest a huge and growing burden on the health service, not only in terms of routine care, but also in terms of specialist follow-up of specific late effects.

Psychological

To some extent, we might use similar arguments to those described previously to justify interest in psychological or behavioral late effects. First, for the individual, identification of psychological late effects is important to direct remedial help. Difficulties in learning or memory following CNS irradiation after ALL or a CNS tumor is a good example. In these cases, it is essential to provide remedial education earlier rather than later.

Second, if it can be shown that certain treatments are more frequently associated with psychological problems, then revised protocols are needed. To some extent, this is what happened when radiation was linked with subsequent learning difficulties; revised protocols recommended use of CNS irradiation only for children with "higher" risk ALL.

Third, identification of psychological effects has implications for education, social, and clinical services. If survivors experience learning problems, then appropriate remedial services need to be provided. In general, the justification is that by determining the type and extent of problems, appropriate education and remedial services can be planned and implemented.

PSYCHOLOGICAL LATE EFFECTS

Psychological Adjustment in Survivors

Koocher and his colleagues can be credited with some of the first major studies of psychological adjustment in survivors of childhood cancer. Koocher et al. (1980) suggested that the most common problem areas included residual depression, anxiety, and self-esteem. In their seminal work, *The Damocles Syndrome*, Koocher and O'Malley (1981) reported that 47% of survivors experienced problems in psychological adjustment in the long term. The consequences of the disease were likened to the "Sword of Damocles," hanging ominously over survivors throughout their lives. This research, and the resulting book, has been extensively cited in later work.

Following from the work of Koocher, a number of subsequent reviews provided further evidence of a significant number of psychiatric or emotional difficulties among survivors. For example, Chang, Nesbit, Youngren, and Robison (1987) reported that 33% of survivors showed clinical evidence of a "moderate" degree of emotional difficulty. Similarly, Chang (1991) concluded that depression, anxiety, and drug dependency were the most common problems among adolescents and young-adult survivors, and school attendance and learning problems among school-age children. Chang's review is especially helpful. He was critical of the prevailing psychopathological model with its emphasis on abnormality, and suggested that the focus on crisis intervention may be of little value in explaining the concerns of families dealing with chronic illness and continuous stress. For these reasons, Chang recommended a shift from deficit-centered models to those that emphasize resilience and QOL.

Zeltzer (1993) described 21 studies, all but 2 of which were published before 1990. Like Chang (1991), Zeltzer identified a number of methodological problems in the literature and made recommendations for future work. In particular, she noted that cancer can affect the adolescent's ability to make the transition to adult life, perhaps by compromising the capacity for intimacy, decisions about career goals, and formation of an adult identity. She emphasized the need to consider survival and maintenance of good QOL at all costs.

Eiser and Havermans (1994) distinguished between three different approaches to measuring psychosocial outcomes in follow-up work. These included assessment of lifestyles (marriage, employment status), psychological outcomes (survivor ratings on standardized tests of anxiety, depression, etc.), and parents' reports of the child's functioning. Their review highlighted methodological difficulties in much published work and problems interpreting some of the lifestyle data. The need for different methodologies depending on the age of the survivor was emphasized. ("Lifestyle" data tend to be reported for older survivors and standardized measures of depression or anxiety used for younger survivors.) Many studies included samples differing widely in age and time since diagnosis. Differences in chronological age mean that it is difficult to assess outcomes with much sensitivity. Furthermore, the practice of including those who had been treated long before current protocols together with more recently treated survivors may limit the relevance of some of the findings for understanding the impact of modern protocols. Like Chang (1991), the authors noted the focus of assessment on maladjustment (depression, anxiety) as opposed to coping and adaptation.

In contrast to some of the earlier reports, Kazak (1994) concluded that most long-term survivors functioned well psychologically and did not have significant emotional problems. However, there was evidence of "more serious adjustment problems in subsets of the survivor population" (p. 188). Criticisms were made of methodologies, particularly the use of global measures of outcome and unstandardized interviews. Kazak emphasized that most work focused on survivors of ALL or Hodgkin's disease and concluded that more work should involve other survivor groups. There should also be more efforts to link biological and psychological variables. Interventions were found to be limited to those for acute distress or school reentry, and more work was advocated to improve adjustment among survivors and their families. It was emphasized that the way in which children cope and reorganize their lives on completion of chemotherapy was a critical but underresearched issue. The transition from a "patient on treatment" to "survivor" can be very difficult. Families come to feel some dependence on treatment and are fearful of relapse when treatment is finished. The concern is justified because risk of relapse does increase at this time. However, the authors concluded that not all survivors experience major adjustment problems and that there is wide variability in outcomes.

Eiser (1998) also emphasized the variability in psychological outcome among survivors and concluded that psychological problems were greater among those who continued to experience residual physical problems as a consequence of treatment. As distinct from previous reviews, more attention was given to issues about informing survivors about their disease, the development of interventions to facilitate school reintegration and academic achievement, and how to promote healthy lifestyles. Continuing psychological concerns among survivors about the possibility of relapse, and need for continuing care for those with fertility problems or chemotherapy and radiotherapy late effects were emphasized. Recommendations were made about the need for psychological support as an integral component of long-term care.

Eiser, J. J. Hill, and Vance (2000) conducted a systematic review of work published after 1990. They identified 20 published papers that fulfilled a minimum set of methodological criteria and attempted to account for inconsistencies in the literature that might be attributable to differences in measures, respondent (parent or child), or the type of cancer. The most frequently used measures included self-esteem (11), anxiety (5), depression (3), social skills (2), body image (2), loneliness (2), mood (2), personality (3), coping (1), health status/quality of life (1), social desirability (2), intrusiveness (4), symptoms (2), and PTSD (4). Three studies included specially developed interviews with standardized questionnaires.

A smaller number of measures were used for completion by parents. These included child behavior (4), family functioning (3), parental distress (1), parental social support (1), parent anxiety (1), and parenting stress (1). Measures used for teachers included the CBCL (teacher report form; Achenbach, 1991), the taxonomy of problem situations (Dodge, McClaskey, & Feldman, 1985), and the cancer-specific teacher behavior rating scale (Deasey-Spinetta & Spinetta, 1980). Almost all studies included only survivors of leukemia or heterogeneous groups of children with different cancers. There remains a need to conduct research that takes into account the different outcomes that are likely to follow depending on the specific cancer.

Differences Between Survivors and Healthy Controls. A number of studies suggest there are no differences between cancer survivors and healthy controls on measures of adjustment (Olson, Boyle, M. W. Evans, & Zug, 1993; T. Sloper, Larcombe, & Charlton, 1994); or self-esteem (Madan-Swain et al., 1994; Olson et al., 1993; T. Sloper et al., 1994).

Good adjustment was also reported by Stern, Norman, and Zevon (1993), but survivors reported a somewhat compromised self-image especially in terms of social and sexual functioning. Madan-Swain et al. (1994) found no major difficulties in social competence, overall coping, and family communication but survivors reported body image disturbance and adjustment difficulties.

An unexpected finding was reported by Elkin, Phipps, Mulhern, and Fairclough (1997), who contacted 161 survivors all of whom had been diagnosed at least 5 years earlier. Survivors were aged between 14 and 18 years on assessment and completed a Symptom Checklist (Derogatis, 1977). In addition, information about major medical events and therapies was taken from medical records. Cosmetic and functional impairments were rated separately as normal, mild, moderate, or severe.

The majority (75%) of patients showed some residual cosmetic impairments (although only 8.1% were rated as severely affected). Slightly fewer (64%) showed some physical impairment but only 2.5% were rated as severely affected. Scores on the Symptom Checklist were compared with norms for the general population and unexpectedly showed that survivors functioned very much *better* than might be expected. Older survivors and those who had experienced a relapse had poorer scores.

This study seriously challenges the assumptions of any deficit-centered approach to assessment of long-term survivors. Future work is needed to replicate these findings and clarify whether these are typical or reflect exceptional adjustment among a small group. Either way, research that clarifies how outcomes can differ *between* survivors may be more informative than work making comparisons with healthy populations.

Survivors, Parents, and Teachers. A second consistent finding is that parents and teachers tend to report that cancer has had a more detrimental impact than survivors do themselves (Olson et al., 1993; T. Sloper et al., 1994). Noll et al. (1997) compared parent and teacher reports of behavior and social competence for survivors of ALL aged between 5 and 18 years of age. These survivors had all been in continuous remission since diagnosis and had completed chemotherapy. The children had been treated by either CNS irradiation plus intrathecal methotrexate or intrathecal methotrexate alone. Parents, but not teachers, reported significantly more somatic symptoms in the children compared with population norms. In this study, variables that have previously been linked with problems, such as CNS irradiation or younger age on diagnosis, were not associated with different outcomes.

The Role of Appraisal. Although survivors with worse physical health tend to report poorer psychological adjustment, individual appraisal or perception of stress associated with the disease appears also to be critical. Varni et al. (1994) drew on the model described by Varni and Wallander (1988) to predict adjustment among survivors of childhood cancer. In this model, described in chapter 6, it is recognized that children treated for chronic and life-threatening conditions are potentially vulnerable, but emphasis is also given to social and family variables that may moderate vulnerability. The authors identified 118 patients who were diagnosed at least 5 years (range = 5–17 years) earlier, although only 39 took part in the study. On assessment, they ranged from 13 to 23 years. Survivors completed measures of perceived stress (Compas, Davis, Forsythe, & Wagner, 1987), psychological distress (Derogatis, 1983), and self-esteem (Harter, 1988). Multiple regression analyses suggested that perceived stress predicted 24% of the variance in overall psychological distress.

Further evidence that appraisal is important in determining adjustment was reported by Stuber et al. (1997). The survivor's subjective appraisal of life threat at the time of treatment was a significant predictor of PTSD in the longer term. Thus, there is some empirical support for the idea that the individual's perception of stress may be as important in determining adjustment as the physical restrictions of the disease.

THE RELATIONSHIP BETWEEN PSYCHOLOGICAL REACTIONS ON DIAGNOSIS WITH LONG-TERM ADJUSTMENT

Children (and families) who experience more problems in the period immediately following diagnosis are also those who report poorer QOL in later years. As described in chapter 10, Kupst and her colleagues studied psychological functioning over a number of years from diagnosis. Kupst et al. (1995) reported the adjustment of these survivors and their families 10 years following diagnosis.

Ten years after diagnosis, 32% had done well in school and were educated to college level. Three were experiencing learning difficulties. Psychological adjustment was poorer among those who had experienced school problems. For the whole group, psychological symptoms were within the normal range. Psychological outcomes were not related to age, gender, or previous coping, but were related to social class and maternal coping. Those from higher social classes and with mothers who coped well were also coping well themselves.

There are, therefore, indications that problems during the acute stages of treatment do predict later difficulties. In particular, work by Kupst et al. (1995) and Sloper et al. (1994) suggests that school-related difficulties can have implications for adult achievement and adjustment.

Body Image

Long-term concerns about body image are similar to those that have been described in the acute phase of the disease. Although body image changes associated with treatment, such as hair loss or weight gain, are not an issue in the longer term, many survivors continue to feel embarrassed about their hair or weight. Although these are essentially cosmetic problems, and may seem trivial in the overall context of surviving cancer, they can still cause considerable stress. In the longer term, cancer can affect other aspects of body image, including those associated with poor growth. Body image can also be compromised by awareness of fertility problems. Thus, simply being aware that you may have fertility problems can adversely affect your views about attractiveness and body image generally. There are many reasons, then, to be concerned about body image in survivors.

In addition to these generic risks to body image, survivors of a bone tumor are additionally vulnerable. With modern chemotherapy, survival rates for osteosarcoma between 60% and 65% can be achieved. Approximately 85% of patients are offered limb salvage and the remainder amputation. In limb salvage, the diseased bone is surgically removed and replaced by a metal prosthesis. Decisions about these treatments are taken partly on patient choice but are also dependent on the site and accessibility of the tumor. Most patients prefer limb salvage (it preserves body image), and amputations are restricted to situations where limb salvage is not possible. Neither treatment is associated with better survival. However, amputation may be preferred by those who wish to participate in contact sports. Participation in contact sports increases the risk of breakages and it is easier to replace an artificial limb than mend a prosthesis. The problem is that salvaged limbs can break, and patients can sometimes adopt sedentary lives rather than risk a breakage. Limb salvage is often recommended on the grounds that body image is less compromised compared with amputation. Attempts to determine differences in body image and QOL depending on the kind of surgery have failed to support this assumption. Some survivors reported wearing special clothes to hide the affected leg (e.g., long skirts or trousers), whereas others (all male) preferred to sport their scars as a sign of masculinity (Eiser, Cool, Grimer, Carter, Cotter et al., 1997).

Social Functioning

Detailed assessment of social functioning has been reported by Noll and his collaborators, in work that extends that with children undergoing treatment described in chapter 7. As described for children in treatment, the work concerned with social functioning in survivors has utilized the Revised Class Play procedure (Masten et al., 1990). During the course of a 2-year longitudinal study, Noll, Bukowski, W. H. Davies, Koontz, and Kulkarni (1993) examined adaptation in 19 survivors (11–18 years). These children had previously participated in studies of social function during treatment (Noll et al., 1990, 1991) and similar measures and procedures were adopted. Comparisons were made with healthy controls ($n = 17$ pairs). (Although all children in this study had completed treatment, follow-up was relatively short; the time since completion of treatment ranged from 14 to 33 months.) Data were collected from teachers, peers, and patients themselves. There were no differences between children with cancer and controls on measures of depression, anxiety, or self-esteem. Depression scores for children with cancer were not significantly different from population norms (Kovacs, 1992) and were in fact slightly lower than might be expected. Neither were there differences on any measures of friendship or popularity. Children treated for cancer rated themselves, and were more likely to be viewed by classmates, as sensitive and isolated. No differences between the groups based on teachers' reports were found.

Eiser, Cool, Grimer, Carter, Cotter et al. (1997) interviewed 34 young people successfully treated for a bone tumor. In addition to the interview, participants completed a cancer-specific (Perceived Illness Experience Scale [PIE]; Eiser et al., 1995) and a generic QOL scale (Ware, Snow, Kosinski, & Gandek, 1993). Further details about the PIE are given in chapter 16. The interviews were coded based on a theoretical schema derived from monitoring–blunting theory (Miller, 1995).

Negativistic monitors (a) sought out threatening information, (b) attended to possible threatening signs, (c) were fearful of injury, loosening or wear of the prosthesis, infection, and cancer recurrence, and (d) made frequent visits to their general practitioner (family doctor). Survivors in this group typically talked about their concerns and anxieties about their future health: "Yes, I did sort of get some lumps here, that sort of worried me, but they were just glands swelling and that but it is just that if suddenly I feel a lump on me I sort of ask my mum and she says 'go to the doctors.' When I sit down and watch TV I might sort of check myself over, it's just sort of a habit now. About three times a month, there is always like something going wrong with me, I go to the doctor" (female, 14 years old).

Adaptive monitors (a) sought out information, but did not always interpret this negatively, (b) appraised information realistically, (c) were aware of their limitations, (d) took adaptive steps to prevent or combat difficulties such as avoiding contact sports, and (e) made rare or occasional visits to their general practitioner. These survivors seemed to accept their potential limitations, but had worked out ways to live life to the full regardless: "So I've always got a good hold on things and you know. I'm very sort of safety conscious like that when I'm doing my work" (male, 21 years old).

Nonmonitors (blunters) (a) refrain from personal responsibility, (b) focus on a less relevant threatening aspect, and (c) withdraw from the situation. These survivors typically suppressed information about their health, and were generally uninformed: "I remember there was a fire in the recovery room. It was a toaster on fire, and they kept changing the sheets every few minutes. They put on a funny sock thing on my leg and I got blisters" (female, 16 years old).

Thirty of the 34 interviews could be clearly categorized into one of the three monitoring groups. In the remaining four instances, the interviews were reread and a global judgment made as to the predominant response being made. The three groups did not differ on clinical measures such as number of surgical procedures or time since diagnosis. However, negativistic monitors reported poorer QOL than the other two groups. This difference was most pronounced on subscales of the PIE measuring interference with activity, food, and preoccupation with illness. The pattern of results obtained using the generic measure mirrored those for PIE but did not reach statistical significance, suggesting that the disease-specific measure was more sensitive in this context.

This study provides some evidence that young people with cancer differ in their attempts to cope with the threatening information associated with treatment, and further that the kinds of coping adopted may mediate survivor-reported QOL. The most disadvantageous approach is one in which the patient seeks information but assumes the worst. In this study, patients who were aware of the possible implications of their condition, but used this information in a constructive way, reported the best QOL.

Posttraumatic Stress Disorder

The possibility of late psychological effects following any trauma in early childhood (e.g., Masten et al., 1990) is now widely recognized. The diagnosis of childhood cancer can predispose individuals to some of the symptoms of PTSD. PTSD has been defined as responses following the experiencing, witnessing, or confronting of an event involving actual or threatened violence or physical injury that evokes intense fear, helplessness, and horror. Cancer may be viewed as a series of potentially traumatic events that might be expected to be associated with PTSD in some survivors. Posttraumatic stress symptoms are categorized as persistent reexperiencing of the trauma (flashbacks); avoidance of reminders of the event or numbing of emotions; and increased arousal or hypervigilance. In children suffering from PTSD, physical symptoms, especially stomachaches, bad dreams, or repetitive play, are common.

Stuber, Christakis, Houskamp, and Kazak (1996) initially identified 179 survivors (7–19 years), although only 65 families were included in the analysis. The survivors were aged between 1 and 13 years on diagnosis and had completed treatment on average 6.7 years earlier. Questionnaires to assess PTSD (Frederick, Pynoos, & Nader, 1992) were sent by mail and families received $10 as payment. Specific symptoms endorsed by more than half the survivors included bad dreams, feeling afraid or upset when thinking about cancer, and feeling alone inside and nervous. Children who were older on diagnosis reported more symptoms. In total, 12.5% of survivors scored at a level that would be considered to indicate a clinical diagnosis of PTSD. The incidence of severe PTSD was even higher for mothers (39.7%) and fathers (33.3%). Further information about PTSD in parents is given in chapter 15.

Kazak et al. (1997) traced 130 survivors of leukemia, ranging in age from 8 to 19 years. Questionnaires were completed by survivors as well as their mothers and fathers. Again questionnaires were mailed and families who took part received $10 as payment. A control group was recruited through hospital clinics but did not include children with a chronic illness. There were no differences between long-term survivors and the control group in the incidence of PTSD. However, parents of survivors reported a higher incidence of PTSD than parents whose children had not had cancer.

In a later study, Stuber et al. (1997) traced 186 survivors aged 8–20 years. All had completed treatment at least 1 year earlier. The purpose of this study was to determine why some survivors show PTSD and others do not. Survivors and their parents completed a measure of PTSD (Frederick et al., 1992). In addition, to assess possible predictor variables, questionnaires were included to assess anxiety (C. R. Reynolds & Richmond, 1985) and social support (Cause, 1986). The authors also developed measures specifically for the study. These included the Assessment of Life Threat, Treatment Intensity, and Stress History. The Assessment of Life Threat included seven items to assess whether the survivor remembered details of the treatment, believed it was intense, and understood that they might have died. The stress history measure was used to assess other life stresses. Treatment intensity (mild, moderate, severe) was based on information about severity of medical late effects (none, mild, significant) and clinical variables such as diagnosis, BMT, and relapse.

Of those survivors who could be traced, 91% agreed to be sent questionnaires. Despite this initial willingness, replies were received from only 246 of 398 families. The sample was further reduced as the youngest children were not able to complete questionnaires alone. As a result, the analyses were based on data from 186 families.

Survivors reported "being afraid" or "upset when thinking about it" (49%), having bad dreams, (60%), "feeling more alone inside" (47%), or "having a changed worldview" (46%). The variables identified as contributing to PTSD included the survivor's subjective appraisal of life threat at the time of treatment, general levels of anxiety, other life stresses, time since completion of treatment, female gender, and family and social support. Thus, predictors of PTSD included anxiety, appraisal of life threat, and perception of treatment toxicity, but not medical variables, such as relapse or BMT. The authors concluded that interventions to reduce anxiety and stress appraisal during treatment are necessary to avert long-standing PTSD.

Problems in interpreting much of this work include the self-selection of survivors. Response rates are often poor, and many families reported that the questionnaires were upsetting or irrelevant or did not wish to be reminded about the illness (Stuber et al., 1997). In part, the lack of relevance is because measures of PTSD were developed to assess symptoms generally and do not necessarily reflect cancer-specific stress. Many of the studies also relied on use of mailed questionnaires. Lack of personal contact or inability to understand the purpose of the study may inevitably result in poorer response rates, compared with other methods.

LIFESTYLE INDICATORS

For older survivors, assessment of functioning has included educational attainment, occupational status, marital status, social relationships, and occasionally place of residence (within or outside the family home). Although much of the work described in the previous section suggests few psychological differences between survivors and healthy controls, the focus on lifestyle indicators points more consistently to a range of problems and difficulties with coping.

Green, Zevon, and Hall (1991) conducted one of the first comprehensive surveys of lifestyles among survivors. They collected data about marital status, employment history, occupation, health and life insurance status, as well as reproductive and family history from 227 survivors. Some 11% reported discrimination at work. Both health and life insurance coverage were lower than that reported for the United States population at the time. Marriage rates were also lower than for the general population. Though a history of childhood cancer did not affect an individual's decisions about getting married, it was cited as important when dissolving a marriage. In addition, a history of cancer was frequently reported to be influential when making decisions about having children. Male survivors were as likely to be employed as would be expected from employment statistics, but females were less likely to be in employment than females with no history of illness.

Gray et al. (1992a, 1992b) criticized much work on the grounds that standardized measures were inadequate to detect the kind of problems that affect survivors of childhood cancer. They argued that qualitative approaches were necessary to understand the impact of cancer on daily life. Both papers are based on the same sample of survivors, all of whom were aged 18 years or more and had completed treatment at least 2 years earlier. Survivors were asked to identify a friend of either gender who might be willing to serve as a comparison. Survivors were asked to discuss the impact of cancer on different areas of their lives including their personality, lifestyle, philosophy of life, religious beliefs, family relations, friendships, and marital relations. They also completed standardized measures of mood, control, and self-esteem. Survivors also completed the Impact of Events scale (Horowitz et al., 1979). Both survivor and comparison wore an electronic pager over a 1-week period and were cued periodically to answer questions about their current thoughts, feelings, and behavior.

Many survivors (63%) identified residual physical problems. These included problems with vision (25%), hearing (17%), hair (12%), bowel or bladder (12%), speech (10%), teeth (10%), skin sensation (7%), smell (7%), and taste (3%). However, despite the prevalence of physical problems, survivors did not differ from controls on standardized measures of perceived control or self-esteem. Among survivors, 20% believed that they had not been offered a job or been promoted because of their cancer history. Altogether 55% felt they had been "very much" affected and another 33% that they had been "somewhat" affected by the illness (but not all these effects were negative). Survivors were more likely to have repeated a school grade, less likely to be drinkers, and less likely to have experienced blackouts following a drinking episode compared with controls. However, they were likely to think more about people and less about ideas, preferred interacting with others, and reported more positive affect interacting with others compared with their peers.

It is perhaps difficult to interpret some of these findings, but Gray and collaborators suggested that the experience of cancer promoted a more serious and concerned approach to life, while at the same time increasing the ability to articulate feelings. Survivors valued relationships but had difficulties establishing and maintaining them. Some looked back on the time when they were ill and recalled intense, emotional, and highly charged relationships. In contrast with the intense emotions experienced during illness, survivors had difficulties accepting the mundaneness of everyday activities. For some survivors, current relationships lacked the intensity of those they remembered during treatment and consequently they were more dissatisfied. Dissatisfaction with relationships was based on what they believed could be possible between people. Although the survivors were not experiencing very different lifestyles from others of a similar age, cancer was nevertheless a major formative experience for the majority.

Mackie et al. (2000) used standardized interviews to assess lifetime psychiatric disorder and interpersonal and social role performance in survivors of ALL (67) or Wilms' tumor (45). Data were compared with individually matched healthy controls. There were no differences between the cancer survivors and controls in terms of major or minor depression. Incidence of major depression was low (4 vs. 3 respectively) although slightly higher for minor depression (15 vs. 16). Neither were there differences in numbers of examinations passed or those entering further education. However, cancer survivors reported poorer functioning in love and sexual relationships, friendship, nonspecific social contact, and day-to-day coping.

Academic Success and Achievements

In addition to the quite extensive and detailed work involving assessments of IQ and academic functioning in survivors of ALL and CNS tumors described in chapters 8 and 9, a limited number of studies have documented academic achievement among survivors generally. In these cases, interest has focused on the level of achievement reached, that is number of exams passed, placement in SEN programs, or involvement in higher education. S. E. Evans and Radford (1995) contacted 48 survivors of different childhood cancers and compared their school results with healthy siblings, and where possible, national statistics. Slightly fewer survivors (55%) compared with siblings (62%) achieved five or more A–C grades at GCSE (national exams completed at school-leaving age in the United Kingdom). Evaluation of this finding needs to be put in the context of the national average at the time (approximately 30% A–C pass rates). Thus, both survivors and siblings achieved higher exam success compared with the national average. Even so, survivors were less likely than peers to go to university. Survivors and siblings were equally likely to be involved in competitive sports and enjoyed an active social life, although more survivors than siblings had passed their driving test. Among the survivors there were three reported cases of employer prejudice. Few differences were found between survivors and their siblings, and there were indications that survivors achieved as well (or considerably better) than the general population at school-leaving age. Similar results were reported in the study described earlier by Mackie et al. (2000), who found no differences between cancer survivors and controls in terms of numbers of examinations passed or numbers entering further education.

Haupt et al. (1994) compared 593 survivors of ALL with 409 sibling controls. This large sample was recruited from 23 centers specializing in care of these children in the United States. Telephone interviews were conducted to determine the highest level of schooling completed, average grades obtained in high school, and enrollment in special-needs or gifted programs. Before diagnosis there were no differences between the groups in terms of SENs. However, after treatment, children with ALL were four times more likely to be placed in a special-needs or learning-disabled program. The relative risk (RR) was higher for females compared with males, but not significantly so. Survivors diagnosed during the preschool period and those who were treated with larger doses of CNS radiotherapy were more likely to be enrolled in special-needs or learning-disabled programs (RR = 2.8 and 2.9, respectively). Despite these problems survivors were as likely as their siblings to finish high school, go to college, or gain a bachelor's degree.

Kingma, Rammeloo, van der Does-van den Berg, Rekers-Mombarg, and Postma (2000) compared the school careers of 94 children treated for ALL with 134 of their siblings. Significantly more survivors had been placed in special educational programs compared with siblings. At the same time, survivors had completed significantly fewer terms of secondary schooling. However, there were no effects of gender on either of these findings. As reported in many previous studies, the most at-risk group were those diagnosed when younger. These findings suggest that school achievements may be compromised in the ALL group, but the response rate (questionnaires by mail) was not very good and the amount of detail limited.

These studies give quite different pictures about educational achievement in survivors. On the one hand, researchers in the United Kingdom (S. E. Evans & Radford, 1995; Mackie et al., 2000) interpret their data to suggest that academic achievement is good, whereas the studies from the United States and the Netherlands highlight difficulties for some. It is possible that some of these differences may be attributable to the organization of educational services in different countries. Schools in the United Kingdom are often reluctant to recommend that a child should repeat a school year and the processes involved in "statementing" and referral to special schools is cumbersome. In addition, there are differences in length of follow-up. In the U.K. studies, children were younger and outcome measures included number of exams passed or numbers entering higher education. In contrast, the other studies included children who were older on assessment and consequently longer since diagnosis. Part of the differences may be attributed to age differences in the survivors who took part. Schools are often very good at managing younger children with physical, psychological, or learning difficulties. However, families experience greater difficulties when the children are due to leave school.

Employment and Insurance

Given that the public often has little accurate information about the cause, treatment, or prognosis of cancer, it is likely that employers have negative expectations, anticipating many absences or that survivors may fail to "pull their weight" or expect to be treated differently from others. Some of the earlier studies (Teta et al., 1986) reported discrimination in the workforce generally and especially by the armed forces.

Hays et al. (1992) located 219 cancer survivors (aged 30–50 years) and compared their educational, occupational, and insurance status with a healthy age-matched control group. Interviews were conducted by phone and covered a range of psychosocial issues. Survivors were asked to identify up to six potential controls. These individuals were initially interviewed by phone to obtain demographic information and ensure the "best match" with the survivor.

No differences were found between survivors (all treated between 1945 and 1975) and matched controls on any of the variables assessed. However, more limited educational achievements and lower rates of marriage and parenthood were found for those treated for CNS tumors. Survivors of CNS tumors also reported greater interpersonal problems.

In a later study that included younger survivors, Hays et al. (1997) conducted telephone interviews with 300 of 986 eligible survivors aged 20 years or more. In 58 cases, where survivors were unable to participate (because of health or disability problems), a proxy was interviewed instead. As in the previous study by Hays and his colleagues (1992), a control was selected from six names originally given by the survivor. Further interviews were conducted with the six survivors to determine a "best match." Results are reported based on mean differences between survivors and their controls, and between survivors treated by CNS radiotherapy and those not treated by radiotherapy.

Cancer survivors had completed fewer years of schooling and consequently had lower educational status, higher rates of unemployment, lower occupational status, and lower annual incomes compared with controls. Within the group of survivors, those who had been treated by CNS irradiation had significantly lower levels of education and employment status compared with those not treated by CNS irradiation. For those in work, there were no differences in terms of number of days of absence or requests for special arrangements at work between cancer survivors and healthy controls.

Marriage

The situation regarding marriage rates is unclear, because different conclusions have been reached in different studies. Survivors experience lower rates of marriage and higher divorce rates compared with sibling controls or U.S. population norms (Byrn, Fears, Steinhorn, & Mulvihill, 1989; Green et al., 1991; Novakovic et al., 1996). These differences are more pronounced for males compared with females. As noted earlier, no differences in marriage rates in comparison with population norms were reported by Hays et al. (1992). Given that the average age on marriage in Western societies is now approaching 30 years, it is doubtful that marriage is a meaningful outcome variable for survivors below this age. This is an example of how psychosocial work needs to be constantly evolving, not only taking into account changes in medical practice, but also changes in societal norms and expectations.

CONCLUSIONS

There have been an increasing number of studies concerned with late psychological effects following treatment for childhood cancer. They have not specifically used measures of QOL, but relied on proxy indicators. A very limited number of proxy indicators have been used in published studies. Generally, these were not developed systematically to target areas that are likely to be of concern for survivors.

Development of measures that reflect issues of concern to survivors, perhaps a specific "late-effects QOL" measure could be useful, not least in ensuring some comparability across studies. Such a measure would also need to be sensitive to issues that reflect the needs and experiences of specific subgroups. Thus, a measure to reflect outcomes in children with a CNS tumor may not necessarily be identical with one needed for survivors of a bone tumor.

Attempts to reconcile discrepant findings in this literature tend to emphasize methodological problems in study design (Eiser & Havermans, 1994). Many studies include survivors of different cancers, thereby failing to take into account differences in severity of the cancer, its treatment, or initial prognosis. Many studies include small sample sizes; there is variation in chronological age of children on diagnosis and at assessment, and length of follow-up. Less often noted are differences in theoretical orientation of researchers. From a traditional deficit-centered approach (Drotar, 1981), it can be predicted that the experience of any chronic illness would be associated with maladjustment, and this indeed has been reported.

Others begin from an adaptive or coping perspective (Gray et al., 1992a, 1992b), and these authors do tend to emphasize the extent to which those with any chronic condition are indistinguishable from the general population, or in some cases, better adjusted.

The extent to which these findings could be accepted as an adequate database on which to develop follow-up clinics depends on the quality of the work and robustness of the findings. It is important to note that the literature very much focuses on those who experience adverse physical or psychological effects following treatment. There has not yet been a satisfactory study that clearly documents the extent of the problems, and the emphasis on negative effects may cloud the fact that some do survive the experience without adverse consequences. In assessing the literature, it is especially important to consider refusal rates. Although it is rarely known exactly why individuals refuse to take part in follow-up studies, it is possible that some do not wish to take part because they do not consider that there are any residual problems. The high mobility of the young population from which survivors are drawn adds to difficulties of recruiting representative samples.

There has been little systematic evidence that survivors of childhood cancer are distinguishable from the rest of the population, at least in terms of the relatively narrow range of measures employed. They tend to score similarly on measures of psychological adjustment such as anxiety or self-esteem. They do as well in school as healthy siblings. However, a number of risk factors associated with greater vulnerability have been identified. Younger children seem to be at greater risk than older children, especially if they were treated with CNS radiotherapy. Girls are more at risk than boys in terms of growth and hormonal problems. They are also more likely to underachieve at school. Although it has received relatively little attention, a child's social or family background may play an important moderating role.

Much of the evidence suggesting that psychological functioning is as good, or occasionally better, than occurs among the general population comes from self-reports. Typically, parents and teachers report more problems. This bias is not restricted to follow-up of survivors, but has also been shown whenever adults, compared with children, describe the effects of disease or treatment. A number of possible explanations have been put forward (see chap. 16), including differences in knowledge between parents and children or differences in expectations.

It is apparent that generalized findings such as these mask a considerable variability in how survivors come to terms with or make sense of their experiences. What matters is how an individual gives meaning to the illness experience. Clinically, these findings are of potential significance. It may not be possible to prevent illness or even to reduce adverse side effects, but it is possible to help an individual toward a cognitive evaluation of the experience that enhances future functioning.

The justification for research is often that identification of vulnerable children is important so that appropriate and timely professional support can be provided. Longitudinal studies from diagnosis till the end of treatment and beyond is important to answer this question. Sufficiently little research is really relevant, although there is some indication that children (and families) who have more psychological difficulties during the early period also show more disturbed subsequent functioning. Difficulties in obtaining funding are a major obstacle to work that is directly relevant to this very important question.

True survival is not just about recovering from cancer, but must include attainment of good general QOL, including opportunities for education, employment, and social relationships. Though children can be protected during their school years, the world of work can be more hazardous. Ignorance and prejudice on the part of career advisers can mean that opportunities that are very possible are denied to the individual survivor (Monaco, 1987). Monaco argued that career advisers and counselors need to overcome their own prejudices, become more informed about survival in childhood cancer, and be more practical and realistic in the advice they offer. Information also needs to be offered to employers. Prejudicial attitudes that survivors will have poor attendance records need to be challenged. There is some work that suggests that survivors of cancer are no more likely to have days absent from work than others (Hays et al., 1997; Stone, 1973), but more work of this kind would be helpful. In addition, the findings need to be communicated to prospective employers, and not simply languish in academic journals. Eiser, Cool, Grimer, Carter, Cotter et al. (1997) found that young people who had been treated for bone cancer had been given little realistic advice about appropriate career opportunities. This is potentially a huge worry for parents.

The findings have clinical implications to the extent that they could be used as the basis for development of appropriate follow-up care. Basic research of the kind reported in this chapter is potentially of huge value in planning and funding follow-up care. At the present time, awareness of physical late effects has driven the organization of follow-up care, with the emphasis on oncological follow-up. Psychological follow-up tends to be more *ad hoc*, with many hospitals being unable to offer very much in the way of psychological support. Yet our conclusions suggest that psychological follow-up is important for a number of reasons. First, there are psychological implications following any trauma and these need to be anticipated and addressed. Second, the incidence of physical late effects is high and will contribute further to psychological vulnerability. Third, psychological functioning is moderated by individual appraisal of the illness and such appraisals are likely to be influenced by appropriated counseling or intervention.

In the next chapter, the implications of this work for the organization of a comprehensive follow-up service for survivors are considered.

14

Lifestyles and Interventions

Summary

On the assumption that survivors may be particularly vulnerable to carcinogenic agents, it follows that they need to understand how their own behavior may influence their future health. For this reason, a number of studies have attempted to identify the incidence of risk behaviors, including tobacco, alcohol, and substance abuse among survivors compared with healthy controls.

Until recently, it was recommended that survivors should be reviewed in clinic on an annual basis. However, as the numbers of survivors has increased, this view has been challenged. There are questions about frequency of follow-up and who should most appropriately conduct it. Many argue that pediatricians are in the best position to provide continuing care and also most interested in determining links between treatment and subsequent late effects. On the other hand, transfer to adult care gives the message that there is a future.

There is undoubtedly a need to ascertain the causes of late effects of treatment, with the hope that successive generations of patients will benefit from informed protocol modifications. It has generally been acknowledged that it is not enough to give people health information but they need also to understand how they themselves can improve their health. This raises special problems in work with survivors to the extent that they have limited control over their future health. Interventions for younger children need to be developed, while they still attend clinic regularly. Information for survivors aged between 11 and 16 years is currently needed.

PROMOTING GOOD HEALTH

We are currently bombarded with information about the relationship between our lifestyles and vulnerability to a wide range of health outcomes. The relationship between smoking and lung cancer has been firmly established for some time (Peto, Lopez, Boreham, Thun, & Heath, 1992), and subsequently links between other lifestyle factors including diet or exercise and cancer have been identified. In fact, these lifestyle behaviors are important for health generally, and not restricted to cancer.

As discussed in chapter 2, the cause of childhood cancer is not known. However, it is known that certain lifestyle behaviors (smoking, sexual activity) are associated with the onset of some cancers in adults. If some behaviors are known to be associated with cancer, it follows that individuals who have had cancer once may be more vulnerable than those who have never had cancer. This assumption underlies work concerned with the lifestyles of survivors, with a clear agenda to target health promotion programs to the specific needs of young cancer survivors. They may feel they know about the link between smoking and cancer, but must accept their own heightened vulnerability. Health promotion therefore needs to be taken very seriously. For some, the message is particularly difficult to accept, as it goes against their view that they "survived cancer once, and could do it again."

Methodological Issues

On the assumption that survivors may be particularly vulnerable to carcinogenic agents, it follows that they need to understand how their own behavior may influence their future health. For this reason, a number of studies have attempted to identify the incidence of risk behaviors, including tobacco, alcohol, and substance abuse among survivors compared with healthy controls. As with any work in this area, there are difficulties about obtaining accurate estimates of substance use. Ideally, data can be obtained through observation studies. These are expensive (in research time) and some behaviors are more amenable to observation than others. (Observation studies have proved useful when studying sunbathing, for example, but pose more difficulties for studying illegal drug use.)

Self-reports, although much criticized, therefore tend to be more popular. There are, of course, questions about how truthful individuals are when reporting such behaviors. There may be temptations to overestimate drug use (if someone thinks it looks grown-up to smoke, for example) or underestimate (if the individual is concerned about the implications of illegal drug use). Because doctors routinely give out information that smoking is bad for you, survivors may be reluctant to be completely honest. Underreporting may also occur where data is collected from parents, because parents may not know whether or not their child is smoking. Ideally, smoking status should be confirmed with biochemical assays.

There are also statistical problems in conducting this research. In part, these reflect the low incidence of legal and illegal drug use (Verrill, Schafer, Vannatta, & Noll, 2000). Coupled with small sample sizes, many studies lack the statistical power to determine differences between groups with confidence.

Smoking, Alcohol, and Drug Use

According to both Gray et al. (1992a, 1992b) and Hollen and Hobbie (1993), survivors do not drink alcohol or engage in unprotected sex more frequently than healthy siblings or the general population. Haupt et al. (1992) concluded that survivors were less likely to begin smoking, but that if they did, they were less likely to give up compared with sibling controls. The authors compared 1,289 survivors with 1,930 sibling controls. After controlling for family factors, they found small to moderate differences between the two groups in terms of smoking status. Survivors were 8% less likely to smoke compared with siblings and 13% less likely to have ever smoked. However, if they were smokers, they were 12% less likely to have tried to give up smoking.

Mulhern et al. (1995) interviewed 110 parents of young survivors (aged 11–17 years) and 40 adult survivors (aged 18–29 years). Parents reported that less than 10% of younger children smoked. Among the older survivors, 47.5% said they had tried smoking, 17.5% were currently smoking, and 15% were using smokeless tobacco products. Parents reported less smoking by young people than might be expected, but this may reflect limited parental knowledge.

Verrill et al. (2000) compared aggression, antisocial behavior, and substance abuse in young-adult survivors and a matched control group. Reports were obtained from survivors and their parents. No differences between survivors and controls were found in aggression or antisocial behavior. Although there were no differences between the groups in self-reported use of tobacco or alcohol, the cancer survivors were less likely to report using illegal drugs. The authors argued that the experience of cancer during adolescence acts as a mild protective factor against illegal drug use. Experimenting with illegal drugs tends to begin at 12–15 years, the same age as when the young adults in this study were very ill. Thus, their illness, with its enforced period at home and away from the influence of peers, may reduce the opportunities to experiment with illegal drugs.

Tyc, Hadley, and Crockett (2001) questioned how well 46 survivors aged 10–18 years were informed about their vulnerability to ill-health if they smoked. Survivors reported that they were unlikely to take up smoking in the future, but they were relatively well informed and perceived themselves to be vulnerable. Older adolescents and those with less knowledge were more likely to express some intentions to smoke in the future.

Exercise

During active periods of treatment, children may lose physical fitness and put on weight. Consequently they find it difficult to participate in sports and exercise when they are well. Concern that survivors may be less active than healthy peers has led to a survey of exercise habits by Elkin, Tyc, Hudson, and Crom (1998). Long-term survivors (n = 251) aged 12–18 years completed questionnaires as part of a routine clinic visit. Participants were asked about their use of alcohol and tobacco and participation in organized sports. Those who stated that they did not participate in any sports were asked if they had more difficulty in sports compared with their friends. All patients were asked for information about insurance coverage and access to a local physician. Information about clinical variables (such as body mass index) was taken from medical records.

On the basis of these self-reports, 51% said they took part in organized sports. Among those who did not, 64% reported that they had no difficulty competing with peers. There were no differences between the groups in demographic or clinical variables including age, race, SES, diagnosis, or body mass index. The only difference was in insurance cover and access to a local physician, with those who took part in sports having better access to both. Self-reported rates of tobacco and alcohol use were very low, and therefore it was not possible to determine the relationship between use of tobacco and alcohol and exercise behavior. As would be expected from studies involving healthy children, more boys were involved in sports compared with girls.

Tillman, Darlington, Eiser, Bishop, and H. A. Davies (2002) found that survivors of ALL (not treated by CNS irradiation) were physically less active than their healthy controls. Furthermore, lower activity correlated with lower body mass density and higher percentage body fat. The worry is that lower body mass density will be associated with an increased risk of bone fractures as the children grow up.

INTERVENTIONS TO IMPROVE LIFESTYLES

Though many survivors of childhood cancer experience no or insignificant late effects, others are not so lucky. The risk of physical and psychosocial late effects, either as a direct result of the initial cancer or as a regrettable but unavoidable consequence of treatment, is very real. Given current knowledge of the likelihood and incidence of late effects, it is important that we consider a systematic approach to intervention.

Robison (1993) distinguished between primary and secondary interventions. Primary interventions include modification of therapy in order to reduce unnecessary toxicity. An example here is the introduction of regimens that do not include CNS irradiation in order to reduce the incidence of neuropsychological or learning problems. A second approach has been to modify the patient's susceptibility to adverse outcome. The hypothesis is that if organ function is suppressed during exposure to radiation or chemotherapy, then damage will be limited. Disappointingly, this approach has had only very limited success. Secondary interventions currently seem to have greater potential. These might include screening for early detection of late effects or developing remedial programs to help the survivor compensate for specific deficits.

FOLLOW-UP CARE

As the number of survivors increase, it is becoming clear that there is wide variation in the quality of survival. A proportion appear to have no or insignificant physical problems. Many also function as well as the general population, achieve as well academically, and appear to have no adverse clinical or psychological sequelae. There is, however, a whole range of outcomes, from minimal or no measurable effects, through to severe physical and/or mental handicap. Given the range of physical and psychological outcomes, and the need for information about survival in the longer term, it is imperative that all survivors are offered the opportunity for systematic follow-up and advice.

The aims of follow-up were summarized by Hawkins and Stevens (1996):

> It has become essential to know the risks of long-term complications, and to understand the specific elements of therapy and biological characteristics of survivors (particularly genetic factors) which are involved in the development of such complications. Such information would provide a sound basis: for counselling survivors and their families; for targeting surveillance of groups of survivors at particular risk with a view to early diagnosis and intervention; and for planning the composition of future protocols to achieve

an optimum balance between the risks and benefits of different treatment strategies. (p. 899)

Recognition of the range of possible late physical effects has prompted a call for continued surveillance of cancer survivors, partly on the assumption that early identification may be associated with better prognosis and partly for collective benefit. It is only by comparing the incidence of problems as a function of different treatment protocols that long-term cure with minimal complications can realistically be achieved.

Questions about the nature and frequency of follow-up for survivors are increasingly being debated. It is important to monitor the late effects of treatment, to provide health-related education for patients in order to enhance their long-term health, and to inform clinicians about the long-term needs of survivors. Those who oppose the establishment of long-term clinics argue that continual monitoring might increase anxiety and potentially create a stigmatized group. There is also a concern that clinics serve a primarily research basis with less emphasis on individual needs.

Transfer From Pediatric to Adult Care

The question of how to care most appropriately for young adults who have survived a chronic or potentially life-threatening condition in childhood is not unique to cancer. The question has recently become an issue in other conditions where survival rates are increasing, such as cystic fibrosis. Pediatricians are keen to continue to care for these patients and argue that their expertise with an essentially pediatric problem makes them better suited to provide care compared with adult physicians who may have very little experience that is directly relevant (Kurtz & Hopkins, 1996).

Survivors' Views of Follow-Up Clinics. As the number of survivors has increased, there have been calls for provision of specialist "late-effect" clinics (Masera et al., 1996). However, the form that such clinics take is dependent on the enthusiasm of staff and availability of space and time. Most clinics are organized in children's hospitals by pediatric oncologists. This can mean that survivors aged 20 years or more are seen routinely in pediatric departments.

The advantages are for the pediatricians in enabling them to monitor late effects of treatment. For patients, the proposed advantages include continuity of care. In theory, it is possible to see the same doctor throughout treatment. In practice, many staff leave or change their responsibilities. The doctor who specializes in diagnosis is not the same person who is skilled in detecting and treating late effects. Other disadvantages include the setting. In a pediatric clinic, the décor and availability of appropriate books or games to pass waiting time are unlikely to be suitable for older patients. Also in a pediatric setting, it may seem entirely appropriate that parents accompany the survivor. The presence of a parent may make it difficult for the survivor to discuss issues of concern. Many survivors will also have to attend other clinics, depending on their own special needs. Attending multiple clinics is time consuming for patients.

Providing appropriate care for survivors is therefore complex. One solution is to organize age-appropriate follow-up in adult hospitals. Another, perhaps overlapping, solution is to establish specialist clinics led by pediatricians and endocrinologists. Such jointly organized clinics should be welcomed, by reducing the number of clinics survivors have to attend and providing the appropriate range of expertise for their needs.

Eiser, Levitt, Leiper, Havermans, and Donovan (1996) attempted to obtain information from survivors about their preferences for different types of follow-up care. The study was prompted by awareness of the increasing number of survivors who failed to keep clinic appointments. (During the course of the study, 17% of survivors failed to attend appointments.) Information was collected from 93 young people (mean age = 16 years) and, where appropriate, their accompanying parent, who were attending a late-effects clinic. Although those who attended and completed the questionnaires were generally positive, some areas in which changes could be made were identified. Females expressed a preference to be seen by female rather than male doctors. Survivors wanted more information about possible complications of treatment, such as growth or fertility problems, and results of diagnostic tests. Survivors reported that doctors were less likely to discuss these issues and spent more time talking about general health promotion and progress at school than they thought necessary. Survivors were almost equally divided between those who felt they gained from attending and those who did not. Those who attended reported that they wanted new knowledge about their illness and reassurance about their current health. Those who perceived it was important to attend also seemed to have a greater understanding of the purpose of follow-up.

These survivors were generally poorly informed about their past illness and unclear about why they were asked to attend. Knowledge of the illness appeared to be poor, with 15 survivors not knowing the name of their illness and 5 only that they had had cancer. In contrast, their parents were more positive and expressed more intentions to continue to encourage their child to attend. These results are based on a single clinic, and as such may not reflect the views of survivors generally. However, knowledge was poor, supporting the idea that survivors need to be educated about the reasons for clinic attendance.

Kadan-Lottick et al. (2002) reported a far more extensive study in which 635 survivors were surveyed about their knowledge of cancer and understanding of how treatment could potentially influence their lives. Overall, 72% were able to describe their disease in some detail and another 19% gave accurate but limited information. As might be expected, survivors of a CNS tumor or neuroblastoma were less informed than survivors of other cancers. The authors explored knowledge of therapies known to be associated with specific late effects. Among those treated by radiotherapy, only 70% knew the site of therapy. Among those treated with anthracyclines, knowledge of the specific drug was limited.

The results of this study document the need to ensure that survivors are up-to-date about their treatment. Without accurate information, survivors may dismiss clinic follow-up as unimportant and fail to appreciate the significance of physical symptoms indicative of relapse or serious late effects. The problems become more acute for those who move or lose contact with the original treatment center. In the absence of information from medical records, the worry is that clinicians who are not familiar with the patient's medical history may fail to appreciate the potential importance of symptoms. With time, the responsibility for seeking appropriate care becomes that of the survivor.

PSYCHOLOGICAL INTERVENTIONS

Early identification of physical late effects is necessarily dependent on how well survivors understand their risk and how willing they are to attend follow-up. Inevitably, attendance at these appointments can decline with time, especially as survivors grow up and are no longer accompanied to follow-up by their parents. Nonattendance is costly for the health service, in that consultant time is not used effectively. Late-effects clinics are labor intensive because it is necessary to discuss complicated issues, such as plans for the future and need for further support. MacLean, Foley, Ruccione, and Sklar (1996) suggested that this side of care could be improved by the provision of written materials and/or video or computer-based instruction.

Although it is possible to identify theoretical reasons why it is appropriate to give survivors and their families information about late effects, there is for the most part very little that survivors can themselves do to reduce the risk in the future. There may be some exceptions. Survivors who are aware that they may have sustained heart damage can help themselves by not participating in extreme physical exercise such as weight lifting. Female survivors should take extra care when pregnant. Survivors can be made aware of dental risks and be encouraged to be very careful about oral hygiene and visit the dentist regularly (Clarkson & Eden, 1998).

But for the most part, survivors must live with the knowledge that they are at greater risk of a variety of physical problems and that there is relatively little that can be done. Very little is known about how survivors react to information of this kind. To date, we know little about how information about infertility, or the possibility of cardiac damage, affects self-esteem or decisions about lifestyle.

For parents, the increase in knowledge about late-effect risks has its costs. Parents often report distress associated with the seemingly endless information regarding possible late-effects damage. There is evidence that some mothers experience significant anxieties long after the original diagnosis (Kazak et al., 1997; van Dongen-Melman, Pruyn et al., 1995).

Clinicians too may be uncertain about how to handle this aspect of cancer treatment. The risks are not quantifiable; it is not always possible to be certain that late effects follow inevitably from treatment. To the extent that risks are very much in the future it does not always seem appropriate to burden families with concerns that may never happen. The possible impact of therapy on later fertility is perhaps the most difficult to handle. The question of how and when to communicate possible future risks associated with therapy is a central issue for those involved with long-term survivors.

New initiatives are constantly being developed and implemented with the goal of reducing the incidence or impact of physical late effects. Despite the relatively large and well-established literature concerned with social and psychological consequences following treatment, there has been little systematic attempt to provide appropriate psychological support. It is essential that new interventions are introduced and formally evaluated, although funding agencies are often reluctant to support such costly and time-consuming work.

Given the heightened vulnerability of survivors to cancer generally, interventions to reduce smoking or sunbathing are especially important (Robison, 1993). This kind of intervention can be particularly difficult, in that information about the dangers of smoking tend to be an integral part of population-based health education. Tyc, Hudson, Hinds, Elliot, and Kibby (1997) argued that existing school-based intervention programs may need some modification to be appropriate for survivors, and particularly need to include information about patients' heightened vulnerability to tobacco-related consequences. They pointed also to the potential role of clinicians in advising survivors about their risk and assisting those who wish to give up smoking. Special consideration needs to be given to young cancer patients in order to influence their beliefs about smoking prior to the peak age of tobacco initiation of 12 to 14 years.

Hudson et al. (1999) developed a simple intervention designed to educate survivors about their risk of late effects and motivate them to practice health-protective behaviors. Survivors attending a long-term follow-up clinic were randomized to standard care or standard care plus intervention conditions. Survivors were aged 12–18 years, had been off therapy for at least 2 years, and had no chronic medical problem requiring them to be seen more than once or twice per year. The educational intervention was integrated in the annual check-up. Survivors were given late-effects risk counseling and a clinical summary of their past treatment. In addition, they made an individually determined commitment to practice a health-protective behavior during the subsequent year and were given relevant training to achieve their chosen goal. A research nurse made telephone follow-ups at 3 and 6 months.

Eighty-six percent of survivors approached agreed to participate in the program. Survivors chose programs to help them reduce dietary fat, take part in regular aerobic exercise, perform monthly breast or testicular examination, lose weight, use sun protection, and give up tobacco.

In a 1-year follow-up study, Hudson et al. (2002) reported limited success. There were no differences between those who had been involved in the intervention and a control group who received standard care in terms of knowledge or health care behavior. For the most part, females showed a bigger improvement in knowledge than males. Those who chose breast or testicular examination as their health-related goal were more likely to report frequent practice. This contrasted with those who chose sun protection or weight control. These patients did not report keeping up the practice throughout the year.

In the intervention group, there was a significant increase in perceived seriousness of health problems associated with cancer treatment over the year, but disappointingly few other differences between the intervention and control groups. In part, these may reflect high-quality care delivered on a regular basis at the hospital. In addition, it must be acknowledged that young people are highly resistant to health promotion of this type. Attention needs to be given to the timing of interventions. Survivors who see themselves to be doing well may be particularly impervious to ideas that they should worry about their long-term health.

What Survivors Need to Know

The evidence available suggests that young-adult survivors are relatively poorly informed about their past illness, the possible implications for their future, and what they themselves can do to ensure as good health as possible. This may be the case, but in fact there has been very little systematic assessment. Survivors vary in their interests in their illness history, though for many, interest seems to be heightened at special times, when they are thinking of marriage or children, for example. Interventions to improve awareness and encourage attendance at follow-up are needed.

A booklet for survivors to increase awareness of vulnerability and clarify the purpose of regular check-ups and screening was recently developed by the UKCCSG. The booklet was well received, at least among those who attended clinic regularly (Blacklay, Eiser, & Ellis, 1998). Evaluation was based on reports of 50 survivors (25 males) aged 14–32 years. Survivors were contacted at follow-up clinic, completed a brief interview to determine their level of information and wish for information, and were then offered the booklet. Follow-up interviews were made by telephone 1–2 weeks later. There was a positive response in that all those who were offered the booklet were keen to read it. Over 75% reported that they learned something. Fears that the information might increase anxiety were unfounded and there was no indication of any adverse psychological reactions to the information. Positive effects included an increase in understanding of the risks associated with sunbathing and greater appreciation of the need for follow-up.

In a subsequent study, Eiser, J. J. Hill, and Blacklay (2000) replicated the aforementioned findings with a larger sample ($n = 263$). They argued that the value of any intervention was partly dependent on the individuals' preparedness to accept new information. To determine this, they borrowed ideas from the theory of stages of change. According to Prochaska et al. (1994), individuals move through a series of stages when contemplating and implementing behavior change. At any given time, an individual may be at any one of seven stages. At Stage 1, the individual is unaware of the problem. At Stage 2, the individual is aware of the problem but has never seriously considered adopting appropriate behavior. At Stage 3, individuals have considered adopting more appropriate behavior but decided against it. At Stage 4, the individual is considering taking up appropriate behavior. At Stage 5, the individual has decided to act, and at Stage 6, is actively participating in appropriate behavior. At Stage 7, the individual has successfully maintained the behavior for some time. Applied to issues in the late-effects clinic, it was hypothesized that the intervention would result in few changes of behavior and be viewed less positively by those in the earlier stages. In contrast, those who were seriously considering the implications of cancer for their future health would be more likely to take on board the recommendations in the booklet and also rate the information more positively.

The findings offered only partial support for these hypotheses to the extent that there were no differences in evaluations or intentions to change behavior depending on the stage identified at the start of the study. However, any effects of stage may have been masked by the positive response overall. There was an increase in professed readiness to change behavior and confidence about how to do this over the course of the study. Those who agreed to take part held more positive attitudes about clinic attendance but also saw themselves to be more vulnerable to future health problems. Thus, they may well have been at higher stages compared with those who were not interested in taking part.

The study raised serious questions about the value of the intervention for male compared with female survivors. Males were less willing to take part in the study at all and less positive about the value of the information. These gender differences are commonly reported in health promotion work; women are more interested in health issues and take them more seriously. This may reflect a view among some men that health is in some way effeminate. Lack of interest and knowledge may well contribute to compromised health in male compared with female survivors.

Some cautions need to be made about this series of studies. Although many survivors welcomed the information, a small number reported that it was very distressing. In addition, survivors did see themselves to be more at risk of future health problems after reading the booklet. Although it is important that survivors understand their vulnerabilities to health problems, it is also important that they are not made to feel unnecessarily vulnerable.

There is also the question of younger survivors. There is an increasing cohort of children who have been treated for cancer at very young ages and may be considered long-term survivors by middle childhood. For a child who is 2 years of age on diagnosis and finished treatment by 4 years, understanding of the illness is likely to be very minimal. In recognizing this, Eiser, Blacklay, and H. Davies (1999) described a simpler version for children aged 10–16 years. Based on social learning theory (Bandura, 1977), the booklet tells the story of Sam, a survivor of childhood cancer who sets out to find out about his cancer history. Sam wants to know what causes cancer, why he comes to follow-up clinic, and why he is always weighed and measured. There are also sections on lifestyle issues; why it is important to exercise or not to bathe in the sun.

Again, evaluation of this booklet for younger survivors suggests that the information is welcome and acceptable (Absolom, Eiser, Greco, & H. Davies, 2003). However, the acceptability of the information was dependent on survivors' perceptions of its personal relevance to them. This is consistent with the argument that as an issue increases in personal relevance, individuals become more motivated to devote the cognitive effort required for a thorough evaluation of the arguments presented. Conversely, when personal relevance is low, people are less motivated to engage in the considerable cognitive work necessary to evaluate the arguments and rely more on peripheral cues to evaluate the information (Petty & Cacioppo, 1984). The implications are that to be maximally useful, survivors need to understand the importance of information before they accept its personal relevance and are prepared to make changes to their own behavior. Thus, there needs to be continuity throughout treatment, so that survivors are not suddenly confronted with potentially threatening information about which they were not previously aware.

Provision of Late-Effects Clinics

It is clear from the preceding sections that the current evidence base to guide the establishment of a structure for long-term clinical follow-up is incomplete. In an ideal world, many pediatric oncologists and hematologists would like to be able to follow up all survivors of childhood cancer indefinitely. In line with this view, it has been recommended that all centers specializing in care of children with cancer establish long-term follow-up clinics (Masera et al., 1996; Neglia & Nesbit, 1993). The establishment of such clinics would enhance clinicians' understanding of the long-term effects of cancer survival and lead to a comprehensive method of assessment for these patients. The long-term commitment raises questions about the setting of such clinics. Establishment of late-effect clinics in pediatric departments assures continuity in care for patients and facilitates the flow of information about late effects back to those involved directly in care of new generations of children. Provision needs to be made, however, to ensure that those providing the service are informed about issues of relevance to adult survivors.

Masera et al. (1996) made a number of recommendations regarding the organization of care in a late-effects clinic: "The goal is to promote long-term physical, psychological and socio-economic health and productivity, not merely to maintain an absence of disease or dysfunction. We need a proactive and preventive set of 'standards for care', ones that offer services for possible clinical problems and regular check-ups" (p. 1). The authors recommended that long-term care must begin as the child completes active therapy. The oncologist, nurse, social worker, and psychologist should meet with the family to review the past and plan the future. It is important to involve the local pediatrician or family doctor at this stage. Counseling needs to be provided and the family must be aware of any likely future problems associated with treatment toxicity. The family needs to be provided with a written summary.

An "off-treatment" clinic should be established "orientated to the preventive medical and psychosocial care of long-term survivors" (Masera et al., 1996, p. 2). This clinic should be managed by pediatric oncologists with the support of specialists as necessary (cardiologists, endocrinologists, etc.). Psychological counseling should be available, as well as information about avoidance of health risks. In parallel with these clinics for survivors,

Masera et al. recommended a public health program to inform the public about childhood cancer and current treatment, overcome discrimination, and educate survivors to be advocates for their own social and economic futures.

As the numbers of survivors increase, it becomes clear that it may not be possible to provide a pediatric-based follow-up service indefinitely. Wallace et al. (2001) raised the question that more targeted follow-up may become increasingly appropriate. It may be possible to identify a group of survivors for whom the benefit of clinical follow-up is not established and for whom postal or telephone follow-up may be all that is required. For those patients who have been treated with surgery alone or with low-risk chemotherapy, postal or telephone follow-up every 1 or 2 years may well be sufficient. Other groups, for instance survivors of BMT or those treated with radiotherapy, are likely to benefit from continued clinical follow-up. The increasing number of survivors means that provision of alternative types of care, including nurse- or general practitioner–led follow-up, may be the way forward.

CONCLUSIONS

It is apparent that many children have an impressive ability to come to terms with the cancer experience and, in adulthood, are indistinguishable from the general population. This has to be seen as a remarkable achievement and should not be trivialized. At the same time, it is important to recognize that a proportion of survivors experience genuine difficulties in adjustment, which may be aggravated by physical complications of the disease or by adverse social circumstances.

Most research on late effects has focused on identification of physical problems. These studies are conducted by oncologists and hematologists. There is a focus on treatment modalities and careful reporting of the measurement and incidence of physical late effects. Though exemplary in many ways, these studies rarely include any measure of the meaning of the illness or disability for the survivor. In contrast, psychological follow-up tends to be conducted by social scientists or social scientists together with clinic staff. Despite this apparent collaboration, there is rarely any detailed analysis of the relationship between physical and psychological late effects. In psychological research, simple clinical data such as diagnosis or duration of treatment is all that is routinely included. Exceptions are studies involving follow-up of intellectual and cognitive late effects, where information about treatment regimens is perceived to be critical. Closer integration of physical and psychological follow-up is essential with specific hypotheses being generated to account for any psychological difficulties associated with the physical complications of a specific treatment regime.

Although systematic information about the physical late effects of cancer treatment is now being coordinated on a national basis, information about emotional or psychological late effects remains fragmentary. Consequently, it is difficult to make accurate predictions regarding the need for formal follow-up among either these patients or their families. It is imperative that national studies are established to determine the incidence of social and psychological problems among survivors, work that should be conducted in parallel with research concerned with identifying the incidence of physical late effects.

Despite the methodological criticisms that can be made of the literature, it is clear that some survivors experience difficulties. Based on this information, it is possible to make some recommendations about the appropriate psychological support necessary in late-effects clinics.

Physical

Survivors with physical late effects need appropriate medical care, but will also benefit from appropriate psychological support. For example, survivors of a bone tumor need routine review to assess the prosthesis. Where there are concerns about fertility, survivors will benefit from appropriate assessment and information about the alternative treatments available.

Recognition of the possibility of physical and psychological late effects places a legal obligation on clinicians to inform survivors and their families and to try to ensure that individuals are sufficiently aware that they do not aggravate that risk further. The communication of this information is difficult, not least because often the risks cannot be quantified in any individual case. In addition, individuals have only limited opportunities to control their future health. Communication of risk information may be required, but we know little about how individuals deal with the knowledge that they are vulnerable to future ill-health as a consequence of past treatment. There are clear roles for psychological support in situations of this kind.

Physical late effects also have implications for emotional and social functioning. For those with fertility problems, discussion of the various alternatives needs to take place sooner rather than later if unnecessary distress is to be avoided. Impartial advice about additional treatments is necessary. Survivors with growth problems need to understand the possible advantages and disadvantages of GHT before embarking on lengthy and costly therapy. It is important that these survivors understand that although the treatment may result in improved height, it is not a panacea for all ills. They may still be bullied and people will still try to put them down. They have to appreciate the limitations of therapy to avoid unnecessary disappointment.

Emotional

All types of emotional outcomes have been reported. Writers such as Chesler (1990) very much emphasize the positive outcomes that can occur. Where positive outcomes are reported, they tend to focus on reappraisal of life, putting things into perspective, and being less bothered by daily hassles. A number of studies conclude that survivors are no different from population norms or control groups. Although these conclusions are based on group mean differences, they may include those who attribute some positive outcomes to the experience as well as those who focus more on negative consequences. At one extreme, studies of PTSD particularly emphasize the negative emotional consequences.

The occurrence of PTSD and needle phobia following treatment has been documented. Provision of appropriate therapy in each case is essential. There is evidence that needle phobia responds well to interventions based on behavior therapy.

A consequence of cancer treatment is the very close relationship that can develop between child and parent. In situations where this becomes damaging, the survivor may have difficulty forming other relationships or be reluctant to leave home and branch out alone. In these situations, sensitive counseling for both survivor and parent may be necessary.

Social

Again, a range of outcomes have been described. Much of the work has been conducted by Noll and his collaborators and points to compromised social function, at least for survivors of school age. However, there are difficulties in measuring social behavior, and inconsistencies between children and adults in their assessment of social functioning. Other work suggests that social difficulties can continue into adult life (Gray et al., 1992a, 1992b).

Education and Employment

There are some reports suggesting few differences in terms of school achievement between survivors and either their healthy siblings or population statistics. These findings, which suggest no significant mean differences between groups, undoubtedly hide considerable variability. Clinically, a whole range of learning outcomes can be identified. However, subgroups of survivors, notably those treated with cranial irradiation, are at considerable risk in terms of learning difficulties. Survivors of a brain tumor, or ALL treated with irradiation, are more likely to repeat a school year or have SENs compared with healthy brothers and sisters. These research findings should be used to target educational resources appropriately.

To ensure optimal adult functioning, assessment of educational, behavioral, and social functioning may be important throughout treatment, especially for those known to be at special risk because of their specific treatment. Counseling with regard to school achievement and future work opportunities is also called for. Survivors may need to accept that certain opportunities are closed to them (work in the armed forces). Survivors with specific handicaps (including survivors of a bone tumor who have difficulties with mobility) need specific and realistic advice about work opportunities.

On diagnosis, there has been concern about the possible implications of cancer for the child's social function, and efforts are made to inform schools and facilitate the child's return and integration in the classroom. These initiatives remain important over time. Schools need to be kept informed about changes in the child's condition, so that they can maintain a balance between the needs of the sick child and goals to optimize participation in school activities. Psychological support in the long-term clinic must therefore include school–hospital liaison, with the goal to facilitate better academic functioning and promote optimal social relationships.

There is ample evidence that children experience school absence and academic difficulties during treatment. Children with ALL or CNS tumors are more likely to need special educational provision than other children. For these children, it is likely that these disadvantages will continue to affect long-term career plans and work opportunities. For children with disabilities generally, there is a lack of support and provision beyond school. It has to be assumed therefore that children with SENs require additional help when leaving school and parents need good information about local opportunities for further education. For children of normal intelligence, the limited data currently available suggest that they are as likely to enter further education as their brothers and sisters. There remains a need to determine longer term outcomes for these children, and more important, to provide a specialist service especially for those with learning difficulties.

Although it is customary to consider late effects as discrete (learning problems or social problems), it is likely that there is considerable interdependence. A survivor with physical problems may be unable to take part in sports, but the effects on this may be to reduce personal confidence and limit social opportunities. (If a survivor is unable to play football, he may also be less likely to be part of the after-match social events.)

As a result, even relatively minor problems in one area can have implications for others.

As more clinics are established specifically for survivors, it is important to recognize that the needs are for psychological as well as physical support. With the increasing number of survivors, the organization of clinics is under review. Such reorganization must adopt a holistic perspective and recognize the interdependence of physical and psychological health and well-being.

15

Long-Term Issues—
The Impact on Parents

Summary

Treatment for cancer is very unpleasant and the prognosis for any individual child is uncertain. Parents have to accept that cancer is a life-threatening disease and that survivors are at risk of residual physical, emotional, and behavioral late effects. Caring for a child with cancer can stretch family emotional and financial resources to the limit and compromise parents' mental health and their opportunities to take part in normal work and social activities. In the final analysis, then, it is important to assess how far all of this takes a toll on parents' own physical and psychological well-being.

In previous chapters, we have seen how much is demanded of parents in the period following diagnosis. Although the everyday demands decrease when treatment ends, there are still many anxieties. Concerns about the child's education, employment, and ability to live independently can take the place of treatment-related worries. For all families, the ultimate fear is of relapse following treatment. In these cases, parents and children must accept the need for further treatment, often with a compromised chance of survival. Diagnosis of relapse and the subsequent need for BMT can impose further burdens on families.

In this chapter, the focus is on parents' views. First, this is considered in relation to their own mental health, well-being, and physical health, and second on their assessment of the impact of cancer on the relationship between them and their child.

PARENTS' VIEWS ABOUT THE IMPACT
OF ILLNESS ON THE CHILD

Treatment for cancer is long, highly distressing, and affects parents in many different ways. With time, it is hoped that anxieties will lessen, but the extent to which life returns to "normal" is not clear. In fact, it is perhaps naive to think that an experience such as having a child diagnosed with cancer can have no lasting psychological impact at all. For parents, who tend to be better informed than their children, worries about possible late effects can continue to be a problem, long after the end of treatment. As we have seen, completion of therapy does not always mean that there are no residual problems. Parents must be very disappointed to learn that completion of therapy often does not mean total cure. In that the child's physical health can be severely compromised by radiotherapy and chemotherapy, there may be a need for further treatment, beyond anyone's initial expectations. Furthermore, many survivors have multiple problems, necessitating follow-up in a range of clinics. Although cancer is cured, children may still need regular medical attention to address some of the physical problems associated with cancer or its treatment. Many families can feel confused, angry, and let-down by this situation. It should not therefore be surprising that, even though treatment has finished, parents may continue to show signs of distress, worry, and poor family functioning, years after diagnosis.

On diagnosis, the child is often very ill and it is clear that medical treatment is vital to save life. The focus is on the day-to-day aspects of treatment, with very limited, if any, glimpses into what the future might hold. This attitude is often encouraged by clinic staff, who understand the child's tenuous hold on life. There is no point in dwelling too much on what might go wrong. Parents have enough to worry about, so that information about future scenarios is not uppermost in their minds. However, for all families, there comes a point, sooner or later, when the future does become an issue. For all that the concern on diagnosis is with saving life at all costs, sooner or later issues about the quality of life saved come to the fore. This can take the form of specific worry about school progress, work opportunities, or fertility problems, or just generalized anxieties.

Many studies attest to the extent and seriousness of parents' concerns and worries. These can include the possibility of future health complications and relapse, delays in the child's social development (Leventhal-Belfer, Bakker, & Russo, 1993), worries about the child's health, and concerns about being overinvolved with the child (W. H. Davies et al., 1991). Overholser and Fritz (1990) reported that parents identified personal distress, marital discord, and financial burden as continuing problems. Lack of support was associated with increased emotional distress among parents. Some parents continued to mourn the psychological losses of the illness, including the health of their child, or the fact that their healthy child has gone and will never return (van Dongen-Melman, van Zuuren, & Verhulst, 1998).

PARENTS' LONG-TERM HEALTH

In that there are often reminders of the illness, in the form of clinic appointments or news stories about other children with cancer, it is difficult for parents to put the whole experience to the back of their minds. Despite all of this, there is evidence that although parents' mental health does not get back to "normal," it does improve with time.

In practice, the experience of having a child with cancer, and the accompanying highs and lows of treatment, have to impact on parents' emotional well-being and attitudes toward life. However, this is not necessarily in a negative direction. Greenberg and A. T. Meadows (1991) reported that although some parents reported many negative comments about the experience (health worries, marital problems, anger, and guilt), they also identified more positive outcomes including the acquisition of new values and attitudes, improved marital adjustment, and social support. Parents often perceived significant changes in relationships during treatment positively, and looked back on people they had known at this time in a positive way (Kvist, Rajantie, & Siimes, 1991).

A number of methods have been reported to determine parents' mental and physical well-being after the child has completed treatment. These include comparisons with groups of parents with a well child, comparisons with parents of a child on treatment, and longitudinal studies tracing changes in mental health throughout treatment.

Comparisons With Normal Populations

Speechley and Noh (1992) reported no differences in depression or anxiety between parents of cancer survivors (who had completed therapy 1–15 years earlier) and healthy controls. However, where parents had little social support, those with a child with cancer were more depressed and anxious. Perceived social support was more important for mothers than fathers.

C. M. Davies, Noll, W. H. Davies, and Bukowski (1993) reported no differences in family functioning between parents of survivors and a matched control group. These authors argued that conflict might be particularly pronounced during mealtimes, because many children remain poor eaters after chemotherapy. Although the children were off treatment and at a low nutritional risk at the time data were collected, all had suffered from nausea and vomiting earlier in treatment. In fact, there were no differences between the two groups in terms of mealtime conflicts, parents' concerns about the child's eating, or satisfaction with the child's food intake.

Paralleling the work with children with cancer and survivors, there has been some recent interest in the incidence of PTSD among parents of survivors. This suggests that parents report more symptoms of PTSD than parents of healthy children, and more than survivors themselves. Stuber et al. (1994) reported that 25% of fathers and 27% of mothers reported moderate levels of PTSD symptoms. Seven percent of mothers reported severe symptoms. For both mothers and fathers, there was a significant correlation between PTSD and anxiety. A relationship was reported between mothers' symptoms of PTSD and their child's appraisal of treatment intensity.

According to Stuber et al. (1996), nearly 40% of mothers and one third of fathers reported symptoms consistent with a severe level of PTSD. Mothers reported reexperiencing disturbing scenes and being afraid when thinking about what happened. Fathers reported experiencing intrusive thoughts, fearing recurrence of cancer in the child, and having difficulties concentrating and remembering.

Barakat et al. (1997) found that 10% of mothers had symptoms of PTSD within the severe range and 27% within the moderate range (compared with 3% and 18.2% of comparison mothers, respectively). They reported intrusive thoughts, hypervigilance, and distress at being reminded of their child's illness. Fathers also reported more PTSD symptoms: 7.1% scored within the severe range and 28.3% were in the moderate range (compared with 0% and 17.3%, respectively, for comparison fathers). Again, parents of survivors reported more long-term stress than survivors themselves.

Not surprisingly, mothers of children who had survived cancer reported significantly higher levels of PTSD than did mothers of healthy children. Mothers of cancer survivors reported intrusive thoughts about the diagnostic interview, impaired sleep, fearing the future, and feeling devastated (Kazak et al., 1997; Pelcovitz et al., 1996).

Van Dongen-Melman, Pruyn et al. (1995) interviewed 133 parents of 8- to 12-year-old children who had completed therapy 6 months to nearly 8 years previously. For both mothers and fathers, uncertainty and loneliness remained problems despite the fact that their child had completed treatment; almost 90% of parents reported feeling uncertain about the future. However, the self-reported incidence of anxiety, depression, disease-related fear, sleep disturbances, and physiological or psychological problems was low (although no comparisons were reported with population norms). There was no relationship between parents' well-being and many characteristics of the disease, such as the length or intensity of treatment or the child's initial prognosis. However, parents of children who underwent surgery reported more residual problems compared with parents of children who did not experience surgery.

Given the nature of the disease, many parents whose child develops cancer may face difficult decisions about whether or not to have more children. Decisions about family planning may be influenced by a number of factors. Lack of information about exactly why the child developed cancer can contribute to feelings that future children may also be vulnerable. Parents may simply feel that the sick child needs so much care and attention that it would be impossible to be able to care adequately for other children. In a small number of cases where there is a known inherited risk (such as retinoblastoma), parents may be anxious not to have another child with the same problem. In other cases, despite the fact that there is little known risk, parents may be reluctant to have other children for fear that they too may develop cancer.

Van Dongen-Melman, De Groot, Hahlen, and Verhulst (1995a) investigated the way in which the diagnosis of cancer in a child affected parents' decisions about having any more children. One hundred and thirty parents of 68 children aged 8–12 years were interviewed about their plans and opinions about having more children. Before diagnosis, parents described their families as: complete ($N = 68$), undecided ($N = 32$), and intending to have more children ($N = 30$). Decisions about future family planning were coded into one of four categories. These included whether family planning (a) was affected and parents decided against having more children, (b) was affected toward parents wanting another baby, (c) was not affected, or (d) was undecided or unknown. Seventy-five percent of parents reported no change in their family planning. Those parents who were undecided about whether or not their family was complete prior to diagnosis were more likely to change their plans because of the experience of cancer in their child. Most (59%) in this group reported being affected, with the majority deciding not to have further children. Among those who had not completed their family before diagnosis, eight reported a change in their intended behavior, with three parents deciding against having more children and two deciding to delay further children. The authors concluded that "an affected rate of 59% in the unsettled group shows that the likelihood of a change in family planning is high when confronted with childhood leukaemia/lymphoma" (p. 195).

Comparisons With On-Treatment Families

As might be expected, mothers of children who were on treatment were more poorly adjusted and had higher levels of anxiety compared with mothers whose child had completed treatment (Moore & Mosher, 1997).

Longitudinal Studies

Although the evidence is not entirely conclusive, the way in which families react on diagnosis and immediately afterward does seem to predict longer term functioning. Parents who reported more emotional strain during treatment were more likely to feel and express anger toward the patient even when treatment had ended (Overholser & Fritz, 1990). Similarly, Kazak and Barakat (1997) found that parents who registered high levels of stress during treatment were more likely to have higher levels of state anxiety after the child completed treatment. Mothers who reported more symptoms of PTSD also felt that their child had a poorer QOL.

RELAPSE

If parents whose child has done well typically report so many worries and concerns, it is not surprising that those whose child relapses will report even more. Despite the potentially devastating implications of relapse, surprisingly little research has focused on the impact of relapse on families. As would be expected, both mothers and fathers of children who relapsed reported more feelings of helplessness and uncertainty than parents whose children were in remission (Grootenhuis & Last, 1997a). Mothers reported extensive feelings of loneliness, which increased with time since diagnosis. As found in other studies, mothers reported more negative emotions than fathers.

Bone Marrow Transplants

Where a child relapses, the hope of cure rests on a successful BMT. In this procedure, the patients' unhealthy bone marrow is eliminated and healthy bone marrow cells infused instead. During the period when the patients' own blood cells have been killed but before the new marrow is engrafted, patients make no new blood cells. Red blood cells and platelets therefore must be transfused, usually for several months. BMT is a very aggressive treatment. Patients are at risk of infections, and critically, graft-versus-host disease. Knowledge that BMT is recommended only when more conventional treatments have failed, that there is little other treatment available in the event of failure, and of the possibility of complications, all contribute to make this a very stressful procedure for patients and their families. In recognizing this, a small number of studies have been published documenting the toll on parents' well-being.

Sormanti, Dungan, and Pieker (1994) asked 73 parents whose child had had a successful BMT 1 to 20 years earlier to complete questionnaires to assess their own outlook on life, relationships, and functional activities. There was evidence that parents' distress decreased with time. Parents reported that the most difficult time had been around the child's hospitalization. Those whose child had been treated within 2 years of the study were most distressed. Despite the relatively long follow-up, parents remained concerned about their child. They also reported difficulties obtaining insurance, with finances, and with their own physical and mental health.

Phipps and Mulhern (1995) conducted a longitudinal study of predictors of child adjustment following BMT. Family conflict, cohesiveness, and expressiveness predicted adjustment post-BMT. The authors concluded that family cohesiveness and expressiveness act as protective factor. In contrast, family conflict is a risk factor and is associated with worse patient adjustment.

The conclusions of these studies are not unexpected: Distress decreases with time since BMT and family variables are associated with adjustment. As BMT becomes more generally available, there will be an increasing need to consider the psychological impact on families.

Terminal Care

One of the most difficult decisions any parent can face concerns when it is inappropriate to continue with care and accept the need for palliative treatment. Hinds et al. (1997) explored the main difficulties faced by 39 parents and 21 health care workers when deciding whether to continue or terminate care. Individuals were asked to describe the factors that most influenced their decisions. For parents, recommendations received from health care professionals were most important, whereas the health care team rated discussion with the family of the patient as the most important factor. Results such as these have implications for helping nurses understand what information parents need in their decision making as well as suggesting ways to communicate with parents.

L. James and Johnson (1997) interviewed parents of eight children with terminal cancer about their needs and concerns. Three needs were highlighted: the need to have the child recognized as special while retaining as much normality in family life as possible; the need for caring and connectedness with health care professionals; and the need to retain responsibility for parenting their dying child. The authors found that these were the main needs of parents, regardless of whether their child died at home or in the hospital. In related work, Martinson, Zhong, and Liang (1994) highlighted the financial worries associated with care of a dying child. Parents face long periods away from work, and incur many additional expenses for travel, care of the child, and care of other children in the family.

Hospital- or Home-Based Care.   Parents whose child received hospital-based terminal care functioned better after the child died than those parents who received home-based terminal care (Birenbaum & M. A. Robinson, 1991). In a subsequent longitudinal study, Birenbaum, Stewart, and Phipps (1996) compared parents' health status over a 1-year period after the child's death with population norms. No differences were found between those whose child received home- or hospital-based care.

Papadatou, Yfantopoulos, and Kosmidis (1996) investigated the experiences of 15 Greek mothers whose child was dying of cancer at home or in hospital. More than half decided to care for their child at home, without having access to home care services. Decisions of this kind were based on the child's desire to die at home, the strength of familial support, and parental preference. Mothers rated the care from the medical team very positively.

When a Child Dies

Martinson, B. Davies, and McClowry (1991) found no mean differences in depression when comparing families at 2 and 9 years after a child's death. However, depression scores at 2 years accounted for 22% of the variance at 9 years after the death. In their follow-up study 7–9 years later (Martinson, McClowry, B. Davies, & Kuhlenkamp, 1994), parents were reported to feel stronger and better prepared for health-threatening situations as a result of their child's death, although a number had fears of developing illnesses and others were frightened by the prospect of death.

Clerico, Ragni, Antimi, and Minori (1995) compared parental health in 44 families where the child had died of cancer and 34 where the child was still alive. The main difference between the two groups was the increased number of pregnancies in the group where the child had died. Within 1 year of the child's death, 17 of 34 women had become pregnant compared with seven pregnancies in the group where the child was still alive. This difference was explained in terms of the "replacement child syndrome."

As part of their longitudinal study, Kupst and Schulman (1988) looked at coping in families whose child had died. Again, they found that the families were coping remarkably well and generally did not differ from a group in remission in terms of their coping practices. They did, however, tend to show more residual anger than did families with survivors. The authors found that time itself did not seem to make a difference either in terms of length of time to anticipate the child's death or in terms of time since the child's death. It seemed more to do with the families' coping strategies during the illness.

Hoesktra-Weebers, Littlewood, Boon, and Postma (1991) investigated parental coping styles following the death of a child from cancer. They compared two groups of parents who differed primarily in terms of the age when the child died (3–9 vs. 13–19 years). Parents in the two groups did not differ from each other in *mean* mental health scores, nor was there a difference between these groups or population norms. However, the bereaved parents seemed reluctant to disclose their emotions and 14 of the 33 parents showed significant mental health problems.

Martinson, McClowry et al. (1994) conducted a longitudinal study with 48 families 7 to 9 years after the death of their child from cancer. Over time, families reported that many changes were made in all aspects of their lives, and that the family was now a top priority in their lives. Some of the changes were considered to be a result of normal development, but others were a direct result of the child's death.

CAN WE IDENTIFY THOSE FAMILIES WHO NEED SUPPORT AFTER TREATMENT ENDS?

Given the limited professional support services available in many busy hospitals, it is important that resources are directed toward those most likely to need help. To this end, there has been some speculation about which families are most likely to benefit from professional support. Intuitively, it might be expected that those who adjust well initially will continue to do so, but relatively small numbers of survivors and limited follow-up means that this hypothesis has not been formally tested. The studies by Kupst and colleagues provided some evidence that those who cope well on diagnosis continue to do so throughout treatment and afterward. The general approach in this kind of work is to correlate general indicators of adjustment or coping before and after treatment ends. Such general indicators may be of limited value in identifying the specific processes by which families achieve satisfactory coping.

Kazak and Barakat (1997) argued that longer term adjustment would be predicted specifically from the degree of parenting stress experienced during treatment. For parents, one of the most stressful aspects of parenting a child with cancer is a consequence of having to watch their child in pain or undergoing repeated invasive procedures. Parents certainly differ in their ability to manage this kind of distress. As the authors expected, parenting stress during treatment was significantly correlated with state anxiety for both mothers and fathers after treatment. For fathers, there was also a correlation between their initial anxiety and subsequent experience of PTSD.

Attempts to set up self-help groups occur frequently, though few of these efforts have been reported in detail or subject to any systematic evaluation. Clinic personnel are often reluctant to encourage communication or friendship between families. Parents themselves often regret this, pointing out that they would both like to receive support from others in the same position as well as give support to other families if required. A survey of parental attitudes by Patno, Young, and Dickerman (1988) showed that many parents (82%) would like greater sharing of information in the clinic and opportunities for parents to support each other.

Last and Grootenhuis (1998) conducted an extensive amount of research detailing coping in children with cancer and their parents. Based on a model originally proposed by Rothbaum (Rothbaum et al., 1982), they conceptualized coping as either *primary* or *secondary*. Primary coping refers to attempts to gain control of the situation by bringing the environment into line with one's own wishes (e.g., seeking treatment for an illness), whereas secondary coping refers to attempts made to bring the self in line with the environment (e.g., seeking explanations for an illness). Last and Grootenhuis showed how the source of stress (in particular, cancer in the child) affects the characteristics of the situation (e.g., uncertainty, uncontrollability) and, in turn, is associated with specific emotions (e.g., guilt, anger, fear). The type of control strategy used to cope with the situation has a direct association with the adjustment of both parents and child. For instance, the authors cited the example of a young girl, Maria, who had been successfully treated for an osteosarcoma. The mother was coping very well and had great faith in the treatment and doctors. However, the father felt the child would ultimately die and was very distressed. The authors concluded that, to help this family out, the father needed to be helped. Specifically, the father's sense of control had to be increased by increasing his understanding of the illness, explaining that because his child had completed treatment, the chances of survival were much greater. He was encouraged to learn this information and apply it in a more realistic way.

Interventions

As often happens, families cope during periods of crisis, but may then experience physical and psychological health problems as the stress recedes. Thus, families report that it is often not until the end of treatment that they have time to think about their ordeal. In part, families are quite unprepared for what to expect. During the time when the child is on treatment, families can feel a degree of security. As treatment ends, this security ends also. Ostroff and Steinglass (1996) noted that the transition from active treatment to off-treatment poses many challenges for patients and families and that both patient and family factors play a role in determining successful adaptation. Consequently, they described a short-term family-focused intervention, involving up to six families including the child with cancer to discuss family problems in a structured discussion format. The program operates on two levels. On the intrafamily level, family members are encouraged to talk among themselves in new ways, with a focus on understanding the impact of the illness on other family members and to hear each other's perspectives. On the interfamily level, family members are allowed to observe and understand their own attitudes and behaviors by comparing themselves with other families. This enables family members to find others who share their views outside the immediate family. The program involves six sessions, focusing on three components: illness impact, family development, and family illness integration. The authors argued strongly for the need to include family members in the post-treatment services for survivors.

Heiney, Wells, Coleman, Swygert, and Ruffin (1990) developed a program, "Lasting Impressions," to help adolescents (aged over 13 years, on- or off-treatment) and their families overcome the stressors of cancer. The aims behind the program were to promote positive mental health and adaptation in the families. The *goals* of the program are threefold: (a) to facilitate coping with the diagnosis and treatment of cancer, (b) to promote community reentry, and (c) to enhance long-term adjustment. Each goal is dealt with individually, with participants accomplishing a set of objectives before moving on to the next goal.

McClowry, E. B. Davies, May, Kulenkamp, and Martinson (1995) further indicated the need for long-term support for families bereaved of a child with cancer. Forty-nine families who experienced a death following childhood cancer were interviewed 7 to 9 years after bereavement. Parents and siblings were still experiencing pain and loss at this time, with the death of a child creating an "empty space" for surviving family members. Families differ in their adjustment to this empty space by either "getting over it," "filling the emptiness," or "keeping the connection."

In a paper to address the needs of the dying child, R. Charlton (1996) also put forward a number of recommendations for the family unit to achieve a "good death." There are a number of shortcomings of under-graduate medical education, one of which is failure to emphasize the importance of caring for the family unit and not just the sick patient. When facing bereavement, siblings (and parents) have needs that should be met in addition to those of the dying child.

Lastly, Goldman (1998) offered an "ABC of palliative care" to address the special problems of children with life-limiting illnesses and their families. Although concerned with the dying child, her recommendations are applicable across family systems in helping the family achieve a better death. Recommendations included: continuing attention be paid to the child's physical, emotional, and cognitive development; recognizing parents as carers and as needing care themselves; assessing and managing the ill child's symptoms; understanding and coping with pain; recognizing the difficulties sometimes encountered feeding a child and the associated emotional problems for parents; and dealing with nausea and vomiting and neurological problems. Particular attention is given to support for the family. Professionals must offer flexible help and address siblings' and grandparents' as well as parents' concerns. In the case of an inherited illness, special difficulties apply and are discussed. It is suggested that families who maintain open communication cope most effectively, but it is acknowledged that this strategy is not appropriate for everyone. Useful resources to facilitate communication are identified. The role of education in maintaining short-term goals for as long as possible is considered to be essential. After bereavement, Goldman pointed out that siblings and parents suffer and may have difficulty adjusting; siblings may feel isolated or neglected and their parents perhaps might be unable to offer their energy or emotion at this time. Helping the bereaved family involves support and assessment through the tasks of normal mourning, access to information sources, referral for specialist bereavement counseling if needed, and (when appropriate) gradual withdrawal of contact.

V

SURVIVAL AND QUALITY OF LIFE

Important work in the 1970s and 1980s by Gerald Koocher, the Spinettas, and van Eys laid the foundations for both subsequent research and clinical practice. It often seems that interest in QOL is a recent phenomenon, but in fact, some of these earliest writers were stressing the need to think about QOL in treatment for childhood cancer. The following was written by van Eys in 1976, but could equally be applied today:

> There are specific problems that need to be addressed, the first being delayed development. Even when cure is a reasonable possibility, parents do not always dare to hope. The result is that the child receives concessions made in the mistaken idea that they contribute to the child's mental comfort.... Clearly this requires constant support of the parents. Discussion groups among parents are essential to hear alternative solutions to common problems. The children should be challenged according to their ability. They should be sent to school and schooling should be provided in the hospital and clinic. Attempts at normalising the child's life through parties and other diversions should never be allowed to have as the main aim the idea that the cancer does not exist, but rather that the cancer is acceptable.
>
> The second problem is poor body image. Much of our current treatment, be it surgery, radiotherapy, chemotherapy, or immunotherapy is physically disfiguring. It is often a devastating problem for children who already have an untested self-

image to absorb these bodily changes. . . . It is the task of all who care for these children to indeed accept them as they are and not as we would like them to be. Self-image has to be tested against peers; thus peer contact is essential, even to the point of having regular teenage group sessions.

Children may have vocational aspirations that are unreasonable to a degree which constitutes denial. Realistic dealing with children needs to be continually emphasised. (p. 222)

Improvements in QOL have resulted in increased awareness of the quality as well as quantity of survival. As was shown in the last section, aggressive treatments necessary to cure cancer can damage healthy tissue, with the result that children are at considerable risk of physical and psychological late effects. For these reasons, the success of treatment has to be considered in terms of both survival rates and QOL. The challenge is to measure QOL.

16

Quality of Life

Summary

The importance of quality as well as quantity of survival must now be clear. Questions of definition and measurement have proved more difficult. The most common definitions of QOL acknowledge the fact that it is multidimensional, includes the impact on the child as well as the family, and must be sensitive to the changes that occur throughout childhood and adolescence. Where possible, ratings of QOL must be made by the individual child rather than a proxy (parent, teacher, or clinician).

In a review of currently available measures, ten were identified that were specifically relevant to cancer. These measures differed on a number of dimensions, including length, number of domains assessed, and whether assessments could be made by children or their parents. Measures also differed in terms of purpose. Some were developed specifically to evaluate QOL in clinical trials, others to determine the impact of different treatment choices, or to evaluate interventions.

Methodological limitations of current measures include the lack of suitable instruments for children below 8 years of age and the focus on parent rather than child report.

BACKGROUND

In previous chapters, it has been shown that cancer effects a child's QOL in many ways. The truly cured child not only is cured of cancer, but also has the opportunity to achieve optimal social, emotional, and physical functioning. Although this is increasingly being acknowledged, there remain many questions about how best to measure QOL. In this chapter, we draw on a wider body of research with the aim to improve understanding of QOL as a concept.

Because the question of QOL is central to this book, issues of definition and measurement are considered in some detail. Currently available measures are reviewed and critiqued. The relationship between child and parent judgments of QOL are important, especially for situations in which children are too ill or unwilling to provide information themselves. In these contexts, it is important to understand how far parents and children agree. This literature is disappointing given the importance of the question, and is largely a reflection of the failure of both researchers and clinicians to agree about how QOL should be measured.

As has been described throughout this book, the child's QOL is potentially compromised by lengthy treatments, lack of opportunities to take part in normal age-related activities, and the emotional concerns associated with a life-threatening disease. During treatment, the child's QOL is likely to be seriously compromised. Perhaps, some might argue, this short-term problem has to be accepted for long-term gain. Certainly, it is hoped that, over time, QOL will improve. For many children, these anticipated improvements in QOL are achieved. For others, residual late effects can compromise the overall success of treatment.

The importance of QOL is clear from the content of interviews conducted with two young people, Tom and Lucy. Both were 19 years of age and had been diagnosed with a bone tumor some 6 years previously. Both had been treated by a limb salvage procedure. This involves surgical removal of the diseased bone and replacement with a metal prosthesis. Given the time since diagnosis, the prognosis for both was good. Tom had left school with no qualifications and had a series of part-time and casual jobs. Lucy, too, had left school with few qualifications and had had difficulties in finding employment. There the similarities ended. Tom lived alone and hardly ever went out. He talked of his dreams of being a professional footballer and how these had been dashed following diagnosis of the tumor. Unable to play football, he had also lost his mates, because they continued to play without him. Thus, at the same time, he lost his mobility, his sport, his dreams, and his mates. Small wonder that he had been unable to find another niche.

Lucy was much more optimistic. Why would she want better mobility? She could drive and therefore get wherever she wanted. She had kept up with all her friends and was happy being with them. Late-night discos were somewhat of a problem, but everyone knew she was unable to stand for long and took turns to sit with her. She would not want to wear a skirt, as this would emphasize her scar and the fact that one leg was thinner than the other, "but everyone wears trousers anyway." She did not feel compromised in her social life, nor did she anticipate that any problems would develop in the future. Thus, apparently the same medical condition and treatment has a substantial and different impact on the lives, and QOL, of these two young people.

Definitions

The scientific study of QOL is complicated by the popular and everyday uses of the term. We talk about QOL in relation to the physical and material aspects of our worlds. QOL is related to access to running water, enough food to eat, and somewhere warm and comfortable to live. There is also an environmental side to QOL. Access to the countryside, the number of birds in the hedgerows, or quality of our beaches have also been used as indicators of the QOL of a nation. In a medical context, researchers have emphasized that we are less interested in this broad definition, but more in a *health-specific* QOL. In all that follows, the discussion is restricted to health-related QOL, though for simplicity the abbreviation QOL is used.

In pediatric medicine, the concept of QOL has had a relatively brief history. In fact, QOL has often been loosely equated with physical symptoms. Clearly a child who is very sick is likely to have a poor QOL, but generally physical symptoms do not relate in any simple way with QOL. Others have suggested that if QOL reflects a child's ability to take part in normal activities, then school attendance might be considered a good proxy indicator. Given the focus on maladjustment rather than adjustment, or problems rather than QOL, school absence has been used on occasions as a proxy indicator of QOL.

Such proxy indicators may be useful, but have limited value. School absence measures school absence. It does not measure the reasons for school absence, how much the child really wants, or is well enough, to be at school, or how the child spends time at home. If a child with leukemia is not at school because of the risk of infection, there may be a huge potential for compromised QOL, especially if the child sits at home and watches television alone while the parents are at work. However, if the parents are able to spend time with the child, carry out some semblance of an educational program, and invite select (infection-free) friends around after school, the impact may be negligible.

Early efforts to describe QOL in children were invariably focused on functional problems and usually relied on assessments made by clinicians. Some of the earliest attempts to assess QOL were provided by Ditesheim and Templeton (1987), Herndon et al. (1986), and Henning, Tomlinson, Rigden, Haycock, and Chanter (1988). Ditesheim and Templeton assessed QOL in infants following surgical repair of high imperforate anus. Their assessment of QOL was based on questionnaire information concerning school attendance, social relationships, and physical abilities. Herndon et al. reported a follow-up of 12 survivors treated for major burns. They included assessments of physical functioning, degree of scarring, and psychological adjustment. One third of the children were very fearful, showing regressive behavior or neurotic symptoms. However, the authors noted that many children showed considerable energy in adapting to their disabilities. Henning et al. measured degree of function, height, and attitudes in children with end-stage renal disease. Although average height was "normal," most children remained disappointed.

The findings of these early studies have implications for modern QOL work in two ways. First, they emphasized that children can adapt to their situation following major stress or injury, and second that children's views about their disability are important. Thus, these early authors might be credited with anticipating the direction in which QOL measurement was to go (even though their measurement of QOL was very simple).

Many doctor–patient consultations begin with simple questions like "how are you?" This is effectively the simplest way to explore a child's QOL. However, as a scientific concept, it leaves much to be desired. Children may see the question as a routine opening remark that is not expected to yield an answer. They may think about the ice cream they had before coming to clinic and respond that they are fine. On another visit, they may be preoccupied with a school test and grunt that things are not so good. If the doctor is to gain any real insight into changes in QOL over time, then more standardized approaches to question asking have to be adopted. In order to understand the impact of cancer on the child's well-being, reliable and valid measures of QOL are needed, in the same way that reliable and valid measures of physiological function are needed to determine the impact of cancer on the child's physical health.

In practice, QOL is often confused on the one hand with related measures favored by clinicians (well-being, functional status, and health status) and on the other with more psychologically oriented concepts such as self-esteem, happiness, or resilience.

Schipper et al. (1996) have attempted to draw together the different approaches to conceptualizing and measuring QOL. They identified five different approaches. First there is the psychological view. This approach emphasizes the importance of the patient's own subjective view of the disease. Individuals have their own unique perspectives on QOL, which depends on present life-style, past experience, hopes for the future, dreams, and ambitions. At the same time, the psychological approach emphasizes the interdependence between physiological and psychological states. Psychological variables can be an important contributor to disease process, and influence the individuals' approach to disease management, adherence to treatment and ultimately QOL.

Second, there is the "utility" approach. This approach, often advocated by health economists, emphasizes the different trade-offs that individuals may be prepared to make. Some want survival at any cost, others consider life to be worth living only in specified circumstances.

Third, there is the community centered approach. This may be understood as a hierarchy, with physical illness at the center of a circle. From the central circle, the impact of illness can be assessed in terms of personal functioning, psychological distress or well-being, general health perceptions and finally social role functioning. This approach emphasizes the impact of individual disease on the wider community and is integral to the SF-36 (Ware et al., 1993), often used as a measure of adult QOL.

Fourth, QOL can be regarded in terms of opportunities for reintegration to normal living. Reintegration to normal living is clearly an important focus for patients and a clear indicator of QOL.

Fifth, an approach favored by a number of authors looks at QOL in terms of a gap between what an individual can and would like to do. Good QOL can be expected when the hopes of an individual are matched and fulfilled by experience. The opposite is also true: poor QOL occurs when hopes do not meet with the experience (Calman, 1987). Similar ideas have been put forward by Bergner (1989) who suggested that QOL is enhanced when the distance between the individual's attained and desired goals is less. However, an individual's goals must be realistic in order that the gap can be narrowed. From a therapeutic point of view, it is as possible to improve QOL by helping a patient give up some dreams and accept reality (and restrictions) as well as work with another patient to achieve more realistically set goals. In both cases, the gap is narrowed. A major limitation of this approach may be in the failure to specify goals as realistic and achievable compared with those that are merely dreams or lack substance (Hayry, 1999).

Common to many of these approaches is the idea that QOL is a multidimensional construct encompassing several domains (Eisen, Ware, Donald, & Brook, 1979; Aaronson, Meyeravitz, Bard, Bloom, Fauzy, Feldstein, Fink, Holland, Johnson, Lowman, Patterson, & Ware, 1991; Gotay, Korn, McCabe, Moore, & Cheson, 1992; Ware, Snow, Kosinski, & Gandek, 1993). These domains, described originally by the World Health Organization (WHO) include "the state of complete physical, mental and social well-being and not merely the absence of disease or infirmity" (WHO, 1947). Common too is the idea that QOL can include both objective and subjective perspectives in each of these domains (Testa & Simonson, 1996). While the objective assessment of QOL focuses on what the individual can do, the subjective assessment includes the individual's perception or appraisal of QOL. Differences in appraisal account for the fact that individuals with the same objective health status can report very different subjective QOL. Thus, the patient's perceptions of, and attributions about, dysfunction are as important as their existence (Schipper et al., 1996).

Gill and Feinstein (1994) distinguish three ways in which QOL may be assessed in the health context. These include objective measures, such as clinical indices that patients would not themselves necessarily use or be aware of (such as blood sugar or peak air flow measurement); functional performance (awareness about their ability to perform certain activities, e.g., climbing stairs); and subjective indicators or the patient's own evaluation of the experience of being able to complete a given activity. This latter subjective rating of health status is frequently considered to be the defining characteristic of QOL.

To go back to the examples at the beginning of the chapter: For Tom, the gap between what he could do and what he wanted to do was wide. He had found no way to begin to achieve this goals. In similar situations, other survivors have talked about how they had taken up a new sport, or were training to be an umpire or coach. The situation was entirely different for Lucy. For her there was no gap; she could do everything she wanted to do, and even though there were difficulties (she could not wear a skirt) she was happy to wear trousers. Both Tom and Lucy shared the experience of being diagnosed with cancer, undergoing surgery and chemotherapy, but beyond this their experiences diverged.

Of special interest here, Bradlyn et al. (1996) have drawn on a number of definitions to provide one with unique potential for work with children with cancer. "Quality of life in pediatric oncology is multidimensional. It includes, but is not limited to, the social, physical, and emotional functioning of the child and adolescent, and when indicated, his/her family. Measurement of QOL must be from the perspective of the child, adolescent, and family, and it must be sensitive to the changes that occur throughout development" (pp. 1333–1334).

MEASURES OF QUALITY OF LIFE

In the absence of QOL measures, some authors have adopted a "battery" approach, in which they use a number of individual measures used as proxy indicators of QOL, (e.g., depression, self-esteem). In essence, much of the work reviewed so far has adopted this approach. Thus, researchers have used measures of physical or emotional functioning to compare children with cancer and healthy controls. Sometimes they have been explicitly interested in differences on the specific measure of physical or emotional functioning. At other times, researchers have assumed that these measures in some way approximate indicators of QOL.

This approach is of limited value. A significant number of proxy measures would be needed in order to provide a comprehensive measure of QOL. Completion of a large number of measures potentially imposes a huge burden on the child. Furthermore, there may be duplication and overlap between the proxy measures, creating redundancy and irritation. At the same time, a battery approach can only be as good as the parts from which it is made up. Thus, assessing QOL with a battery of measures is subject to the same criticisms that might be made of the individual measures. For both these reasons, there has been a huge interest in developing comprehensive measures of QOL.

Choices

For researchers and clinicians wanting to measure the child's QOL, the choice between different measures currently available can be confusing. Two related but separate approaches can be identified. The first involved development of generic measures or "health scales" for use in population surveys of children. A second approach involved assessment of children with a specific chronic disease or undergoing a particular treatment. Often, QOL was used interchangeably with "social and psychological problems" or was restricted to demographic or clinical indicators. Studies that attempted to evaluate the impact of a disease on lifestyle (Mok, Laing, & Ferguhar, 1984) or compare marriage rates between individuals differing in disease status (Ahlfield, Soler, & Marcus, 1983) might be considered to be precursors of the contemporary interest in QOL.

In order to determine current approaches to measuring QOL in children with cancer, we conducted a computer-based search. A total of 11 measures were identified (see Table 16.1). Some of these are cancer specific; that is, they were developed solely to assess QOL in children with cancer. Others are thought to be appropriate for children with a range of conditions although the development work relied heavily on involvement of children with cancer (Barr, Petrie, Furlong, Rothney, & Feeny, 1997; Bradlyn, C. V. Harris, Warner, Ritchey, & Zaboy, 1993; Calaminus, Weispach, Teske, & Gobel, 2000). One of the measures (Phipps, Hinds, Channell, & Bell, 1994) was developed specifically for use in the BMT clinic.

TABLE 16.1
The Main Domains Assessed by Cancer-Specific Measures of QOL

Domain	Physical	Social	Psychological	Cognitive	Treatment-Related Measure
Lansky et al. (1985)	•				
Bradlyn et al. (1993)	•	•			
Feeny et al. (1995)	•		•	•	•
Goodwin et al. (1994)	•		•		
Armstrong et al. (1999)		•	•		
Varni et al. (1998)	•	•	•	•	•
Eiser et al. (1995)	•	•	•	•	•
Calaminus et al. (2000)	•	•	•	•	
Zebrack & Chesler (2001)	•	•	•		
Bhatia et al. (2002)	•	•	•	•	
Phipps et al. (1994)	•	•	•		•

PARENT-COMPLETED MEASURES

The Play Performance Scale for Children

The Play Performance Scale for Children (PPSC; L. L. Lansky, List, S. B. Lansky, M. E. Cohen, & Sinks, 1985) is the original, most simple, and most frequently cited indicator of QOL used for children with cancer. It is a relatively simple "downward extension" of the Performance Scale described by Karnofsky and Burchenal (1949) for work with adult cancer patients. Parents are asked to record play activity in terms of 10 graded statements ("fully active, normal," scored as 100, through to "unresponsive," scored as 0). It is quick to administer and easy to score. It was originally considered suitable for a relatively wide age range (1–16 years) though has recently been thought to lack sensitivity, particularly for older children and those functioning at near normal levels.

Mulhern, Fairclough, Friedman, and Leigh (1990) compared the efficacy of the PPSC over a simple visual analog scale. Comparisons were made between children who were hospitalized, treated as outpatients, or had completed therapy. The PPSC discriminated between the groups better than the visual analog scale. Scores on the PPSC were lower for hospitalized patients compared with outpatients or those who had completed therapy, suggesting a degree of validity. However, there were no differences between the two nonhospitalized groups, indicating less sensitivity for those functioning near normal levels.

This scale has been used widely in research and remains popular. At a clinical level, it is quick and easy to administer and can be used by those with no special training. More critically, it is not a sensitive instrument and there is no facility for children to make ratings for themselves. The

PPSC is frequently treated as a kind of "gold standard" against which new measures are compared, although the wisdom of this is hard to accept given its clear limitations.

The Quality of Well-Being Scale

The Quality of Well-Being Scale (Bradlyn et al., 1993) is a slightly modified version of the Quality of Well-Being Scale for adults (R. M. Kaplan & J. P. Anderson, 1988). Four areas of QOL were measured: physical functioning, social/role functioning, mobility, and symptoms. Estimates of the level of impairment in each area are based on interview responses.

Clinicians rated treatment toxicity on a global score (1 = mild to 5 = severe), based on information about bone marrow suppression, nausea and vomiting, acute and long-term risk of hematopoietic functioning, and nutritional status. The scale was found to distinguish between children on the basis of medical data as would be expected. Criticisms of this scale include the fact that data collection is complex and time consuming, and there is no parallel form for children to make their own ratings. The domains of QOL that are assessed are different from those used in other measures.

Multiattribute Health Status Classification System

The multiattribute health status classification system (Feeny et al., 1995), based on the Health Utilities Index (HUI; Torrance, Boyle, & Horwood, 1982), has been used especially for work in neonatal intensive care and oncology. In development work, four attributes or components of health were identified with each attribute consisting of between four and eight levels of function. Proponents of this schema argue that one of its merits lies in the potential to determine almost a thousand health states, by combining the scores on each level from each attribute.

In developing the multiattribute health status classification, Feeny, Furlong, Boyle, and Torrance (1995) began by asking parents in the general population to identify important components of health for their children. From these data, six domains were identified: sensation, emotion, cognition, mobility, self-care, and pain. A seventh domain, fertility, was added, as this was felt to be important to parents of children treated for cancer, though not an issue for parents of healthy children. For each attribute, three to five levels of functioning were identified. The child's health status score is a computation of functioning on the different levels for each domain.

The link between these health status measurements and QOL is assessed using a technique called the standard gamble. Respondents are asked to consider a specific health state. Then they must choose between remaining in this health state or take a gamble, the gamble being between sudden death and enjoying perfect health. These preferences are then varied until the respondent is unable to choose between the two. This is called the utility score; the better the state of health the higher the utility score.

Criticisms of this approach include the fact that the attributes are not completely independent. (If you score badly on the mobility attribute, it is almost inevitable that you will also score badly in terms of self-care.) In part recognition of some of these problems, later versions dropped the self-care attribute. In addition, the system does not allow for better than average functioning. Thus, in terms of cognition, for example, ratings are made from severe morbidity to normality. Thus, the system fails to recognize children who function better than average.

In subsequent work, the scale has been modified and completed by parents and older children. Glaser, K. Davies, Walker, and Brazier (1997) assessed health status in 37 survivors of CNS tumors. Outcome measures included the HUI, the PPSC (Lansky et al., 1985), and the Karnofsky Performance Index (Karnofsky & Burchenal, 1949). Comparisons were reported between ratings made by parents and by patients themselves, and between whether data were collected at home or in the clinic. Doctors and physiotherapists also provided ratings for some patients. The focus of the study was to determine the level of agreement between different raters rather than provide information about the level of functioning. There was good agreement between patients and parents on some attributes of the HUI but not for vision or pain.

Billson and D. A. Walker (1994) used the multiattribute system (Feeney et al., 1992) to assess health status in a group of 63 survivors of different cancers. Assessments were made for six attributes (senses, mobility, emotion, cognition, self-care, and pain). Consultations with the doctor were informally structured to facilitate assessment of the child's health status in each of the six attributes assessed. Some modifications were made to the initial instrument to ease comprehension for parents and children. Parents completed the instrument for children under 8 years of age whereas parents and children together completed the measure for those aged 8–14 years. Children over 14 years completed the measure themselves.

A total of 48 assessment pairs were collected. No deficits on any of the six attributes were identified for 16 patients (33%) on the basis of their own assessments or those of their parents and for 19 patients (40%) on the basis of doctor's assessments. Assessments by doctors identified fewer deficits than those made by parents or patients and this difference was most pronounced for pain. In 17 cases, there was no difference between assessment by the doctor and patient or parent. Disagreements were found on only one attribute for 15 patients and on two attributes for 10 patients. There were no differences in health status scores made by patients/parents and by doctors. Based on this study, there seems to be good agreement between doctors and patients/parents regarding the health status of survivors. From both doctor and patient/parent ratings, some 33%–40% of survivors were found to have no measurable deficits. Problems in at least one attribute were identified for the remainder.

This system has been adopted by a number of workers and is especially popular with pediatricians. It is most commonly used to compare alternative treatments. The main advantages include brevity and ease of administration. It is possible for a clinician to complete the instrument within a few minutes. From this point of view, it seems ideal for work in a busy clinic. It may prove useful as a very brief screening instrument in the comparison of different therapies, but is unlikely to yield a comprehensive picture of QOL unless supplemented by additional measures.

The Pediatric Oncology Quality of Life Scale

The original items for the Pediatric Oncology Quality of Life Scale (Goodwin, Boggs, & Graham-Pole, 1994) were generated by health professionals, parents of cancer patients, and patients themselves. Parents were asked to generate written statements about how their child's life was affected by cancer. Adolescents were asked to report the impact themselves. Younger children were simply asked to describe the "good" and "bad" things about having cancer. From the original item pool, 44 items were selected as representative of the most commonly reported themes.

A questionnaire was then constructed using these 44 items and respondents were asked to rate each one on a series of 7-point scales ("never" to "very frequently") and was completed by 210 parents. On the basis of factor analysis and further refinement of the scale, Goodwin et al. (1994) finally developed a 21-item scale. Validity was established in relation to the PPSC (Lansky et al., 1985), the CBCL (Achenbach & Edelbrock, 1983), and depression (W. M. Reynolds, G. Anderson, & Bartell, 1985).

The final scale measures three components of QOL: "physical functioning and restriction from normal activity," "emotional distress," and "response to active medical treatment." Although there were no age differences in total scores, there were significant age differences on two of the three subscales. Adolescents felt they were more restricted in terms of "physical functioning and restriction from normal activity" than younger children. On the subscale measuring "emotional distress," children aged 8–12 years showed more distress compared with younger or older children. There were no age effects on the subscale measuring "response to active treatment."

Goodwin et al. (1994) reported good internal reliability for the total score and for the three separate subscales. The measure also appears to have adequate validity, at least in terms of discriminating between children depending on time since diagnosis. In addition, scores on the subscales correlated with the validity measures as expected. For example, scores on the physical functioning subscale correlated with the PPSC (Lansky et al., 1985) but not with the CBCL (Achenbach & Edelbrock, 1983) or depression (W. M. Reynolds et al., 1985).

This measure was designed for use by parents of children from preschool through to adolescence. Age differences on subscale scores suggest that the impact of cancer on QOL may be age-dependent, at least as far as parents are concerned. There are indications that adolescents are more affected in terms of physical functioning compared with younger children, whereas children between the ages of 8 and 12 years are most affected in terms of emotional functioning.

Goodwin et al. (1994) argued that parents are a reliable and accurate source of information about their children and that parent-completed measures have some advantages over child-completed measures. This is clearly a point of view, and many would see the lack of a child version to be a major limitation of this measure. The content of the measure also highlights disagreements about the key domains that contribute to QOL. Whereas Goodwin and colleagues defined subscales to measure "physical functioning and restriction from normal activity," "emotional distress," and "response to active medical treatment," Bradlyn et al. (1993) identified three somewhat different domains: physical functioning, social/role functioning, and mobility.

The Miami Pediatric Quality of Life Questionnaire: Parent Scale

The development of the Miami Pediatric Quality of Life Questionnaire: Parent Scale (F. D. Armstrong et al., 1999) was based on interviews conducted with 30 families of children with cancer; 10 of preschool age, 10 of school age, and 10 of adolescent age. Responses were videotaped, transcribed, and categorized to develop a pool of 56 items. Items are rated twice. The first yields an Objective scale; parents rate how much each item was true for their child (1 = much less than other children the same age and 5 = much more than children the same age). If an item is not deemed appropriate by the parent, they are instructed to give the item a rating of 3. A second rating yields a Subjective scale based on the importance of each item for the parent (1 = not important to 5 = extremely important).

These data were related to information from clinicians about the child's diagnosis, date of diagnosis, history of relapse and subsequent treatment, type of treatment, and known side effects. In addition, each clinician rated the child's overall QOL on 5-point Likert scales. Clinicians also rated how far the child was affected by common side effects, again on 5-point scales.

Questionnaires were completed by 132 children and their parents. Three primary factors on the Parent form were identified through factor analysis: self-competence, emotional stability, and social competence. The questionnaire differentiated between children treated for leukemia and those treated for solid tumors. Those treated for leukemia were rated as having a better QOL overall. They also reported better QOL on two of the three separate factors (self-competence and social competence). There were no significant differences in terms of emotional stability. Neither were there any significant correlations between clinician and parents' ratings of the child's QOL.

MEASURES FOR CHILDREN AND PARENTS

The Pediatric Cancer Quality of Life Inventory

The Pediatric Cancer Quality of Life Inventory (PCQOL; Varni et al., 1998) includes 84 items organized around five domains: physical functioning (8 items), disease-related and treatment-related symptoms (28 items), psychological functioning (13 items), social functioning (23 items), and cognitive functioning (12 items). Ratings are made on a series of 4-point Likert scales (where 0 = never a problem to 3 = always a problem) and respondents are asked to think back over a 1-month period. The PCQOL includes a child form for 8- to 12-year-olds and an adolescent form for 13- to 18-year-olds. There are identical forms for parents, which differ only in terms of the use of "developmentally appropriate language" and whether they are written in the first or third person. Initial psychometric data were based on responses from 291 children, aged 8–18 years.

With any measure for children and parents, questions arise as to how far there is agreement or concordance, or whether children and parents differ substantially in their views about QOL. Concordance is often reported in terms of simple correlations between the two sets of ratings (though some argue that intraclass correlations are more appropriate). Varni and colleagues (1998) reported that, for both children and adolescents, concordance with parents' ratings was mostly in the medium effect size range (suggesting parents have a different perception from their children/adolescents, but there is still a correlation between the values). Lower concordance was found for more subjective domains (psychological functioning) compared with objective domains such as physical functioning.

A potential problem relates to the length of the scale (which includes 84 items). In anticipation of this, the same group (Varni et al., 1999) subsequently reported a short form (the PCQOL-32). The number of items in each domain was reduced (disease- and treatment-related symptoms = 9 items, physical functioning = 5 items, psychological functioning = 6 items, social functioning = 5 items, cognitive functioning = 7 items). Ratings were made on 4-point scales as before.

Varni et al. (1999) reported satisfactory internal consistency as well as clinical and construct validity, and suggested that the brief form is potentially suitable for research involving evaluation of RCTs. It should be noted that the item means were mostly under 1.0. These low item means suggest that patients did not consider their QOL to be seriously compromised, at least on the domains assessed. It is not clear if this is because patients included in the study were well and not severely affected or if the items used were not entirely appropriate. However, inspection of the standard deviations suggests that there was considerable variability in response.

The Perceived Illness Experience Scale

The Perceived Illness Experience Scale (PIE; Eiser et al., 1995) represents an attempt to develop a measure of QOL that captures the specific interests and concerns of the child with cancer. Following the approach recommended by Oppenheim (1992), a series of in-depth interviews were first conducted with children and adolescents to determine their own perceptions of the impact of cancer.

The interviews were analyzed using a content analysis guided by a review of the literature. Nine major themes were identified. These included physical activity (pleasure and competence in sports), appearance (concern about physical appearance), peer relationships (feelings of being bullied or getting on well with others), integration in school (participation in various aspects of school life), emotion and manipulation (fear of relapse or becoming ill again), parental behavior (perceptions that parents restrict activities), disclosure (not wanting people to know about the illness), preoccupation with illness (worries and concerns), and impact of treatment (extent to which they are bothered by treatment or hospital visits). Apart from physical activity, each theme was assessed by four items and ratings were made on 5-point Likert scales. The items were rated by 41 children (mean age = 14.6 years) and 35 of their parents. In addition, they also completed a set of related measures in order to obtain preliminary validation data. These included measures of physical functioning (Walker & Greene, 1991) and physical and psychological symptoms (Watson, Law, & Maguire, 1992).

The Flesch (1948) scoring system was used to determine the ease of readability of the scale. A "reading ease" score is calculated based on the average number of words in each sentence and the average number of syllables in each 100 words. Reading ease scores range from "very easy" (90–100; equivalent to 4 years of schooling) to "very difficult" (0–30; equivalent to 15 years of schooling). Analysis suggested that readability of the scale was within a range from "fairly easy" to "standard" (Flesch reading ease = 60–70).

Disappointingly, the scale failed to distinguish between children who were on therapy and those who had completed treatment. The only exception was the school subscale where those who had completed treatment reported better QOL than those on treatment. Significant correlations between mothers' and children's ratings were found on all but two subscales (disclosure and impact of treatment). In both cases, mothers reported less impact on QOL compared with their children.

Modifications to the PIE scale have since been made. It was felt that the two items to measure activity were insufficient and two further items were added. In addition, a subscale to measure attitudes to food was added, because many children, including those who had been off treatment for some time, suggested that their diets remained restricted because of changes in taste and food habits resulting from chemotherapy.

Further work with this revised scale provides additional evidence for the reliability and validity of the scale (Eiser, Kopel, Cool, & Grimer, 1999). Internal reliability for the separate subscales and total scale were confirmed. There were significant correlations between mothers' and children's ratings, suggesting that the instrument can be used as a good proxy measure. High correlations between the PIE and other established scales (Ware et al., 1993) and a measure of function (Enneking, Dunham, Gebhardt, Malawar, & Pritchard, 1993) were taken as evidence of construct validity.

The PEDQOL

Calaminus, Weinspach, Teske, and Gobel (2000) reported the development of a 34-item questionnaire, the PEDQOL, organized around seven domains to determine how children with cancer perceived their QOL compared with healthy children. The domains included some that are typically included in QOL measures, such as physical functioning, emotional functioning, cognition, social functioning/friends, and social functioning/family. Others were introduced because of their assumed relevance to adolescents (autonomy and body image). Results have been reported for 49 survivors of cancer aged between 8 and 17 years and a group of 62 healthy children of similar age. There were few differences between the groups, although children with cancer described their QOL in the domains measuring physical functioning, social functioning/peers, and body image to be worse. These differences were, however, very small. There were also some differences in reported QOL between survivors of leukemia compared with survivors of a solid tumor, but these varied somewhat unpredictably across the different domains.

One of the main merits of this measure is its relative brevity. On the downside, development of this measure was conducted without any systematic involvement of children. Failure to distinguish between children with cancer and healthy peers is also a problem.

MEASURES FOR SURVIVORS

The QOL-CS

Ideally, a measure of QOL would be useful to track changes occurring from diagnosis through to adult life. In practice, many of the scales currently available are more sensitive during specific stages of treatment. The Pediatric Cancer Quality of Life Inventory (Varni et al., 1998), for example, is more appropriate during the early stages of treatment, as it includes items about how the child views the impact of injections (needles) on QOL. For some survivors, fear of needles can remain a problem long after completion of treatment. However, for others who have completed therapy, needles are hopefully relegated to the past. For these patients, questions about injections may not be sensitive to current QOL.

Given the different experiences of children on treatment and survivors, some advocate that specific measures are needed to assess QOL appropriately. Zebrack and Chesler (2001) based their measure, the QOL-CS, on one previously developed for survivors of adult cancers (Ferrell, Hassey Dow, & Grant, 1995). The aim is to assess both positive and negative outcomes reflecting physical, psychological, social, and spiritual dimensions of QOL.

The QOL-CS for cancer survivors is a 41-item scale that includes four subscales: physical well-being (8 items), psychological well-being (18 items), social well-being (8 items), and spiritual well-being (7 items). The psychological scale can be further divided into two subcomponents assessing distress and fear. Survivors are asked to rate each item on a scale from 0 to 10. Four scale scores, two subcomponent scores (distress and fear), and a total QOL can be computed, with higher scores indicating better QOL. In assessing the validity of the scale for work with childhood cancer survivors, Zebrack and Chesler (2001) also asked patients to complete three worry scales (cancer-specific worries, worries about general psychosocial issues, and worries about general health). The data were also compared with clinical variables such as age on diagnosis, type of cancer, and presence of any other chronic health condition, as well as demographic variables such as age, gender, income, and marital status. The questionnaires were mailed to 335 survivors, of whom 53% responded.

Good internal reliability was reported for all scales and subscales. However, attempts to confirm the factor structure using factor analysis were less successful. As a result, Zebrack and Chesler (2001) concluded that there was evidence for only five scales (psychological, psychosocial, physical, spiritual, and the fears subcomponent of the psychosocial scale), and raised questions about the appropriateness of considering QOL in terms of separate subscales. In many ways, overlap between scales has to be expected. Poor physical well-being may limit employment and opportunities to maximize social QOL. These findings may well challenge the established dictum that QOL should be measured in relation to specific domains. For the future, a more profitable approach may be to consider how QOL in one domain has an impact on another.

This study also questions the appropriateness of using a measure to assess adult QOL as the model for QOL in children, including survivors, of childhood cancer. Zebrack and Chesler (2001) particularly pointed to "the potentially greater vitality in this age-group, the greater probability of a physical 'cure' for childhood cancer survivors, and the likelihood that they have not yet attained certain developmental milestones (e.g. childbearing) may affect their responses differently from adults" (p. 327). In addition, they noted that the religious or spiritual dimension of QOL appears less relevant to childhood cancer survivors compared with adults. More careful work needs to be done to define the spiritual aspects of QOL as experienced by these young-adult survivors.

A second measure specifically suitable for survivors was reported by Bhatia et al. (2002). To date a version for adolescents (13–20 years) has been described, but parallel forms for youth (8–12 years) and young adults (21–45 years) are proposed. These different versions offer opportunities for longitudinal work, tracing the impact of cancer over time. The domains of QOL defined by the WHO were taken as a starting point, and additional domains thought relevant for this age-group added (body image, outlook on life, and intimate relations). The final measure includes eight domains (physical, cognitive, psychological, social functioning and physical symptoms and the three above).

Although specific details about items and response scales are not provided in the published paper, the measure has been subject to fairly extensive psychometric analyses. Results were reported for 129 healthy adolescents, 110 undergoing treatment for cancer, and 158 who had completed treatment at least 1 year ago. Concurrent validity was established in relation to a generic measure of QOL.

Differences as predicted between the three groups were found for the physical, cognitive, psychological and social functioning domains, but disappointingly not for those measuring body image, intimate relations or outlook on life.

Quality of Life Following Bone Marrow Transplant

In recognition of the specific difficulties experienced by children undergoing BMT, Phipps et al. (1994) reported the Behavioral, Affective, and Somatic Experiences Scale (BASES). Three versions were developed; for parent, nurse, and child report. The BASES is a 38-item questionnaire that includes five subscales, which assess somatic distress (disease state and physical symptoms), mood disturbance (psychological functioning), quality of interactions (social functioning), activity (functional status), and compliance. Although compliance is not usually considered a component of QOL, it was included given the clinical importance in the context of BMT. Responses are made on 5-point scales and the measure takes about 5 minutes to complete (by adults). Phipps et al. reported good internal consistency and interrater reliability (based on nurse pairs and nurse–parent report). The child version (Phipps, Dunavant, Jayawardene, & Srivastiva, 1999) includes just 14 items organized around five scales: somatic distress (three items), compliance (three items), mood/behavior (four items), interactions (two items), and activity (two items). Again ratings are made on 5-point scales.

Preliminary analyses involved 105 children and suggested that the measure had good reliability and discriminant validity. This means that the measure discriminated in expected directions between children undergoing treatments differing in severity of physical consequences. The inclusion of a number of items to assess physical symptoms and the general focus on acute aspects of treatment suggests that the measure could potentially also be useful in other situations. These might include comparison of different trials, or assessment of the impact of high-dose chemotherapy.

Childhood Cancer Stressors Inventory and Children's Adjustment to Cancer Index

The Childhood Cancer Stressors Inventory and Children's Adjustment to Cancer Index (Hockenberry-Eaton, Manteuffel, & Bottomley, 1997) were developed to assess the child's perceptions of the cancer experience. Items for both were developed from a review of the literature and discussions with pediatric nurse specialists. The Childhood Cancer Stressors Inventory includes physical, emotional, and psychosocial concerns thought to affect children with cancer. It includes eight items rated "true" or "false." If an item is rated to be "true," children are also asked to rate its bothersomeness on a 4-point scale from "not at all a bother" to "a lot of bother." The Children's Adjustment to Cancer Index was developed in a similar way and includes 30 items, each rated on a 5-point scale from "never" to "always." Reliability and validity were reported for 75 children, 41 aged between 7 and 9 years and 34 aged between 10 and 13 years.

Moderately good internal reliability was reported for both scales. The two correlated negatively with each other, suggesting that children who perceived more disease-related stress had poorer adjustment. There were no correlations between age, gender, diagnosis, and whether or not the child had relapsed with either measure. Adjustment correlated negatively with number of days school missed and positively with number of friends. Scores on the Stressors scale also correlated with number of days off school.

CHARACTERISTICS OF MEASURES

The number of QOL measures developed in recent years might be taken as a broad criticism of the area. In some ways, it is true that the number of measures and diversity of approaches is indicative of the lack of agreement between researchers, and between researchers and clinicians. An alternative, and more optimistic view, is that the number of measures provides a degree of choice. The question then becomes one of choosing between measures in order to select the most appropriate for the particular purpose in mind. Measures differ in terms of a number of characteristics, as summarized in Table 16.1.

Purpose

Four QOL measures (F. D. Armstrong et al., 1999; Goodwin et al., 1994; Lansky et al., 1985; Varni et al., 1998) were developed with the expressed goal of assessing the efficacy of clinical trials. Other measures were developed for the assessment of symptoms (Lansky et al., 1985; Phipps et al., 1994), provision of anticipatory guidance (Phipps et al., 1994); comparison of populations at different risk (Varni et al., 1998), identification of children at special risk (Goodwin et al., 1994), and understanding the child's perspective (Calaminus et al., 2000). Bhatia et al. (2002) anticipate that their measure will provide "help in the decision-making process regarding selection of therapy, appropriate follow-up, and interventions where needed to prevent or manage sequelae that could negatively impact on QOL" (Bhatia et al., 2002, p. 4697).

Respondent

Of the 10 measures, four allowed for completion by both parents and child, compared with those that made provision for responses by parents (four) or children and adolescents only (two). Only one measure includes a version suitable for nurse report (Phipps et al., 1994). The HUI was originally developed for use by pediatricians but was subsequently shown to be usable by parents and children (Billson & Walker, 1994).

Age Ranges

Four measures were designed to be suitable for children of any age (F. D. Armstrong et al., 1999; Bradlyn et al., 1993; Goodwin et al., 1994; Lansky et al., 1985). All these are necessarily parent completed, because very young children are unable to provide information themselves. Parallel versions for children of different ages are provided in the measures reported by Varni et al. (1998, 1999). Others focus specifically on older children or adolescents (Bhatia et al., 2002; Calaminus et al., 2000; Eiser et al., 1994).

Number of Domains

The number of domains assessed ranged from 1 (Lansky et al., 1985) to 34 (Calaminus et al., 2000) and 38 (Phipps et al., 1994).

Domains Assessed

Examination of the domains summarized in Table 16.1 shows that more important than variation in number of domains may be the variation in content of domains. Some assessment of physical QOL is included in all measures. Measures by F. D. Armstrong et al. (1999), Varni et al. (1998), and Calaminus et al. (2000) include a social domain. Those by Varni et al., Bhatia et al. (2002), Calaminus et al., and Feeny et al. (1992) include a cognitive domain. In addition, some measures include unique domains; compliance was measured by Phipps et al. (1994), externalizing behavior by Goodwin et al. (1994), and body image by Calaminus et al. (2000) and Bhatia (2002). Thus, despite the frequently endorsed statement that QOL includes assessment of physical, social, and emotional functioning, researchers may add additional domains. On occasions, measures do not include core domains.

Rating Scales

Most measures use standard Likert-type scales involving three to five re-sponse categories. The HUI adopts a multiple-choice response format. Authors have not typically sought to justify the number of response cate-gories chosen.

Administration Time

One of the requirements of a "good" measure has always been brevity. It is argued that it should be possible to complete a good measure quickly, in order to allow for completion in a busy clinic or prevent boredom in chil-dren. Thus, the HUI involves just 2 minutes or so for pediatrician comple-tion. The Pediatric Quality of Life Inventory (PedsQL) can take 4 minutes for completion by parents. Phipps, Dunavant, Jayawardene, and Sriva-stiva (1999) reported that completion of BASES takes approximately 5 minutes. It can take longer for children or adolescents to complete a mea-sure. Calaminus et al. (2000) reported that adolescent cancer patients could complete her measure within 20 minutes.

Psychometric Properties

Reliability. Internal reliability, or the extent to which the individual items measure the same construct, as measured by Cronbach's alpha is re-ported in most measures with test–retest reliability assessed less fre-quently.

Clinical Validity. In reality we might expect QOL to depend on the specific diagnosis and stage in the treatment cycle. QOL may be more compromised for cancers involving more intensive treatments and for children in the immediate period after diagnosis. These assumptions have most frequently been used as a basis for determining the clinical validity of a new measure. Thus, Varni et al. (1998) reported that children who had completed treatment had a better QOL than those who were still on treat-ment. F. D. Armstrong et al. (1999) reported that children with a brain tu-mor had poorer QOL compared with those with either leukemia/lym-phoma or solid tumors, although there were no differences between the latter two groups. QOL was also more compromised where children were treated by whole-brain radiation. Mulhern et al. (1990), using the PPSC by Lansky et al. (1985), reported that children who were inpatients had poorer QOL than those who were outpatients, although the measure did not discriminate between outpatients and healthy controls. In general, children who had been diagnosed for a shorter time had poorer QOL than those diagnosed for longer (Goodwin et al., 1994). In a number of studies, the HUI has been reported to discriminate between children differing in cancers or time since diagnosis (Barr et al., 1999, 2000; Felder-Puig et al., 1998). Calaminus et al. (2000) reported poorer QOL for children with solid tumors compared with leukemias, but the quality of the measure may be compromised by the lack of significant differences between children with cancer and healthy controls. Bhatia et al. (2002) reported better QOL among healthy adolescents compared with those with cancer, and between those on treatment and those who had completed therapy.

Face Validity. Measures differ according to the extent to which the initial selection of items and domains and thus the content of the measure involved children or their families. At one extreme, measures rely heavily or exclusively on input from professional staff (Calaminus et al., 2000; Phipps et al., 1994; Varni et al. 1998, 1999). In contrast, others report extensive interview procedures with children and their parents to determine the content of items (F. D. Armstrong et al., 1999; Eiser et al., 1994; Goodwin et al., 1994). Unusually, F. D. Armstrong et al. also reported procedures for coding these interviews and determining the specific items included in the final version. The HUI was originally based on interview data obtained from a population sample of Canadian parents, although other items (e.g., fertility) were added to address issues thought to be of concern to parents of children with cancer.

The PPSC (Lansky et al., 1985) is often described as a QOL measure, though was not labeled as such by Lansky herself. In style, the measure borrowed heavily from the Karnofsky scale for adults with cancer. However, the PPSC is exceptional in that the content was based on a theoretical account of developmental changes in children's play developed by Gesell and Ilg (1946).

Concurrent Validity. A further question involves overlap between domains purporting to measure the same aspect of QOL. For example, how far do the different measures assess physical functioning in the same way? Papers vary in the extent to which they give details of the specific items to be completed. Pressures on journal space further limit the amount of detail. Some papers (Calaminus et al., 2000) give no information about specific questions, whereas the most common strategy involves providing an example for each domain. More complete information is given by some authors (Goodwin et al., 1994; Phipps et al., 1994; Varni et al., 1998). A full description of items is given by F. D. Armstrong et al. (1999), and merits some discussion because the domains identified differ markedly from those described in other measures. The social competence scale includes not only a number of items about friendships and getting on with others, but also items referring to body image, participation in sports, and school attendance. The emotional stability scale includes items that would be expected about mood, worries, and emotionality. The self-competence scale includes items about positive attitude, motivation, autonomy, and decision making, as well as items about ability to remember and maintain attention to task, items that might well be included in cognitive scales by others. Interestingly, these scales were confirmed through factor analysis, suggesting a degree of robustness, even though the specific content does not entirely reflect the domains of QOL normally thought relevant.

Sensitivity. Barr et al. (1997) used the HUI (marks 2 and 3) to track QOL in children with ALL in remission during postinduction chemotherapy. The children ($N = 18$) ranged in age from 11 months to 14 years. Ratings were made by nurses, parents, and, where possible, by children themselves. They concluded, as might be expected, that the burden of morbidity is cyclical in nature, mirroring the schedule of chemotherapy. The impact on QOL was least at the onset of the treatment cycle (following a week of no treatment) and greatest at the beginning of the second week (following use of steroids). Pain was the most frequently reported indicator of morbidity, followed by emotion and mobility. This study documents the close relationship between treatment and QOL, and suggests also that HUI is sufficiently sensitive to detect these changes.

Kazak, Penati, Boyer, and Himelstein (1996) devised an intervention to reduce distress among children undergoing BMAs and LPs. Children were compared in two arms of a randomized, controlled prospective study. One group ($n = 45$) received a pharmacological intervention only, and the other group a combined pharmacological and psychological intervention ($n = 47$). Outcome measures included child distress, parent-rated assessment of child QOL, and parenting stress. Child distress was lower in the combined intervention group, but there were no differences in QOL scores. (Subsidiary analyses suggested that QOL for both groups improved over the 6-month course of the study. Thus there is evidence that this QOL measure lacks sensitivity to identify differences as a function of the intervention, but may more adequately reflect changes over time.)

Predictive Validity. One of the main justifications for developing measures of QOL has always been to predict changes in QOL over time, with a goal to provide appropriate support to those most in need. This predictive aspect of validity has rarely, if at all, been investigated.

CLINICAL IMPLICATIONS

As we have seen, the truly cured child is free of cancer, but also competent socially and psychologically (van Eys, 1991). Thus, the goals of treatment are about quality as well as quantity of survival. Measurement of quality poses considerable problems, but is nevertheless an integral part of the overall evaluation of the success of treatment.

Clinical Trials

Because current treatment protocols are not expected to be associated with significant improvements in survival, it follows that any changes to protocols must have implications for QOL. Although measures of QOL are routinely included in trials involving adult patients with cancer, they have not been included in trials involving children. Such omissions are unacceptable.

Pollock (1999) made a number of points about why QOL measures are not routinely used in clinical trial work involving children. These include the added financial costs incurred by addition of QOL measures, which may be substantial in international trials where care must be taken to ensure comparability of different versions. Greater use of new technologies and use of self-administered questionnaires that can be directly scanned into a computer would offset costs somewhat, and are increasingly being used in work with adults. Assessment of the child's QOL is necessarily more complex and may inevitably involve more costly and laborintensive methods. In addition, it is essential that clinicians are committed to QOL assessment in order to ensure successful completion of the project. Finally, collaboration across centers is essential to ensure adequate statistical power. In conclusion, Pollock argued that:

> It is important that clinical investigators become familiar with [QOL] assessment. Demonstration of the usefulness of this process should be made a high priority to encourage acceptance of measures. Additional financial resources are needed to further the development and validation of measures as well as to enhance the ongoing evaluation of existing instruments used for new clinical applications. Investigators should be encouraged to take advantage of the existing infrastructure provided by clinical trial groups as these groups provide a platform to evaluate the performance of measures efficiently. Selection of measures should be based on common sense, internal and external validity considerations, cost and ultimate clinical applicability. These issues must be addressed before [QOL] assessment becomes a standard outcome component for pediatric cancer clinical trials. (p. 153)

Evaluation of Interventions

The focus on QOL measures in evaluating clinical trials should not cloud the issue that the measures have other potential uses. Measurement of QOL has also been seen to be relevant in determining the efficacy of physical and psychological interventions, and understanding the child's perspective about the disease (Eiser & Morse, 2001). The development of a BMT-specific measure is to be welcomed given the increasing use of BMT for children with cancer. Using this measure, Phipps, Dunavant, Lensing, and Rai (2002) were able to identify groups at special risk during BMT. Children undergoing unrelated donor transplants experienced greater distress, followed by those undergoing matched-sibling BMT, and both groups experienced greater distress than those undergoing autologous transplant. Furthermore, these authors reported that younger children reported less distress and higher QOL than older children. Those from lower socioeconomic backgrounds also reported worse QOL during the course of treatment. For all these reasons, Phipps et al. concluded that interventions should target the most vulnerable groups, specifically those undergoing allogenic transplant, older children and adolescents, and those from lower socioeconomic backgrounds. Thus, information about the potential impact during and after BMT on QOL may be useful for parents in enabling them to anticipate the child's reactions, and descriptive work of this kind may usefully form the basis of future interventions.

Treatment Choices

In addition to its role as an outcome measure in trials, QOL needs to be considered in situations where children and families make decisions about different treatment protocols. Perhaps the most difficult decisions are those involving treatment alternatives on diagnosis. These have to be taken quickly and at times when families are stressed anyway.

For example, parents of children newly diagnosed with rhabdomyosarcoma are currently confronted by very difficult choices. Orbital rhabdomyosarcoma affects very young children (less than 7 years) but the prognosis is excellent (almost 90% survival rate over a 10-year period). As noted previously, survival rates hide the true costs of the impact of treatment on child and family. In this case, the choice is between radiotherapy or chemotherapy only. Children treated with radiotherapy are at risk of reduced vision, cataracts, orbital hypoplasia, and facial asymmetry. A small number of patients may require late enucleation (removal of the eye) for the complications of therapy. The majority of patients receiving radiation to an orbital field also show evidence of growth impairment as a result of pituitary damage and growth hormone insufficiency (Heyn et al., 1986; Raney et al., 2000).

Patients treated with chemotherapy alone have a high risk of relapse and may then require further treatment (Rousseau, Flamant, Quintana, Voute, & Gentet, 1994). Some of those who survive will then not only receive radiotherapy but will also be exposed to significantly more chemotherapy including higher doses of alkylating agents and, possibly, anthracycline drugs.

The decision, therefore, is between sparing of radiotherapy in some patients against the psychological burden and additional risk involved in treatment of relapse in another subset of the same patients. This decision is particularly difficult as the overall survival rate seems to be the same whether or not radiotherapy is incorporated as part of the initial treatment.

The concept of the "total burden of therapy" is important in considering the overall "cost" of survival for any disease. In this scenario, it is particularly important to be able to assess and compare patients who survive with or without additional treatment after relapse. Any assessment must include an attempt to measure the overall experience of the child (and family) during and after treatment.

It is not only on diagnosis that complex and difficult decisions may need to be made. Similar situations can arise at any time during treatment. Again, this can be illustrated with an example. Most children are fitted with a Hickman or similar line. This has the advantage of facilitating procedures. It is possible to deliver chemotherapy or withdraw blood without injection. In itself, the Hickman line has revolutionized care and contributed massively to the child's QOL. However, there are disadvantages. Children are not able to swim with a Hickman line, and even bathing is complicated, as it is important the line does not get wet. There are also fears that the line may come out, especially as the child feels better and takes part in more boisterous play. Decisions to continue with the line therefore involve an assessment of the importance of keeping the line and ensuring pain-free procedures, against the negative implications of no swimming or fear of the line coming out. For young children especially, the decision is not easy.

There are also QOL decisions to be made at the end of treatment. GHT is commonly recommended following treatment by radiotherapy. Prescription of GHT is considered primarily where children fail to grow, but has also been linked with improved energy and vitality, muscle tone, and memory. The potential disadvantages include daily injections, more frequent trips to the hospital, and a slight risk of cancer recurrence. The decision about whether or not to begin GHT is entirely based on QOL issues. There are no implications for long-term survival. (The possibility of recurrence is considered negligible by clinicians.) Decisions therefore need to be made on the basis of the child's current height and the possible importance of height in the future. There are still height requirements for some types of work, and if a child is set on a career in the police force, GHT may seem more essential than if the child wants to be a ballet dancer. For parents, the decision may be especially difficult where a child is currently well and involved in lots of activities. Beginning GHT after years of cancer treatment can seem a backward step, not worth the possible gains in future height. Parents' decisions are further complicated because their actions may be held against them at some future time. A child who does not want to bother with the extra injections now may nevertheless be full of criticism in later years when unable to pursue a particular career.

Many treatment alternatives have implications for both current as well as future QOL. Often new methods of treatment delivery are introduced on the assumption that the new method will prove superior, but in the absence of any empirical data, such assumptions are rarely confirmed. For example, wherever possible, arrangements are made for children to have treatment at home, rather than in the hospital. On the surface, there are considerable advantages to treatment at home, the most critical being the reduced disruption to everyday life, for both the child and family. In practice, there may also be some disadvantages to home-based care. These include the greater responsibility placed on parents. Where children are very uncooperative with treatment, the burden on parents can be considerable. On the one hand, they know that treatment is vital; on the other hand, they may find it very distressing to "force" the reluctant child to undergo care at home.

Dilemmas between home- and hospital-based care are not unique to care of children with cancer but are shared with families caring for children with many other chronic conditions. In the treatment of cystic fibrosis, for example, children may be well enough to go home but require antibiotics. However, the advantages of home-based care, in the case of cystic fibrosis, include the freeing-up of hospital beds and avoidance of cross-infection.

There is evidence of improved clinical outcomes and preferences for home-based care among both families of children with cystic fibrosis and clinic staff (Donati, Guenette, & Auerbaech, 1987; Gilbert, T. Robinson, & Littlewood, 1988; Pond, Newport, Jones, & Conway, 1994). Wolter, Bowler, Nolan, and McCormack (1997) used a QOL measure (Guyatt, Berman, Townsend, Pugsley, & Chambers, 1987) to assess adolescents and young adults on three separate occasions during the course of treatment. At the end of treatment, patients were also asked to rate the degree of disruption to various domains of life, including family and personal relationships, sleeping, and eating.

There were no differences between home- and hospital-based groups in duration of treatment or clinical outcomes (respiratory function). However, home-based patients reported more fatigue, less feelings of mastery, and reduced overall QOL compared with those treated in the hospital. At the same time, the home-based-care group reported improvements in personal, family, sleeping, and eating aspects of QOL. Wolter et al. (1997) suggested that increased fatigue was a consequence of trying to keep up with normal life as well as administer treatments at home.

These studies suggest that QOL considerations can improve our understanding of the merits of home-based over hospital-based care. It is not that either method of treatment delivery will have a positive impact on all aspects of QOL, but careful measurement and research can give insights into how patients manage different kinds of care. This is potentially useful in explaining details to new patients and helping them make balanced decisions about treatment alternatives.

These studies also demonstrate that understanding the QOL implications of different diseases might be facilitated by greater collaboration between researchers involved with different disease groups. Interest in QOL implications of home- or hospital-based care, for example, is not unique to those looking after children with cystic fibrosis but also is an issue for those working with children with cancer. We stand to learn much from work with other disease groups, both about research methodology and about the implications of treatment for families of a child with cancer.

DISCUSSION

Requirements for a Child-Centered Measure

Measures have variously been developed for completion by parents, by the child, and less often, by both. Measures differ also in quality. This is normally defined in terms of psychometric properties; the reliability, validity, or sensitivity of the measure. The issue of establishing validity is problematic, because to date, there is no widely accepted gold standard. The validity of new measures is sometimes reported in relation to the PPSC (Lansky et al., 1985). Yet this scale is widely criticized, particularly in that it lacks sensitivity for work with children functioning at near normal levels. Thus, choice of the PPSC as the key instrument against which to determine the validity of a new instrument does little more than establish a correlation between the two measures. Because it is not clear that the PPSC is a comprehensive measure of QOL for children, it follows that establishing a correlation between the PPSC and any other measure does not satisfactorily establish the validity of the new instrument.

There are also difficulties in establishing the psychometric properties of new scales in that conventional statistical procedures (e.g., factor analysis) require relatively large samples of respondents. Given the low incidence of cancer in children, it is only possible to collect adequate sample sizes through collaboration. Small sample sizes mean that only two currently available QOL measures (F. D. Armstrong et al., 1999; Goodwin et al., 1994) have been subject to factor analysis (and both are based on parent- rather than child-completed report). In other cases, the different themes or domains have been defined intuitively and are not supported by statistical techniques.

Early measures of QOL were simple downward extensions of adult measures (e.g., Bradlyn et al., 1993; Lansky et al., 1985). More recently, the approach has been more child centered, with researchers going to some pains to collect preliminary data from children in order to ensure that their views are represented (e.g., Eiser et al., 1995; Bhatia et al., 2002). Issues of quality may also relate therefore to how involved children have been in determining the content of a measure.

The range of measures developed in recent years poses a problem for researchers and clinicians wanting to measure the child's QOL. Decisions need to be made about the *purpose* of the assessment, the most suitable *respondent* (parents, the child, or both), and the *appropriateness* of the measure for work with children. Other considerations relate to the *psychometric properties* of the measure and method of development. In particular, however good the psychometric properties, the critical question refers to whether or not the items in a measure are sensitive to issues concerning the child or family. Typically QOL measures tap general achievements (e.g., can you climb the stairs?) or general concerns (are you sad or worried?). They do not assess parents' anxieties about whether or not they are administering medication correctly, or children's cooperation with treatment. Manne et al. (1999) showed that parents experience difficulties with (a) administration of oral medications, (b) administration of mouth care, (c) administration of central-access-line care, (d) getting the child to drink fluids and (e) getting the child ready for clinic visits. QOL measures typically do not include items such as these. General items such as "feel sad" are likely to occur in all children treated for cancer and may not distinguish between children on different protocols. In contrast, the frequency of medication and complexity of regimens may contribute to differences in QOL. Thus, comprehensive evaluation of QOL also needs to take into account parents' ability or willingness to carry out home-based treatments. It is important therefore not only to determine the relative difficulties of different aspects of home-based care, but also to determine how far such reported difficulties are a function of parental attitudes.

Currently available measures have considerable limitations. Though some information about reliability and validity is often available, critical questions about sensitivity and predictive validity remain. Measures have not been proven to be sensitive to changes over time or to the specific issues of importance to children. Early measures of QOL were simple downward extensions of adult measures (e.g., Bradlyn et al., 1993; Lansky et al., 1985). More recently, the approach has been more child centered, with researchers recognizing the need to collect preliminary data from children in order to ensure that their views are represented (e.g., Eiser et al., 1995; Jenney et al., 1995). Issues of quality may also relate therefore to how involved children have been in determining the content of a measure. It is regrettable that new measures continue to be published even though there has been little if any consultation with children or their families. At the same time, it is crucial that developers are clear about how information gained from children is translated into the items that make up a published scale.

At the present time there is a lack of measures for self-completion even by children above 8 years of age, with many measures relying on parent report. Where measures are for use in evaluation following diagnosis, this may well be appropriate or indeed the only way to collect information given that many children will be too young or too ill to respond themselves at this time. However, differences between children and their parents in ratings of QOL need to be considered, and for this reason greater attention needs to be given to development of measures for child completion. There is no suggestion that parent or child views are more accurate, but a complete picture of QOL needs to include both.

The situation is more complex where younger children are involved. There are considerable difficulties in developing measures for work with children less than 8 years of age (Eiser, Mohay, & Morse, 2000). These include limitations in the child's reading and language skills, and understanding of rating scales. Measures to assess QOL in children below 8 years of age may be possible and have been reported for children with asthma (French, Christie, & West, 1994). These will necessarily involve a different format from that adopted in adult work.

Perhaps it is because QOL is so important that so much heat has been generated about measurement. This would not be a problem, except insofar as we have reached a sort of stalemate and have become expert at criticizing measures. Such criticism is at the expense of progress. As emphasized by Gill and Feinstein (1994), QOL can refer to both clinical and objective measures in addition to the subjective. Future development must attempt to integrate these different views in order to provide a truly comprehensive assessment of QOL. In the pediatric field, progress may best be achieved where a battery of measures that includes key clinical, behavioral, and subjective indices of QOL is agreed upon.

17

Conclusions

Quality of Life in Children With Cancer

Cancer in children is a rare and life-threatening disease. Improvements in survival have only been possible through the development of long and aggressive treatment protocols. As described earlier, the increasing success of these treatments is evident in improved survival rates for many childhood cancers. With these improvements in survival rates comes the luxury of considering quality, as well as quantity of survival.

There are many reasons to be concerned about the QOL of children with cancer. Although adults may accept that the physical side effects typical of treatment are temporary, and the long-term goal is cure, children experience the discomfort of chemotherapy and pain associated with LPs and other procedures. They may be unable to focus on the potential long-term benefits nor understand the reasons for their current pain and sickness. For all of these reasons, it is important to weigh quantity and quality of survival from the child's perspective.

Although the question of QOL has been central in pediatric oncology since the 1960s, there has been much disagreement about what constitutes QOL. The gold standard has traditionally been inferred from scores on the PPSC, but as discussed in chapter 16, this is little more than an index of basic activity. Others have assumed a simple relationship between clinical parameters and QOL. Yet it is clear that for any disease, there is no simple relationship between clinical variables and QOL. The experience of physical symptoms is associated with, but not the same as, QOL.

Is QOL the same as participation in daily activities? Again, the answer is only partly yes. Children who do not regularly attend school probably do have compromised QOL. They lack structure to their day, lack social contacts, and ultimately experience compromised adult QOL. Similarly, children who do not take part in regular sports activities probably have compromised QOL. Yet many children do not enjoy physical sports. More critically, where children are unable to take part in sports, they become skilled in defining alternative interests. Within a short time, QOL is no longer compromised by inability to take part in sports.

We must therefore recognize the subjective nature of QOL. My QOL is uniquely defined by my interests, my experiences, my goals and ambitions. Furthermore, key components and determinants of QOL will change with age and with other changes in circumstances. We should not underestimate the challenge of measuring QOL, and critically, should not cut corners by assuming that easily measurable concepts (e.g., school absence) will provide viable alternatives.

The challenge in measuring QOL is clearly brought out in the literature reviewed in this book. We have moved from a focus on clinical symptoms to a simple assumption that participation in everyday activities such as going to school is an indicator of QOL. However, we have frequently assumed that established measures of affect (depression, anxiety, or loneliness) are good proxy indicators.

Perhaps we are not really interested in *quality of life*, but in the *lack* of quality of life. The result is that QOL is more often measured in terms of problems rather than a reflection of the processes underlying adjustment. This bias to the negative is evident in almost all current measures of QOL and is a major limitation.

These criticisms of method are partly off-set by the undoubted advantages of considering QOL. Discussion about QOL has brought to the fore the importance to children and their families of quality and not just quantity of survival. The focus on QOL has led to an acknowledgment of the potential impact of illness on all aspects of the child's life.

Our understanding of the QOL implications of cancer for the child is, however, limited by these issues of conceptualization and associated measurement. With these reservations in mind, it is still possible to draw some conclusions. These are presented first in terms of what we can infer about QOL and second in terms of what we cannot.

First of all, we know there are critical differences between parents and their child in assessment of the child's QOL. This has been shown consistently, and not only for children with cancer. It is a typical finding and is not dependent on any specific disease. In addition, mothers who evaluate their own QOL poorly also rate their child's QOL to be low. Other family variables may also moderate the impact of the disease on the child's QOL.

Socioeconomic class, mother's education, and family financial resources are probably closely linked and have all been implicated. The attitudes and behaviors of friends is also very important.

Although many adults accept that a child's QOL will inevitably be compromised after diagnosis, they also assume that life will return to normal with time. It is more difficult to find the evidence for this. Long-term follow-up of survivors, and separate studies involving their siblings, suggest there is considerable variability in outcome. In truth, long-term outcomes are multiply determined. The type of cancer and treatment are critical but the extent to which individual resources can modify the effects of treatment are not known.

A further enigma concerns how far appropriate education and rehabilitation can alleviate the disadvantages of treatment. We have done so little intervention work that we cannot begin to answer this question. Undoubtedly, some families seem to know intuitively what needs to be done for their child. Within a brief time of diagnosis, some families accept that their child is not going to be able to play on the school football team, and efficiently maneuver him into some new, less aggressive activity before he realizes that he can't play. Others acknowledge the potential damage of a CNS tumor for the child's balance and coordination, and they introduce piano lessons with an aim to improve motor skills. The development of a range of intervention programs is essential for the potential benefit of the child. In addition, understanding how far children can benefit from interventions and recover function will greatly enhance our current knowledge of brain development.

EVALUATION OF CURRENT RESEARCH

In writing a book of this kind, the question of how to evaluate the quality of research is paramount. In the final analysis, how can the work reviewed in this book be judged? It is important that the literature concerned with child and family coping with cancer is of the highest caliber. Traditionally, the quality of research can be evaluated against three criteria.

First of all, we can consider the theoretical value of research. To a large extent, the work reviewed in this book is not characterized by theoretical quality. Yet without theory, it may be difficult to interpret findings and our results may be dismissed as trivial or obvious. Second, we can evaluate research against methodological criteria. As we have seen throughout this book, if methods are of poor quality, contradictory results are obtained. Third, research can be evaluated against clinical criteria. Do the results contribute to our understanding of the impact of childhood cancer on the family, and critically, is it possible to reorganize services so as to minimize distress?

Relationships Between Applied and Theoretical Work

An overriding question is whether research has really contributed to the promotion of well-being or QOL in children with cancer and their families. Compared with the 1950s, there is now a much greater recognition of the potentially adverse psychological consequences of illness for children. However, it cannot be argued that this is entirely due to the research findings. Recognizing the need for holistic care of the child has to be seen within a much wider context. Two important influences can be identified. First, there have been changes in legislation that have emphasized parents' rights to be with their sick child, and second, there is increasing recognition of children's rights to be involved in decisions about their medical treatment and care. Relevant, too, are changes in public attitudes to health care, including greater confidence to challenge the views of doctors. In the extreme, we have become a society in which litigation actions against medical staff have become commonplace. The growth of self-help and patient organizations has also contributed to a shift in power away from doctors to the greater empowerment of individuals. Finally, changes in nurse training have included greater emphasis on the psychological as well as the physical care of patients. The media, and cancer charities, too, have played a role in redefining how the ordinary citizen views cancer, particularly cancer in children. Publicity campaigns orchestrated by cancer charities have contributed to more open discussion of cancer and the promotion of a more informed public.

So greater public awareness of cancer can be attributable to a number of different events. Most of the high-profile interventions (e.g., the Hole-in-the-Wall gangs) are the inspiration of individuals, driven to do something themselves. These approaches are a response to personal experience or "gut" feelings, and rarely do these individuals begin by conducting a literature review. The strength of their approaches is in the huge diversity and extent of types of interventions. The weakness is the lack of coherence and failure to build on more successful approaches. We are in danger of continually rediscovering the wheel.

At a clinical level, the lack of theory limits the progress and development of innovative ideas. The apparent haphazard nature of this approach also leaves us open to criticism from those who are committed to a more traditional, experimental type of research. Consequently, this work can be dismissed as unsophisticated.

These criticisms are common to most applied work, and reflect an unhelpful distinction between theoretical or basic research on the one hand,

and applied research on the other. "The experimental method now dictates rather than serves the research questions we value, fund, and pursue; as a result the process of development as it naturally transpires in children growing up in actual life circumstances is largely ignored" (McCall, 1997, p. 334).

The distinction between applied work on the one hand, and basic or theoretical research on the other, has been a problem generally (Schwebel, Plumert, & Pick, 2000), and particularly in the study of children with cancer and their families. The goal of basic research is to provide information about processes of development whether or not this is relevant for solving any problem of practical significance. The goal of applied research is to provide information that will help solve problems that have immediate practical consequences for children regardless of whether this has relevance for understanding the processes of development. "Researchers have tended to array themselves on one side or the other of the basic–applied distinction as if their paths by definition diverged and an uncrossable chasm gaped between them" (Zigler, 1980, p. 1).

In attempting to reconcile these approaches, theorists sometimes try to consider how their work could have practical implications. Conversely, applied researchers look to theories that could underpin their work. Both approaches are commendable, but result in limited cross-fertilization of ideas. Just as the study of child development grew out of practical concerns for children, so, too, the impetus for much work involving children with cancer has been justified in clinical terms. Though clinical implications are important, there are limitations if these are studied in complete isolation of any theoretical context.

This is especially clear when considering interpretation of findings in QOL work. Without theory, it is impossible to understand the processes underlying differences in QOL. Thus, as reviewed in the previous chapter, QOL is better for children with ALL compared with those with a neuroblastoma (Barr et al., 2000). Without theory, it is difficult to account for this. Children with ALL tend to have a better prognosis and fewer complications than those with neuroblastoma.

At the time, the approaches taken by Wallander and Varni (1992) and Thompson and colleagues (R. J. Thompson & Gustaffson, 1996) to attempt to account for behavior in this very complex area were highly innovative. Both emphasized the risk and resistance variables involved and challenged the assumptions of the deficit-centered approaches. However, though both document the range of possible influences on the child's psychological outcome, they shed little light on the processes underlying psychological outcomes. Despite the popularity of these theories in work with children with chronic illness, they have not attained general use in work with children with cancer.

The failure to use theoretical criteria either to guide research or as a means of evaluation is a major limitation of work in this area. In the absence of theory, it is too easy to think of *post hoc* explanations of findings, which do little to contribute to the overall development of the field. A theory of QOL in children with cancer is needed to underpin the next generation of QOL measures, and lend greater scientific merit to research.

Toward a Model of QOL for Children With Cancer

Research involving children with cancer has to move away from the simple questions that have dominated work to date. It is much too simple to ask "do children with cancer generally have a poorer QOL than healthy children?" At one level, of course they do. Those who argue otherwise would be fooling themselves. Development occurs through interaction between the child and their environment. Where the environment includes treatment for cancer, the developmental trajectory will be affected. Studies that suggest there are no effects, or that children with cancer do not differ from healthy controls, are not using sufficiently sensitive measures.

The simplest model of QOL assumes a direct relationship between physical health (presence or absence of disease) and QOL. The custom of validating new measures of QOL against disease severity is based on the assumption of a one-to-one correspondence between the two, as are comparisons between children with cancer and healthy peers.

There can be no doubt that physical health is a huge and significant contributor to QOL. Anyone who has a cold knows that the physical symptoms can make them feel miserable, unattractive, tired, and sluggish. Children on steroids are routinely moody, aggressive, and quite unlike themselves. Yet a few weeks later, at a different phase of treatment, the same children can have fun and be almost indistinguishable from any other child. If this were the whole story, we could accept the linear model. However, this model does not account for the substantial differences in QOL that can emerge between children undergoing apparently similar treatment. More adequate accounts need to explain the causal links between indicators and the expression of QOL.

According to Wilson and Cleary (1995), a major barrier to use of QOL measures stems from differences between clinicians and social scientists in perceived value of the work. For clinicians, the value of QOL is in the potential role to understand causation and guide diagnosis and treatment. In contrast, social scientists emphasize the value of QOL in describing and classifying, as a means to measure complex feelings. For Wilson and Cleary, greater use of QOL measures is dependent on greater links between QOL measurement and implications for intervention. Their model describes potential linkages between biological and physiological variables, symptoms, functional status, health perceptions, and QOL. The model is an attempt to bridge distinct conceptual systems and suggests links between biological symptoms and impairment with QOL.

In a limited amount of previous work, it has been noted that it is *perceptions* of difficulties rather than real difficulties that can compromise adjustment following illness. Ireys et al. (1994) suggested that individuals differ in the extent to which they perceive their condition to be responsible for ongoing difficulties and handicaps, regardless of more objective indicators of disease. This "perceived impact" mediates the relationship between condition characteristics and psychological symptoms. Some support for this perceived impact model was obtained in a study involving 600 young people born between 1966 and 1970 who had been diagnosed with a range of conditions. Of the total sample, 286 young adults and their parents (*n* = 138) agreed to take part. In addition to collecting information about the severity and course of the illness and any impairments still experienced, the authors developed a four-item scale to assess perceived impact.

These young-adult survivors reported a high incidence of physical symptoms (relative to figures for population norms). The risk of psychological symptoms was greater for those with restricted activity days, unpredictable symptoms, poor prognosis, presence of more than one condition, and presence of speech and hearing problems; that is, there was a positive relationship between physical and psychological health. However, the effect of these risk factors was moderated by the young adult's perception of the impact of the disease. The more the individual perceived there to be a problem associated with the illness, the more they also reported psychological symptoms.

The next question is what determines an individual's perception of illness or appraisal of consequences. How is it that, confronted with cancer, one individual sees it as a challenge to all previous hopes and ambitions, whereas another sees it as an opportunity? For children, the expression of physical symptoms is defined by the family environment. The way the family handles the illness is vital. Families mediate between the child and clinic staff. They also communicate their own fears and anxieties to the child. Parenting the child is a balancing act. What seems to be in the best interest of the sick child today may not be conducive to optimal development and a well-functioning adult in the future. How parents maintain this balance, or tip it to needs of today or the future, has massive implications for the child's QOL. What, then, do we know about how parents manage this dilemma?

Perceptions of difficulties or limitations are not made in a vacuum, but depend on our reference points. It is not so much of a problem if a survivor is unable to go to university if no one else in the family or neighborhood is going either. It is a big problem if everyone else who matters is going. As also noted by van Eys (1976), self-image needs to be tested against peers. This idea can be taken further to suggest that individual decisions about QOL must in large part depend on social comparison processes. According to Festinger (1954), all humans have a drive to evaluate their opinions and abilities. To function effectively, they need to know their own limitations and be accurate in their opinions of other people. Festinger suggested that this could be best achieved by comparison against objective indices, but failing these, individuals compare themselves with other people. Individuals prefer to evaluate themselves against similar others. At the same time, individuals drive to be at a point slightly above comparison others.

Social comparison theory (Festinger, 1954) has proved useful in accounting for adjustment to cancer in adults. In one of the first examples of this, Wood, S. E. Taylor, and Lichtman (1985) showed that women with breast cancer made comparisons between themselves and others who were doing less well. It was assumed that these "downward comparisons" enable individuals to maintain self-esteem or "situated optimism" about their own circumstances or prospects (Armor & S. E. Taylor, 1998, p. 309). Though it may be possible to maintain self-esteem by comparing oneself with people who are worse off, such comparisons are not always possible. In practice, choice of comparison standard is complex. Comparison of oneself against friends without cancer can potentially be a very distressing experience, because it highlights limitations in activities and opportunities. QOL may well be very compromised where such comparisons are made because the child with cancer will inevitably come off worse. The individual therefore has a choice: to change the comparison standard or to change the dimension of comparison. Change in comparison standard involves a shift from the individual's original peer group to one including children who also have a disease or disability. Such a shift potentially allows individuals to see themselves in a more positive light. It is possible to achieve a positive self-image also by changing the dimension along which comparisons are made. It is still possible to compare oneself with healthy peers if the comparison is made along dimensions where you are better. This might include recognition of increased empathy or social skill. The elements of comparison processes have been described in children from 4 years of age (Butler, 1995). Consequently, both children and their parents can potentially use social comparison processes to maintain QOL.

Thus, there is some evidence that social comparison processes play a large part in determining an individual's decisions about their QOL. Consider, for example, this father deciding whether or not he wanted his child to begin GHT following treatment for a brain tumor:

> Dan is so well now. If only you could see him. He is always out and about. There is nothing he can't do. He came second in the 100 metres at school last week. He may be small but he is very strong. He's been helping me with the new kitchen I am building and he is as good a mate as I could find anywhere. There is nothing he can't lend a hand with. He's as strong as a grown man. And when we take the dog out now, he can walk as well as anyone; it's never Dan we're waiting for. If his QOL was not so good, then I could see the point maybe, but you know his QOL now is so good.

Or again, a mother discussing how ALL had affected her daughter:

> The problem is worse because of Abigail (a sister 2 years younger). Abigail is 18 now and she is really independent. She has a car and she's working part time at the moment to earn enough to go to university next year. So you know, it's all where will Abi go? How much choice does she have? She could go anywhere, study whatever she wants. And then there's Beth, who doesn't go anywhere at all. If Beth goes anywhere, I put her on the bus here and make sure someone sees her off at the other end, and that's only happened once. She'll never be able to drive. And there just isn't anything she can do. Who would want to employ her?

In the first example, the comparison is with the recent past. The father was remembering how ill his son had been. His current view, that his son's current QOL was so good, was very much a reflection of how things used to be. The comparison was with the child's past self. Choice of this comparison standard led the dad to conclude that life was as good as it could be, and he did not want anything to change. In this particular case, choice of past self as a comparison standard enabled the family to feel very positive. If they chose a sibling or healthy peer, they would be forced to acknowledge that the child was extremely small, on considerable daily medication to compensate for thyroid dysfunction following treatment, and less independent than most boys of a similar age.

However, comparisons with past self are not inevitably associated with positive implications. Both children and their parents can focus on the time before the diagnosis and contrast the current QOL negatively in comparison: "I was really excellent at football. I would have been playing for Man. U. by now if this hadn't happened."

In the second example, the comparison is with the healthy unaffected sibling. Comparisons are more difficult for brothers and sisters, but where there are two children in the family of the same gender, it is easy to make unfavorable comparisons and conclude that the differences are entirely due to cancer. Such comparisons are unhelpful because they accentuate the negative consequences of cancer, but also do not suggest any solutions. On the other hand, comparisons with siblings can also result in more positive views of QOL: "We often say it was a good job it was Ruth and not Mary. Ruth is a real toughie and just gets on with things. She has never been any problem over taking medication or going to the hospital. She just accepts whatever they throw at her. But she never gives up. Mary would never have managed so well."

We are all free to choose our comparison standards, but whom we choose can have consequences for our QOL. Families can achieve good QOL by comparing themselves favorably with other families of sick children. Emphasizing how well the child is doing compared with others is part of a process of maintaining good QOL despite the illness. Good QOL can also be achieved if comparisons are made along appropriate dimensions. Comparisons with families of well children have to challenge QOL. Healthy families have more freedom and flexibility, they do not have to go to the hospital, and they have no real worries about the child's health or future. However, we do not have complete freedom to choose whom we compare ourselves with, and therefore these challenging comparisons have to be met. The solution is that families of a child with cancer look to other dimensions along which comparisons can be made: "It seems crazy to say this but in some ways it's been a good thing. Bill [the dad] was working all hours. We were in such a rat-race, making money for this and that. But when this happened, we just asked ourselves, did it really matter? Bill set up his own company and works from home now. It's been hard but it means he's around so much more. He has seen the children grow up, and we think really that that is what it's all about."

There are other points to be made about QOL. It is not a static trait but a dynamic process. Some disease restrictions can be accommodated in the early stages of disease and accepted, but become much less acceptable over time. Our emphasis on research involving single time points, and lack of follow-up data, means that we have little information about changes in QOL over time, or crucially, how individuals adjust over time. The concept of QOL as the discrepancy between what an individual can do, and wants to be able to do, has some potential here: "I used to play hockey at university but I am not fit enough anymore. I really enjoy helping at the local school though. They have just started a team and I coach on Saturday mornings."

In this example, the discrepancy between what one can do now and used to be able to do is painfully clear. The potential discrepancy between what one can't do now but would like to do (play hockey) is resolved by becoming interested in coaching. Assessment of QOL on only one occasion is unlikely to have identified the problem, and certainly paper-and-pencil measures currently available would not identify the solution.

The second point to emerge from the literature reviewed is that QOL is not entirely an individual phenomenon. From the beginning, parents make decisions about how much to tell their child about cancer and how far to involve them about decisions about treatment. The way parents behave in clinics, and especially how they support the child through painful treatments, establishes a symbiotic approach to management of the illness. Mothers who report poor QOL themselves rate their child's QOL to be poor too. Despite these obvious ways in which children and their families are linked, QOL is typically viewed as an individual concept—"How far has your child had a problem with the following?" In practice, the extent to which any behavior is viewed as a problem is a function of family values and expectations.

First of all, it must be acknowledged that cancer and its treatment poses a huge challenge to the attainment of quality QOL. At a general level, the more serious the disease, the more aggressive the treatment, and the more handicapping the late effects, the more the challenge. However, superimposed on this continuum of physical risk is a parallel continuum of social risk. This is determined by the attitudes and coping strategies of those with whom the child comes into contact, and can include medical staff, parents, teachers, and friends. Where there is little risk to physical health and parenting is good, we can predict good to excellent child outcomes. Conversely, where the risk to physical health is high and parenting poor, outcomes may be universally negative. This model raises interesting questions about how far good parenting can offset the consequences of disease involving considerable risk to physical health. The dearth of intervention studies makes it difficult to answer this question. However, it may be that no amount of good parenting can offset the deletrious consequences.

Method. Conducting exemplary work in this area is difficult. Psychologists and pediatricians have been trained to conduct research within a traditional scientific paradigm. The RCT is the gold standard for work in the clinical sciences. Thus, the gold standard to which we are trained to aspire stresses that research should be evaluated in terms of control groups, placebo interventions, and valid and reliable outcome indicators. There are huge problems with this design if the focus of interest is QOL. It is not ethical to withhold treatment from some children in order to create a control group and a scientifically acceptable study. At the same time, there are no sophisticated outcome measures with exemplary reliability and validity.

Although the RCT may not be the method of choice, it may still be desirable to model some of the assumptions. Debate about the psychometric properties of measures is common, as was shown clearly in the discussion in chapter 16 about development of measures of QOL. Reference to source books extolling the virtues of measurement theory in the physical sciences is essential reading for all those interested in measurement issues.

Whether or not we can apply the same criteria to evaluation of measures in the social, compared with the physical, sciences is less resolved. The point is that there are methodological standards against which research can be judged, and these are often cited. Indeed, in discussing contradictory findings, researchers most frequently point to methodological differences in procedures. Specific methodological problems routinely identified include the limited number of measures, small samples, choice of control groups, and impact of moderating variables.

Measures. In terms of the quality of research, one of the biggest difficulties in work in this area is the very limited number of measures that are available and appropriate. As was clear in chapter 6, evaluation of outcomes in children with cancer have tended to rely on a limited number of measures. These include the CBCL (Achenbach & Edelbrock, 1983), anxiety (Spielberger, Gorsuch, Luschene, Vagg, & Jacobs, 1970), depression (Beck, Ward, Mendelson, Mock, & Erbaugh, 1961; Kovacs, 1981), and hopelessness (Kazdin, French, Unis, & Esveldt-Dawson, 1983). None of these measures was developed specifically for work with sick children. Almost without exception, these are parent-completed paper-and-pencil measures, chosen more for their psychometric properties than any consideration of their appropriateness or sensitivity for this group of children. The focus has been on *parents'* perceptions of the impact of the disease on the child, and very rarely has consideration been given to the child's own perspective.

Thus, researchers have relied on a handful of measures developed for purposes other than to assess the impact of cancer on the child. These measures have often been selected for their apparent psychometric rigor rather than their relevance or sensitivity to the issue. Few measures have been developed specifically to assess the impact of cancer. At least partly for this reason, results have been at best inconclusive and at worst contradictory. It has not been consistently shown that children with cancer differ from healthy peers, siblings, or children with other chronic diseases on any generic measure of adjustment or behavior.

The measurement of health status and QOL is a major growth industry in health care, whether for children or adults. Judgments about the "quality" of QOL measures tend to focus on psychometric properties, based on some unwritten assumption that if a measure has good reliability then it is without question a suitable and acceptable means of assessing outcomes. However, this reliance on psychometric properties has come under some criticism:

> Ultimately, any judgement about whether or not a measure is "valid" or "reliable" rests on what "validity" and "reliability" are said to mean. And be-

yond the obvious fact that sets of simple questions about how people are coping with disease (How long do you sit during the day? Do you take tablets to help you sleep? Do you need help with eating, dressing, bathing, or using the toilet?) undoubtedly ought to produce similar results when asked of similar types of patient, there are no gold standards of reliability and validity. (Seedhouse, 1996, p. 261)

It is important that these limitations inherent in all currently available measures are recognized, because otherwise myths grow up ascribing virtues to certain measures, resulting in their use above all others. In reality, their virtues may consist of nothing more than reasonable internal reliability and good marketing. The bottom line is that we have to invest in developing quality measures that really tap the behaviors we are concerned about. This will cost money and take time, but lack of investment in the past remains the single most important obstacle to developing quality research in this area.

Samples. The relatively small numbers of children diagnosed with cancer has proved a considerable barrier to the conduct of research that meets traditional standards of scientific rigor. Despite the big differences in prognosis and treatment most studies have included heterogeneous groups of children differing in specific diagnosis, age of onset, treatment intensity, and prognosis. The result has been to increase sample size but at the cost of reducing interpretability. Other studies have involved smaller numbers of children with insufficient power to identify differences between groups. Such studies increase the risk of Type 1 errors.

Survivors with any obvious handicap or visible disfigurement are routinely excluded from much published work. There has been a bias to include survivors of some cancers almost to the exclusion of others. As a result, much is known about the consequences of ALL, but very little about most other cancers. Long-term psychological functioning and QOL will be intimately associated with physical consequences of the disease, and for this reason, follow-up of homogeneous groups is to be recommended. Exclusion of subgroups of children, especially those with special difficulties or problems, severely limits the value of findings.

Also of importance is the issue of respondent bias; not all children with cancer or survivors want to be involved. In order to feel confident about the representativeness of our results, we strive to achieve 100% accrual to our research studies. In reality, we may be lucky to recruit 50% or 60%. Medical records are not perfect, and many survivors are lost to follow-up. They move, change their name, or don't want to be found. Others may be happy to take part at certain times, but not right at the time they are asked. They are too busy, not well, or experiencing difficulties in other aspects of their lives that leave them unwilling or unable to take part. Others don't want to take part because they are doing very well; life is good and they do not want to be reminded of the past. Because current ethics guidelines do not allow researchers to ask why patients do not wish to take part in research, it is impossible to tell how biased the recruited sample is. Without a change in basic thinking about ethics, it will remain impossible for us to be certain about the representativeness of any sample accrued.

Control Groups.   The standard experimental method involves comparison of a group of interest against a control group, and this approach is typical of much work in this area. Thus, groups of children with cancer are compared with groups of healthy children. This approach can be appropriate in some situations. It has proved useful, for example, when describing school achievement after treatment. Comparisons with healthy children facilitate decisions about the kind of remedial programs that should be offered in order for children to reach the required school-leaving standards. Comparisons with norms (in terms of educational level, for example) can tell us that the population has specific problems and that remedial services may be necessary. Though some questions can be answered by research designs where children with cancer are compared with healthy controls, others really cannot. Showing differences on a measure of self-esteem or depression tells us nothing about the processes whereby the problems arose. Indeed, taken to an extreme, this kind of approach is subject to the criticism that the differences were always there; that is, depressed children get cancer.

In other contexts, the method has limitations, not least because recruitment of control groups is very difficult. Whereas children or young-adult survivors may see some personal reason for taking part in the study, and perhaps feel some obligation to take part in work initiated by the hospital where they were treated, healthy control groups have no such incentives. As a consequence, control groups can be highly selective. As an example, Spirito et al. (1990) reported that the control group in their study represented only 29% of those invited to participate.

In efforts to address recruitment problems, authors have adopted a variety of techniques. Pendley et al. (1997) recruited volunteers from advertisements; Gray et al. (1992a, 1992b) asked patients to recommend friends. Small financial incentives have been offered in other studies. Results can be distorted by anomalies in the control group. For example, Allen et al. (1997) reported that newly diagnosed adolescents were not more depressed than a control group of healthy young people. However, it was unfortunate that incidence of depression in the control group was much higher than would normally be expected.

Moderating Variables.   As it has been recognized that the way children react to cancer is multiply determined, there have been attempts to identify key moderating variables. The simplest accounts draw on demographic or clinical variables. However, these are often not well reported. For example, in many studies of survivors, time since completion of treatment may be described simply as "more than 2 years." Others report mean years for the total group, which may include those who have recently completed treatment and those who completed treatment many years previously. In practice, there may be huge differences depending on the length of time since end of treatment. In addition to demographic or clinical variables, family or social variables are expected to make considerable differences to how children cope. However, measurement of family variables is very complex, and for the most part has been restricted to established generic measures of family interaction. Family attitudes to the illness, expectations about the future, or long-standing family conflict are less often considered. Family access to economic or social resources are also likely to be important. Access to a car can make hospital visits much less trying. Employers who are generous in allowing paid time for parents can also be critical. Families also differ in their own resources, and the extent to which they can integrate new patterns of care into their everyday lives.

In the absence of appropriate measures, the question arises as to how to identify family variables. The simplest approach may simply be to ask families about their experiences, but such an approach is usually dismissed as unscientific. The objection is that individual families cannot provide a "representative" view, and they may exaggerate or distort their reports depending on the listener.

In conclusion, there are considerable methodological challenges in conducting research in this area. This has been bemoaned by many authors, and can severely curtail the extent to which research findings are accepted as any kind of evidence for the organization of clinical practice. A major difficulty stems from adoption of the experimental method as the gold standard for research in such an applied context. It is inappropriate to hold up the RCT as the only research paradigm in this area. Given the diverse ways in which children and families function, the key question has to focus on intra- rather than intergroup comparisons. That is, in most situations, we are interested in differences within the group of children with cancer rather than between them and others.

The problems about measurement also need to be addressed. In recognizing the lack of measures, especially to determine QOL, there has been a spate of recent attempts to describe new measures. Typically, researchers have decried the reliance on adults as informants and argued that children must answer for themselves whenever possible. Consequently, they tend to start by eliciting basic information from children about their experiences, and then identifying themes in the data to fit around often predetermined scales and subscales. The result is a burgeoning literature in which we are confronted with a number of measures, all developed in a similar way but resulting in often diverse conclusions. Though acknowledging the value of involving children and their families in research, this approach has to be married with a more theoretical orientation that directs the underlying assumptions.

Clinical Implications

For many people who conduct research with sick children, the question of clinical significance is much more important than that of methodological rigor or theoretical value. The desire to improve things for these children is the ultimate justification for this work. In addition, the need to collaborate with pediatricians and justify proposals to ethics committees forces researchers to specify the practical benefits of the work. Convincing an ethics committee of the value of a proposed study is very different from convincing a university department or research council.

There has undoubtedly been a heightened interest in studying the QOL implications of childhood cancer. This research has enjoyed a degree of success to the extent that those involved in the care of childhood cancer patients are aware of the potential psychosocial consequences of the condition. It is customary for specialists centers to hold regular psychosocial meetings, at which issues about the impact on the child's family and school relationships are considered alongside medical concerns. Voluntary organizations have worked hard to provide an important service and have been very instrumental in raising awareness of the need to consider the psychosocial, as well as the medical care of the child. Thus, children can take part in activity holidays, affording them a degree of independence from their families, and parents the opportunity for time free of worry about daily care. Community nurses are employed to visit children at home or school, freeing them from some hospital visits.

Much of this, however, is based on intelligent guesses about what might work or be beneficial for families; these are not theory-driven interventions, evaluated against hard outcomes. Perhaps, it might be argued, as long as they work, interventions do not need to be theory-driven or evaluated in any scientific way. Such arguments are limited. Interventions cost money. If they really work, they should be available to all children with cancer, and this could only happen if the intervention was really proven. We also need to understand how interventions work, in order to provide the best fit between the program and the individual.

No intervention will work equally effectively for all individuals at any stage of the disease.

Thus, many of the interventions that have been put in place are based on general ideas about helping, rather than flowing directly from research findings. Many of the very practical and helpful activities can be credited to the insight and vision of individuals or groups of individuals, establishing charities, raising funds, and making things happen. There are many examples, and the current list is far from exhaustive. In the United Kingdom, Sir Malcolm Sargant, the famous conductor, established the Sargant Cancer Care for children with cancer. This highly successful organization now funds social workers in all major centers. These highly specialized social workers are able to provide information and practical support for families throughout the child's treatment. As nonmedical staff, they can act as informal sources of information about the disease, giving families the opportunity to ask questions they would rather not bother consultants with. They also provide practical information regarding financial rights and benefits. In the United States, Paul Newman established the Hole in the Wall Gangs (www.holeinthewallgang.org), activity camps for children where they could experience some independence from their families while also receiving appropriate treatment for their cancer. These camps offer children a variety of more physical experiences and activities than they might otherwise. As discussed in chapter 6, camps can improve children's knowledge of cancer, as well as promote self-esteem and independence. Camps offer children a normalizing experience, and this can be very valuable, especially for those who are too handicapped to take part in social activities that are not supported by professional care.

Other examples that relate more directly to research include changes in use of CNS irradiation following the extensive work suggesting links between irradiation and subsequent achievement and learning (see chap. 8). Despite the methodological difficulties in conducting this research and the lack of guiding theory, the bulk of the evidence points to learning difficulties following CNS irradiation. As a procedure, there are reasons to avoid CNS irradiation wherever possible. However, the risks do vary with the child's age, and suggest that care is needed especially for younger children. CNS irradiation remains the only treatment for some conditions. There remains therefore a need to establish if appropriate remedial education can offset the adverse effects of CNS irradiation.

Research has also documented the extent to which children experience difficulties on return to school after diagnosis. Absences can be long; 6 months is not unusual for children with bone cancer or a CNS tumor. As treatment for ALL has become more intense, long absences for these children are also the norm. Even after the first inevitably long absence following diagnosis, children can continue to miss a lot of school. Fear of infections is a major barrier to the resumption of normal life. Return to school has been identified as a critical time, and as a consequence, community nurses or social workers visit schools to talk to children and teachers. The goals are to inform children and teachers about the illness, thereby facilitating the child's return to school and integration in the classroom. As was discussed in chapter 7, such programs do improve teachers' knowledge, but it has not conclusively been established that this leads to greater acceptance of the sick child by others in the class. More systematic work developing programs to facilitate the child's return to school after diagnosis by Varni et al. (1993) has been described and evaluated.

Research has much greater clinical potential than these examples suggest. There is evidence of behavioral and emotional problems in healthy brothers and sisters. Parents recognize this to be a problem, and there have been reports of groups for siblings being established in large hospitals. These groups aim to help siblings understand that they are not alone in their situation, on the assumption that peer support will be beneficial. In addition, the opportunity to air their concerns away from parents is thought to be helpful. The program described by Meyer, Vadasy, and Lassen (1994) is exemplary in drawing on research findings to direct the content of an intervention.

To the extent that the work involves sick children and their families, we must also consider the pay-off for them. What are the benefits when families take part in research? Indeed, why do they agree in the first place? The benefits of previous research to children in hospital today are undoubtedly enormous. Before the Second World War, hospitals for children were very grim places. Staff were not specially trained or sympathetic to the needs of children compared with adults. Parents were not welcome on wards and there were certainly no opportunities for them to stay with their child. It took the vision of J. Robertson (1952) to highlight the plight of children in hospital. His work filming the distress of young children in hospital was the trigger for changes in care of sick children. Changes in legislation in the United Kingdom (Platt Committee, 1959) and the United States resulted in more child-friendly care in hospitals. Among the recommendations of the Platt report were ideas that children should be nursed on pediatric wards staffed by specially trained nurses, that provision should be made for play and education, and that parents should be entitled to unrestricted visiting of their child. Similarly, the U.S. report documented specific ways to reduce the stress of children in hospitals. The subsequent establishment of voluntary agencies such as NAWCH (National Association for the Welfare of Children in Hospital) in the United Kingdom and ACCH (Association for the Care of Children's Health) in the United States cemented the trend toward more child-centered care in hospitals. Partly as a consequence of these innovations, pediatric oncology wards now offer a friendly atmosphere for child patients. Specialist staff can provide play and educational opportunities. Wards are decorated to be attractive places for children to stay. Voluntary organizations provide clowns for entertainment. Thus, awareness of the close relationship between physical and psychological health has resulted in some very practical changes for children.

For those participating in research today, there may not be any immediate benefits. However, there is a hope that participation in research will lead to psychological benefits resulting from the opportunity to describe their experiences. The opportunity to talk may in itself be valuable. Work by Pennebaker, Mayne, and Francis (1997) suggests in fact that there can be tangible benefits to taking part in research. In one study, patients with arthritis who were given the opportunity to write about their feelings about their disease showed better mental health than those patients who did not have this opportunity (Kelley, Lumley, & Leisen, 1997). The implication is that families may benefit from involvement in research, simply because, for some at least, talking helps.

Disappointingly, there has been very little formal evaluation of family views about participation in research in pediatric oncology. As a consequence, we cannot be certain that this does constitute a positive benefit for all, or even some, families. Some may agree to participate as a means to gain some help for their own problem. If a family has struggled to get a child with learning problems assessed, they may reasonably hope that involvement in research may bring the problem to the attention of others and hasten some resolution. More often, families must content themselves that their involvement will lead to benefits for those diagnosed in the future. Informal discussions with families who have taken part in research suggest that this essentially altruistic appraisal is typical. If families take part for the benefits of future families, it is imperative that research is evaluated against this criterion, that is, that work really will contribute to improved care of children in the future.

EPILOGUE

For the future, the dream is to cure cancers in children with minimal risk to QOL. The aim is to achieve improvements in survival by better matching of treatment to tumor type. The dilemma is always to maximize the likelihood of cure while minimizing any risks of iatrogenic treatment effects. As described in the previous chapter, this is exemplified in current debates about the best approach to treatment of rhabdomyosarcoma. New techniques based on gene expression seem to have potential in facilitating understanding of the pathogenesis of tumors. Thus, clinical outcomes in medulloblastoma appear to be predictable on the basis of gene expression profiles of tumors on diagnosis (Pomeroy et al., 2002).

Just as some children may be more or less sensitive to different drugs, so some will have more or less resilience to cope with the traumas of treatment. Innovations in treatment do not guarantee QOL. Indeed, it may be that new treatments pose increasingly complex dilemmas for families and doctors to resolve.

Despite all of the criticisms that have been made about measuring QOL in children, these are, in my view, offset by what has been achieved. Discussion about QOL has brought to the fore the importance to children and their families of quality and not just quantity of survival. This awareness of QOL has resulted in acknowledgment of the potential impact of illness on all aspects of the child's life.

Though it may not be possible to cure cancer for all children in the foreseeable future, it is nevertheless vital to attempt to optimize QOL. This requires attention to QOL during treatment, and establishment of comprehensive social, educational, and physical follow-up in the longer term.

References

Aaronson, N. K., Meyeravitz, B. E., Bard, M., Bloom, J. R., Fauzy, F. I., Feldstein, M., Fink, D., Holland, J. C., Johnson, J. E., Lowman, J. T., Patterson, B., & Ware, J. E. (1991). Quality of life research in oncology: Past achievements and future priorities. *Cancer, 67*, 839–843.

Abidin, R. R., Jenkins, L. L., & McGaughey, M. C. (1992). The relationship of early family variables to children's subsequent behavioral adjustment. *Journal of Clinical Child Psychology, 21*, 60–69.

Absolom, K., Eiser, C., Greco, V., & Davies, H. (2003). Health promotion for survivors of childhood cancer: A minimal intervention. *Patient Education and Counselling* (in press).

Achenbach, T. M. (1991). *Manual for the Child Behavior Checklist/4–18 and 1991 profile.* Burlington: University of Vermont, Department of Psychiatry.

Achenbach, T. M., & Edelbrock, C. S. (1979). The child behavior profile: II. Boys aged 12–16 and girls aged 6–11 and 12–16. *Journal of Consulting and Clinical Psychology, 47*, 223–233.

Achenbach, T. M., & Edelbrock, C. (1983). *Manual for the Child Behavior Checklist and revised child behavior profile.* Burlington, VT: Queen City Printers.

Achenbach, T. M., & Edelbrock, C. (1987). *Manual for the youth self-report form.* Burlington: University of Vermont Press.

Acheson Report. (1998). *Independent inquiry into inequalities in health report.* London: The Stationery Office.

Adamoli, L., Deasy-Spinetta, P., Corbetta, A., Jankovik, M., Lia, R., Locati, A., Fraschini, D., Masera, G., & Spinetta, J. J. (1997). School functioning for the child with leukemia in continuous first remission: Screening high risk children. *Pediatric Hematology and Oncology, 14*, 121–131.

Ahlfield, J. E., Soler, N. G., & Marcus, S. D. (1983). Adolescent diabetes mellitus: parent/child perspectives of the effect of the disease on family and social interactions. *Diabetes Care, 6*, 393–398.

Allen, R., Newman, S. P., & Souhami, R. L. (1997). Anxiety and depression in adolescent cancer: Findings in patients and parents at the time of diagnosis. *European Journal of Cancer, 33*, 1250–1255.

Altschuler, J. (1997). *Working with chronic illness.* London: Macmillan.

American Cancer Society. (1997). *Cancer facts and figures.* Atlanta, GA.

American Psychiatric Association. (1994). *Diagnostic and statistical manual of mental disorders* (4th ed.). Washington, DC: Author.

Anderson, B. J. (1990). Diabetes and adaptations in family systems. In C. S. Holmes (Ed.), *Neuropsychological and behavioural aspects of diabetes* (pp. 85–101). New York: Springer-Verlag.

Anderson, V., Smibert, E., Ekert, H., & Godber, T. (1994). Intellectual, educational, and behavioural sequelae after cranial irradiation and chemotherapy. *Archives of Disease in Childhood, 70,* 476–483.

Anholt, U. V., Fritz, G. K., & Keener, M. (1993). Self-concept in survivors of childhood and adolescent cancer. *Journal of Psychosocial Oncology, 11,* 1–16.

Armor, D. A., & Taylor, S. E. (1998). Situated optimism: Specific outcome expectancies and self-regulation. In M. P. Zanna (Eds.), *Advances in experimental social psychology* (pp. 309–379). New York: Academic Press.

Armstrong, F. D., & Horn, M. (1995). Educational issues in childhood cancer. *School Psychology Quarterly, 10,* 292–304.

Armstrong, F. D., Toledano, S. R., Miloslavich, K., Lackman-Zeman, L., Levy, J. D., Gay, C. L., Schuman, W. B., & Fishkin, P. E. (1999). The Miami Pediatric Quality of Life Questionnaire: Parent Scale. *International Journal of Cancer, Supplement 12,* 11–17.

Armstrong, G. D., Wirt, R. D., Nesbit, M. E., & Martinson, I. M. (1982). Multidimensional assessment of psychological problems in children with cancer. *Research in Nursing and Health, 5,* 205–211.

Asher, S., & Coie, J. (1990). *Peer rejection in childhood.* Cambridge, England: Cambridge University Press.

Asher, S. R., Hymel, S., & Renshaw, P. D. (1984). Loneliness in children. *Child Development, 55,* 1456–1464.

Aur, R. J., Simone, J., Hustu, H. O., Walters, T., Borella, L., Pratt, C., & Pinkel, D. (1971). Central nervous system therapy and combination chemotherapy of childhood lymphocytic leukemia. *Blood, 37,* 272–281.

Balen, R., Fielding, D., & Lewis, I. (1996). Activity camps for children with cancer. *Children and Society, 10,* 317–323.

Bandura, A. (1977). *Social learning theory.* Englewood Cliffs, NJ: Prentice-Hall.

Bannister, M., Stewart, S. M., Kennard, B. D., Benser, M., Andrews, W. S., & Moore, P. E. (1995). *Developmental and physical growth status of pediatric liver transplantation patients at least 5 years after surgery.* Paper presented at the meeting of the Joint Congress on Liver Transplantation, London.

Barakat, L., Kazak, A. E., Meadows, A., Casey, R., Meeske, K., & Stuber, M. L. (1997). Families surviving childhood cancer: A comparison of posttraumatic stress symptoms with families of healthy children. *Journal of Pediatric Psychology, 22,* 6843–6859.

Barbarin, O. A., Sargent, J. R., Sahler, O. J., & Carpenter, P. J. (1995). Sibling adaptation of childhood cancer collaborative study: Parental views of pre- and post diagnosis adjustment of siblings of children with cancer. *Journal of Psychosocial Oncology, 13,* 1–20.

Barr, R. D., Chalmers, D., DePauw, S., Furlong, W., Weitzman, S., & Feeny, D. (2000). Health-related quality of life in survivors of Wilms' tumor and advanced neuroblastoma: A cross-sectional study. *Journal of Clinical Oncology, 18,* 3280–3287.

Barr, R. D., Petrie, C., Furlong, W., Rothney, M., & Feeny, D. (1997). Health-related quality of life during post-induction chemotherapy in children with acute lymphoblastic leukemia in remission: An influence of corticosteroid therapy. *International Journal of Oncology, 11,* 333–339.

Barr, R. D., Simpson, T., Whitton, A., Rush, B., Furlong, W., & Feeny, D. H. (1999). Health-related quality of life in survivors of tumors of the central nervous system in childhood—A preference-based approach to measurement in a cross-sectional study. *European Journal of Cancer, 35,* 248–255.

Baysinger, M., Heiney, S. P., Creed, J. M., & Ettinger, R. S. (1993). A trajectory approach for education of the child/adolescent with cancer. *Journal of Pediatric Oncology Nursing, 10,* 133–138.

Bearison, D. J., & Pacifici, C. (1989). Children's event knowledge of cancer treatment. *Journal of Applied Developmental Psychology, 10,* 469–486.

Bearison, D. J., Sadow, A. J., Granowetter, L., & Winkel, G. (1993). Patients' and parents' causal attributions for childhood cancer. *Journal of Psychosocial Oncology, 11,* 47–61.

Beck, A. T., Ward, C. H., Mendelson, M., Mock, J., & Erbaugh, J. (1961). An inventory for measuring depression. *Archives of General Psychiatry, 4,* 561–571.

Bennett, D. S. (1994). Depression among children with chronic medical problems: a meta-analysis. *Journal of Pediatric Psychology, 19,* 149–169.

Benton, A. L., Varney, N. R., & Hamsher, K. D. (1978). Visuospatial judgement. A clinical test. *Archives of Neurology, 35,* 364–367.

Ben-Tovim, D. I., & Walker, M. K. (1995). Body image, disfigurement and disability. *Journal of Psychosomatic Research, 39,* 283–291.

Bergner, M. (1989). Quality of life, health status and clinical research. *Medical Care, 27,* S148–S156.

Bernstein, A. C., & Cowan, P. A. (1981). Children's conceptions of birth and sexuality. In R. Bibace & M. E. Walsh (Eds.), *New directions for child development: No. 14. Children's conceptions of health, illness and bodily functions* (pp. 9–30). San Francisco: Jossey Bass.

Bernstein, J. H. (2000). Developmental neuropsychological assessment. In K. O. Yeates, M. D. Ris, & H. D. Taylor (Eds.), *Pediatric neuropsychology: Research, theory and practice* (pp. 405–438). New York: Guilford.

Bhatia, S., Jenney, M. E. M., Bogue, M. K., Rockwood, T. H., Feusner, J. H., Friedman, D. L., Robison, L. L., & Kane, R. L. (2002). The Minneapolis-Manchester Quality of Life instrument: Reliability and validity of the adolescent form. *Journal of Clinical Oncology, 29,* 4692–4698.

Bibace, R., & Walsh, M. E. (1979). Developmental stages in children's conceptions of illness. In G. C. Stone, F. Cohen, & N. E. Adler (Eds.), *Health psychology* (pp. 285–301). San Francisco: Jossey-Bass.

Bibace, R., & Walsh, M. E. (1981). Children's conceptions of illness. In R. Bibace & M. E. Walsh (Eds.), *New directions for child development: Children's conceptions of health, illness and bodily functions.* New Directions in Developmental Psychology Series (pp. 312–348). San Fransisco: Jossey-Bass.

Billson, A. L., & Walker, D. A. (1994). Assessment of health status in survivors of cancer. *Archives of Disease in Childhood, 70,* 200–204.

Birenbaum, L. K., & Robinson, M. A. (1991). Family relationships in two types of terminal care. International Conference on Community Nursing. *Social Science and Medicine, 32,* 95–102.

Birenbaum, L. K., Stewart, B. J., & Phipps, D. S. (1996). Health status of bereaved parents. *Nursing Research, 45,* 105–109.

Blacklay, A., Eiser, C., & Ellis, A. (1998). Development and evaluation of an information booklet for adult survivors of cancer in childhood. *Archives of Disease in Childhood, 78,* 1–6.

Bleyer, W. A. (1988). Central nervous system leukemia. *Pediatric Clinics of North America, 35,* 789–814.

Bleyer, W. A., Fallavollita, J., Robison, L., Balsom, W., Meadows, A., Heyn, R., Sitarz, A., Ortega, J., Miller, D., Constine, L., Nesbit, M., Sather, H., & Hammond, D. (1990). Influence of age, sex, and concurrent intrathecal methotrexate therapy on intellectual function after cranial irradiation during childhood: A report from the Children's Cancer Study Group. *Pediatric Hematology and Oncology, 7,* 329–338.

Block, J. H. (1965). *The Child-Rearing Practices Report (CRPR): A set of Q items for the description of parental socialization attitudes and values.* Unpublished manual, University of California, Institute of Human Development, Berkeley.

Blotcky, A. D., Raczynski, J. M., Gurwitch, R., & Smith, K. (1985). Family influences on hopelessness among children early in the cancer experience. *Journal of Pediatric Psychology, 10,* 479–493.

Blount, R. I., Landolf-Fritsche, B., Powers, S. W., & Sturges, J. W. (1991). Differences between high and low coping children and between parent and staff behaviors during painful medical procedures. *Journal of Pediatric Psychology, 16,* 795–809.

Blount, R. L., Corbin, S. M., Sturges, J. W., Wolfe, V. V., Prater, J. M., & James, L. D. (1989). The relationship between adults' behaviour and child coping and distress during BMA/LP procedures: a sequential analysis. *Behavior Therapy, 20,* 585–601.

Bluebond-Langner, M., Perkel, D., Goertzel, T., Nelson, K., & McGeary, J. (1990). Children's knowledge of cancer and its treatment: Impact of an oncology camp experience. *Journal of Pediatrics, 116,* 207–272.

Bolton, A. (1997). *Losing the thread: Pupils' and parents' voices about education for sick children.* London: NAESC/PRESENT.

Boogerd, W. (1995). Neurological complications of chemotherapy. In F. A. de Wolff (Ed.), *Handbook of clinical neurology: Vol. 21. Intoxications of the nervous system, Part II* (pp. 527–546). Amsterdam: Elsevier Science.

Bowlby, J. (1969). *Attachment and loss.* New York: Basic Books.

Boyle, M. H., Offord, D. R., Racine, Y. A., Szatmari, P., Fleming, J. E., & Links, P. S. (1992). Predicting substance use in later adolescence: Results from the Ontario Health Study follow-up. *American Journal of Psychiatry, 149,* 761–767.

Bradlyn, A. S., Harris, C. V., Warner, J. E., Ritchey, A. K., & Zaboy, K. (1993). An investigation of the validity of the quality of Well-Being Scale with pediatric oncology patients. *Health Psychology, 12,* 246–250.

Bradlyn, A. S., Ritchey, A. K., Harris, C. V., Moore, I. M., O'Brien, R. T., Parsons, S. K., Patterson, K., & Pollock, B. H. (1996). Quality of life research in pediatric oncology—Research methods and barriers. *Cancer, 78,* 1333–1339.

Breslau, N., & Marshall, S. (1985). Psychiatric disorder in children with physical disabilities. *Journal of the American Academy of Child Psychiatry, 24,* 87–94.

Briery, B. G., & Rabian, B. (1999). Psychosocial changes associated with participation in a pediatric summer camp. *Journal of Pediatric Psychology, 24,* 183–190.

Brodie, B. (1974). Views of healthy children toward illness. *American Journal of Public Health, 64,* 1156–1159.

Broome, M., Lillis, P., McGahee, T., & Bates, T. (1992). Reduction of procedural pain in pediatric oncology patients. *Oncology Nursing Forum, 19,* 499–502.

Broome, M. E., & Stieglitz, K. A. (1992). The consent process and children. *Research in Nursing and Health, 15,* 147–152.

Brouwers, P. (1987). *Neuropsychological abilities of long-term survivors of childhood cancer.* Bethesda, MD: National Cancer Institute, Pediatric Branch.

Brouwers, P., & Poplack, D. (1990). Memory and learning sequelae in long-term survivors of acute lymphoblastic leukemia: association with attention deficits. *American Journal of Pediatric Hematology and Oncology, 12,* 174–181.

Brouwers, P., Riccardi, R., Fedio, P., & Poplack, D. (1985). Long-term neuropsychologic sequelae of childhood leukemia: Correlation with CT brain scan abnormalities. *Journal of Pediatrics, 106,* 723–728.

Brown, K. A., & Barbarin, O. A. (1996). Gender differences in parenting a child with cancer. *Social Work in Health Care, 22,* 53–71.

Brown, R. T., Kaslow, N. J., Hazzard, A. P., Madan-Swain, A., Sexson, S. B., Lambert, R., & Baldwin, K. (1992). Psychiatric and family functioning in children with leukemia and their parents. *Journal of the American Academy of Child and Adolescent Psychiatry, 31,* 495–502.

Brown, R. T., Kaslow, N. J., Madan-Swain, A., Doepke, K. J., Sexson, S. B., & Hill, L. J. (1993). Parental psychopathology and children's adjustment to leukemia. *Journal of the American Academy of Child and Adolescent Psychiatry, 32,* 554–561.

Brown, R. T., Madan-Swain, A., Pais, R., Lambert, R. G., Sexson, S., & Ragab, A. (1992). Chemotherapy for acute lymphocytic leukemia: Cognitive and academic sequelae. *Journal of Pediatrics, 121,* 885–889.

Brown, R. T., Sawyer, M. B., Antoniou, G., Toogood, I., Rice, M., Thompson, N., & Madan-Swain, A. (1996). A 3-year follow-up of the intellectual and the academic functioning of children receiving central nervous system prophylactic chemotherapy for leukemia. *Journal of Developmental and Behavioral Pediatrics, 17,* 392–398.

Buhrmester, D., & Furman, W. (1990). Perceptions of sibling relationships during middle childhood and adolescence. *Child Development, 61,* 1387–1398.

Bull, B. A., & Drotar, D. (1991). Coping with cancer in remission: Stressors and strategies reported by children and adolescents. *Journal of Pediatric Psychology, 16,* 767–782.

Butler, R. (1998). Age trends in the use of social and temporal comparison for self-evaluation: Examination of a novel developmental hypothesis. *Child Development, 69,* 1054–1073.

Butler, R., Hill, J. M., Steinherz, P. G., Meyers, P. A., & Finlay, J. L. (1994). Neuropsychologic effects of cranial irradiation, intrathecal methotrexate, and systemic methotrexate in childhood cancer. *Journal of Clinical Oncology, 12,* 2621–2629.

Butler, R. W., Rizzi, L. P., & Handwerger, B. A. (1996). Brief report: The assessment of posttraumatic stress disorder in pediatric cancer patients and survivors. *Journal of Pediatric Psychology, 21,* 499–504.

Buttsworth, D. L., Murdoch, B. E., & Ozanne, A. E. (1993). Acute lymphoblastic leukaemia: Language deficits in children post-treatment. *Disability and Rehabilitation, 15,* 67–75.

Byrn, J., Fears, T. R., Steinhorn, S. C., & Mulvihill, J. J. (1989). Marriage and divorce after childhood and adolescent cancer. *Journal of American Medical Association, 262,* 2693–2699.

Cadman, D., Boyle, M., Szatmari, P., & Offord, D. R. (1987). Chronic Illness, disability, and mental and social well-being: Findings of the Ontario child health study. *Pediatrics, 79,* 705–712.

Calaminus, G., Weispach, S., Teske, C., & Gobel, U. (2000). Quality of life in children and adolescents with cancer. *Klinische Padiatrie, 212,* 211–215.

Callery, P. (1997). Maternal knowledge and professional knowledge: Co-operation and conflict in the care of sick children. *International Journal of Nursing Studies, 34,* 27–34.

Calman, K. C. (1987). Definitions and dimensions of quality of life. In N. K. Aaronson & J. Beckmann (Eds.), *The quality of life of cancer patients* (pp. 1–9). New York: Raven Press.

Canning, E. H., Canning, R. D., & Boyce, T. (1992). Depressive symptoms and adaptive style in children with cancer. *Journal of American Academy of Child and Adolescent Psychiatry, 31,* 1120–1124.

Carey, S. (1985). *Conceptual change in childhood.* Cambridge, MA: MIT Press.

Carlson-Green, B., Morris, R. D., & Krawiecki, N. (1995). Family and illness predictors of outcome in pediatric brain tumors. *Journal of Pediatric Psychology, 20,* 769–784.

Carpenter, P. J., & Levant, C. S. (1994). Sibling adaptation to the family crisis of childhood cancer. In D. J. Bearison & R. K. Mulhern (Eds.), *Pediatric psycho-oncology: Psychological perspectives on children with cancer* (pp. 122–142). New York: Oxford University Press.

Carpenter, P. J., & Sahler, O. J. Z. (1991). Sibling perception and adaptation to childhood cancer. In J. H. Johnson & S. B. Johnson (Eds.), *Advances in child health psychology* (pp. 193–205). Gainesville: University of Florida Press.

Carpentieri, S. C., Mulhern, R. K., Douglas, S., Hanna, S., & Fairclough D. (1993). Behavioral resiliency among children surviving brain tumors: A longitudinal study. *Journal of Clinical Child Psychology, 22,* 236–246.

Cash, T. F. (1991). Binge-eating and body images among the obese: A further evaluation. *Journal of Social Behavior and Personality, 6,* 367–376.

Cause, A. M. (1986). Social networks and social competence: Exploring the effects of early adolescent friendships. *American Journal of Community Psychology, 14,* 607–628.

Cayse, L. N. (1994). Fathers of children with cancer: A descriptive study of their stressors and coping strategies. *Journal of Pediatric Oncology Nursing, 11,* 102–108.

Celcalupo, A. (1994). Childhood cancers: Medical issues. In R. A. Olson, L. L. Mullins, J. B. Gillman, & J. M. Chaney (Eds.), *The sourcebook of pediatric psychology* (pp. 90–97). Boston: Allyn & Bacon.

Chang, P., Nesbit, M. E., Youngren, N., & Robison, L. L. (1987). Personality characteristics and psychosocial adjustment of long-term survivors of childhood cancer. *Journal of Psychosocial Oncology, 5,* 43–58.

Chang, P.-N. (1991). Psychosocial needs of long-term childhood cancer survivors: A review of literature. *Pediatrician, 18,* 20–24.

Charlton, A., Larcombe, I. J., Meller, S. T., Morris-Jones, P. H., Mott, M. G., Potton, M. W., Tranmer, M. D., & Walker, J. J. P. (1991). Absence from school related to cancer and other chronic conditions. *Archives of Disease in Childhood, 66,* 1217–1222.

Charlton, R. (1996). Medical education: Addressing the needs of the dying child. *Palliative Medicine (BYQ), 10,* 240–246.

Chen, E., Zeltzer, L. K., Craske, M. G., & Katz, E. R. (2000). Children's memories for painful cancer treatment procedures: Implications for distress. *Child Development, 71,* 933–947.

Chesler, M. (1990). Survivng childhood cancer: The struggle goes on. *Journal of Pediatric Oncology Nursing, 7,* 57–59.

Chesler, M. A., Allswede, J., & Barbarin, O. O. (1991). Voices from the margin of the family: Siblings of children with cancer. *Journal of Psychosocial Oncology, 9,* 19–42.

Chesler, M. A., & Barbarin, O. A. (1986). Parents' perspectives on the school experiences of children with cancer. *Topics in Early Childhood Special Education, 5,* 36–48.

Chesler, M. A., Paris, J., & Barbarin, O. A. (1986). "Telling" the child with cancer: Parental choices to share information with ill children. *Journal of Pediatric Psychology, 11,* 497–516.

Chessells, J. M. (2000). Recent advances in management of acute leukaemia. *Archives of Disease in Childhood, 82,* 438–442.

Chessells, J. M., Richards, S. M., Bailey, C. C., Lilleyman, J. S., & Eden, O. B. (1995). Gender and treatment outcome in childhood lymphoblastic leukaemia: Report from the MRC UKALL trials. *British Journal of Haematology, 89,* 364–372.

Childhood ALL Collaborative Group. (1996). Duration and intensity of maintenance chemotherapy in acute lymphoblastic leukaemia: Overview of 42 trials involving 12,000 randomised children. *The Lancet, 347,* 1783–1788.

Christie, D., Leiper, A. D., Chessells, J. M., & Vargha-Khadem, F. (1995). Intellectual performance after presymptomatic cranial radiotherapy for leukaemia: Effects of age and sex. *Archives of Disease in Childhood, 73,* 136–140.

Cicirelli, V. G. (1972). The effect of sibling relationships on concept learning of young children taught by child teachers. *Child Development, 43,* 282–287.

Claflin, C. J., & Barbarin, O. A. (1991). Does "telling" less protect more? Relationships among age, information disclosure, and what children with cancer see and feel. *Journal of Pediatric Psychology, 16,* 169–191.

Clarkson, J. E., & Eden, O. B. (1998). Dental health in children with cancer. *Archives of Disease in Childhood, 78,* 560–561.

Cleave, H., & Charlton, A. (1997). Evaluation of a cancer-based coping and caring course used in three different settings. *Child: Care, Health and Development, 23,* 399–413.

Clerico, A., Ragni, G., Antimi, A., & Minori, A. (1995). Behaviour after cancer death in offspring: Coping attitude and replacement dynamics. *New Trends in Experimental and Clinical Psychiatry, 11,* 87–89.

Closs, A. (2000). *The education of children with medical conditions.* London: David Fulton Publishers.

Closs, A., & Norris, C. (1997). *Outlook uncertain: Enabling the education of children with chronic and/or deteriorating conditions.* Edinburgh, Scotland: Moray House Institute of Education.

Cobb, S. (1976). Social support as a moderator of life stress. *Psychosomatic Medicine, 38,* 300–314.

Cohen, D. S., Freidrich, W. N., Jaworski, T. M., & Copeland, D. (1994). Pediatric cancer: Predicting sibling adjustment. *Journal of Clinical Psychology, 50,* 303–319.

Cohen, J. (1993). Attentional disorders in adolescence: integrating psychoanalytic and neuropsychological diagnostic and developmental considerations. *Adolescent Psychiatry, 19,* 301–342.

Cohen, M. J. (1997). *Children's memory scale.* New York: Psychological Corporation.

Cohen, S., & Wills, T. A. (1985). Stress, social support and the buffering hypothesis. *Psychological Bulletin, 98,* 310–357.

Compas, B. E., Connor-Smith, J. K., Saltzman, H., Thomsen, A. H., & Wadsworth, M. E. (2001). Coping with stress during childhood and adolescence: Problems, progress, and potential in theory and research. *Psychological Bulletin, 127,* 87–127.

Compas, B. E., Davis, G. E., Forsythe, C. J., & Wagner, B. M. (1987). Assessment of major and daily stressful events during adolescence: The Adolescent Perceived Events Scale. *Journal of Consulting and Clinical Psychology, 55,* 534–541.

Cook, S. D. (1975). *The development of causal thinking with regard to physical illness among French children.* Lawrence: University of Kansas Press.

Copeland, D. R., Dowell, R. E., Fletcher, J. M., Sullivan, M. P., Jaffee, N., Cangir, A., Frankel, L. S., & Judd, B. W. (1988). Neuropsychological test performance of pediatric cancer patients at diagnosis and one year later. *Journal of Pediatric Psychology, 13,* 183–196.

Cousens, P. (1997). Specific learning problems among children treated for acute lymphoblastic leukaemia. *International Journal of Pediatric Hemotology/Oncology, 4,* 353–362.

Cousens, P., Ungerer, J. A., Crawford, J. A., & Stevens, M. M. (1991). Cognitive effects of childhood leukemia therapy: A case for four specific deficits. *Journal of Pediatric Psychology, 16,* 475–488.

Cousens, P., Waters, B., Said, J., & Stevens, M. (1988). Cognitive effects of cranial irradiation in leukaemia: A survey and meta-analysis. *Journal of Child Psychology and Psychiatry, 29,* 839–852.

Cox, C. N., Dahlquist, L. M., & Fernbach, D. J. (1987). *Parenting and children's distress during invasive medical procedures.* Paper presented at the meeting of the Society of Behavioral Medicine, Washington, DC.

Craft, A. W. (2000). Childhood cancer—Mainly curable so where next? *Acta Paediatrica, 89,* 386–392.

Crandall, V. C. (1966). Personality characteristics and social and achievement behaviors associated with children's social desirability response tendencies. *Journal of Personality and Social Psychology, 4,* 477–486.

Creasey, G., & Jarvis, P. (1994). Relationships between parenting stress and developmental functioning among 2-year-olds. *Infant Behavior and Development, 17,* 419–425.

Crider, C. (1981). Children's conceptions of the body interior. In R. Bibace & M. Walsh (Eds.), *New directions for child development: Childrens' conceptions of health and illness, and body functions* (pp. 49–65). San Francisco: Jossey-Bass.

Crisp, J., Ungerer, J. A., & Goodnow, J. J. (1996). The impact of experience on children's understanding of illness. *Journal of Pediatric Psychology, 21,* 57–72.

Dahlquist, L. M., Czyzewski, Copeland, K. G., Jones, C. L., Taub, E., & Vaughan, J. K. (1993). Parents of children newly diagnosed with cancer: Anxiety, coping and marital distress. *Journal of Pediatric Psychology, 3,* 365–376.

Dahlquist, L. M., Czyzewski, D. I., & Jones, C. L. (1996). Parents of children with cancer: A longitudinal study of emotional distress, coping style, and marital adjustment two and twenty months after diagnosis. *Journal of Pediatric Psychology, 21,* 541–554.

Dahlquist, L. M., Power, T. G., & Carlson, L. (1995). Physician and parent behavior during invasive pediatric cancer procedures: Relationships to child behavioral distress. *Journal of Pediatric Psychology, 20,* 477–490.

Dahlquist, L. M., Power, T. G., Cox, C. N., & Fernbach, D. J. (1994). Parenting and child distress during cancer procedures: A multidimensional assessment. *Child Health Care, 23,* 149–166.

Daniels, D., Dunn, J., Furstenberg, F. F., & Plomin, R. (1985). Environmental differences within the family and adjustment differences within pairs of adolescent siblings. *Child Development, 56,* 764–774.

Danoff, B. F., Cowchock, S., Marquette, C., Mulgrew, L., & Kramer, S. (1982). Assessment of the long-term effects of primary radiation therapy for brain tumors in children. *Cancer, 49,* 1580–1586.

Darbyshire, P. (1994). Skilled expert practice: Is it "all in the mind"?: A response to English critque of Benner novice to expert model. *Journal of Advanced Nursing, 19,* 755–761.

Darling, N., & Steinberg, L. (1993). Parenting style as context: An integrative model. *Psychological Bulletin, 113,* 487–496.

Davey, G. C. L. (1989). Dental phobias and anxieties: Evidence for conducting processesin the acquisition and modulation of a learned fear. *Behaviour Research and Therapy, 27,* 51–58.

Davies, C. M., Noll, R. B., Davies, W. H., & Bukowski, W. M. (1993). Mealtime interactions and family relationships of families with children who have cancer in long-term remissions and controls. *Journal of the American Dietetic Association, 93,* 773–776.

Davies, H. A., Didcock, E., Didi, M., Ogilivy-Stuart, A., Wales, J. K. H., & Shalet, S. M. (1995). Growth, puberty and obesity after treatment for leukaemia. *Acta Paediatrica (Supplement), 411,* 45–50.

Davies, W. H., Noll, R. B., De Stefano, L., Bukowski, W. N., & Kulkarni, R. (1991). Differences in the child-rearing practices of parents of children with cancer and controls: The perspectives of parents and professionals. *Journal of Pediatric Psychology, 16,* 295–306.

Deasy-Spinetta, P. (1993). School issues and the child with cancer. *Cancer, 71,* 3261–3264.

Deasy-Spinetta, P., & Spinetta, J. J. (1980). The child with cancer in school: Teachers' appraisal. *The American Journal of Pediatric Hematology/Oncology, 2,* 89–94.

Deater-Deckard, K., Dodge, K. A., Bates, J. E., & Pettit, G. S. (1996). Physical discipline among African American and European American mothers: Links to children's externalizing behaviors. *Developmental Psychology, 32,* 1065–1072.

Dennis, M., Hetherington, C. R., & Spiegler, B. J. (1988). Memory and attention after childhood brain tumours. *Medical and Pediatric Oncology Supplement, 1,* 25–33.

Dennis, M., Spiegler, B. J., Hetherington, C. R., & Greenberg, M. L. (1996). Neuropsychological sequelae of the treatment of children with medulloblastoma. *Journal of Neuro-Oncology, 29,* 91–101.

Dennis, M., Spiegler, B. J., Hoffman, H. J., Hendrick, E. B., Humphreys, R. P., & Becker, L. E. (1991). Brain tumors in children and adolescents—I. Effects on working, associative and serial-order memory of IQ, age at tumor onset and age of tumor. *Neuropsychologia, 29,* 813–827.

Dens, F., Boute, P., Otten, J., Vinckier, F., & Declerck, D. (1995). Dental caries, gingival health, and oral hygiene of long term survivors of paediatric malignant diseases. *Archives of Disease in Childhood, 72,* 129–132.

Derogatis, L. R. (1977). *The SCL-90–R administration, scoring and procedures manual—I.* Baltimore: Clinical Psychometric Research.

Derogatis, L. R. (1983). Misuse of the symptom checklist 90. *Archives of General Psychiatry, 40,* 1152–1153.

Dibenedetto, S. P., Ragusa, R., Vaccaro, A., Ippolito, A. M., Miraglia, V., D'Amico, S., Nigro, L. L., Luca, G., & Schiliro, G. (1997). Neurocognitive function in children with acute lymphoblastic leukaemia according to central nervous system treatment type and age. *International Journal of Pediatric Hematology/Oncology, 4*, 385–391.

Ditesheim, J. A., & Templeton, J. M. (1987). Short-term v long-term quality of life in children following repair of high imperforate anus. *Journal of Pediatric Surgery, 22*, 581–587.

Dobkin, P. L., Tremblay, R. E., Masse, L. C., & Vitaro, F. (1995). Individual and peer characteristics in predicting boys' early onset of substance abuse: A seven-year longitudinal study. *Child Development, 66*, 1198–1214.

Dodge, K. A., McClaskey, C. L., & Feldman, E. (1985). Situational approach to the assessment of social competence in children. *Journal of Consulting and Clinical Psychology, 53*, 344–353.

Dolgin, M. J., Blumensohn, R., Mulhern, R. K., Orbach, J., Sahler, O. J., Roghman, K. J., Carpenter, P. J., Barbarin, O. A., Sargent, J. R., Zeltzer, L. K., & Copeland, D. R. (1997). Sibling adaptation to childhood cancer collaborative study: Cross-cultural aspects. *Journal of Psychosocial Oncology, 15*, 1–14.

Dolgin, M. J., Somer, E., Zaidel, N., & Zaizov, R. (1997). A structured group intervention of children with cancer. *Journal of Child and Adolescent Group Therapy, 7*, 3–18.

Doll, R. (1996). Trends in adolescent cancer with time. In P. Selby & C. Bailey (Eds.), *Cancer and the adolescent* (pp. 30–36). London: BMJ Publishing Group.

Donati, M. A., Guenette, G., & Auerbaech, H. (1987). Prospective controlled study at home and hospital therapy of cystic fibrosis pulmonary disease. *Journal of Pediatrics, 111*, 28–33.

Dorn, L. D., Susman, E. J., & Fletcher, J. C. (1995). Informed consent in children and adolescents: Age, maturation and psychological state. *Journal of Adolescent Health, 16*, 185–190.

Drigan, R., Spirito, A., & Gelber, R. D. (1992). Behavioural effects of corticosteroids in children with acute lymphoblastic leukemia. *Medical and Pediatric Oncology, 20*, 13–21.

Drotar, D. (1981). Psychological perspectives in chronic childhood illness. *Journal of Pediatric Psychology, 6*, 211–228.

Drotar, D. (1989). Psychological research in pediatric settings: Lessons from the field. *Journal of Pediatric Psychology, 14*, 63–74.

Duffner, P. K., Cohen, M. E., & Thomas, P. (1983). Late effects of treatment on the intelligence of children with posterior-fossa tumors. *Cancer, 51*, 233–237.

Dunn, J. (1988). Annotation: Sibling influences on childhood development. *Journal of Child Psychology and Psychiatry, 29*, 119–127.

Dunn, J., & McGuire, S. (1992). Sibling and peer relationships in childhood. *Journal of Child Psychology and Psychiatry, 33*, 67–105.

Dunn, J., & Stocker, C. (1989). The significance of differences in siblings' experiences within the family. In K. Kreppner & R. Lerner (Eds.), *Family systems and life-span development* (pp. 289–301). Hillsdale, NJ: Lawrence Erlbaum Associates.

Dunn, J., Stocker, C., & Plomin, R. (1990). Nonshared experiences within the family: Correlates of behavioral problems in middle childhood. *Development and Psychopathology, 2*, 113–126.

Eisen, M., Ware, J. E., Donald, C. A., & Brook, R. H. (1979). Measuring components of children's health status. *Medical Care, XVII*, 902–921.

Eiser, C. (1980). Effects of chronic illness on intellectual development. A comparison of normal children with those treated for childhood leukaemia and solid tumours. *Archives of Disease in Childhood, 55*, 766–770.

Eiser, C. (1991). Cognitive deficits in children treated for leukaemia. *Archives of Disease in Childhood, 66*, 164–168.

Eiser, C. (1993). *Growing up with a chronic disease: The impact on children and their families*. London: Jessica Kingsley Publishers.

Eiser, C. (1998). Practitioner review: Long-term consequences of childhood cancer. *Journal of Child Psychology and Psychiatry, 39*, 621–633.

Eiser, C., Blacklay, A., & Davies, H. (1999). *What's the point of coming to the clinic: A guide for young people who have had cancer*. London: The Cancer Research Campaign.

Eiser, C., Cool, P., Grimer, R. J., Carter, S. R., Cotter, I. M., Ellis, A. J., & Kopel, S. (1997). Quality of life in children following treatment for a malignant primary bone tumour around the knee. *Sarcoma, 1,* 39–45.

Eiser, C., Cool, P., Grimer, R., Carter, S., Ellis, A., Kopel, S., & Eiser, J. R. (1997). The role of monitoring in determining quality of life following treatment for a bone tumor. *International Journal of Behavioral Medicine, 4,* 397–414.

Eiser, C., & Havermans, T. (1994). Long-term social adjustment after treatment for childhood cancer. *Archives of Disease in Childhood, 70,* 66–70.

Eiser, C., Havermans, T., Craft, A., & Kernahan, J. (1995). Development of a measure to assess the perceived illness experience (PIE) after treatment for cancer. *Archives of Disease in Childhood, 72,* 302–307.

Eiser, C., Hill, J. J., & Blacklay, A. (2000). Surviving cancer; what does it mean for you? An evaluation of a clinic based intervention for survivors of childhood cancer. *Psycho-Oncology, 9,* 214–220.

Eiser, C., Hill, J. J., & Vance, Y. H. (2000). Examining the psychological consequences of surviving childhood cancer: Systematic review as a research method in pediatric psychology. *Journal of Pediatric Psychology, 25,* 449–460.

Eiser, C., Kopel, S., Cool, P., & Grimer, R. (1999). The perceived illness experience scale (PIE): Reliability and validity revisited. *Child: Care, Health and Development, 25,* 179–190.

Eiser, C., & Lansdown, R. (1977). Retrospective study of intellectual development in children treated for acute lymphoblastic leukaemia. *Archives of Disease in Childhood, 52,* 525–529.

Eiser, C., Levitt, A., Leiper, A., Havermans, T., & Donovan, C. (1996). Clinic audit for long term survivors of childhood cancer. *Archives of Disease in Childhood, 75,* 405–409.

Eiser, C., Mohay, H., & Morse, R. (2000). The measurement of quality of life in young children. *Child: Care, Health and Development, 26,* 401–414.

Eiser, C., & Morse, R. (2001). The measurement of quality of life in children: Past and future perspectives. *Developmental and Behavioral Pediatrics, 22,* 1–9.

Eiser, C., Parkyn, T., Havermans, T., & McNinch, A. (1994). Parents' recall on the diagnosis of cancer in their child. *Psycho-Oncology, 3,* 197–203.

Eiser, C., & Town, C. (1987). Teachers' concerns about chronically sick children: Implications for paediatricians. *Developmental Medicine and Child Neurology, 29,* 56–63.

Elkin, T. D., Phipps, S., Mulhern, R. K., & Fairclough, D. (1997). Psychological functioning of adolescent and young adult survivors of pediatric malignancy. *Medical and Pediatric Oncology, 29,* 582–588.

Elkin, T. D., Tyc, V. L., Hudson, M., & Crom, D. (1998). Participation in sports by long-term survivors of childhood cancer. *Journal of Psychosocial Oncology, 16,* 63–73.

Elkin, T. D., Whelan, J. P., Meyers, A. W., Phipps, S., & Glaser, R. R. (1998). The effect of achievement orientation on response to success and failure in pediatric cancer patients. *Journal of Pediatric Psychology, 23,* 67–76.

Ellenberg, L., McComb, G., Siegal, S. E., & Stowe, S. (1987). Factors affecting intellectual outcome in pediatric brain tumor patients. *Neurosurgery, 21,* 638–644.

Elliott, G., Murray, D., & Pearson, L. (1978). *British Ability Scales.* Windsor, England: NFER Publishing.

Ellis, R., & Leventhal, B. (1993). Information needs and decision-making preferences of children with cancer. *Psycho-Oncology, 2,* 277–284.

Enneking, W. F., Dunham, W., Gebhardt, M. C., Malawar, M., & Pritchard, D. J. (1993). A system for the functional evaluation of reconstructive procedures after surgical treatment of tumors of the musculoskeletal system. *Clinical Orthopedics and Related Research, 286,* 241–246.

Erikson, E. H. (1959). Identity and the life cycle. *Psychological Issues, 1,* 164.

Evans, C. A., Stevens, M., Cushway, D., & Houghton, J. (1992). Sibling response to childhood cancer: A new approach. *Child: Care, Health and Development, 18,* 229–244.

Evans, S. E., & Radford, M. (1995). Current lifestyle of young adults treated for cancer in childhood. *Archives of Disease in Childhood, 72,* 423–426.

Favrot, M., Frappaz, D., Saltel, P., & Cochat, P. (1992). To break the isolation. Telecommunication to help the schooling of sick children (French). *Bulletin Cancer, 79,* 855–863.

Feeny, D., Furlong, W., Barr, R. D., Torrance, G. W., Rosenbaum, P., & Weitzman, S. (1992). A comprehensive multiattribute system for classifying the health status of survivors of childhood cancer. *Journal of Clinical Oncology, 10,* 923–928.

Feeny, D., Furlong, W., Boyle, M., & Torrance, G. W. (1995). Multiattribute health-status classification systems: Health utilities index. *Pharmacoeconomics, 7,* 490–502.

Felder-Puig, R., Formann, A. K., Bretschneider, W., Bucher, B., Windhager, R., Zoubek, A., Puig, S., & Topf, R. (1998). Quality of life and psychosocial adjustment of young patients after treatment of bone cancer. *Cancer, 83,* 69–75.

Ferrell, B. R., Hassey Dow, K., & Grant, M. (1995). Measurement of the quality of life in cancer survivors. *Quality of Life Research, 4,* 523–531.

Festinger, L. (1954). A theory of social comparison processes. *Human Relations, 7,* 117–140.

Flesch, R. F. (1948). A new readability yardstick. *Journal of Applied Psychology, 32,* 221–233.

Fletcher, J. M., & Copeland, D. R. (1988). Neurobehavioral effects of central nervous system prophylactic treatment of cancer in children. *Journal of Clinical and Experimental Neuropsychology, 10,* 495–538.

Folkman, S., & Lazarus, R. S. (1988). Coping as a mediator of emotion. *Journal of Personality and Social Psychology, 54,* 466–475.

Fowler, M., Johnson, R., & Atkinson, S. (1985). School achievement and absence in children with chronic health conditions. *Journal of Pediatrics, 106,* 683–687.

Frank, N. C., Blount, R. L., & Brown, R. T. (1997). Attributions, coping, and adjustment in children with cancer. *Journal of Pediatric Psychology, 22,* 563–576.

Frederick, C. J., Pynoos, R. S., & Nader, K. (1992). The child post-traumatic stress disorder reaction index. Copyrighted Index.

Freeman, A. I., Boyett, J. M., Glicksman, A. S., Brecher, M. L., Leventhal, B. G., Sinks, L. F., & Holland, J. F. (1997). Intermediate-dose methotrexate versus cranial irradiation in childhood acute lymphoblastic leukemia: A ten-year follow-up. *Medical and Pediatric Oncology, 28,* 98–107.

French, D. J., Christie, M. J., & West, A. (1994). Quality of life in childhood asthma: Development of the childhood asthma questionnaires. In M. Christie & D. French (Eds.), *Assessment of quality of life in childhood asthma* (pp. 147–154). London: Harwood.

Futterman, E., & Hoffman, I. (1973). Crises and adaptation in the families of fatally ill children. In E. J. Anthony & C. Koupernick (Eds.), *The child in his family II: The impact of disease and death* (pp. 127–143). New York: Wiley.

Gallo, A. M., Breitmayer, B. J., Knafl, K. A., & Zoeller, L. H. (1992). Well siblings of children with chronic illness: Parents' reports of their psychologic adjustment. *Pediatric Nursing, 18,* 23–27.

Gallo, C., Perrone, F., DePlacido, S., & Giusti, C. (1995). Informed consent versus randomized consent to clinical trials. *The Lancet, 346,* 1060–1064.

Gesell, A., & Ilg, F. (1946). *The child from five to ten.* New York: Harper & Row.

Gilbert, J., Robinson, T., & Littlewood, J. M. (1988). Home intravenous antibiotic treatment in cystic fibrosis. *Archives of Disease in Childhood, 63,* 512–517.

Gill, T. M., & Feinstein, A. R. (1994). A critical appraisal of the quality of quality-of-life measurements. *Journal of American Medical Association, 272,* 619–626.

Glaser, A. W., Davies, K., Walker, D., & Brazier, D. (1997). Influence of proxy respondents and mode of administration on health status assessment following central nervous system tumours in childhood. *Quality of Life Research, 6,* 43–53.

Glaser, A. W., Rashid, A. N. F., Chin Lyn, U., & Walker, D. A. (1997). School behaviour and health status after central nervous system tumours in childhood. *British Journal of Cancer, 76,* 643–650.

Glasgow, K. L., Dornbusch, S. M., Troyer, L., & Steinberg, L. (1997). Parenting styles, adolescents' attributions and educational outcomes in nine heterogenous high schools. *Child Development, 68,* 507–529.

Goertzel, L., & Goertzel, T. (1991). Health locus of control, self-concept, and anxiety in pediatric cancer patients. *Psychological Reports, 68,* 531–540.

Goff, J. R., Anderson, H. R., & Cooper, P. F. (1980). Distractibility and memory deficits in long-term survivors of acute lymphoblastic leukemia. *Journal of Developmental and Behavioral Pediatrics, 1,* 158–163.

Goldman, A. (1998). ABC of palliative care: Special problems of children. *British Medical Journal, 316,* 49–52.

Goodwin, D. A. J., Boggs, S. R., & Graham-Pole, J. (1994). Development and validation of the Pediatric Oncology Quality of Life Scale. *Psychological Assessment, 6,* 321–328.

Gortmaker, S. L., Walker, D. K., Weitzman, M., & Sobol, A. M. (1990). Chronic conditions, socio-economic risks, and behavior problems in children and adolescents. *Pediatrics, 85,* 267–276.

Gotay, C. C., Korn, E. L., McCabe, M. S., Moore, T. D., & Cheson, B. D. (1992). Quality of life assessment in cancer treatment protocols: Research issues in protocol development. *Journal of the National Cancer Institute, 84,* 575–579.

Gray, R. E., Doan, B. D., Shermer, P., Fitzgerald, A. V., Berry, M. P., Jenkin, D., & Doherty, M. A. (1992a). Psychological adaptation of survivors of childhood cancer. *Cancer, 70,* 2713–2721.

Gray, R. E., Doan, B. D., Shermer, P., Fitzgerald, A. V., Berry, M. P., Jenkin, D., & Doherty, M. A. (1992b). Surviving childhood cancer: A descriptive approach to understanding the impact of life-threatening illness. *Psycho-Oncology, 1,* 235–245.

Green, D. M., Zevon, M. A., & Hall, B. (1991). Achievement of life goals by adult survivors of modern treatment for childhood cancer. *Cancer, 67,* 206–213.

Greenberg, H. S., Kazak, A. E., & Meadows, A. T. (1989). Psychologic functioning in 8- to 16-year-old cancer survivors and their parents. *Journal of Pediatrics, 114,* 488–493.

Greenberg, H. S., & Meadows, A. T. (1991). Psychosocial impact of cancer survival on school-age children and their parents. *Journal of Psychosocial Oncology, 9,* 43–56.

Gregory, K., Parker, L., & Craft, A. W. (1994). Returning to primary school after treatment for cancer. *Pediatric Hematology and Oncology, 11,* 105–109.

Grootenhuis, M. A. (1996). *Coping with childhood cancer—Strategies of parents and hospital staff.* Enshede, Netherlands: PrintPartners Ipskamp.

Grootenhuis, M. A., & Last, B. F. (1997a). Parents' emotional reactions related to different prospects for the survival of their children with cancer. *Journal of Psychosocial Oncology, 15,* 43–62.

Grootenhuis, M. A., & Last, B. F. (1997b). Predictors of parental emotional adjustment to childhood cancer. *Psycho-Oncology, 6,* 115–128.

Grootenhuis, M. A., Last, B. F., De Graaf-Nukerk, J. H., & Van Der Wel, M. (1996). Secondary control strategies used by parents of children with cancer. *Psycho-Oncology, 5,* 91–102.

Grotevant, H. D., & Cooper, C. R. (1985). Patterns of interaction in family relationships and the development of identity exploration in adolescence. *Child Development, 56,* 415–28.

Gurney, J. G., Severson, R. K., Davis, S., & Robinson, L. L. (1995). Incidence of cancer in children in the United States: Sex-, race- and 1 year age-specific rates by histologic type. *Cancer, 75,* 2186–2195.

Guyatt, G. H., Berman, L. B., Townsend, M., Pugsley, S. O., & Chambers, L. W. (1987). A measure of quality of life for clinical trials in chronic lung disease. *Thorax, 42,* 773–778.

Haberle, H., Schwarz, R., & Mathes, L. A. P. N. (1997). Family-oriented management of children and adolescents with cancer. *Journal of Child Psychology and Psychiatry, 46,* 405–419.

Hain, R. D. W., & Campbell, C. (2001). Invasive procedures carried out in conscious children: contrast between North American and European paediatric oncology centres. *Archives of Disease in Childhood, 85,* 12–14.

Hann, I., Vora, A., Richards, S., Hill, F., Gibson, B., Lilleyman, J., Kinsey, S., Mitchell, C., & Eden, O. B. (2000). Benefit of intensified treatment for all children with acute lympho-blastic leukaemia: Results from MRC UKALL XI and MRC ALL97 randomised trials. UK Medical Research Council's Working Party on Childhood Leukaemia. *Leukemia, 14,* 356–363.

Hanson, C. L., Henggeler, S. W., Harris, M. A., Burghen, G. A., & Moore, M. (1989). Family systems variables and the health status of adolescents with insulin-dependent diabetes mellitus. *Health Psychology, 8,* 239–253.

Hardy, M. S., Armstrong, F. D., Routh, D. K., & Albrecht, J. (1994). Coping and communica-tion among parents and children with human immunodeficiency virus and cancer. *Jour-nal of Developmental and Behavioral Pediatrics, 15,* S49–S53.

Harris, A., & Curnick, S. (1995). Group work with bereaved children. In S. C. Smith & M. Pennells (Eds.), *Interventions with bereaved children* (pp. 193–203). London: Jessica Kingsley Publishers.

Harter, S. (1985). *Manual for the self-perception profile for children.* Denver: University of Den-ver.

Harter, S. (1988). *Manual for the self-perception profile for adolescents.* Denver: University of Denver.

Harter, S., & Pike, R. (1984). The pictorial scale of perceived competence and social accep-tance of young children. *Child Development, 55,* 1969–1982.

Harth, S. C., & Thong, Y. H. (1995). Parental perceptions and attitudes about informed con-sent in clinical research involving children. *Social Science and Medicine, 41,* 1647–1651.

Haupt, R., Byrne, J., Connelly, R. R., Mostow, E. N., Austin, D. F., Holmes, G. R., Holmes, F. F., Latourette, H. B., Teta, M. J., Strong, L. C., Myers, M. H., & Mulvihill, J. J. (1992). Smoking habits in survivors of childhood and adolescent cancer. *Medical and Pediatric On-cology, 20,* 301–306.

Haupt, R., Fears, T. R., Robison, L. L., Mills, J. L., Nicholoson, S., Zeltzer, L. K., Meadows, A. T., & Byrne, J. (1994). Educational attainment in long-term survivors of childhood acute lymphoblastic leukemia. *Journal of American Medical Association, 272,* 1427–1432.

Hauser, S. T., Book, B. K., Houlihan, J., Powers, S. I., Weissperry, B., Follansbee, D., Jacobsen, A. M., & Noam, G. G. (1987). Sex differences within the family: Studies of adolescent and parent family interactions. *Journal of Youth and Adolescence, 16,* 199–220.

Hauser, S. T., DiPlacido, J., Jacobson, A. M., Willett, J., & Cole, C. (1993). Family coping with an adolescent's chronic illness: An approach and three studies. *Journal of Adolescence, 16,* 305–329.

Hauser, S. T., Jacobsen, A. M., Benes, K. A., & Anderson, B. J. (1997). Psychological aspects of diabetes mellitus in children and adolescents: Implications and interventions. In N. E. Alessi (Eds.), *Handbook of child and adolescent psychiatry* (pp. 340–354). New York: Wiley.

Havermans, T., & Eiser, C. (1994). Siblings of a child with cancer. *Child: Care, Health and De-velopment, 20,* 309–322.

Hawkins, M. M., Draper, G. J., & Kingston, J. E. (1987). Incidence of second primary tumours among childhood cancer survivors. *British Journal of Cancer, 56,* 339–347.

Hawkins, M. M., & Stevens, M. C. G. (1996). The long-term survivors. *British Medical Journal, 52,* 898–923.

Hayry, M. (1999). *Measuring quality of life: Why, how and what?* Australia: Harwood Academic Publishers.

Hays, D. M., Dolgin, M., Steele, L. L., Patenaude, A. F., Hewitt, K., Ruymann, F., Ruccione, K., Sallan, S. E., & Siegal, S. E. (1997). Educational achievement, employment and work-place experience of adult survivors of childhood cancer. *International Journal of Pediatric Hematology/Oncology, 4,* 327–337.

Hays, D. M., Landsverk, J., Sallan, S. E., Hewitt, K. D., Patenaude, A. F., Schoonover, D., Zilber, S. L., Ruccione, K., & Siegal, S. E. (1992). Educational, occupational, and insurance status of childhood cancer survivors in their fourth and fifth decades of life. *Journal of Clinical Oncology, 10,* 1397–1406.

Heaton, R. K. (1981). *Wisconsin Sort Coding Manual.* Odessa, FL: Psychological Assessment Resources.

Heiney, S. P., Wells, L. M., Coleman, B., Swygert, E., & Ruffin, J. (1990). Lasting impressions: A psychosocial support program for adolescents with cancer and their parents. *Cancer Nursing, 13,* 13–20.

Henning, P., Tomlinson, L., Rigden, S. P. A., Haycock, G. B., & Chantler, C. (1988). Long-term outcome of treatment of end-stage renal failure. *Archives of Disease in Childhood, 63,* 35–40.

Herndon, D. N., LeMaster, J., Beard, S., Bernstein, N., Lewis, S. R., Rutan, T. C., Winkler, J. B., Cole, M., Bjarnason, D., & Gore, D. (1986). The quality of life after major thermal injury in children: an analysis of 12 survivors with greater than or equal to 80% total body, 70% third-degree burns. *Journal of Trauma, 26,* 609–619.

Hernstein, R. J., & Murray, C. (1994). *The bell curve: Intelligence and class structure in American life.* New York: The Free Press.

Heyn, R., Ragab, A., Raney, R. B., Ruymann, D., Tefft, M., Lawrence, W., Soule, E., & Maurer, H. (1986). Late effects of therapy in orbital rhabdomyosarcoma in children. A report from the Intergroup Rhabdomyosarcoma Study. *Cancer, 57,* 1738–1743.

Hicks, S. P., & D'Amato, C. J. (1966). Effects of ionising radiations on mammalian development. *Advances in Teratology, 1,* 195–250.

Hiemenz, J. R., Hynd, G. W., & Jimenez, M. (1999). Seizure disorders. In R. T. Brown (Eds.), *Cognitive aspects of chronic illness in children* (pp. 238–261). New York: Guilford.

Hill, D. E., Ciesielski, K. T., Sethre-Hofstad, L., Duncan, M. H., & Lorenzi, M. (1997). Visual and verbal short-term memory deficits in childhood leukemia survivors after intrathecal chemotherapy. *Journal of Pediatric Psychology, 22,* 861–870.

Hill, J., Kornblith, A. B., Jones, D., Freeman, A., Holland, J. F., Glicksman, A. S., Boyett, J. M., Lenherr, B., Brecher, M. L., Dubowy, R., Kung, F., Maurer, H., & Holland, J. C. (1998). A comparative study of the long-term psychosocial functioning of childhood acute lymphoblastic leukemia survivors treated by intrathecal methotrexate with or without cranial radiation. *Cancer, 82,* 208–218.

Hillman, K. A. (1997). Comparing child-rearing practices in parents of children with cancer and parents of healthy children. *Journal of Pediatric Oncology Nursing, 14,* 53–67.

Hinds, P. S., Oakes, L., Furman, W., Foppiano, P., Olson, M. S., Quargnenti, A., Powell, B., Srivastiva, D. K., Jayawardene, D., Sandlund, J. T., & Strong, C. A. D. (1997). Decision making by parents and healthcare professionals when considering continued care for pediatric patients with cancer. *Oncology Nursing Forum, 24,* 1523–1528.

Hobbs, N., & Perrin, J. M. (1985). *Issues in the care of children with chronic illness.* San Francisco: Jossey-Bass.

Hockenberry-Eaton, M., Manteuffel, M., & Bottomley, S. (1997). Development of two instruments examining stress and adjustment in children with cancer. *Journal of Pediatric Oncology Nursing, 14,* 178–175.

Hockenberry-Eaton, M., Dilorio, C., & Kemp, V. (1995). The relationship of illness longevity and relapse with self-perception, cancer stressors, anxiety, and coping strategies in children with cancer. *Journal of Pediatric Oncology Nursing, 12,* 71–79.

Hockenberry-Eaton, M., Kemp, V., & Dilorio, C. (1994). Cancer stressors and protective factors: predictors of stress experienced during treatment for childhood cancer. *Research in Nursing and Health, 17,* 351–361.

Hoekstra-Weebers, J. E. H. M., Heuvel, F., Jaspers, J. P. C., Kamps, W. A., & Klip, E. C. (1998). Brief report: An intervention program for parents of pediatric cancer patients: A randomised controlled trial. *Journal of Pediatric Psychology, 23,* 207–214.

Hoekstra-Weebers, J. E., Littlewood, J. L., Boon, C. M., & Postma, A. (1991). A comparison of parental coping styles following the death of adolescent and preadolescent children. *Death Studies, 15,* 565–575.

Holden, G. W., & Miller, P. C. (1999). Enduring and different: A meta-analysis of the similarity in parents' child rearing. *Psychological Bulletin, 125,* 223–254.

Hollen, P. J., & Hobbie, W. L. (1993). Risk taking and decision-making of adolescent long-term survivors of cancer. *Oncology Nursing Forum, 20,* 769–776.

Holmes, H. A., & Holmes, F. F. (1975). After ten years, what are the handicaps and life styles of children treated for cancer?: An examination of the present status of 124 such survivors. *Clinical Pediatrics, 14,* 819–823.

Hoppehirsch, E., Renier, D., Lellouchtubiana, A., Saintrose, C., Pierrekahn, A., & Hirsch, J. F. (1990). Medulloblastoma in childhood—progressive intellectual deterioration. *Child's Nervous System, 6,* 60–65.

Hopwood, P. (1993). The assessment of body image in cancer patients. *European Journal of Cancer, 29A,* 276–281.

Horowitz, M. J. (1976). *Stress response symptoms.* New York: Aronson.

Horowitz, M., Wilner, N., & Alvarez, W. (1979). Impact of events scale: a measure of subjective stress. *Psychosomatic Medicine, 41,* 209–218.

Horwitz, W. A., & Kazak, A. E. (1990). Family adaptation to childhood cancer: Sibling and family systems variables. *Journal of Clinical Child Psychology, 15,* 221–228.

Howe, M. L. (1997). Children's memory for traumatic experiences. *Learning and Individual Differences, 9,* 153–174.

Howe, M. L., Courage, M. L., & Peterson, C. (1995). Intrusions in preschoolers' recall of traumatic childhood events. *Psychonomic Bulletin and Review, 2,* 130–134.

Hudson, M., Tyc, V. L., Jayawardene, D., Gattuso, J., Quargnenti, A., Greenwald, C., Crom, D. B., Mason, C., Srivastiva, D. K., & Hinds, P. (1999). Feasibility of implementing health promotion interventions to improve health-related quality of life. *International Journal of Cancer (Supplement), 12,* 138–142.

Hudson, M. M., Tyc, V. L., Srivastava, D. K., Gattuso, J., Quarngenti, A., Crom, D. B., & Hinds, P. (2002). Multi-component behavioral intervention to promote health protective behaviors in childhood cancer survivors: The protect study. *Medical and Pediatric Oncology, 39,* 2–11.

Hymel, S., Rubin, K. H., Rowden, L., & LeMare, L. (1990). Children's peer relationships: Longitudinal prediction of internalising and externalising problems from middle childhood. *Child Development, 61,* 2004–2021.

Ireys, H. T., Werthamer-Larsson, L. A., Koloner, K. B., & Gross, S. S. (1994). Mental heath of young adults with chronic illness: The mediating effect of perceived impact. *Journal of Pediatric Psychology, 19,* 205–222.

Jaakkola, R. (1997). *The development of scientific understanding: Children's construction of their first biological theory.* Cambridge, MA: MIT Press.

Jacobsen, P. B., Manne, S. L., Gorfinkle, K., Schorr, O., Rapkin, B., & Redd, W. H. (1990). Analysis of child and parent behavior during painful medical procedures. *Health Psychology, 9,* 559–576.

James, A. (1993). *Childhood identities: Self and social relationships in the experience of the child.* Edinburgh, Scotland: Edinburgh University Press.

James, L., & Johnson, B. (1997). The needs of parents of pediatric oncology patients during the palliative care phase. *Journal of Pediatric Oncology Nursing, 14,* 83–95.

Jankovic, M., Brouwers, P., Valsecchi, M. G., Van Veldhuizen, A., Huisman, J., Kamphuis, R., Kingma, A., Mor, W., Van Dongen-Melman, J., Ferronato, L., Mancini, M. A., Spinetta, J. J., & Masera, G. (1994). Association of 1800 cGy cranial irradiation with intellectual functioning in children with acute lymphoblastic leukemia. *The Lancet, 344,* 224–227.

Jannoun, L. (1983). Are cognitive and educational development affected by age at which prophylactic therapy is given in acute lymphoblastic leukaemia? *Archives of Disease in Childhood, 58,* 953–958.

Janoff-Bulman, R., & Frieze, I. H. (1983). A theoretical perspective for understanding reactions to victimization. *Journal of Social Issues, 39,* 1–17.

Jay, S. M., & Elliot, C. H. (1990). A stress inoculation program for parents whose children are undergoing medical procedures. *Journal of Consulting and Clinical Psychology, 58,* 799–804.

Jelalian, E., Stark, L. J., & Miller, D. (1997). Maternal attitudes towards discipline: A comparison of children with cancer and non-chronically ill peers. *Child Health Care, 26,* 169–182.

Jenney, M. E., Kane, R. L., & Lurie, N. (1995). Developing a measure of health outcomes in survivors of childhood cancer: A review of the issues. *Medical and Pediatric Oncology, 24,* 145–153.

Johnson, D. L., McCabe, M. A., Nicholson, H. S., Joseph, A. L., Getson, P. R., & Byrne, J. (1994). Quality of long-term survival in young children with medulloblastoma. *Journal of Neurosurgery, 80,* 1004–1010.

Jones, B., Freeman, A. I., Shuster, J. J., Jacquillat, C., Weil, M., Pochedly, C., Sinks, L., Chevalier, L., Maurer, H. M., Koch, K., Falkson, G., Patterson, R., Seligman, B., Sartorius, J., Kung, F., Haurani, F., Stuart, M., Burgert, E. O., Ruymann, F., Sawitsky, A., Forman, E., Pluess, H., Truman, J., Hakami, N., Glidewell, O., Glicksman, A. S., & Holland, J. F. (1991). Lower incidence of meningeal leukemia when prednisone is replaced by dexamethasone in the treatment of acute lymphocytic leukemia. *Medical and Pediatric Oncology, 19,* 269–275.

Kadan-Lottick, N. S., Robison, L. L., Gurney, J. G., Neglia, J. P., Yutaka, Y., Hayashi, R., Hudson, M., Greenberg, M., & Mertens, A. C. (2002). Childhood cancer survivors knowledge about their past diagnosis and treatment—Childhood cancer survivor study. *Journal of the American Medical Association, 287,* 1832–1839.

Kaplan, B. M., Goodglass, H., & Weintraub, S. (1983). *The Boston Naming Test.* Philadelphia: Lea & Febiger.

Kaplan, R. M., & Anderson, J. P. (1988). The general health policy model: Update and applications. *Health Services Research, 23,* 203–235.

Karnofsky, D., & Burchenal, J. (1949). Clinical evaluation of chemotherapeutic agents in cancer. In C. M. Macleod (Eds.), *Evaluation of chemotherapeutic agents* (pp. 191–205). New York: Columbia University Press.

Kashani, J., & Hakami, N. (1982). Depression in children and adolescents with malignancy. *Canadian Journal of Psychiatry, 27,* 474–477.

Kato, M., Azuma, E., Ido, M., Ito, M., Nii, R., Higuchi, K., Ihara, T., Kamiya, H., & Sakurai, M. (1993). Ten-year survey of the intellectual deficits in children with acute lymphoblastic leukaemia receiving chemoimmunotherapy. *Medical and Pediatric Oncology, 21,* 435–440.

Katz, E., Rubenstein, C. L., Hubert, N. C., & Blew, A. (1988). School and social reintegration of children with cancer. *Journal of Psychosocial Oncology, 6,* 123–140.

Katz, E., Varni, J. W., Rubenstein, C. L., Blew, A., & Hubert, N. C. (1992). Teacher, parent and child evaluative ratings of a school reintegration intervention for children with newly diagnosed cancer. *Child Health Care, 21,* 69–75.

Katz, J., & Melzack, R. (1990). Pain "memories" in phantom limb: Review and clinical observations. *Pain, 43,* 319–336.

Kazak, A. E. (1992). The social context of coping with childhood chronic illness: Family systems and social support. In A. M. La Greca, L. J. Siegel, J. L. Wallander, & C. E. Walker (Eds.), *Stress and coping in child health* (pp. 262–278). New York: Guilford.

Kazak, A. E. (1994). Implications of survival: Pediatric oncology patients and their families. In D. J. Bearison & R. K. Mulhern (Eds.), *Pediatric psycho-oncology* (pp. 173–192). New York: Oxford University Press.

Kazak, A. E. (1998). Posttraumatic distress in childhood cancer survivors and their parents. *Medical and Pediatric Oncology, 1,* 60–68.

Kazak, A. E., & Barakat, L. P. (1997). Brief report: Parenting stress and quality of life during treatment for childhood leukaemia predicts child and parent adjustment after treatment ends. *Journal of Pediatric Psychology, 22,* 749–758.

Kazak, A. E., & Christakis, D. A. (1996). The intense stress of childhood cancer: A systems perspective. In C. R. Pfeffer (Ed.), *Severe stress and mental disturbance in children* (pp. 277–305). Washington, DC: American Psychiatric Press.

Kazak, A. E., Christakis, D., Alderfer, M., & Coiro, M. J. (1994). Young adolescent cancer survivors and their parents: Adjustment, learning problems and gender. *Journal of Family Psychology, 8,* 74–84.

Kazak, A. E., Meeske, K., Penati, B., Barakat, L. P., Christakis, D., Meadows, A. T., Casey, R., & Stuber, M. L. (1997). Posttraumatic stress, family functioning, and social support in survivors of childhood leukaemia and their mothers and fathers. *Journal of Consulting and Clinical Psychology, 65,* 120–129.

Kazak, A. E., & Nachman, G. S. (1991). Family research on childhood chronic illness: Pediatric oncology as an example. *Journal of Family Psychology, 4,* 462–483.

Kazak, A. E., Penati, B., Boyer, B. A., & Himelstein, B. (1996). A randomized controlled prospective outcome study of a psychological and pharmacological intervention protocol for procedural distress in pediatric leukemia. *Journal of Pediatric Psychology, 21,* 615–631.

Kazdin, A. E., French, N. H., Unis, A. S., & Esveldt-Dawson, K. (1983). Assessment of childhood depression: Correspondence of child and parent ratings. *Journal of the American Academy of Child and Adolescent Psychiatry, 22,* 157–164.

Kelley, J. E., Lumley, M. A., & Leisen, J. C. C. (1997). Health effects of emotional disclosure in rheumatoid arthritis patients. *Health Psychology, 16,* 331–340.

Kendrick, C., Culling, J., Oakhill, T., & Mott, M. (1986). Children's understanding of their illness and its treatment within a paediatric oncology unit. *Association for Child Psychology and Psychiatry* [Newsletter], *8,* 16–20.

Kingma, A., Rammeloo, L. A. L., van der Does-van den Berg, A., Rekers-Mombarg, L., & Postma, A. (2000). Academic career after treatment for acute lymphoblastic leukaemia. *Archives of Disease in Childhood, 82,* 353–357.

Koch, U., Harter, M., Jakob, U., & Siegrist, B. (1996). Parental reactions to cancer in their children. In L. Baider, C. L. Cooper, & A. K. De-Nour (Eds.), *Cancer and the family* (pp. 149–170). London: Wiley.

Koocher, G. P., & O'Malley, J. E. (1981). *The Damocles Syndrome. Psychosocial consequences of surviving childhood cancer.* New York: McGraw-Hill.

Koocher, G. P., O'Malley, J. E., Gogan, J. L., & Foster, D. J. (1980). Psychological adjustment among pediatric cancer survivors. *Journal of Child Psychology and Psychiatry, 21,* 163–175.

Koopman, C., Classen, C., & Speigel, D. (1994). Predictors of posttraumatic stress symptoms among survivors of the Oakland/Berkeley, California, Firestorm. *American Journal of Psychiatry, 6,* 888–894.

Kopel, S. J., Eiser, C., Cool, P., Grimer, R. J., & Carter, S. R. (1998). Brief report: Assessment of body image in survivors of childhood cancer. *Journal of Pediatric Psychology, 23,* 141–147.

Kovacs, M. (1981). Rating scale to assess depression in school-aged children. *Acta Paediatrica, 46,* 305–315.

Kovacs, M. (1983). *The children's depression inventory: A self rated depression scale for school aged youngsters.* Unpublished manuscript, University of Pittsburgh School of Medicine.

Kovacs, M. (1992). *Children's depression inventory, CDI manual.* North Tonawanda, NY: Multi-Health Systems.

Kovacs, M., Iyengar, S., Goldston, D., Obrosky, D. S., Stewart, J., & Marsh, J. (1990). Psychological functioning among mothers of children with insulin-dependent diabetes mellitus: A longitudinal study. *Journal of Consulting and Clinical Psychology, 58,* 189–195.

Kun, L., Camitta, B., Mulhern, R. K., Lauer, S., Kline, R. W., Casper, J., Kamen, B. A., Kaplan, B. M., & Barber, S. W. (1984). Treatment of meningeal relapse in childhood acute lymphoblastic leukemia. I. Results of craniospinal irradiation. *Journal of Clinical Oncology, 2,* 359–364.

Kun, L. E., Mulhern, R. K., & Crisco, J. J. (1983). Quality of life in children treated for brain tumors. Intellectual, emotional, and academic function. *Journal of Neurosurgery, 58,* 1–6.

Kupst, M. J. (1992). Long-term family coping with acute lymphoblastic leukaemia in childhood. In A. M. La Greca, L. J. Siegel, J. L. Wallander, & C. E. Walker (Eds.), *Stress and coping in child health* (pp. 242–261). New York: Guilford.

Kupst, M. J., Natta, M. B., Richardson, C. C., Schulman, J. L., Lavigne, J. V., & Das, L. (1995). Family coping with pediatric leukemia: Ten years after treatment. *Journal of Pediatric Psychology, 20,* 601–617.

Kupst, M. J., & Schulman, J. L. (1988). Long-term coping with pediatric leukemia: A six-year follow-up study. *Journal of Pediatric Psychology, 13,* 7–22.

Kupst, M. J., Schulman, J. L., Maurer, H., Honig, G., Morgan, E., & Fochtman, D. (1984). Coping with pediatric leukemia: A two-year follow-up. *Journal of Pediatric Psychology, 9,* 149–163.

Kurtz, Z., & Hopkins, A. (1996). *Services for young people with chronic disorders in their transition from childhood to adult life.* London: Royal College of Physicians of London.

Kvist, B., Rajantie, J., Kvist, M., & Siimes, M. A. (1991). Perceptions of problematic events and quality of care among patients and parents after successful therapy of the child's malignant disease. *Social Science and Medicine, 33,* 249–256.

La Greca, A. M. (1990). Social consequences of pediatric conditions: Fertile area for future investigation and intervention? *Journal of Pediatric Psychology, 15,* 285–307.

La Greca, A. M. (1992). Peer influences in pediatric chronic illness: An update. *Journal of Pediatric Psychology, 17,* 775–784.

La Greca, A. M., Dandes, S. K., Wick, P., Shaw, K., & Stone, W. L. (1988). Development of the social anxiety scale for children: Reliability and concurrent validity. *Journal of Clinical Child Psychology, 17,* 84–91.

Lamborn, S. D., Mounts, N. S., Steinberg, L., & Dornbusch, S. M. (1991). Patterns of competence and adjustment among adolescents from authoritative, authoritarian, indulgent, and neglectful families. *Child Development, 62,* 1049–1065.

Landgraf, J. L., Abetz, L., & Ware, J. E. (1996). *The CHQ User's Manual.* Boston: The Health Institute, New England Medical Center.

Langford, W. S. (1948). Physical illness and convalescence: Their meaning to the child. *Journal of Pediatrics, 33,* 242–250.

Lannering, B., Marky, I., Lundberg, A., & Olsson, E. (1990). Long-term sequelae after pediatric brain tumors: Their effect on disability and quality of life. *Medical and Pediatric Oncology, 18,* 304–310.

Lansdown, R., & Goldman, A. (1988). The psychological care of children with malignant disease. *Journal of Child Psychology and Psychiatry, 29,* 555–567.

Lansky, L. L., List, M. A., Lansky, S. B., Cohen, M. E., & Sinks, L. F. (1985). Toward the development of a Play Performance Scale for Children (PPSC). *Cancer, 56,* 1837.

Lansky, S. B., Lowman, J. T., Vats, T., & Gyulay, J.-E. (1975). School phobia in children with malignant neoplasms. *American Journal of Disease of Children, 129,* 42–46.

Larcombe, I. (1995). *Reintegration to school after hospital treatment: Needs and services.* Aldershot, England: Avebury.

Larcombe, I. J., & Charlton, A. (1996). Children's return to school after treatment for cancer. *Journal of Cancer Education, 11,* 102–105.

Larcombe, I. J., Walker, J., Charlton, A., Meller, S., Morris-Jones, P., & Mott, M. G. (1990). Impact of childhood cancer on return to normal schooling. *British Medical Journal, 301,* 169–171.

Larson, L. S., Wittrock, D. A., & Sandgren, A. (1994). When a child is diagnosed with cancer: I. Sex differences in parental adjustment. *Journal of Psychosocial Oncology, 12,* 123–142.

Last, B. F., & Grootenhuis, M. A. (1998). Emotions, coping and the need for support in families of children with cancer: A model for psychological care. *Patient Education and Counselling, 33,* 169–179.

Last, B. F., & van Veldhuizen, A. M. H. (1995). Information about diagnosis and prognosis related to anxiety and depression in children with cancer aged 8–16 years. *European Journal of Cancer, 32A,* 290–294.

Lavigne, J. V., & Faier-Routman, J. (1992). Psychological adjustment to pediatric physical disorders: A meta-analytic review. *Journal of Pediatric Psychology, 17,* 133–157.

Lazarus, R. S., & Folkman, S. (1984). *Stress, appraisal and coping.* New York: Springer.

Lebaron, S., Zeltzer, L. K., Lebaron, C., Scott, S. E., & Zeltzer, P. M. (1998). Chemotherapy side-effects in pediatric oncology patients—drugs, age, and sex as risk-factors. *Medical and Pediatric Oncology, 16,* 263–268.

Lesko, L. M., Dermatis, H., Penman, D., & Holland, J. C. (1989). Patients', parents' and oncologists' perceptions of informed consent for bone marrow transplantation. *Medical and Pediatric Oncology, 17,* 181–187.

Leventhal-Belfer, L., Bakker, A. M., & Russo, C. L. (1993). Parents of childhood cancer survivors: A descriptive look at their concerns and needs. *Journal of Psychosocial Oncology, 11,* 19–41.

Levi, F., La Vecchia, C., Negri, E., & Lucchini, F. (2001). Childhood cancer mortality in Europe, 1955–1995. *European Journal of Cancer, 37,* 785–809.

Leviton, J. (1994). Principles of epidemiology. In M. E. Cohen & P. K. Duffner (Eds.), *Brain tumors in children: Principles of diagnosis and management* (2nd ed.). New York: Raven Press.

Lockwood, K. A., Bell, T. S., & Colegrove, R. W. (1999). Long-term effects of cranial radiation therapy on attention functioning in survivors of childhood leukemia. *Journal of Pediatric Psychology, 24,* 55–66.

Longeway, K., Mulhern, R. K., Crisco, J. J., Kun, L., Lauer, S., Casper, J., Camitta, B., & Hoffman, R. G. (1990). Treatment of meningeal relapse in childhood acute lymphoblastic leukemia: II. A prospective study of intellectual loss specific to CNS relapse and therapy. *American Journal of Pediatric Hematology and Oncology, 12,* 45–50.

Lozowski, S., Chesler, M. A., & Chesney, B. K. (1993). Parental intervention in the medical care of children with cancer. *Journal of Psychosocial Oncology, 11,* 63–88.

Maccoby, E. E. (1984). Socialization and developmental change. *Child Development, 55,* 317–328.

Mackie, E., Hill, J., Kondryn, H., & McNally, R. (2000). Adult psychosocial outcomes in long-term survivors of acute lymphoblastic leukaemia and Wilm's tumour: A controlled study. *The Lancet, 355,* 1310–1314.

MacLean, W. E., Foley, G. V., Ruccione, K., & Sklar, C. (1996). Transitions in the care of adolescent and young adult survivors of childhood cancer. *Cancer, 78,* 1340–1344.

Madan-Swain, A., & Brown, R. T. (1991). Cognitive and psychosocial sequelae for children with acute lymphoblastic leukemia and their families. *Clinical Psychology Review, 11,* 267–294.

Madan-Swain, A., Brown, R. T., Sexson, S., Balwin, K., Pais, R., & Ragab, A. (1994). Adolescent cancer survivors: Psychosocial and familial adaption. *Psychosomatics, 35,* 453–459.

Madan-Swain, A., Sexson, S. B., Brown, R. T., & Ragab, A. (1993). Family adaptation and coping among siblings of cancer patients, their brothers and sisters, and nonclinical controls. *American Journal of Family Therapy, 21,* 60–70.

Malcolm, H., Thorpe, G., & Lowden, K. (1996). *Understanding truancy: Links between attendance, truancy and performance.* Edinburgh, Scotland: SCRE.

Manne, S. L., Bakeman, R., Jacobsen, P. B., Gorfinkle, K., Bernstein, D., & Redd, W. H. (1992). Adult–child interaction during invasive medical procedures. *Health Psychology, 11,* 241–249.

Manne, S., Bakeman, R., Jacobsen, P., Gorfinkle, K., & Redd, W. H. (1994). An analysis of an intervention to reduce children's distress during venipuncture. *Health Psychology, 13,* 556–566.

Manne, S., Jacobsen, P. B., Gorfinkle, K., Gerstein, F., & Redd, W. H. (1993). Treatment adherence difficulties among children with cancer: The role of parenting style. *Journal of Pediatric Psychology, 18,* 47–62.

Manne, S. L., Lesanics, D., Meyers, P., Wollner, N., Steinherz, P., & Redd, W. (1995). Predictors of depressive symptomatology among parents of newly diagnosed children with cancer. *Journal of Pediatric Psychology, 20,* 491–510.

Manne, S., Miller, D., Meyers, P., Wollner, N., Steinherz, P., & Redd, W. H. (1996). Depressive symptoms among parents of newly diagnosed children with cancer: A 6-month follow-up study. *Children's Health Care, 25,* 191–209.

Manne, S., Miller, D. L., Meyers, P., Wollner, N., Steinherz, P., & Redd, W. (1999). Difficulties completing treatment tasks among newly diagnosed children with cancer. *Children's Health Care, 28,* 255–276.

Manne, S. L., Redd, W. H., Jacobsen, P. B., Gorfinkle, K., & Schorr, O. (1990). Behavioral intervention to reduce child and parent distress during venipuncture. *Journal of Consulting and Clinical Psychology, 58,* 565–572.

Martinson, I., Chong, Y. L., & Liang, Y. H. (1997). Distress symptoms and support systems of Chinese parents of children with cancer. *Cancer Nursing, 20,* 94–99.

Martinson, I. M., Davies, B., & McClowry, S. (1991). Parental depression following the death of a child. *Death Studies, 15,* 259–267.

Martinson, I. M., McClowry, S. G., Davies, B., & Kuhlenkamp, E. J. (1994). Changes over time: A study of family bereavement following childhood cancer. *Journal of Palliative Care, 10,* 19–25.

Martinson, I. M., Zhong, B. H., & Liang, Y. H. (1994). The reaction of Chinese patients to terminally ill children with cancer. *Cancer Nursing, 17,* 72–76.

Masera, G., Chesler, M. A., Jankovic, M., Ablin, A. R., Ben Arush, M. W., Breatnach, F., McDowell, H. P., Eden, T., Epelman, C., Fossati Bellani, F., Green, D. M., Kosmidis, H. V., Nesbit, M. E., Wandzura, C., Wilbur, J. R., & Spinetta, J. J. (1997). SIOP working committee on psychosocial issues in pediatric oncology: Guidelines for communication of the diagnosis. *Medical and Pediatric Oncology, 28,* 382–385.

Masera, G., Chesler, M., Jankovic, M., Eden, T., Nesbit, M. E., van Dongen-Melman, J. E. W. M., Epelman, C., Ben Arush, M. W., Schuler, D., Mulhern, R. K., Adamoli, L., Wilbur, J., & Spinetta, J. J. (1996). SIOP Working committee on psychosocial issues in pediatric oncology: Guidelines for care of long-term survivors. *Medical and Pediatric Oncology, 27,* 1–2.

Masera, G., Spinetta, J. J., D'Angio, G. J., Green, D. M., Marky, I., Jankovic, M., Karamoschoglou, L. D., Mor, W., Morris Jones, P., Stocker, M., Postma, A., Nesbit, M. E., Schuler, D., Stevens, M., & Wilbur, J. (1993). SIOP working committee on psychosocial issues in pediatric oncology. *Medical and Pediatric Oncology, 21,* 627–628.

Masten, A. S., Best, K. M., & Garmezy, N. (1990). Resilience and development: Contributions from the study of children who overcome adversity. *Development and Psychopathology, 2,* 425–444.

Masten, A. S., Morison, P., & Pellegrini, D. S. (1985). A revised class play method of peer assessment. *Developmental Psychology, 21,* 523–533.

McCabe, M., & Weisz, J. R. (1988). *Psychological adjustment in children with leukemia: The role of personal and social resources.* Unpublished doctoral dissertation, Catholic University of America, Washington, D.C.

McCabe, M. A. (1996). Involving children and adolescents in medical decision making: Developmental and clinical considerations. *Journal of Pediatric Psychology, 21,* 505–516.

McCall, R. B. (1997). Challenges to a science of developmental psychology. *Child Development, 48,* 333–344.

McCarthy, A. M., Williams, J. K., & Eidahl, L. (1996). Children with chronic conditions: educators' views. *Journal of Pediatric Health Care, 10,* 272–279.

McCarthy, A. M., Williams, J. M., & Plumer, C. (1998). Evaluation of a school re-entry nursing intervention for children with cancer. *Journal of Pediatric Oncology Nursing, 15,* 143–152.

McCarthy, D. (1970). *McCarthy Scales of Children's Abilities.* New York: Psychological Corporation.

McClowry, S. G., Davies, E. B., May, K. A., Kulenkamp, E. J., & Martinson, I. M. (1995). The empty space phenomenon: The process of grief in the bereaved family. In K. J. Doka (Eds.), *Children mourning, mourning the children* (pp.). Washington DC: Hospice Foundation of America.

McNally, R. J. Q., Cairns, D. P., Eden, O. B., Alexander, F. E., Taylor, G. M., Kelsey, A. M., & Birch, J. M. (2002). An infectious aetiology for childhood brain tumours? Evidence from space-time clustering and seasonality analyses. *British Journal of Cancer, 86,* 1070–1077.

McNemar, Q. (1962). *Psychological statistics.* New York: Wiley.

Meadows, A. M., Kramer, S., Hopson, R., Lustbader, E., Jarrett, P., & Evans, A. E. (1983). Survival in childhood acute lymphocytic leukemia: Effect of protocol and place of treatment. *Cancer Investigations, 1,* 49–55.

Meadows, A. T., & Evans, A. E. (1976). Effects of chemotherapy on the central nervous system. *Cancer, 37,* 1079–1085.

Meadows, A. T., Gordon, J., Massari, D. J., Littman, P., Fergusson, J., & Moss, K. (1981). Declines in IQ scores and cognitive disfunctions in children with acute lymphoblastic leukaemia treated with cranial irradiation. *The Lancet,* pp. 1015–1018.

Meadows, A. T., & Hobbie, W. L. (1986). The medical consequences of cure. *Cancer, 58,* 524–528.

Meadows, A. T., Krejmas, N. L., & Belasco, J. B. (1980). The medical cost of cure: Sequelae in survivors of childhood cancer. In J. van Eys & M. P. Sullivan (Eds.), *Status of the curability of childhood cancers* (pp. 263–276). New York: Raven Press.

Melamed, B. G. (1992). Family factors predicting children's reaction to anesthesia induction. In A. M. LaGreca, L. J. Siegel, J. L. Wallander, & C. E. Walker (Eds.), *Stress and coping in child health: Advances in pediatric psychology* (pp. 140–156). New York: Guilford.

Merritt, K. A., Ornstein, P. A., & Spicker, B. (1994). Children's memory for a salient medical procedure: Implications for testimony. *Pediatrics, 94,* 17–23.

Meyer, D. J., Vadasy, P. F., & Lassen, C. P. (1994). *Sibshops: Workshops for siblings of children with special needs.* Baltimore, MD: Paul H. Brookes Publishing.

Middleton, J. A. (2001). Practitioner review: Psychological sequelae of head injury in children and adolescents. *Journal of Child Psychology and Psychiatry, 42,* 165–180.

Miller, S. M. (1987). Monitoring and blunting: validation of a questionnaire to assess styles of information seeking under threat. *Journal of Personality and Social Psychology, 52,* 345–353.

Miller, S. M. (1995). Monitoring versus blunting styles of coping with cancer influence the information patients want and need about their disease. *Cancer, 76,* 167–177.

Miller, S. M., & Mangan, C. E. (1983). Interacting effects of information and coping style in adapting to gynecologic stress: Should the doctor tell all? *Journal of Personality and Social Psychology, 45,* 223–236.

Miller, S. M., Rodoletz, M., Schroeder, C. M., Mangan, C. E., & Sedlacek, T. V. (1996). Applications of the monitoring process model to coping with severe long-term medical threats. *Health Psychology, 15,* 216–225.

Miller, S. M., Sherman, H. D., Caputo, G. C., Kruus, L., & Combs, C. (1993). *Patterns of coping with threat: Dispositional and situational aspects.* Unpublished manuscript, Temple University, Philadelphia.

Mok, J. Y., Laing, I. A., & Ferguhar, J. W. (1984). Young diabetics: Memories, current lifestyles and attitudes. *Diabetic Medicine, 1,* 227–230.

Monaco, G. P. (1987). Socioeconomic considerations in childhood cancer survival: Society's obligations. *The American Journal of Pediatric Hematology/Oncology, 9,* 92–98.

Moore, J. B., & Mosher, R. B. (1997). Adjustment responses of children and their mothers to cancer: Self-care and anxiety. *Oncology Nursing Forum, 24,* 519–525.

Moore, I. M. K., Kramer, J. H., Wara, W., Halberg, F., & Ablin, A. R. (1991). Cognitive function in children with leukemia: Effect of radiation dose and time since irradiation. *Cancer, 68,* 1913–1917.

Morris, J. A. B., Blount, R. L., Cohen, L. C., Frank, N. C., Madan-Swain, A., & Brown, R. T. (1997). Family functioning and behavioral adjustment in children with leukemia and their healthy peers. *Child Health Care, 26,* 61–75.

Mostow, E. N., Byrne, J., Connelly, R. R., & Mulvihill, J. J. (1991). Quality of life in long-term survivors of CNS tumors of childhood and adolescence. *Journal of Clinical Oncology, 9,* 592–599.

Mott, M. G., Mann, J. R., & Stiller, C. A. (1997). The United Kingdom Children's Cancer Study Group—the first 20 years of growth and development. *European Journal of Cancer, 33,* 1448–1452.

Mulhern, R. K. (1994). Neuropsychological late effects. In D. J. Bearison & R. K. Mulhern (Eds.), *Pediatric psycho-oncology: Psychological perspectives on children with cancer* (pp. 99–121). New York: Oxford University Press.

Mulhern, R. K., Armstong, N., & Thompson, S. J. (1998). Function specific neuropsychological assessment. *Medical and Pediatric Oncology (Supplement), 1,* 34–40.

Mulhern, R. K., Carpentieri, S., Shema, S., Stone, P., & Fairclough, D. (1993). Factors associated with social and behavioural problems among children recently diagnosed with brain tumor. *Journal of Pediatric Psychology, 18,* 339–350.

Mulhern, R. K., Fairclough, D. L., Friedman, A. G., & Leigh, L. D. (1990). Play performance scale as an index of quality of life in children with cancer. *Psychological Assessment, 2,* 149–155.

Mulhern, R. K., Fairclough, D., & Ochs, J. J. (1991). A prospective comparison of neuropsychologic performance of children surviving leukemia who received 18-Gy, 24-Gy, or no cranial irradiation. *Journal of Clinical Oncology, 9,* 1348–1356.

Mulhern, R. K., Fairclough, D. L., Smith, B., & Douglas, S. M. (1992). Maternal depression, assessment methods, and physical symptoms affect estimates of depressive symptomatology among children with cancer. *Journal of Pediatric Psychology, 17,* 313–326.

Mulhern, R. K., Hancock, J. L., Fairclough, D., & Kun, L. (1992). Neuropsychological status of children treated for brain tumors: A critical review and integrative analysis. *Medical and Pediatric Oncology, 20,* 181–191.

Mulhern, R. K., Kovnar, E. H., Kun, L., Crisco, J. J., & Williams, J. M. (1988). Psychologic and neurologic function following treatment for childhood temporal lobe astrocytoma. *Journal of Child Neurology, 3,* 47–52.

Mulhern, R. K., Kovnar, E., Langston, J., Carter, M., Fairclough, D., Leigh, L., & Kun, L. E. (1992). Long-term survivors of leukaemia treated in infancy: Factors associated with neuropsychological status. *Journal of Clinical Oncology, 10,* 1095–1102.

Mulhern, R. K., Ochs, J. J., Fairclough, D., Wasserman, A. L., Davis, K. S., & Williams, J. M. (1987). Intellectual and academic achievement status affter CNS relapse: A retrospective analysis of 40 children treated for acute lymphoblastic leukemia. *Journal of Clinical Oncology, 5,* 933–940.

Mulhern, R. K., Tyc, V. L., Phipps, S., Crom, D., Barclay, D., Greenwald, C., Hudson, M., & Thompson, E. I. (1995). Health-related behaviors of survivors of childhood cancer. *Medical and Pediatric Oncology, 25,* 159–165.

Mulhern, R. K., Wasserman, A. L., Fairclough, D., & Ochs, J. J. (1988). Memory function in disease-free survivors of childhood acute lymphoblastic leukemia given CNS prophylaxis with or without 1,800 cGy cranial irradiation. *Journal of Clinical Oncology, 6,* 315–320.

Murdoch, B. E., & Boon, D. L. (1999). Language disorders in children treated for acute lymphoblastic leukaemia. In B. E. Murdoch (Eds.), *Communication disorders in childhood cancer* (pp. 126–157). London: Whurr Publishers.

Murdoch, B. E., Boon, D. L., & Ozanne, A. E. (1994). Variability of language outcomes in children treated for acute lymphoblastic leukaemia: An examination of 23 cases. *Journal of Medical Speech/Language Pathology, 2,* 113–123.

Muris, P., van Zuuren, F. J., de Jong, P. J., De Beurs, E., & Hanewald, G. (1994). Monitoring and blunting coping styles: The Miller Behavior Style Scale and its correlates, and the development of an alternative questionnaire. *Personality and Individual Differences, 17,* 9–19.

Murray, L., McCarron, P., Bailie, K., Middleton, R., Davey Smith, G., Dempsey, S., McCarthy, A., & Gavin, A. (2002). Association of early life factors and acute lymphoblastic leukaemia in childhood: Historical cohort study. *British Journal of Cancer, 86,* 356–361.

Nagy, S., & Ungerer, J. (1990). The adaptation of mothers and fathers to children with cystic fibrosis: A comparison. *Children's Health Care, 19,* 147–154.

Neff, E. J., & Beardslee, C. I. (1990). Body knowledge and concerns of children with cancer as compared with the knowledge and concerns of other children. *Journal of Pediatric Nursing, 5,* 179–189.

Neglia, J. P., Meadows, A. T., Robison, L. L., Kim, T. H., Newton, W. A., Ruymann, F. B., Sather, H. N., & Hammond, G. D. (1991). Second neoplasms after acute lymphoblastic leukemia in childhood. *The New England Journal of Medicine, 325,* 1330–1336.

Neglia, J. P., & Nesbit, M. E. (1993). Care and treatment of long-term survivors of childhood cancer. *Cancer, 71,* 3386–3391.

Nelson, A. E., Miles, M. S., Reed, S. B., Davis, C. P., & Cooper, H. (1994). Depressive symptomatology in parents of children with chronic oncologic or hematologic disease. *Journal of Psychosocial Oncology, 12,* 61–75.

Newburger, J. W., Silbert, A. R., Buckley, L. P., & Fyler, D. C. (1984). Cognitive function and age at repair of transportation of the great arteries in children. *New England Journal of Medicine, 310,* 1495–1499.

Nir, Y. (1985). Post-traumatic stress disorder in children with cancer. In S. Eth & R. Pynoos (Eds.), *Post traumatic stress disorder in children* (pp. 121–132). Washington, DC: American Psychiatric Press.

Noll, R. B., Bukowski, W. M., Davies, W. H., Koontz, K., & Kulkarni, R. (1993). Adjustment in the peer system of adolescents with cancer: A two-year study. *Journal of Pediatric Psychology, 18,* 351–364.

Noll, R. B., Bukowski, W. M., Rogosch, F. A., LeRoy, S., & Kulkarni, R. (1990). Social interactions between children with cancer and their peers: Teacher ratings. *Journal of Pediatric Psychology, 15,* 43–56.

Noll, R. B., Gartstein, M. A., Hawkins, A., Vannatta, K., Davies, W. H., & Bukowski, W. M. (1995). Comparing parental distress for families with children who have cancer and matched comparison families without children with cancer. *Family Systems Medicine, 13,* 11–27.

Noll, R. B., LeRoy, S., Bukowski, W. M., Rogosch, F. A., & Kulkarni, R. (1991). Peer relationships and adjustment in children with cancer. *Journal of Pediatric Psychology, 16,* 307–326.

Noll, R. B., MacLean, W. E., Whitt, J. K., Kaleita, T. A., Stebbens, J. A., Waskerwitz, M. J., Ruymann, F. B., & Hammond, G. D. (1997). Behavioral adjustment and social functioning of long-term survivors of childhood leukaemia: Parent and teacher reports. *Journal of Pediatric Psychology, 22,* 827–841.

Noll, R. B., Ris, M. D., Davies, W. H., Bukowski, W. M., & Koontz, K. (1992). Social interactions between children with cancer or sickle cell disease and their peers: Teacher ratings. *Developmental and Behavioral Pediatrics, 13,* 187–193.

Novakovic, B., Fears, T. R., Wexler, L. H., McClure, L. L., Wilson, D. L., McCalla, J. L., & Tucker, M. A. (1996). Experiences of cancer in children and adolescents. *Cancer Nursing, 19,* 54–59.

Nutbrown, C., & Hannon, P. (1997). *Preparing for early literacy development with parents: A professional development manual.* Nottingham: NES Arnold.

Nysom, K., Colan, S. D., & Lipshultz, S. E. (1998). Late cardiotoxicity following anthracycline therapy for childhood cancer. *Progress Pediatric Cardiology, 8,* 121–138.

Oakhill, A., & Mann, J. R. (1983). Poor prognosis of acute lymphoblastic leukaemia in Asian children living in the United Kingdom. *British Medical Journal, 286,* 839–841.

Ochs, J. J., Brecher, M. L., Mahoney, D., Vega, R., B. H., P., Buchanan, G. R., Whitehead, V. M., Ravindranath, Y., & Freeman, A. I. (1991). Recombinant interferon alfa given before and in combination with standard chemotherapy in children with acute lymphoblastic leukemia in first marrow relapse: A Pediatric Oncology Group pilot study. *Journal of Clinical Oncology, 9,* 777–782.

Ochs, J. J., Rivera, G., Aur, R. J., Hustu, H. O., Berg, R., & Simone, J. V. (1985). Central nervous system morbidity following an initial isolated central nervous system relapse and its subsequent therapy in childhood acute lymphoblastic leukemia. *Journal of Clinical Oncology, 3,* 622–626.

Offer, L. D., Ostrov, E., & Howard, K. I. (1982). *The Offer self-image questionnaire for adolescents: A manual (revised).* Chicago: Michael Reese Hospital.

Olson, A. L., Boyle, W. E., Evans, M. W., & Zug, L. A. (1993). Overall function in rural childhood cancer survivors: The role of social competence and emotional health. *Clinical Pediatrics, 32,* 334–342.

Oppenheim, A. N. (1992). *Questionnaire design, interviewing and attitude measurement.* London: Pinter Publications.

Ostroff, J., & Steinglass, P. (1996). Psychosocial adaptation following treatment: A family systems perspective on childhood cancer survivorship. In L. Baider, C. L. Cooper, & A. Kaplan De-Nour (Eds.), *Cancer and the family* (pp. 129–147). London: Wiley.

Overholser, J. C., & Fritz, G. K. (1990). The impact of childhood cancer on the family. *Journal of Psychosocial Oncology, 8,* 71–85.

Packer, R. J., Meadows, A. T., Rorke, L. B., Goldwein, J. L., & D'Angio, G. (1987). Long-term sequelae of cancer treatment on the central nervous system in childhood. *Medical and Pediatric Oncology, 15,* 241–253.

Packer, R. J., Sutton, L. N., Atkins, T. E., Radcliffe, J., Bunin, G. R., & D'Angio, G. (1989). A prospective study of cognitive function in children receiving whole-brain radiotherapy and chemotherapy: 2-year results. *Journal of Neurosurgery, 70,* 707–713.

Papadatou, D., Yfantopoulos, J., & Kosmidis, H. V. (1996). Death of a child at home or in hospital: Experiences of Greek mothers. *Death Studies, 20,* 215–235.

Patno, K. M., Young, P. C., & Dickerman, J. D. (1988). Parental attitudes about confidentiality in a pediatric oncology clinic. *Pediatrics, 81,* 296–300.

Peckham, V. C., Meadows, A. T., Bartel, N., & Marrero, O. (1988). Educational late effects in long-term survivors of childhood acute lymphocytic leukemia. *Pediatrics, 81,* 127–133.

Pelcovitz, D., Goldenberg, B., Kaplan, S., Weinblatt, M., Mandel, F., Meyers, B., & Vinciguerra, V. (1996). Posttraumatic stress disorder in mothers of pediatric cancer survivors. *Psychosomatics, 37,* 116–126.

Pendley, J. S., Dahlquist, L. M., & Dreyer, Z. (1997). Body image and psychosocial adjustment in adolescent cancer survivors. *Journal of Pediatric Psychology, 22,* 29–43.

Pennebaker, J. W., Mayne, T. J., & Francis, M. E. (1997). Linguistic predictors of adaptive bereavement. *Journal of Personality and Social Psychology, 72,* 863–871.

Perrin, E. C., & Gerrity, P. S. (1981). There's a demon in your belly: Children's understanding of illness. *Pediatrics, 67,* 841–849.

Perrin, E. C., & Gerrity, P. S. (1984). Development of children with a chronic illness. *Pediatric Clinics of North America, 31,* 19–31.

Perrin, E. C., Stein, R. E. K., & Drotar, D. (1991). Cautions in using the Child Behavior Checklist: Observations based on research about children with a chronic illness. *Journal of Pediatric Psychology, 16,* 411–421.

Petersen, A. C., Schulenberg, J. E., Abramowitz, R. H., Offer, D., & Jarcho, H. D. (1984). A self-image questionnaire for young adolescents (SIQYA): Reliability and validity studies. *Journal of Youth and Adolescence, 13,* 93–111.

Peterson, C., & Bell, M. (1996). Children's memory for traumatic injury. *Child Development, 67,* 3045–3070.

Peto, R., Lopez, A. D., Boreham, J., Thun, M., & Heath, C. (1992). Mortality from tobacco in developed countries: Indirect estimation from national vital statistics. *Lancet, 339,* 1268–1278.

Petty, R. E., & Cacioppo, J. T. (1984). The effects of involvement on response to argument quantity and quality: Central and peripheral routes to persuasion. *Journal of Personality and Social Psychology, 46,* 69–81.

Pfefferbaum-Levine, B., Copeland, D. R., Fletcher, J. M., Ried, H. L., Jaffe, N., & McKinnon, W. R. (1984). Neuropsychologic assessment of childhood leukemia. *American Journal of Pediatric Hematology and Oncology, 12,* 174–181.

Phillips, P. C., Dhawan, V., Strother, S. C., Stieltis, J. J., Evans, A. C., Allen, J. C., & Rottenberg, D. A. (1987). Reduced cerebral glucose metabolism and increased brain capillary permeability following high-dose methotrexate chemotherapy: A positron emission tomographic study. *Annals of Neurology, 21,* 59–63.

Phipps, S., Dunavant, M., Jayawardene, D., & Srivastiva, D. K. (1999). Assessment of health-related quality of life in acute in-patient settings: Use of the BASES instrument in children undergoing bone marrow transplantation. *International Journal of Cancer (Supplement), 12,* 18–24.

Phipps, S., Dunavant, M., Lensing, S., & Rai, S. N. (2002). Acute health-related quality of life in children undergoing stem cell transplant: II. Medical and demographic determinants. *Bone Marrow Transplantation, 29,* 435–442.

Phipps, S., Fairclough, D., & Mulhern, R. K. (1995). Avoidant coping in children with cancer. *Journal of Pediatric Psychology, 20,* 217–232.

Phipps, S., Hinds, P. S., Channell, S., & Bell, G. L. (1994). Measurement of behavioural, affective, and somatic responses to pediatric bone marrow transplantation: Development of the BASES scale. *Journal of Pediatric Oncology Nursing, 11,* 109–117.

Phipps, S., & Mulhern, R. K. (1995). Family cohesion and expressiveness promote resilience to the stress of pediatric bone marrow transplant: A preliminary report. *Journal of Developmental and Behavioral Pediatrics, 16,* 257–263.

Phipps, S., & Srivastava, D. K. (1997). Repressive adaptation in children with cancer. *Health Psychology, 16,* 521–528.

Piaget, J. (1929). *The childs' conception of the world.* New York: International Universities Press.

Piaget, J. (1952). *The childs' conception of number.* London: Routledge and Kegan Paul.

Piers, E. V., & Harris, D. (1969). *The Piers–Harris children's self-concept scale.* Nashville, TN: Counsellor Recordings and Tests.

Pinkerton, C. R., Cushing, P., & Sepion, B. (1994). *Childhood cancer management.* London: Chapman & Hall.

Platt Committee. (1959). *The welfare of children in hospital.* London: Her Majesty's Stationery Office.

Pless, I. B., Cripps, H. A., Davies, J. M., & Wadsworth, M. E. (1989). Chronic physical illness in childhood: Psychological and social effects in adolescence and adult life. *Developmental Medicine and Child Neurology, 31,* 746–55.

Pless, I. B., & Pinkerton, P. (1975). *Chronic childhood disorder: Promoting patterns of adjustment.* London: Henry Kimpton.

Pless, I. B., Power, C., & Peckham, C. S. (1993). Long-term psychosocial sequelae of chronic physical disorders in childhood. *Pediatrics, 91,* 1131–1136.

Pollock, B. H. (1999). Obstacles and opportunities for the use of health-related quality-of-life assessment in pediatric cancer clinical trials (discussion). *International Journal of Cancer (Supplement), 12,* 151–153.

Pomeroy, S. L., Tamayo, P., Gaasenbeek, M., Sturla, L. M., Angelo, M., McLaughlin, M. E., Kim, J. Y. H., Goumnerova, L. C., Black, P. M., Lau, C., Allen, J. C., Zagzag, D., Olson, J. M., Curran, T., Wetmore, C., Biegel, J. A., Possio, T., Mukherjee, S., Rifkin, R., Califano, A., Stolovitzky, G., Louis, D. N., Mesirov, J. P., Lander, E. S., & Golub, T. R. (2002). Prediction of central nervous system embryonal tumor outcome based on gene expression. *Nature, 415,* 436–442.

Pond, M. N., Newport, M., Jones, D., & Conway, S. P. (1994). Home versus hospital intravenous antibiotic therapy in treatment of young adults with cystic fibrosis. *European Respiratory Journal, 7,* 1640–1644.

Postlethwaite, R. J., Reynolds, J. M., Wood, A. J., Evans, J. H., Lewis, M. A., & Eminson, D. M. (1995). Recruiting patients to clinical trials: lessons from studies of growth hormone treatment in renal failure. *Archives of Disease in Childhood, 73,* 30–35.

Pot-Mees, C. (1989). *The psychosocial effects of bone marrow transplantation in children.* Delft, Netherlands: Eburon Publisher.

Potter, P. C., & Roberts, M. C. (1984). Children's perceptions of chronic illness: The roles of disease symptoms, cognitive development and information. *Journal of Pediatric Psychology, 9,* 13–28.

Powers, S. W., Blount, R. L., Bachanas, P. J., Cotter, M. W., & Swan, S. C. (1993). Helping preschool leukemia patients and their parents cope during injections. *Journal of Pediatric Psychology, 18,* 681–695.

Price, B. (1992). Living with altered body image: The cancer experience. *British Journal of Nursing, 1,* 263–273.

Prochaska, J. O., Velicer, W. F., Rossi, J. S., Goldstein, M. G., Marcus, B. H., Rakowski, W., Fiore, C., Harlow, L. L., Redding, C. A., Rosenbloom, D., & Rossi, S. R. (1994). Stages of change and decisional balance for 12 problem behaviors. *Health Psychology, 13,* 39–46.

Pui, C. H., & Evans, W. E. (1998). Acute lymphoblastic leukemia. *New England Journal of Medicine, 339,* 605–615.

Punnett, A. F., & Thurber, S. (1993). Evaluation of the asthma camp experience for children. *Journal of Asthma, 30,* 195–198.

Puukko, L., Sammallahti, P. R., Siimes, M. A., & Aalberg, V. A. (1997). Childhood leukaemia and body image: Interview reveals impairment not found with a questionnaire. *Journal of Clinical Psychology, 53,* 133–137.

Quittner, A. L., Tolbert, V. E., Regoli, M. J., Orenstein, D. M., Hollingsworth, J. L., & Eigen, H. (1996). Development of the role-play inventory of situations and coping strategies for parents of children with cystic fibrosis. *Journal of Pediatric Psychology, 21,* 209–235.

Radcliffe, J. R., Bennett, D., Kazak, A., Foley, B., Goldwein, J., Sutton, L. N., Lange, B., & Phillips, P. C. (1994). *Child and family adjustment among childhood brain tumour survivors.* Unpublished manuscript.

Radcliffe, J., Bennett, D., Kazak, A. E., Foley, B., & Phillips, P. C. (1996). Adjustment in childhood brain tumor survival: Child, mother, and teacher report. *Journal of Pediatric Psychology, 21,* 529–539.

Radcliffe, J., Packer, R. J., Atkins, T. E., Bunin, G. R., Schut, L., & Goldwein, J. W. (1992). Three- and four-year cognitive outcome in children with noncortical brain tumors treated with whole-brain radiotherapy. *Annals of Neurology, 32,* 551–554.

Ramsey, P. (1991). *Making friends in school.* New York: Teachers College Press.

Raney, R. B., Anderson, J. R., Kollath, J., Vassipoloulou-Sellin, R., Klein, M. J., Heyn, R., Glicksman, A. S., Wharam, M., Crist, W. M., & Maurer, H. M. (2000). Late effects of therapy in 94 patients with localized rhabdomyosarcoma of the orbit: Report from the Intergroup Rhabdomyosarcoma Study (IRS)–III, 1984–1991. *Medical and Pediatric Oncology, 34,* 413–420.

Recklitis, C., O'Leary, T., & Diller, L. (2003). Utility of routine psychological screening in the childhood cancer survivor clinic. *Journal of Clinical Oncology, 5,* 787–792.

Rey, A. (1964). *L'examin clinique en psychologie* [Clinical examination in psychology]. Paris: Presses Universitaires de France.

Reynolds, C. R., & Richmond, B. O. (1985). *Manual for the revised children's manifest anxiety scale*. Los Angeles: Western Psychological Services.

Reynolds, W. M. (1985). Depression in childhood and adolescence: Diagnosis, assessment, intervention strategies and research. In T. Kratochwill (Ed.), *Advances in school psychology* (pp. 133–189). Hillsdale, NJ: Lawrence Erlbaum Associates.

Reynolds, W. M., Anderson, G., & Bartell, N. (1985). Measuring depression in children: A multimethod assessment investigation. *Journal of Abnormal Child Psychology, 13,* 513–526.

Ris, M. D., & Noll, R. B. (1994). Long-term neurobehavioral outcome in pediatric brain-tumor patients: Review and methodological critique. *Journal of Clinical and Experimental Neuropsychology, 16,* 21–42.

Robertson, C. M., Hawkins, M. M., & Kingston, J. E. (1994). Late deaths and survival after childhood cancer: Implications for cure. *British Medical Journal, 309,* 162–166.

Robertson, J. (1952). *A two year old goes to hospital*. New York: New York University Film Library.

Robison, L. L. (1993). Issues in the consideration of intervention strategies in long-term survivors of childhood cancer. *Cancer Supplement, 71,* 3406–3410.

Robison, L. L., Nesbit, M. E., Sather, H. N., Meadows, A. T., Ortega, J. A., & Hammond, G. D. (1984). Factors associated with IQ scores in long-term survivors of childhood acute lymphoblastic leukemia. *American Journal of Pediatric Hematology and Oncology, 6,* 115–121.

Rodgers, J., Britton, P. G., Kernanhan, J., & Craft, A. W. (1991). Cognitive function after two doses of cranial irradiation for acute lymphoblastic leukaemia. *Archives of Disease in Childhood, 66,* 1245–1246.

Rodin, G., Daneman, D., & deGroot, J. (1993). The interaction of chronic medical illness and eating disorders. In A. S. Kaplan & P. E. Garkinkel (Eds.), *Medical issues and the eating disorders: The interface* (pp. 176–192). New York: Brunnel/Mazel.

Rosen, J. C., Srebnik, D., Saltzberg, E., & Wendt, S. (1991). Development of a body image avoidance questionnaire. *Psychological Assessment, 3,* 32–37.

Ross, D. M., & Ross, S. A. (1984). The importance of type of question, psychological climate and subject set in interviewing children with pain. *Pain, 19,* 71–79.

Rothbaum, F., Weisz, J. R., & Snyder, S. S. (1982). Changing the world and changing the self: A two-process model of perceived control. *Journal of Personality and Social Psychology, 42,* 5–37.

Rousseau, P., Flamant, F., Quintana, E., Voute, P. A., & Gentet, J. C. (1994). Primary chemotherapy in rhabdomyosarcomas and other malignant mesenchymal tumors of the orbit: Results of the international society of pediatric oncology MMT 84 study. *Journal of Clinical Oncology, 12,* 516–521.

Rovet, J., & Fernandes, C. (1999). Insulin-dependent diabetes mellitus. In R. T. Brown (Eds.), *Cognitive aspects of chronic illness in children* (pp. 142–171). New York: Guilford.

Royal College of Paediatrics and Child Health. (1997). *A guide to developing paediatric palliative care services*. London.

Rubenstein, C. L., Varni, J. W., & Katz, E. R. (1990). Cognitive functioning in long-term survivors of childhood leukemia: A prospective analysis. *Developmental and Behavioral Pediatrics, 11,* 301–305.

Rubin, K. H., Chen, X., McDougall, P., Bowker, A., & McKinnon, J. (1995). The Waterloo Longitudinal Project: Predicting adolescent internalizing and externalizing problems from early and mid-childhood. *Development and Psychopathology, 7,* 751–764.

Ruccione, K., Kramer, R. F., Moore, I. K., & Perrin, G. (1991). Informed consent for treatment of childhood cancer: Factors affecting parents' decision making. *Journal of Pediatric Oncology Nursing, 8,* 112–121.

Russell, A., & Saebel, J. (1997). Mother–son, mother–daughter, father–son, and father–daughter: Are they distinct relationships? *Developmental Review, 17,* 111–147.

Rutter, M. (1981). Stress, coping and development: Some issues and some questions. *Journal of Child Psychology and Psychiatry, 22,* 323–356.

Rutter, M., Graham, P., & Yule, W. (1970). *A neuropsychiatric study in childhood.* London: Heinemann.

Ryan, C. M. (1990). Neuropsychological consequences and correlates of diabetes in childhood. In C. S. Holmes (Eds.), *Neuropsychological and behavioural aspects of diabetes.* New York: Springer-Verlag.

Saha, V., Love, S., Eden, T., Micallef-Eynaud, P., & MacKinlay, G. (1993). Determinants of symptom interval in childhood cancer. *Archives of Disease in Childhood, 68,* 771–774.

Sahler, O. J., Roghman, K. J., Carpenter, P. J., & Mulhern, R. K. (1994). Sibling adaptation to childhood cancer collaborative study: Prevalence of sibling distress and definition of adaptation levels. *Journal of Developmental and Behavioral Pediatrics, 15,* 353–366.

Sahler, O. J., Roghman, K. J., Mulhern, R. K., & Carpenter, P. J. (1997). Sibling adaptation to childhood cancer collaborative study: The association of sibling adaptation with maternal well-being, physical health, and resource use. *Journal of Developmental and Behavioral Pediatrics, 18,* 233–243.

Said, J. A., Waters, B. G. H., Cousens, P., & Stevens, M. M. (1989). Neuropsychological sequelae of central nervous system prophylaxis in survivors of childhood acute lymphoblastic leukaemia. *Journal of Consulting and Clinical Psychology, 57,* 251–256.

Sanger, M. S., Copeland, D. R., & Davidson, E. R. (1991). Psychosocial adjustment among pediatric cancer patients: A multidimensional assessment. *Journal of Pediatric Psychology, 16,* 463–474.

Sargent, J. R., Sahler, O. J. Z., Roghman, K. J., Mulhern, R. K., Barbarian, O. A., Carpenter, P. J., Copeland, D. R., Dolgin, M. J., & Zeltzer, L. K. (1995). Sibling adaptation to childhood cancer collaborative study: Siblings' perceptions of the cancer experience. Special issue: Pediatric chronic conditions. *Journal of Pediatric Psychology, 20,* 151–164.

Sattler, J. M. (1988). *Assessment of children's abilities.* San Diego.

Sawyer, M. G., Antoniou, G., Toogood, I., & Rice, M. (1997). Childhood cancer: A two-year prospective study of the psychological adjustment of children and parents. *Journal of American Academy of Child and Adolescent Psychiatry, 36,* 1736–1743.

Sawyer, M. G., Antoniou, G., Toogood, I., Rice, M., & Baghurst, P. A. (1993). A prospective study of the psychological adjustment of parents and families of children with cancer. *Journal of Pediatric Child Health Care, 29,* 352–356.

Sawyer, M. G., Streiner, D. L., Antoniou, G., Toogood, I., & Rice, M. (1998). Influence of parental and family adjustment on the later psychological adjustment of children treated for cancer. *Journal of American Academy of Child and Adolescent Psychiatry, 37,* 815–822.

Schipper, H., Clinch, J. J., & Olweny, C. L. M. (1996). Quality of life studies: Definitions and conceptual issues. In B. Spilker (Ed.), *Quality of life and pharmacoeconomics in clinical trials* (pp. 11–23). Philadelphia: Lippincott-Raven Publishers.

Schwartz, C. L. (1995). Late effects of treatment in long-term survivors of cancer. *Cancer Treatment Reviews, 21,* 355–366.

Schwebel, D. C., Plumert, J. M., & Pick, H. L. (2000). Integrating basic and applied developmental research: A new model for the twenty-first century. *Child Development, 71,* 222–230.

Secord, P. F., & Jourard, S. M. (1953). The appraisal of body-cathexis: Body cathexis and the self. *Journal of Consulting Psychology, 17,* 343–347.

Seedhouse, D. (1996). Measuring health: An exercise in social pseudoscience and political naivety. *Health Care Analysis, 4,* 261–264.

Shalet, S. M., Clayton, P. E., & Price, D. A. (1988). Growth and pituitary function in children treated for brain tumours or acute lymphoblastic leukaemia. *Hormone Research, 30,* 53–61.

Share, L. (1972). Family communication in the crisis of a child's fatal illness: A literature review and analysis. *Omega, 3,* 187–201.

Sherwin, E. D., & O'Shanick, G. J. (2000). The trauma of paediatric and adolescent brain injury: Issues and implications for rehabilitation specialists. *Brain Injury, 14,* 267–284.

Sheslow, D., & Adams, W. (1990). *Wide range assessment of memory and learning: Administration manual.* Wilmington, DE: Jastak Assessment Systems.

Siegel, L. J., & Graham-Pole, J. (1991). Stress, immunity, and disease outcome in children undergoing cancer chemotherapy. In J. H. Johnson & S. B. Johnson (Eds.), *Advances in child health psychology* (pp. 28–41). Gainesville: University of Florida Press.

Slavc, I., Salchegger, C., Hauer, C., Urban, C., Oberbauer, R., & Pakisch, B. (1994). Follow-up and quality of survival of 67 consecutive children with CNS tumors. *Child's Nervous System, 10,* 433–443.

Slavin, L. A., O'Malley, J. E., Koocher, G. P., & Foster, D. J. (1982). Communication of the cancer diagnosis to pediatric patients: Impact on long-term adjustment. *American Journal of Psychiatry, 139,* 179–183.

Sloper, P. (1996). Needs and responses of parents following the diagnosis of childhood cancer. *Child: Care, Health and Development, 22,* 187–202.

Sloper, P., & While, D. (1996). Risk factors associated with the adjustment of siblings of children with cancer. *Journal of Child Psychology and Psychiatry, 37,* 597–607.

Sloper, P., Larcombe, I. J., & Charlton, A. (1994). Psychosocial adjustment of five-year survivors of childhood cancer. *Journal of Cancer Education, 9,* 163–169.

Smith, K. E., Gotlieb, S., Gurwitch, R. H., & Blotcky, A. D. (1987). The impact of a summer camp experience on daily activity and family interaction among children with cancer. *Journal of Pediatric Psychology, 12,* 533–542.

Soni, S. S., Marten, G. W., Pitner, S. E., Duenas, D. A., & Powazek, M. (1975). Effects of central nervous system irradiation on neuropsychologic functioning of children with acute lymphocytic leukaemia. *The New England Journal of Medicine, 293,* 113–118.

Sormanti, M., Dungan, S., & Pieker, P. P. (1994). Pediatric bone marrow transplantation: Psychosocial issues for parents after a child's hospitalization. *Journal of Psychosocial Oncology, 12,* 23–42.

Sourkes, B. M. (1991). Truth to life: Art therapy with pediatric oncology patients and their siblings. *Journal of Psychosocial Oncology, 9,* 81–96.

Sparrow, S. S., Carter, A. S., & Cicchetti, D. V. (2000). *Comprehensive psychological and psychoeducational assessment of children and adolescents—A developmental approach.* Boston: Allyn & Bacon.

Speechley, K. N., & Noh, S. (1992). Surviving childhood cancer, social support, and parents' psychological adjustment. *Journal of Pediatric Psychology, 17,* 15–31.

Spielberger, C. D. (1973). *Manual for the State–Trait Anxiety Inventory for children.* Palo Alto, CA: Consulting Psychologists Press.

Spielberger, C. D., Gorsuch, R. L., Luschene, R. E., Vagg, P. R., & Jacobs, G. A. (1970). *Manual for the State–Trait inventory.* Palo Alto, CA: Consulting Psychologists Press.

Spinetta, J. J., & Deasy-Spinetta, P. C. (1981). *Living with childhood cancer.* St. Louis, MO: Mosby.

Spinetta, J. J., Rigler, D., & Karon, M. (1974). Personal space as a measure of a dying child's sense of isolation. *Journal of Consulting and Clinical Psychology, 42,* 751–756.

Spirito, A., Stark, L. J., Cobiella, C., Drigan, R., Androkites, A., & Hewitt, K. (1990). Social adjustment of children successfully treated for cancer. *Journal of Pediatric Psychology, 15,* 359–371.

Spirito, A., Stark, L., & Williams, C. (1988). Development of a brief coping checklist for use with pediatric populations. *Journal of Pediatric Psychology, 13,* 555–574.

Springer, K. (1994). Beliefs about illness causality among preschoolers with cancer: Evidence against immanent justice. *Journal of Pediatric Psychology, 19,* 91–101.

Stallard, P., Mastroyannopoulou, K., Lewis, M., & Lenton, S. (1997). The siblings of children with life threatening conditions. *Child Psychology and Psychiatry Review, 2,* 26–33.

Stehbens, J. A., Ford, M. E., Kisker, C. T., Clarke, W. R., & Strayer, F. (1981). WISC–R verbal/performance discrepancies in pediatric cancer patients. *Journal of Pediatric Psychology, 6,* 61–68.

Stehbens, J. A., Kaleita, T. A., Noll, R. B., MacLean, W. E., O'Brien, R. T., Waskerwitz, M. J., & Hammond, G. D. (1991). CNS prophylaxis of childhood leukemia: What are the long-term neurological, neuropsychological, and behavioral effects. *Neuropsychology Review, 2,* 147–176.

Stehbens, J. A., Kisker, C. T., & Wilson, B. K. (1983). Achievement and intelligence test–retest performance in pediatric cancer patients at diagnosis and one year later. *Journal of Pediatric Psychology, 8,* 47–56.

Stein, R. E. K., & Jessop, D. J. (1984). Relationship between health status and psychological adjustment among children with chronic conditions. *Pediatrics, 73,* 169–174.

Steptoe, A. (1989). An abbreviated version of the Miller Behavioral Style Scale. *British Journal of Clinical Psychology, 28,* 183–184.

Stern, M., Norman, S. L., & Zevon, M. A. (1993). Adolescents with cancer—Self-image and perceived social support as indexes of adaptation. *Journal of Adolescent Research, 8,* 124–142.

Stevens, M. C. G., Kaye, J. I., Kenwood, C. F., & Mann, J. R. (1988). Facts for teachers of children with cancer. *Archives of Disease in Childhood, 63,* 456–458.

Steward, M. S., & Steward, D. S. (1981). Children's conceptions of medical procedures. In R. Bibace & M. Walsh (Eds.), *Children's conceptions of health, illness and bodily functions* (pp. 67–84). San Francisco: Jossey-Bass.

Stiller, C. A. (1994). Cancer in adolescence—Special problems and special solutions. *British Medical Journal, 308,* 1382–1383.

Stiller, C. A., & Bunch, K. J. (1994). Trends in survival for childhood cancer in Britain diagnosed 1971–85. *British Journal of Cancer, 62,* 806–815.

Stiller, C. A., Bunch, K. J., & Lewis, I. J. (2000). Ethnic group and survival from childhood cancer: Report from the UK Children's Cancer Study Group. *British Journal of Cancer, 82,* 1339–1343.

Stiller, C. A., & Draper, G. J. (1989). Treatment centre size, entry to trials, and survival in acute lymphoblastic leukemia. *Archives of Disease in Childhood, 64,* 657–661.

Stiller, C. A., & Eatock, E. M. (1999). Patterns of care and survival for children with acute lymphoblastic leukemia diagnosed between 1980–1994. *Archives of Disease in Childhood, 81,* 202–208.

Stone, R. (1973). Employing the recovered cancer patient. In *Proceedings of the American Cancer Society National Conference on Human Values and Cancer.* New York: American Cancer Society.

Stuber, M. L., Christakis, D. A., Houskamp, B., & Kazak, A. E. (1996). Posttrauma symptoms in childhood leukemia survivors and their parents. *Psychosomatics, 37,* 254–261.

Stuber, M. L., Gonzalez, S., Meeske, K., Guthrie, D., Houskamp, B. H., Pynoos, R., & Kazak, A. E. (1994). Post-traumatic stress after childhood cancer II: A family model. *Psycho-oncology, 3,* 313–319.

Stuber, M. L., Kazak, A. E., Meeske, K., Barakat, L., Guthrie, D., Garnier, H., Pynoos, R., & Meadows, A. (1997). Predictors of posttraumatic stress symptoms in childhood cancer survivors. *Pediatrics, 100,* 958–964.

Sulmont, V., Brauner, R., Fontura, M., & Rappaport, R. (1990). Response to growth hormone treatment and final height after cranial or craniospinal irradiation. *Acta Paediatrica Scandinavia, 79,* 542–549.

Susman, E. J., Dorn, L. D., & Fletcher, J. C. (1992). Participation in biomedical research: The consent process as viewed by children, adolescents, young adults and physicians. *Journal of Pediatrics, 121,* 547–552.

Susman, E. J., Hersh, S. P., Nannis, E. D., Strope, B. E., Woodruff, P. J., Pizzo, P. A., & Levine, A. S. (1982). Conceptions of cancer: The perspectives of child and adolescent patients and their families. *Journal of Pediatric Psychology, 7,* 253–261.

Swenson, T. G. (1988). A dose of Camp Dost: Meeting the psychosocial needs of children with cancer. *Issues in Comprehensive Pediatric Nursing, 11,* 29–32.

Taylor, H. G., & Fletcher, J. M. (1994). Progress in pediatric neuropsychology. *Journal of Pediatric Psychology, 20,* 695–701.

Taylor, S. C. (1980). The effect of chronic childhood illnesses upon well siblings. *Maternal-Child Nursing Journal, 9,* 109–116.

Tebbi, C. K., Bromberg, C., & Mallon, J. C. (1988). Self-reported depression in adolescent cancer patients. *American Journal of Pediatric Hematology and Oncology, 10,* 185–190.

Testa, M. A., & Simonson, D. C. (1996). Assessment of quality-of-life outcomes. *The New England Journal of Medicine, 334,* 835–840.

Teta, M. J., Del Po, M. C., Kasl, S. V., Meigs, J. W., Myers, M. H., & Mulvihill, J. J. (1986). Psychosocial consequences of childhood and adolescent cancer survival. *Journal of Chronic Disease, 39,* 751–759.

Thoma, M. E., Hockenberry-Eaton, M., & Kemp, V. (1993). Life change events and coping behaviors in families of children with cancer. *Journal of Pediatric Oncology Nursing, 10,* 105–111.

Thompson, J. K., Penner, L. A., & Altabe, M. N. (1990). Procedures, problems, and progress in the assessment of body images. In T. F. Cash & T. Pruzinsky (Eds.), *Body images: Development, deviance, and change* (pp. 21–48). New York: Guilford.

Thompson, R. J., & Gustafson, K. E. (1996). *Adaption to chronic childhood illness.* Washington, DC: American Psychological Society.

Thompson, S. J., Leigh, L., Christensen, R., Xiong, X., Kun, L. E., Heideman, R. L., Reddick, W. E., Gajjar, A., Merchant, T., Pui, T.-H., Hudson, M. M., & Mulhern, R. K. (2001). Immediate neurocognitive effects of methylphenidate on learning-impaired survivors of childhood cancer. *Journal of Clinical Oncology, 19,* 1802–1808.

Tillman, V., Darlington, A. S. E., Eiser, C., Bishop, N. J., & Davies, H. A. (2002). Male sex and low physical activity are associated with reduced spine bone mineral density in survivors of childhood acute lymphoblastic leukemia. *Journal of Bone and Mineral Research, 17,* 1073–1080.

Torrance, G. W., Boyle, M. H., & Horwood, S. P. (1982). Application of multi-attribute utility theory to measure social preferences for health states. *Operations Research, 30,* 1043–1069.

Tucker, M. A., D'Angio, G. J., Boice, J. D., Strong, L. C., Li, F. P., Stovall, M., Stone, B. J., Green, D. M., Lombardi, F., Newton, W., Hoover, R. N., & Fraumeni, J. F. (1987). Bone sarcomas linked to radiotherapy and chemotherapy in children. *New England Journal of Medicine, 317,* 588–593.

Twaddle, V., Britton, P. G., Craft, A. C., Noble, T. C., & Kernanhan, J. (1983). Intellectual function after treatment for leukaemia or solid tumours. *Archives of Disease in Childhood, 58,* 949–992.

Tyc, V. L., Hadley, W., & Crockett, G. (2001). Brief report: Predictors of intentions to use tobacco among adolescent survivors of cancer. *Journal of Pediatric Psychology, 26,* 117–121.

Tyc, V. L., Hudson, M. M., Hinds, P., Elliot, V., & Kibby, M. Y. (1997). Tobacco use among pediatric cancer patients: Recommendations for developing clinical smoking interventions. *Journal of Clinical Oncology, 15,* 2194–2204.

Vamos, M. (1993). Body image in chronic illness—A re-conceptualization. *International Journal of Psychiatry in Medicine, 23,* 163–178.

van Dongen-Melman, J. (1997). Information booklet for parents of children surviving cancer. *Leukaemia, 11,* 1799–1806.

van Dongen-Melman, J. E. W. M., De Groot, A., Hahlen, K., & Verhulst, F. C. (1995a). Impact of childhood leukaemia on family planning. In J. E. W. M. van Dongen-Melman (Ed.), *On surviving childhood cancer* (pp. 189–198). Alblasserdam, Netherlands: Haveka.

van Dongen-Melman, J. E. W. M., De Groot, A., Hahlen, K., & Verhulst, F. C. (1995b). Siblings of childhood cancer survivors: How does this forgotten group of children adjust after cessation of sucessful cancer treatment? In J. E. W. M. van Dongen-Melman (Ed.), *On surviving childhood cancer: Late psychosocial consequences for patients, parents and siblings* (pp. 231–243). Alblasserdam, Netherlands: Haveka.

van Dongen-Melman, J. E., De Groot, A., Hahlen, K., & Verhulst, F. C. (1996). Potential pitfalls of using illness specific measures. *Journal of Pediatric Psychology, 21,* 103–106.

van Dongen-Melman, J. E. W. M., Pruyn, J. F. A., De Groot, A., Koot, H. M., Hahlen, K., & Verhulst, F. C. (1995). Late psychosocial consequences for parents of children who survived cancer. *Journal of Pediatric Psychology, 20,* 567–586.

van Dongen-Melman, J. E. W. M., & Sanders-Woudstra, J. A. R. (1986). Psychosocial aspects of childhood cancer: A review of the literature. *Journal of Child Psychology and Psychiatry, 27,* 145–180.

van Dongen-Melman, J. E. W. M., van Zuuren, F. J., & Verhulst, F. C. (1998). Experiences of parents of childhood cancer survivors: A qualitative analysis. *Patient Education and Counselling, 34,* 185–200.

van Eys, J. (1976). Supportive care for the child with cancer. *Pediatric Clinics of North America, 23,* 215–224.

van Eys, J. (1991). The truly cured child? *Pediatrician, 18,* 90–95.

van Zuuren, F. J. (1994). Cognitive confrontation and avoidance during a naturalistic medical stressor. *European Journal of Personality, 8,* 371–384.

van Zuuren, F. J., & Wolfs, H. M. (1991). Styles of information seeking under threat: Personal and situational aspects of monitoring and blunting. *Personality and Individual Differences, 12,* 141–149.

Vannatta, K., Gartstein, M. A., Short, A., & Noll, R. B. (1998). A controlled study of peer relationships of children surviving brain tumors: Teacher, peer, and self ratings. *Journal of Pediatric Psychology, 23,* 279–287.

Vannatta, K., Zeller, M., Noll, R. B., & Koontz, K. (1998). Social functioning of children surviving bone marrow transplantation. *Journal of Pediatric Psychology, 23,* 169–178.

Varni, J. W., Katz, E. R., Colegrove, R., & Dolgin, M. (1993). The impact of social skills training on the adjustment of children with newly diagnosed cancer. *Journal of Pediatric Psychology, 18,* 751–767.

Varni, J. W., Katz, E. R., Colegrove, R., & Dolgin, M. (1994). Perceived stress and adjustment of long-term survivors of childhood cancer. *Journal of Psychosocial Oncology, 12,* 1–16.

Varni, J. W., Katz, E. R., Colegrove, R., & Dolgin, M. (1996). Family functioning predictors of adjustment in children with newly diagnosed cancer: a prospective analysis. *Journal of Child Psychology and Psychiatry, 37,* 321–328.

Varni, J. W., Katz, E. R., Seid, M., Quiggins, D. J., Friedman-Bender, A., & Castro, C. M. (1998). The Pediatric Cancer Quality of Life Inventory (PCQL). I. Instrument development, descriptive statistics, and cross-informant variance. *Journal of Behavioral Medicine, 21,* 179–204.

Varni, J. W., Seid, M., & Rode, C. A. (1999). The Peds QL (TM): Measurement model for the pediatric quality of life inventory. *Medical Care, 37,* 126–139.

Varni, J. W., & Setoguchi, Y. (1991). Correlates of perceived physical appearance in children with congenital/acquired limb deficiencies. *Developmental and Behavioral Pediatrics, 12,* 171–176.

Varni, J. W., & Setoguchi (1993). Effects of parental adjustment on the adaptation of children with congenital or acquired limb deficiencies. *Developmental and Behavioral Pediatrics, 14,* 13–20.

Varni, J. W., & Wallander, J. L. (1988). Pediatric chronic disabilities: Hemophilia and spina bifida as examples. In D. Routh (Eds.), *Handbook of pediatric psychology* (pp. 190–221). New York: Guilford.

Vernick, J., & Karon, M. (1965). Who's afraid of death on a leukemia ward? *American Journal of Diseases of Children, 109,* 393–397.

Verrill, J. R., Schafer, J., Vannatta, K., & Noll, R. B. (2000). Aggression, antisocial behavior, and substance abuse in survivors of pediatric cancer: Possible protective effects of cancer and its treatment. *Journal of Pediatric Psychology, 25,* 493–502.

Verzosa, M. S., Aur, R. J., Simone, J., Hustu, H. O., & Pinkel, D. P. (1976). Five years after central nervous system irradiation of children with leukemia. *International Journal of Radiation Oncology, Biology and Physiology, 1,* 209–215.

Waber, D. P., Gioia, G., Paccia, J., Sherman, B., Dinklage, D., Sollee, N., Urion, D. K., Tarbell, N. J., & Sallan, S. E. (1990). Sex differences in cognitive processing in children treated with CNS prophylaxis for acute lymphoblastic leukemia. *Journal of Pediatric Psychology, 15,* 105–122.

Waber, D. P., Urion, D. K., Tarbell, N. J., Niemeyer, C., Gelber, R., & Sallan, S. E. (1990). Late effects of central nervous system treatment of acute lymphoblastic leukemia in childhood are sex-dependent. *Developmental Medicine and Child Neurology, 32,* 238–248.

Walker, L. S., Garber, J., & Greene, J. W. (1991). Somatization symptoms in pediatric abdominal pain patients: Relation to chronicity of abdominal pain and parent somatization. *Journal of Abnormal Child Psychology, 19,* 379–394.

Walker, L. S., & Greene, J. W. (1991). The Functional Disability Inventory: Measuring a neglected dimension of child heath status. *Journal of Pediatric Psychology, 16,* 39–58.

Wallace, W. H. B., Blacklay, A., Eiser, C., Davis, H. A., Hawkins, M. M., Levitt, G. A., & Jenney, M. E. M. (2001). Developing strategies for long-term follow up of survivors of childhood cancer. *British Medical Journal, 323,* 271–274.

Wallander, J. L., & Thompson, R. J. (1995). Psychosocial adjustment of children with chronic physical conditions. In M. C. Roberts (Eds.), *Handbook of pediatric psychology* (pp. 124–141). New York: Guilford.

Wallander, J. L., & Varni, J. W. (1992). Adjustment in children with chronic physical disorders: Programmatic research on a disability-stress-coping model. In A. M. La Greca, L. J. Siegel, J. L. Wallander, & C. E. Walker (Eds.), *Advances in pediatric psychology: Stress and coping in child health* (pp. 279–297). New York: Guilford.

Wallander, J. L., Varni, J. W., Babani, L., Banis, H. T., & Wilcox, K. T. (1989). Family resources as resistance factors for psychological maladjustment in chronically ill and handicapped children. *Journal of Pediatric Psychology, 14,* 157–173.

Ware, J. E., Snow, K. K., Kosinski, M., & Gandek, B. (1993). *SF-36 health survey: Manual and interpretation guide.* Boston: The Health Institute, New England Medical Center.

Waring, W. H. B., & Wallace, W. H. B. (2000). Subfertility following treatment of childhood cancer. *Hospital Medicine, 61,* 550–557.

Watson, M., Law, M., & Maguire, G. P. (1992). Further development of a quality of life measure for cancer patients: The Rotterdam symptom checklist (revised). *Psycho-Oncology, 1,* 35–44.

Wechsler, D. (1991). *Wechsler Intelligence Scale for Children.* New York: Harcourt Brace.

Weithorn, L. A., & Campbell, S. B. (1982). The competency of children and adolescents to make informed treatment decisions. *Child Development, 53,* 1589–1598.

Wellman, H. M. (1990). *The child's theory of mind.* Cambridge, MA: MIT Press.

Wertlieb, D., Weigel, C., & Feldstein, M. (1987). Measuring children's coping. *American Journal of Orthopsychiatry, 57,* 548–560.

Williams, J. M., & Davis, K. S. (1986). Central nervous system prophylactic treatment for childhood leukemia: Neuropsychological outcome studies. *Cancer Treatment Review, 13,* 113–127.

Williams, K. S., Ochs, J. J., Williams, J. M., & Mulhern, R. K. (1991). Parental report of everyday cognitive abilities among children treated for ALL. *Journal of Pediatric Psychology, 16,* 13–26.

Wilson, I., & Cleary, P. D. (1995). Linking clinical variables with health-related quality of life: A conceptual model of patient outcomes. *Journal of the American Medical Association, 273,* 59–65.

Wingo, P. A., Tong, T., & Bolden, S. (1995). Cancer statistics, 1995. *Cancer Journal for Clinicians, 45,* 8–30.

Wittrock, D. A., Larson, L. S., & Sandgren, A. (1994). When a child is diagnosed with cancer: II. Parental coping, psychological adjustment, and relationships with medical personnel. *Journal of Psychosocial Oncology, 12,* 17–32.

Wolter, J. M., Bowler, S. D., Nolan, P. J., & McCormack, J. G. (1997). Home intravenous therapy in cystic fibrosis: A prospective randomised trial examining clinical, quality of life and cost aspects. *European Respiratory Journal, 10,* 896–900.

Wood, J. V., Taylor, S. E., & Lichtman, R. R. (1985). Social comparison in adjustment to breast cancer. *Journal of Personality and Social Psychology, 49,* 1169–1183.

Worchel, F. F., Nolan, B. F., Willson, V. L., Purser, J. S., Copeland, D. R., & Pfefferbaum, B. (1988). Assessment of depression in children with cancer. *Journal of Pediatric Psychology, 13,* 101–112.

Wordsworth, W. (1888). *The complete poetical works. With an introduction by John Morley.* London: Macmillan.

World Health Organization. (1947). *World health organization constitution.* Geneva, Switzerland: Author.

Youniss, J. (1980). *Parents and peers in social development: A Sullivan–Piaget perspective.* Chicago: University of Chicago Press.

Youniss, J., & Smollar, J. (1985). *Adolescent relations with mothers, fathers, and friends.* Chicago: University of Chicago Press.

Yule, W. (1999). Post-traumatic stress disorder. *Archives of Disease in Childhood, 80,* 107–109.

Zabin, M. A., & Melamed, B. G. (1980). Relationship between parental discipline and children's ability to cope with stress. *Journal of Behavioral Assessment, 2,* 17–38.

Zebrack, B. J., & Chesler, M. A. (2001). A psychometric analysis of the quality of life-cancer survivors (QOL-CS) in survivors of childhood cancer. *Quality of Life Research, 10,* 319–329.

Zeltzer, L. K. (1993). Cancer in adolescents and young adults psychosocial aspects in long-term survivors. *Cancer Supplement, 71,* 3463–3468.

Zeltzer, L. K., Dolgin, M. J., Sahler, O. Z., Roghman, K., Barbarin, O. A., Carpenter, P. J., Copeland, D. R., Mulhern, R. K., & Sargent, J. R. (1996). Sibling adaptation to childhood cancer collaborative study: Health outcomes of siblings of children with cancer. *Medical and Pediatric Oncology, 27,* 98–107.

Zigler, E. (1980). Welcoming a new journal. *Journal of Applied Developmental Psychology, 1,* 1–6.

Author Index

Doll, R., 16
Donald, C. A., 249
Donati, M. A., 271
Donovan, C., 219
Dorn, L. D., 143
Dornbusch, S. M., 158
Douglas, S. M., 70, 126
Dow, K., 261
Dowell, R. E., 107, 114
Draper, G. J., 21, 191
Dreyer, Z., 73
Drigan, R., 22
Drotar, D., 26, 41, 75, 209
Duenas, D. A., 103
Duffner, P, K., 129
Dunavant, M., 263, 265, 269
Duncan, M. H., 105
Dungan, S., 236
Dunham, W., 259
Dunn, J., 170, 171, 182

E

Eatock, E. M., 16
Edelbrock, C., 41, 69, 112, 255, 256, 286
Eden, O. B., 17, 220
Eidahl, L., 85
Eisen, M., 249
Eiser, C., 37, 45, 52, 56, 92, 97, 102, 103,
    108, 138, 174, 196, 197, 200,
    201, 209, 211, 216, 219, 223,
    224, 258, 259, 264, 266, 269,
    273, 274
Ekert, H., 112
Elkin, T. D., 119, 198, 216
Ellenberg, L., 125, 127
Elliot, C. H., 161
Elliot, V., 221
Elliott, G., 101, 110
Ellis, A., 223
Ellis, R., 60
Enneking, W. F., 259
Erbaugh, J., 286
Erickson, E. H., 49, 51, 53
Esveldt-Dawson, K., 286
Ettinger, R. S., 93
Evans, A. E., 102
Evans, C. A., 175, 178
Evans, M. W., 197
Evans, S. E., 206, 207
Evans, W. E., 18

F

Faier-Routman, J., 67
Fairclough, D., 70, 78, 104, 126, 127,
    154, 198, 252
Fauzy, F. I., 249
Favrot, M., 118
Fears, T. R., 209
Fedio, P., 104
Feeny, D., 251, 253, 254, 264
Feinstein, A. R., 250, 274
Felder-Puig, R., 266
Feldman, E., 197
Feldstein, M., 75, 249
Ferguhar, J. W., 251
Fernandes, C., 108
Fernbach, D. J, 159, 160
Ferrell, B. R., 261
Festinger, L., 282
Fielding, D., 92
Fink, D., 249
Finlay, J. L., 112
Flamant, F., 270
Fletcher, J. C., 143
Fletcher, J. M., 102, 107, 108, 114, 124
Foley, G. V., 220
Folkman, S., 26, 75
Fontura, M., 193
Forsythe, C. J., 199
Foster, D. J., 51, 56
Fowler, M., 83
Francis, M. E., 293
Frappaz, D., 118
Frederick, C. J., 203
Freeman, A. I., 113
Freidrich, W. N., 177
French, D. J., 274
French, N. H., 286
Friedman, A. G., 252
Frieze, I. H., 38
Fritz, G. K., 34, 232, 236
Furlong, W., 251, 253
Furman, W., 170
Furstenberg, F. F., 171
Futterman, E., 138
Fyler, D. C., 108

G

Gallo, A. M., 178
Gallo, C., 140
Gandek, B., 201, 249

Subject Index